History

of

Economic

Relations

between

Russia&China

History

Of **Economic Relations**

between

Russia&China

From Modernization to Maoism

M.I. Sladkovskii

Routledge
Taylor & Francis Group

LONDON AND NEW YORK

Originally published in 1966 by Israel Prograr
Ltd.

Published 2008 by Transaction Publishers

Published 2017 by Routledge
2 Park Square, Milton Park, Abingdon, Oxon OX
605 Third Avenue, New York, NY 10017

Routledge is an imprint of the Taylor & Francis

Library of Congress Catalog Number: 20070316

Library of Congress Cataloging-in-

Sladkovskii, M. I. (Mikhail Iosifovich)
[Ocherki ekonomicheskikh otnoshenii SSSR s
History of economic relations between Russia
tion to Maoism / M.I. Sladkovskii. p. cm.
Originally published: Jerusalem : Israel Progra
1966.
Includes bibliographical references.
ISBN 978-1-4128-0639-8
1. Soviet Union—Commerce—China. 2.
Union. I. Title.

HF3628.C6S613   2007
382.0947'051—dc22

ISBN 13: 978-1-4128-0639-8 (pbk)
ISBN 13: 978-0-87855-193-4 (hbk)

TABLE OF CONTENTS

FOREWORD

THIS work is an attempt to survey the economic relations of China with tsarist Russia and, more recently, with the Soviet Union over a period of almost 300 years—from the middle of the 17th century to the present day. I have utilized official treaties and agreements, letters and other diplomatic documents, statistical data on foreign trade and banking, as well as historical and economic studies which throw light on the development of economic ties between the two neighboring states.

Data on foreign trade have been furnished mainly by the available Russian statistical records of customs duties, and the historical literature of prerevolutionary Russia and the Soviet Union. Russian sources have been used because no statistical data pertaining to the initial period of Sino-Russian trade, i.e., from the end of the 17th to the middle of the 19th centuries, could be found in the Chinese literature on the subject. Even after 1862, when regular publication of customs returns in China was started, no data are available on the border trade with Russia. The Chinese customs were controlled by a British Inspector General, and duties were sporadically collected only in areas visited by the inspectors; this explains, in particular, the lack of information in prerevolutionary Chinese customs records on trade between Russia and the Sinkiang province,[1] and between the Soviet Union and Manchuria following its occupation by the Japanese.

With regard to the most recent stage in Sino-Russian trade, i.e., following the establishment of the Chinese People's Republic, as yet no official statistics have been published by the Chinese government. However, as far as I can see from a partial survey of the available Chinese records, no serious discrepancies are revealed in a comparison with Soviet data. I therefore decided to utilize Soviet statistics to provide further light on this latest period.

Treaties, agreements and other diplomatic documents are cited from official Russian and Soviet publications. They have been collated with the Chinese versions published in China or with Russian translations officially recognized by the Chinese government. Sino-Russian treaties, agreements and other diplomatic documents relating to the prerevolutionary period in Russia have been published in Russian and Chinese by the Inspector General of Chinese Customs (*Treaties, Conventions, etc..., between China and Foreign States,* Vol. I. Shanghai, 1917); they are based on official publications of the Chinese government. These for all practical purposes may be considered to be identical with the Russian versions, since the discrepancies between them are insignificant, consisting merely of differences in style, and in the

---

[1] [Now the Sinkiang-Uighur Autonomous Region.]

orthography of certain terms. Treaties, agreements and other diplomatic documents relating to the period after the October Revolution have been collated with the official publications of the People's Commissariat of Foreign Affairs and the Soviet Ministry of Foreign Affairs, the authenticity of which has been acknowledged by the Chinese.

Statistics on Sino-Russian trade from the end of the 17th to the middle of the 19th centuries have been compiled from two Russian works: *A Historical-Statistical Survey of Trade between Russia and China*[2] and *Diplomatic and Commercial Relations between Russia and China to the 19th Century*.[3] Subsequent data on Sino-Russian and Sino-Soviet trade up to 1939, excepting the period of World War I for which I have used Chinese statistical customs records (Russian statistics for this period were not published), have been compiled from the official customs returns of prerevolutionary Russia and the Soviet Union. Data on Sino-Soviet trade for the period 1939-1955, published here for the first time, have been obtained from the archives of the Soviet Ministry of Foreign Trade.

All documents relating to the 17th and 18th centuries cited without reference are furnished by *Collected Diplomatic Papers on the Relations between the Russian and Chinese Governments from 1619 to 1792*[4] or by the above-mentioned work by Trusevich.

Sino-Russian trade figures for the period under review are supplied in the appended table, *Foreign Trade of the U.S.S.R. with China*.

The volume of trade has been denoted by showing its value in both current prices of year in question and their equivalents in 1955 rubles. Since in practice it would be hardly possible to calculate 1955 prices for all the commodities throughout the entire period (because of differences in quality between products bearing the same name and varying market conditions), I have attempted to calculate coefficients by a comparison of the price of gold in the given year with its 1955 price.

An objective analysis of the facts and data presented in this work leads to the inevitable conclusion, that the development of economic ties between the Soviet Union and China is the logical outcome of a centuries-old friendship between these two neighboring peoples, a friendship which accords with their fundamental interests and is of general benefit to mankind.

The Author.

---

[2] Korsak, A. Kazan'. 1857. [Russ.].
[3] Trusevich, Moskva. 1882. [Russ.].
[4] Bantysh-Kamenskii, Kazan'. 1882. [Russ.].

CHAPTER ONE

FIRST EMBASSIES AND THE PRELIMINARY (CARAVAN) PERIOD OF TRADE BETWEEN RUSSIA AND CHINA

DISCOVERY OF CHINA BY RUSSIA

THE earliest ties between the peoples inhabiting the present territories of the Soviet Union and China were formed in antiquity. The Chinese encountered the peoples of Central Asia during the struggle against the Huns in the 2nd century B.C., and subsequently relations with this area were more or less constantly maintained. The itinerary of the Chinese traveler Chang Kien (160-110 B.C.) included a visit to Bactria (the territory of Eastern Turkmenia and Uzbekistan), where he found Chinese wares, which had been imported through India.

The trade between China and Rome, which had been initiated some centuries before the Christian era, was conducted through the territory of the present Central Asian and Caucasian Soviet Republics, along the 'silk routes' through Tashkent and Bukhara and near Yerevan.

Russian historians[1] assume that information about China first reached Russia toward the end of the Mongol invasions, when Russian princes traveled to the Khan of the Golden Horde in order to obtain the *yarlyk* confirming them in office (Alexander Nevskii reached the headquarters of the Mongol Khan at Karakorum [Holin] in the 60's of the 13th century). In 1404 Russian merchants are found living in close proximity to their Indian and Chinese counterparts in Samarkand, where Chinese caravans brought silks, precious stones, pearls and rhubarb.[2]

In the eyes of 16th-century Russia, China was the richest country of the East. In 1557 Ivan the Terrible authorized an Englishman, named in the records as Jackson,[3] to proceed through Russian territory to Bukhara in order to open up trade routes to China.

In 1567 (according to Karamzin) Ivan the Terrible, wishing to obtain information about China, dispatched 'beyond Siberia to the south' the two Cossack hetmans Ivan Petrov and Burnash Yalychev. On their return the two envoys presented a *rospis* (description) of the countries they had visited, including China; it gives an account of the lands lying along the further shore of Lake Baikal, and mentions Bukhara, Tibet, Turkistan and Kashgaria, and the 'Mongol land,' and its cities; the occupations and religions of its inhabitants are described in detail, and mention is

---

[1] Solov'ev, S. *A History of Russia from the Earliest Times*, 5th ed., Vol. 3. Moskva. 1880 [Russ.].
Andreev, M. *History of the Relations between Russia and China from the 17th to the 20th Centuries.* 1925 [Russ.].
[2] Aristov, N. *Industry in Ancient Rus*, pp. 194-196. Sankt Petersburg. 1886 [Russ.].
[3] [The name is erroneous; the reference points undoubtedly to Anthony Jenkinson.]

made of Chinese cities, in particular 'Great China,'[4] the residence of the Khan Taibun, whom the Russian envoys, lacking suitable gifts, did not succeed in meeting.

The Chinese history of the Ch'ing dynasty *(Ch'ingch'aoch'üanshih)* also mentions the arrival in 1567 (the first year of Lung Ch'ing's reign)[5] of the Russian envoys Petrov and Yalychev, to whom an imperial audience was refused, reportedly because they bore no gifts. [6]

There is, however, some doubt as to the authenticity of this mission of Petrov and Yalychev. Kh. Trusevich adduces the following contentions: a) the 'description' attributed to this mission bears a marked resemblance to the subsequent 'description' brought back by the legation of Ivan Petlin. Despite an interval of 52 years, this *rospis* mentions persons of the same name and similar towns, etc.; moreover, while no confirmation of Ivan Petrov's mission could be found in the archives of the Russian Ministry of Foreign Affairs, the authenticity of Petlin's mission is corroborated by the official records *(stateinyi spisok)* and other documents; b) the 'description' furnished by Petrov and Yalychev makes no mention of the Siberian territory lying between the Urals and Lake Baikal, although this territory was not controlled by Russia at the time and should have been considered highly important by the Russian envoys. A similar conclusion is reached by another Russian historian, F. I. Pokrovskii.[7]

In 1582 the Moscow authorities sent representatives to Siberian towns and to the Ob River, ordering them to find out 'where the Chinese state is, how rich it is and whether anything may be obtained from it.'[8]

More reliable information on China began to reach Russia only after hunters and freemen, led by Cossacks in their quest for free land and attracted by the fabulous furs of the Siberian taiga, had pushed through Siberia for some 50 to 60 years. Having succeeded in traversing the almost impenetrable forests, tundras, and swamps, these adventurers reached the Mongolian border and came into contact with the vassal states of China.

RUSSIAN POSITION AT THE END OF THE 16TH AND IN THE FIRST HALF OF THE 17TH CENTURIES

The annexation of the Kazan and Astrakhan khanates to Russia was accomplished in the middle of the 16th century (1552-1556). This opened a convenient trade route

---

[4] [An incorrect translation of the Chinese name for *Peking*, which under the Mongol dynasty was designated *Tatu*, or *Great Capital*. *Tatu* is the translation of the Mongol name *Khanbalig*, i.e., the Khan's capital.]

[5] [The Ch'ing (Manchu) dynasty began its rule in 1644; Lung Ch'ing was an emperor of the preceding (Ming) dynasty.]

[6] *Ch'ingch'aoch'uanshih*, Vol. 1, section 4, p. 59. Shanghai. 1914 [Chin.].

[7] Pokrovskii, F. I. 'Travels of the Siberian Cossack Ivan Petlin to Mongolia and China in 1618—the Supposed Voyage of the Hetmans Ivan Petrov and Burnash Yalychev in 1567.'—*Izvestiya Otdela Russkogo Yazyka i Slovesnosti Imperatorskoi Akademii Nauk*, Vol. 18, Book 4, pp. 258 and 260. Sankt Petersburg. 1914 [Russ.].

[8] Bartol'd, V. *History of the Study of the East in Europe and Russia*, p. 187. Leningrad. 1925 [Russ.].

from Central Russial along the Volga to the Caspian Sea and thence to the markets of Azerbaidzhan and Iran, or by caravan through the Caspian steppes to the merchant cities of Central Asia (Bukhara and Khiva) and along the Kama to the lands lying beyond the Urals. The period marks the beginning of gradual Russian penetration into the rich fur regions of Siberia: the northern districts to the Ob River had already been explored in the 14th century by the Novgorodians.

In addition to their activity in the fur trade, Russian entrepreneurs also began to mine the lands beyond the Urals. In the middle of the 16th century the famous Stroganovs, who owned salt mines near the Kama River, discovered ore deposits on the Sosva River from which they began to extract silver ore, and also mined iron ore from the upper reaches of the Tura River. In 1558, having obtained letters patent from Ivan IV granting them the territories around the Kama River and authorizing them to form an armed guard, recruit Cossacks and build forts, the Stroganovs rapidly began to increase their holdings in the region of the Tura, Lozva, Tovda and Tobol rivers. In 1574 Ivan authorized them to equip an armed expedition beyond the Urals 'to the Siberian sultan.' A group of fugitive Volga Cossacks headed by Ermak (Ermolai Timofeevich) appeared in the Stroganovs' territory in the 1570's. Backed by the Stroganovs, these adventurers attacked the Siberian Khan Kuchum in 1581. They fought their way along the Chusova, Tagil and Tura rivers and finally broke through to the heart of the Siberian khanate, on the Irtysh River, in the fall of 1582. The Cossacks stormed Kuchum's main forts and occupied his capital, Kashlyk, or Sibir. Seeing that his army was destroyed, Kuchum retreated southward into the steppe; his vassals submitted to the Russian Tsar and agreed to payment of *yasak* (tribute).

Kuchum continued his operations against the Cossacks for the next 15 years, but Ermak's campaign had aroused general interest in the lands beyond the Urals, and an increasing number of Russians reached the area. The first Russian settlements appeared on the communication routes along the Tobol, Irtysh, Ob and Taz rivers: Tyumen (1586), Tobolsk (1587), Berezov (1593), Surgut (1594), Tara (1594), Mangazeya (1601), Tomsk (1604), and others.

The last two settlements, Mangazeya and Tomsk, played a leading role in furthering the Russian advance to the east. The northern outpost of Mangazeya became an important center for the sable trade; the fur *yasak* from the northern regions of Siberia was collected there. The *yasak* was brought to Mangazeya as early as 1603 by the Samoyeds (Nenets), who dwelt not only along the Taz River, but also much further to the east, along the Yenisei and its tributary the Lower Tunguska. Tomsk, situated to the south, was as important as Mangazeya, for it was through this town that relations were maintained with the Kalmucks, Dzungars and Kirghizes. Starting out from Mangazeya, and following a portage from the Taz to the Turukhan, the Russians reached the Yenisei and in 1607 founded the town of Turukhansk. The Russian advance to the east was then facilitated by the wide Yenisei River and its tributaries. After the founding of Krasnoyarsk in 1628, Russian boats could follow the main Siberian waterway—Yenisei River—Angara River—Lake Baikal—Selenga River—from the Arctic Ocean to the Mongolian borders.

The Lena River could be reached by two routes: along the Lower Tunguska and by portage to the Vilyui (a tributary of the Lena) as well as along the Angara and Ilim and by portage to the Kuta River. The exploration of the Lena and its tributaries led to the discovery of a direct outlet to the Pacific and northeast Asia. The fort built in 1632 at Yakutsk, which became the new administrative center of the Yakutsk government, played an important role in the conquest of northeastern and eastern Siberia.

The upper Yenisei and the region of Lake Baikal were also annexed to Russia in the 17th century.

Merchants, hunters, fugitive peasants, free Cossacks, as well as elements from the poorer classes, migrated in great numbers to these territories, and were followed by tsarist officials and administrators sent to enforce the central authority and exact its accompanying heavy tribute—the *yasak*. This and other similar requisitions weighed heavily on both the indigenous population and the Russian immigrants. They caused widespread dissatisfaction among the working people, and led to uprisings against the administration in which both Russians and local inhabitants participated.[9]

The Amur, the legendary 'grain river,' began at this time to attract the attention of the Russian 'wayfarers' [as the explorers were then called], for it reputedly lay between highly fertile grainlands. Such land would be of great importance to the Russian settlers who were remote from the agricultural regions of Russia and therefore felt greatly the lack of bread—which constituted the main element of their diet.

Expansion toward the Amur followed two routes. Russian freemen started out from the Upper Lena and in 1640 reached Lake Baikal; they crossed the lake and in 1642 built on its eastern shore the fort of Barguzin, used as a base for the exploration of the Selenga River and of the Shilka, a tributary of the Amur. At almost the same time expansion began from Yakutsk; in 1643 an expedition led by Vasilii Poyarkov set out to the Amur from this locality along the Lena and Aldan rivers. In the spring of 1644 he arrived at the upper reaches of the Zeya, another tributary of the Amur, with his detachment, after crossing the Stanovoi mountain range.

The only Manchurian or Chinese nationals living in this territory were itinerant merchants, who were engaged in barter for furs, obtained for a trifle from the local inhabitants (Daurs, Duchers, Golds [Nanay], Giliaks [Nivkhs]), and who by various contrivances drew the whole population of some neighborhoods they entered, and even entire clans, into economic bondage.

Poyarkov proceeded down the Amur to the Sea of Okhotsk and wintered on the coast among the Giliaks. The expedition took to the sea in the spring of 1645, but the sinking of one of its boats forced it back to shore; it then reached the Ulya River overland and returned to Yakutsk on 12 July 1646, having traced the courses of the Maya and the Aldan. Poyarkov brought back a large consignment of sables and a detailed itinerary including maps of the rivers.

[9] The small merchants and artisans of Mangazeya rebelled in 1630, besieging the fort occupied by the chief voivode and rich merchants; the Russian garrison of Krasnoyarsk mutinied in 1695-1698, and the Kachin Tatars sided with the rebels.

Erofei Pavlovich Khabarov, a peasant from Veliki Ustyug in Vologda province, who had become a trapper and occasionally ventured into commerce and salt extraction, recruited 'hunting people' at his own expense, with the assistance of the Yakutsk voivode, and in 1649 set out for the conquest of the Daur lands. This expedition, numbering approximately 70 men, followed the Olekma and its tributary the Tugira and crossed to the Amur by the Tugirsk portage. Khabarov then returned to Yakutsk, leaving some of his party on the Amur. In 1651, having by that time succeeded in collecting about 400 men, he set out on a new campaign and occupied several settlements along the Amur.

Khabarov's treks to the Amur coincided with the Manchu conquest of China and the founding of the Ch'ing dynasty. Simultaneously with their southward movement into China, the Manchus strove to expand to the north, into the Amur region.

Russian farmers settled during this period around Albazin [Yaksa] and other towns, and many hunters' lodges were built in the forest region of the Amur.

The consolidation of free Cossack settlements along the Amur increased the Russian government's interest in these territories. In 1653 the Tsar commissioned the nobleman Zinov'ev, who set out to join Khabarov with a detachment of 200 men; he was later followed by numerous adventurers. However, as with the other regions of Siberia, no effort was made by government officials to consolidate the Russian settlements of the Amur, which were regarded merely as new sources of *yasak* for the Treasury. The small garrison of Albazin was not reinforced and in 1658 had to abandon the site under pressure from Manchu detachments. However, in 1665 Albazin was recaptured by a group of fugitive Cossacks led by Nikifor of Chernigov.

From time to time Manchu troops appeared in the vicinity of Albazin, demanding its evacuation and the abolishment of the *yasak*.

CHINA IN THE FIRST HALF OF THE 17TH CENTURY

The beginning of the 17th century was marked in China by severe internal upheavals caused by the oppressive conditions in which the peasantry and poorer urban sectors were living. The seizure by the feudal aristocracy of state-owned land which had previously been allotted to peasants for cultivation was already increasing in the 16th century. The peasants were forced to use their own implements for tilling the fields of landowners, aristocrats and members of the imperial court, while having to hand over as much as four-fifths or more of their produce. In the words of Mao Tse-Tung, 'Such peasants were, in fact, serfs.'[10] The feudal lords confiscated not only the products of the peasants' agricultural labor but also that of their domestic industry. The imperial court levied an annual tax of 100,000 pieces of cotton fabric on peasant cotton industries.[11] Peasant labor was extensively used in manufactories owned by

---

[10] Mao Tse-Tung. *Selected Works*, Vol.3, p.139.—Izdatel'stvo inostrannoi literatury, Moskva. 1953 [Russ.].
[11] Yang Chung-p'ing. *Essays on the History of the Cotton Textile Industry in China* (1289-1937).—Kohsü-ehch'upansheh Publishing House. Peking. 1955 [Chin.].

the landlords and the imperial court, and this retarded the development of China's domestic industries and urban growth.

In their constant pursuit of the gratuitous produce of peasant labor, the feudal aristocracy increased land rents and taxes, as well as the forced labor impressed from the population. The dispossession of the peasantry and mass pauperization resulted.

Chinese merchants, who for centuries had maintained commercial ties with the countries and peoples of southeast Asia and the Near East, were gradually supplanted in the middle of the 16th century by European colonizers who reached the sealanes of the Pacific and Indian Oceans.

As opponents the Chinese junks encountered the powerful modern sailing fleets of the Spanish, the Dutch and later the British. The annexation of the Philippines by Spain (1565) and of the Spice Islands by Holland (1598-1600), and the appearance of the first vessels of the East India Company off the shores of China, considerably weakened Chinese trade in these regions. The European merchants not only ousted Chinese goods but also behaved brutally toward the Chinese traders, driving them out and ruthlessly annihilating them.[12]

The severance of commercial ties with southeast Asia had severe consequences for the internal commerce of China and its craft industry. The decrease in foreign trade discouraged the production and flow of merchandise and predetermined the development of an autarkic economy.

Internal social problems and setbacks in foreign affairs weakened the authority of the Ming dynasty and led to open mass revolt against feudal oppression. An insurrection which broke out in 1628 in Shensi province spread to the neighboring regions and developed into an antifeudal peasant war. The insurgent army of almost a million men, whose primary commander was Li Tzy-ch'eng, was successful in overcoming the imperial forces, and captured Peking in 1644.

The insurgents expropriated the property of the rich in favor of the poor, reduced taxes and consistently campaigned against bribery and corruption in the administration. In order to maintain their authority over the people the alarmed Chinese feudal lords then entered into a compact with the Manchu princes.[13]

The Manchus occupied Peking in 1644 and then, with the help of the Chinese feudal aristocracy, set off on a further campaign. Even after their conquest of the southern provinces however, they were forced to wage a prolonged struggle against the Chinese masses, particularly in the southwest and southeast of the country. In the Fukien province the Chinese navy, commanded by Cheng Ch'eng-kung (known

---

[12] Chinese merchants of Manila were annihilated by the Spanish in 1603 and again in 1662.

[13] A movement for the creation of an independent Manchurian empire developed in northern China, on the territory of modern Manchuria, then mostly settled by Manchu tribes in vassalage to China. Unification of the separate Manchu tribes had begun at the end of the 16th century. As agriculture developed, the division of labor was accelerated, commodity circulation among the various tribes and regions of Manchuria increased and a centralized political leadership became a necessity.

Nurhachi (1559-1626), one of the Manchu princelings, united several tribes at the beginning of the 17th century. The Manchu Chin ('Golden') Kingdom was established in 1616.

in Europe by the name of Koxinga,[14] stubbornly resisted the Manchus. When he had ousted the Dutch from Taiwan [Formosa], he proclaimed the establishment of a new Chinese state which included the Fukien province as well as a number of islands, among them Taiwan. However, this opposition movement, headed also by Cheng Ching, the son of Cheng Ch'eng-kung, was eventually crushed by the Manchus with the help of the Dutch. The authority of the Manchu Ch'ing dynasty (originally named the Chin dynasty) was recognized throughout China only in 1683.

The Manchu dynasty, supported by the Chinese feudal landowners, strove to strengthen the feudal system which had been shaken by the peasant insurrections. A large part of the land holdings were appropriated by the Manchu aristocracy and soldiery.

In the field of foreign relations, including trade, the Manchus sought to isolate China from foreign influences. All Chinese merchants were forbidden to participate in foreign trade; only certain organizations granted a monopoly by the imperial court were excepted. The construction of large seagoing vessels was also forbidden to them and the merchants were not allowed to hold high posts in the administration.

Manchu policy toward neighboring states was hostile and agressive. Intoxicated by their successes in China, they attempted to occupy the territories surrounding the Amur River as well as other regions by force.

FIRST RUSSIAN EMBASSIES TO CHINA

Even after the Russian annexation of western Siberia, Russia and China were still separated by territories settled by Mongols, Kalmucks and other peoples. Relations with China could only be maintained through the territories of the Mongol and Kalmuck khanates. The Mongol state of Altan Khan (the 'Golden' Khan) (1507-1582) and his successors, through which lay the shortest and most convenient route from western Siberia to China, was of particular significance in this respect.

According to Miller,[15] the first embassy to the Altan khans to establish relations with China was dispatched by Volynskii, voivode of Tomsk, in 1608; however, in his conversations with the Russian envoys who reached him in 1616, the Altan Khan[16] stated that this embassy had been dispatched in 1606. It reached its destination at a time when the khan was struggling against the invading Karakalpaks, and the Russian envoys were killed on their way home. We possess more reliable information concerning the Russian embassy of 1616, that of Tyumenets, a Cossack, and of Petrov, a minor official, dispatched to the Altan Khan in that year by Prince Kurakin, the voivode of Tobolsk. This embassy was not so much concerned with reaching China as in persuading the Altan Khan to accept Russian suzerainty, and in this respect it succeeded. Tyumenets learned from the khan that the distance to China

---

[14][*Kuohsingyeh* in Chinese; this is not a name, but a type of honorary title, i.e., 'Head of the State' or 'Father of the Country.']

[15] Miller. *First Russian Travelers and Embassies to China.* 1755 [Russ.].

[16] The successors of Altan Khan continue to bear the same name in the Russian sources.

was 'a month's travel by foot,' that this obscure country possessed cannon and har-quebuses, and velvet, satin and other precious wares, and that it traded with its neighbors.

It could be concluded from Prince Kurakin's report to the Tsar in 1617 that Tyumenets and Petrov continued their voyage from the Altan Khan's court to China. In Kurakin's report he informs the Tsar: 'The Altyn-Tsar gave orders that your officers, whom we, your servant, had dispatched as an embassy, should be sent off and accompanied to China so that the Chinese Emperor might in return send his high envoys to you, Sire, in the company of your officers, in order to honor and exalt Your Imperial Majesty and so as to learn of the greatness of your state.' This version of events, however, is not corroborated by subsequent information, according to which Tyumenets and Petrov returned to Tobolsk in 1617 accompanied by envoys of the Altan Khan, and set out from there for Moscow. Consequently, if we accept these two dates, Trumenets could not have traveled to China, and Prince Kurakin's report would have been sent before the former's return to Tobolsk, when the Prince had as yet no information as to the result of the embassy. Tyumenets, who regarded himself as the first Russian to visit the court of Altan Khan, relates that he 'drank milk heated with butter, containing some unknown plants...and certain other un-known red herbs.' Accompanied by the Altan Khan's envoys, he brought presents to Moscow from the Khan to the Tsar, among which were the first samples of China tea.

After the return of the Tyumenets—Petrov mission, Prince Kurakin decided to obtain direct information about China, without the help of the Mongols; to this end he dispatched in 1618 a new embassy, that of the Cossack Ivan Petlin and Petrun'ka Kozylov, to China in 1618. Petlin's route through the Russian lands lay through Tomsk and Kuznetsk, and from there he entered Mongolia, cutting through the upper Yenisei in the approximate direction of Ulan Bator [Urga], Kalgan [Chang-kiakow and Peking.

In Peking Petlin was given a letter addressed to the Tsar, in which the Chinese expressed their desire to establish trade with Russia. The letter stated: 'From Valli[17] the Chinese Emperor. Two men have come to us from Russia, and Valli, Emperor of China, said to them, the Russians: Come with merchandise and trade; and leave and come again. You are the high sovereign of those lands and I am no small king, therefore let the way between us be open; travel from north and from south, and I shall bestow upon you precious stones in exchange for the valuable wares that you will bring. And now go back, and if you come here again or if His Majesty's men come, let them bring me a letter from His Majesty, and I shall send a letter in return. And when I receive your letters I shall order your men to be received with great honor. But I cannot send my envoys to you, Your Majesty, for the way is long and they do not know your language...If there were a route open for my envoys to travel to you, Your Majesty, I would send you my envoys. I also am an emperor in my own

---

[17] [A distortion of *Wan Li*, the designation for the reign of Emperor Shen Tzung (1573-1620) of the Ming dynasty.]

right, and do not travel out of my realm or allow my envoys and merchants to leave it.'

This letter was not brought to Moscow, but remained with the voivode of Tobolsk, where it was not translated into Russian for 56 years for lack of an interpreter.

Russian dealings with China were broken off after Petlin's first embassy, owing to tension in relations with the Altan Khan as well as to the beginnings of internal strife in China. It is clear from data on trade at Tomsk in 1640, 1652 and 1653 (when the town was the center for Russian trade with the Kalmucks, Bukharans, Mongols and Persians) that no Chinese goods penetrated into Russia at that time, either directly or through middlemen. Even such commodities as rhubarb, silks and nutgall, which were to play an important role in Sino-Russian trade, were not then recognised as being of Chinese origin.

A new stage in the relations between Russia and China was reached when Russian expansion had encompassed Lake Baikal and penetrated to the Amur. Permanent contact was then established between the Russian settlements in the Nerchinsk area and along the Amur and the Manchurian inhabitants of the border region. It became an urgent matter to establish regulations governing the border areas and to determine the boundary between the two states with precision. The instructions sent by the Russian government to the voivode of Nerchinsk, who represented Russian authority in the territories lying beyond Lake Baikal and along the Amur, stringently enjoined him to maintain friendly relations with China and avoid clashes with the Chinese inhabitants of the border area.

Kabarov's voyage to Moscow, and his report to Tsar Alexis on the movements of the Russian Cossacks along the Amur and the clashes with the Manchus, induced the Russian government to dispatch an embassy to China to settle border conflicts and establish trade relations. Fedor Isakovich Baikov, a boyar's son, was dispatched from Moscow to Tobolsk in 1653 by order of Tsar Alexis. Fifty thousand rubles rubles were alloted to him by the Treasury to buy wares in Moscow and other cities in order to resell them in China.

Before setting out on his embassy, Baikov was to gather information at Tobolsk concerning the routes leading to China, the Russian goods which could be sold there, and the Chinese merchandise to be brought back. On 2 February 1654, having gathered the necessary information and prepared the expedition, Baikov received the order to proceed to Khanbalig (as the Russians then called Peking), the capital of China.

From Tobolsk Baikov sent out ahead of him the Tatar Sektul Ablin, who was to give advance notice of the arrival of the Tsar's envoy. Baikov's route from Tobolsk to China lay along the Irtysh River and through the lands of the Kalmuck khan, Ablai Taishe. After staying at Ablai's court for four and a half months, Baikov reached the first Chinese city of Kokotan on 12 January 1656 and entered the Chinese capital on March 3. He bore a letter from the Tsar to the Emperor of China which stated: 'Because of the great distance between our countries there have been no presents or friendship and no exchange of envoys between your forefathers, the emperors of the Chinese state, or yourself, Great Khan, and our forefathers the great sovereigns and our father of blessed memory the mighty sovereign... Hearing that you are wont to send envoys of friendship and love, and since our state has become a neighbor of yours, we wish to establish from this time on a fitting, proper and firm friendship.' The Baikov embassy was to collect detailed information on China's commerce (in particular, to ascertain whether silk and velvet were produced in the country or if these commodities were imported by China from abroad), to sample Chinese merchandise and buy small amounts of certain wares.

With him Baikov brought the first batch of Russian merchandise consisting of Russian leather, pelts and diamonds, of which he was to present part to the Emperor and exchange the rest for Chinese goods. Although Baikov succeeded in learning a good deal about Chinese conditions and trade, in selling his wares, and in buying 30,000 rubles worth of Chinese merchandise, the main objects of his embassy could not be attained. The armed clashes along the border between Russian Cossacks and Manchu troops intensified during Baikov's stay in Peking.

Having enforced its authority in Central and Southern China and transformed Korea and eastern Mongolia into vassal states, the Manchu dynasty maintained an arrogant attitude in relations with neighboring countries. The Baikov embassy was treated with contempt by the authorities. The courtiers demanded that Baikov 'fall on his knees and bow' [kow-tow] to the arms and seal of the Great Khan; they tried to take the Tsar's letter from Baikov before he could enter the palace, and prevented him from meeting the Emperor. Having refused to submit to this humiliating ceremonial, Baikov was obliged to return to Russia in 1658 without having met the Emperor, to whom he had been ordered to hand over in person the Tsar's letter and obtain an answer. Although it did not fully succeed, Baikov's embassy played an important role in the establishment of Sino-Russian relations. The envoy compiled a detailed description of his itinerary from Tobolsk along the Irtysh River, past Lake Zaisan and through Mongolia to Peking; he carried out the first sizable commercial transactions and provided a description of conditions in China.[18]

Despite the failure of this first embassy, Russia continued attempts to establish normal relations with China. A second official Russian embassy headed by Perfil'ev was dispatched in 1658 along the same route taken by Baikov. Perfil'ev was empowered to assure the Chinese Emperor that the Russian government was prepared to seek a peaceful solution to the Amur conflict and to abstain from sending Russian troops to that area. At the same time, the envoy was to obtain an authorization for trading with China. Tsar Alexis' instructions stated: 'We shall not send any of our soldiers to Dauria,[19] and you will authorize us to bring our wares there.' In addition to the costly presents sent to the Emperor with Perfil'ev (40 sables, 13 silver

---

[18] Baikov wrote a journal of his travels, first published in *Sibirskii Vestnik* ('Siberian Herald') in 1820.

[19] [The territory which included (in the 17th century) the eastern Transbaikal area and a part of the Amur region, with the basins of the Shilka, Argun, Zeya, Bureya, and partly the Sungari and Ussuri rivers. After the 17th century the name is mainly applied to the Transbaikal area. The territory between Lake Baikal and the Yablonovoi range is called Baikal Dauria, that to the east of the Yablonovoi range Nerchinsk Dauria; the basin of the Selenga River (southern part of Baikal Dauria) is called Selenga Dauria.]

fox pelts, four pieces of cloth and one ermine), the envoy also carried merchandise to Peking, the proceeds of its sale to be used for buying Chinese commodities.

Perfil'ev was received much more hospitably in Peking than his predecessor; however, although he returned to Moscow bearing gifts from the Emperor to the Tsar (24 pieces of silk, one *pood* 12 *funty* 45 *zolotniki* of silver,[20] 3 pelts each of beaver, snow leopard and seal, a certain quantity of velvet and 3 *poods* of 'tea herb'), accompanied by an answering letter; no agreement was reached on the establishment of permanent commercial ties.

Meanwhile, in the Amur region, the recovery of Albazin in 1665 was followed by the reconstruction of Fort Zeya, situated at the mouth of the Zeya River. A group of peasants settled in the Albazin region in 1671, which became a government under voivode Tolbuzin and his aide Oskol'kov. Several settlements and villages were soon founded around Albazin, and the fort itself grew into a fortified town.

The Manchus, on the other hand, founded the military outpost of Aigun [Heilungki angcheng][21] on the left bank of the Amur (region of the modern Heiho or Sahalien), from which attacks were launched against the Russian inhabitants of the area. The conflict over Albazin, which again flared up, threatened to develop into a largescale war between the Manchus and Russian settlers.

Meanwhile, in another border region further removed from the Manchu military bases, the area of the Nerchinsk government, permanent political and commercial relations were established between the Russian administration and the Manchu Emperor's Mongolian Office (Mengkulifanyüan).[22] In 1669 the Emperor ordered the border princeling Mankadii to send a representative to Nerchinsk for the opening of talks over the return of the fugitive Gantimur[23] to the Manchus. On 19 April 1670 the voivode of Nerchinsk, Danil Arshinskii (known in the Chinese documents by the name of Danil), dispatched an answering embassy to Peking, consisting of Ignatii Milovanov, Anton Filev and Grigorii Kobyakov with 'three companions.' Acting on the Tsar's instructions, Arshinskii ordered Milovanov to inform the Manchu Emperor of Russia's desire to establish trade relations with China, and that with this in view, 'His Majesty's subjects and the Emperor's subjects would be permitted to trade on both sides [of the frontier].'

The Emperor's answer, transmitted to the Tsar through Milovanov, demanded the return of Gantimur and the recall from the Amur of all the Russians settled at Albazin and other outposts. The Emperor promised that if his demands were met 'it would be so done and then there would be peace.'

[20] [47 lb 5 oz, or approximately 21.5 kg.]

[21] [The town of Aigun was later transfered to the right bank of the Amur. Now known as Aihwei.]

[22] This was the 'Chamber of Foreign Relations,' which dealt with the affairs of Mongolia, Turkistan and Tibet; this was also the body through which Russia and China maintained relations up to 1860, since Mongolia served as the link between the two countries.

[23] Prince Gantimur, a Tungus who had held high military rank in the Manchu army, fled to Russian territory in 1667. Together with his family, numbering 40 persons, Gantimur settled in Nerchinsk, becoming a Russian subject and assuming the Christian faith. His sons Lazar and Larion were to receive the title of *stol'nik* [a rank of the lesser nobility] in 1710, at which date they owned large tracts of land beyond Lake Baikal.

Despite the continuing border disputes, trade between Russia and China became a more or less permanent feature after the 1650's. During this period the Russian border town of Nerchinsk and the Manchurian town of Naun [Nunkiang or Mergen] grew into important trading centers, visited by merchants not only from Peking and other northern Chinese cities but even from neighboring Korea.

At the same time Russian trade caravans began to visit Peking. They were sent out either by the various voivodes in the name of the Russian Treasury or by private merchants. In addition to the state-owned caravans which accompanied the Paikov and Perfil'ev embassies, the literature on the subject mentions the dispatch to Peking in 1670 of a state-owned caravan led by Krasikov bearing 280 sables, 180 otter pelts, 100 pieces of Russian leather, metal articles, and other wares; the caravan brought back to Russia 3 pounds of spun silk thread and 315 pieces of silk. Visiting Chinese merchants in Nerchinsk and Albazin, where clashes with the Manchus continued, are often mentioned during this period.

A group of 43 Russian merchants, including Ivan Proshennikov, Evstafii Filat'ev and Gavril Romanov, set out from Selenginsk to Peking in August 1674, and traded for seven weeks in the Chinese capital.

However, this spontaneous development of trade encountered several obstacles. The Mongol tribes roving through the territory lying between Nerchinsk and Peking, who were not subjugated by the Manchu emperor until the end of the 17th century, frequently raided the caravans of both Russian and Chinese merchants; these caravans therefore had to be accompanied by large escorts, expensive to maintain. It also has to be borne in mind in this connection that the Manchu authorities gave little attention to the development of trade.

The further development of Sino-Russian trade required drastic measures on the part of both governments, and, first, the settlement of the border disputes. With this object, the Russian authorities dispatched the envoy Nikolai Spafarii[24] to China in 1675. The Tsar's instructions to Spafarii enjoined him to assure the Chinese Emperor Kang Hsi that 'His Majesty the Tsar wishes always to maintain perpetual friendship and amity with His Majesty the Emperor.' The other eleven points in the instructions empowered Spafarii to reach an agreement with Kang Hsi concerning the dispatch of a Chinese embassy to Moscow, and to obtain his authorization for 'trade people to travel freely on both sides,' and to 'let out 4,000 poods of silver from China to Russia every year in payment for Russian wares, according to the merchants' wishes,' as well as the Emperor's promise not to prevent Russian merchants from bartering Russian wares for precious stones, to allow Russian merchandise unimpeded entry into China after duties had been paid, and to permit Chinese expert craftsmen to travel to Russia.

---

[24] Nikolai Gavrilovich Spafarii, a Moldavian Greek, was an interpreter of the Ministry of Foreign Affairs. The mission included Konstantin Grechanin and Fedor Livanov (both Greeks), Nikifor Venyukov, Ivan Favorov, six other servants and a retinue of 40 Cossacks. Having left Moscow on 4 March 1675, the Spafarii mission arrived at Tobolsk on March 30 and set out for Yeniseisk after the ice had broken on the Irtysh, Ob and Ket rivers, reaching the town on July 9. On December 19 the mission departed from Nerchinsk to Naun, residence of the Manchu border administrator.

On his way to China, Spafarii conferred with the Russian defenders of Albazin, whom he instructed to refrain from hostile acts against the Manchus and in particular to stop collection of the *yasak* from Manchu subjects dwelling along the Amur. In Irkutsk he visited the fugitive Gantimur, who pleaded with the envoy not to hand him over to the Manchu authorities, for 'he and his parents had been born on the Nercha [River],' urging that 'even were His Majesty to return him to the Chinese, he would not reach Peking alive but kill himself instead.' Spafarii assured Gantimur that he would never be delivered by Russia into Chinese hands.

While still at Yeniseisk, Spafarii dispatched the envoy Milovanov to inform the Chinese Emperor that a Russian mission was on its way. Having reached the Manchurian River Nonni Ula [Nun Kiang] on 26 January 1676, Spafarii awaited Milovanov's return from Peking. Prolonged arguments with the Manchu border authorities over the order of precedence and the handing over of the Tsar's letters to the Chinese emperor[25] ensued before he could continue his journey, and, he reached Peking on 15 May 1676.

In Spafarii's discussions with the Manchu mandarins he encountered considerable difficulties. The mandarins demanded that he submit to a humiliating ceremonial; they were arrogant and disrespectful, and finally subjected the mission's entourage to irritating regulations: the Russian merchants accompanying the embassy were forbidden to associate with Chinese merchants and were authorized to buy Chinese wares only from a specially designated store; fixed low prices were set by the authorities for the imported Russian commodities, and Chinese merchants who did not respect this ruling were severely punished.

When Spafarii insisted that an answer be given to the twelve points in the Tsar's instructions, the President of the Mongolian Office declared on 29 August 1676 through his Jesuit interpreter: 'The Emperor does not wish to answer His Majesty's letter, in the first place because he, Spafarii, disobeyed by receiving the gifts while standing instead of falling on his knees as is customary; secondly, because there is nothing to write about since, despite the Emperor's repeated demands, Prince Gantimur, who fled to Russia, has not been returned (although it was so promised by Danil Arshinskii), and until this matter is concluded he [the Emperor] has no intention of discussing anything else; and in the future not only will he refrain from writing but he will not receive envoys, ambassadors or Russian merchants until the following three demands have been met: 1) that Prince Gantimur be sent to Peking with a Russian envoy; 2) that this envoy be an intelligent man who will do all that he is ordered, according to custom, without objection; 3) that the Russians who have settled along the border always live peacefully. And when these things have been done by the Russian side, then the Chinese nobles will answer not only the twelve points presented by the envoy but even one hundred and twenty points; but as long as these

---

[25] The Manchu administrator Askhani-Amban demanded that Spafarii first appear before him and hand over the Tsar's letters. The dispute was settled by setting up a nomad's tent near the house in which Spafarii dwelt; the encounter took place in this tent, but the Tsar's letters remained in Spafarii's possession.

three demands are not met, no persons whatsoever, either from Moscow or from the border towns, even if bearing merchandise, shall come here.'

The mandarins of the Mongolian Office menaced Spafarii with threats that if the Russian government neglected the Emperor's demands, the Manchus would dispatch their troops against the Russian forts along the Amur and destroy Nerchinsk and Albazin. Further arguments with the mandarins only introduced greater confusion into the talks, and the mission was forced to leave Peking on September 1 without reaching agreement on any of the points under discussion.

After they had broken off the talks with the Spafarii mission, the Manchus began to implement their threats on the Russian settlements along the Amur; this policy had been decided upon although, by that time peaceful relations had become established in the area and no provocation had been offered by the Russian side to induce hostilities.

In October 1682 the Emperor Kang Hsi dispatched a letter to Aleksei Tolbuzin, the voivode of Albazin, in which he demanded that the town be ceded without conflict, and proposed that the Russians should either retreat from the Amur or proffer their allegiance to the Manchu Emperor. The Albazin area again became the scene of protracted fighting between the attacking Manchu forces and the defenders of the settlements. The latter were favored by the situation inside China; Kang Hsi, who was mounting a campaign against the western Mongols, was apprehensive lest the conflict with Russia might spread since this country did not constitute a direct threat to China. To Russia, also, a peaceful solution of the dispute was no less important.

On 15 November 1685 a letter from Kang Hsi reached Moscow with the Albazin Cossacks Yakim Ivanov and Grishka Fomin, who had been taken prisoner by the Chinese. In this letter the Emperor declared that he had dispatched 'a large force' to the Amur and continued to insist that the Russians abandon the river, as though this constituted the main obstacle to the establishment of peace between China and Russia. He proposed at the same time that the frontier between the two states should pass some distance from the Amur, through territories about which the Manchus themselves possessed no information. 'Take back your Russian subjects of Albazin,' wrote Kang Hsi. 'Wherever the border between us shall be fixed, be it at Yakutsk or elsewhere, we shall both dwell there, each in his own land, and develop our crafts. You shall take the *yasak* from the inhabitants living there and shall not send Russian people to my lands; do not order my subjects to be oppressed or taxes to be levied without cause; and on your reply to this letter we shall seek counsel with one another. The troops that I have sent to Albazin I shall order back and shall position at the border; and that shall be the border between us, and our subjects along the border shall begin to live in peace and mutual counsel.'[26]

---

[26] In his *Diplomaticheskoe sobranie del mezhdu Rossiiskim i Kitaiskim gosudarstrami c 1619 do 1792 g.* ('Collected Diplomatic Papers on the Relations between the Russian and Chinese Governments from 1619 to 1792') (Kazan'. 1882) N. Bantysh-Kamenskii states that Kang Hsi also sent two letters to the Tsar through Dutch missionaries. The first letter, dispatched from Peking on 7 September 1687 reached Moscow on 2 January 1690, and the second left Peking on 12 October 1687 and was received in Moscow on 18 March 1690. Both touched upon the same problems as those raised in the letter dispatched

The Russian Tsars Ivan and Peter (then reigning together) took advantage of Kang Hsi's peace proposals; on 10 December 1685 they dispatched a letter to China with Nikifor Venyukov and Ivan Favorov, two minor officials of the Ministry of Foreign Affairs. In this letter the Tsars indicated that they had heard of the entry of Manchu troops into Russian territory, and that hostilities had begun without preliminary diplomatic discussion of the disputed issues. Notifying Kang Hsi that Russia had also decided to 'send to the border countless troops with valiant voivodes in order to pacify her adversaries,' the letter stressed that 'Their Imperial Majesties had ordered their troops to refrain from shedding blood and had sent their envoys, the *okol'nichii*[27] Golovin and his companions, to confer at Albazin, commanding them to pacify with justice and to punish obstinate and disobedient Russians, wherever such are found.'

The letter proposed that Kang Hsi should order his troops to 'fall back to their own land;' that he should designate envoys for the negotiations and 'give all satisfaction concerning ravaged property,' [it continued, stipulating], 'that which has been settled anew [by the Chinese] should be returned and ceded to the Russian side; that the initiators of the dispute be executed; and that friendship and love would then be brought about between the two powers and their subjects could live in peace and tranquillity.'

Upon receiving the Tsar's answer, on 4 November 1686, Kang Hsi ordered his forces to fall back two *versts*[28] from Albazin and to cease all hostilities against the Russians, and he consented to the opening of negotiations. He instructed the Russian messengers 'when they shall confer with their official envoy Golovin, to invite him to travel with all speed to China in order to put an end to the war.'

The two governments thus agreed to regulate their border conflicts peacefully and establish friendly relations.

THE SINO-RUSSIAN TREATY OF NERCHINSK, 1689

Even before the reply from Kang Hsi to the Russian proposals for negotiations on the border question and on the opening up of unrestricted and regular trade had arrived, the Russian authorities had dispatched an embassy to the Chinese border to meet the Chinese envoys.[29]

The viceroy [*namestnik*] of Bryansk, Fedor Alekseevich Golovin, was designated ambassador to China (with the title of Ambassador Extraordinary and Minister Plenipotentiary); he was assisted by Ivan Astaf'evich Vlasov, voivode of Nerchinsk, and by the clerk Ivan Yudin from Yeniseisk (shortly afterwards replaced by the clerk

with the Cossacks Ivanov and Fomin. The letters sent through the missionaries did not contribute toward speeding up the peace talks between Russia and China as they reached Moscow after the end of the negotiations and the conclusion of the Sino-Russian Treaty of Nerchinsk.

[27] [One of the higher-ranking boyars.]

[28] [One verst = 1,066 m or 3,556 ft.]

[29] The edicts designating the Golovin embassy were signed on 12 and 16 December 1685 by Tsars Ivan and Peter and Tsarevna Sophie.

Semen Kornitskii). The embassy was to be accompanied from Moscow by 506 archers, commanded by two colonels, one lieutenant colonel, and five captains; 1,400 servants were to join this caravan on its passage through Siberia.

On 26 January 1686 the embassy left Moscow and on September 28 reached the Rybnyi fort on the Tunguska River, where it wintered. From there, messengers were dispatched on November 16, to the Mongolian khan Gegen Khutukhtu, whose lands Golovin would have to cross on his way to China.[30] At the Rybnyi fort Golovin also met the Cossacks Shaparov and Bushkov, who had been sent from Peking by the Russian heralds Venyukov and Favorov. Shaparov informed the ambassador that when passing through Albazin he had heard of the arrival of the messengers from the Emperor Kang Hsi, who had ordered the Manchu troops to fall back from Albazin and lift their siege of that town.

The Golovin embassy set out on May 15 [of the following year] and traveled by the Tunguska River to Fort Bratskii, by wagon to Irkutsk and again by boat on the Angara River, Lake Baikal and the Selenga up to Udinsk, reaching Selenginsk on the Russian-Mongolian border on October 25. Golovin had been given wide latitude to settle the Amur conflict and had been instructed to seek a solution of other questions of mutual interest to Russia and China. In particular, he was to obtain agreement that 'Chinese merchants be authorized to export to Russia, if they possess it, unalloyed silver, either with or without official envoys, in amounts of 1,000 and 3,000 *poods,* and to give it to and exchange it at its real price in His Majesty's Treasury, and [to export] white and yellow silk.'

The Russian heralds' reports, as well as Kang Hsi's letters, showed that the Manchus were attempting to bring pressure to bear on the Russian embassy. After he had reached Selenginsk, Golovin dispatched the herald Stepan Korovin to the Manchu governor of the border regions on 19 November 1687; Korovin was to inform the Emperor Kang Hsi that a Russian ambassador had reached the frontier and to request that Chinese envoys be sent there to open discussions for the conclusion of an agreement and the 'settlement of mutual disputes.' The Manchus retorted by instigating a Mongol attack on Golovin's camp. In January 1688 the Mongol Khans Ochiroi and Khutukhtu sent a force of 4,000 men with Manchu firearms and cannon to destroy Golovin's camps at Selenginsk and Udinsk. This provocation did not succeed, however, and the Mongols were completely routed by the Russians.

The Chinese embassy which reached Nerchinsk to conduct the peace talks consisted of Sangotu, a high court official, Head of the Chamber for Internal Affairs, Tumke-Kamon, First Prince of the Chamber for Internal Affairs and Chief of the Khan's Standard, and Ilmat, the Emperor's uncle. The Chinese embassy was accompanied by two interpreters, the Jesuits Thomas Pereyra and Jean François Gerbillon.

The Treaty of Nerchinsk, the first treaty between Russia and China, was signed on 24 August 1689. It was also the first treaty to be signed by China with a European state. It included the stipulation that 'the town of Albazin, built by His Majesty the

---

[30] Golovin informed Khutukhtu that he had been dispatched to open talks with China and asked him to cooperate with Russia.

Tsar, is to be entirely demolished, and the people residing there shall be moved with all military and other effects into the lands of His Majesty the Tsar without suffering any loss of property or damage whatsoever' (article 3).

In agreeing to abandon Albazin Russia showed its desire to put an end to the border clashes that had continued for more than 20 years and had prevented the establishment of friendly relations between the two great states.

The Treaty of Nerchinsk regulated the problem of fugitives hiding in the territory of either of the contracting states. The Manchu representatives, who were more concerned than the Russian side in finding a solution to this problem, agreed, that they would not press demands for the return of fugitives who had already found asylum from the Manchus on Russian territory, in exchange for the Russian ambassador's assurance that no asylum would be granted in the future. Article 4 of the treaty stated: 'Fugitives from either side who may have settled in the other country prior to the date of this treaty may remain where they are; no claim for their extradition will be made on either side. But those who take refuge in either country after the date of this treaty of amity are to be sent without delay to the frontier and at once handed over to the authorities.'

Regarding the establishment of commercial relations between the contracting states, the treaty stipulated the right of subjects of either country to unrestricted passage through the territory of the other for the purpose of freely buying and selling any wares whatsoever. In the words of article 5: 'It is to be understood that from the time when this treaty of amity is contracted, the subjects of either nation, if provided with proper passports, may come and go freely on both sides on their private business, and may engage in commerce.'

This article established equal trade rights for both nations, without exception or limitation. The conditions contrast favorably with the commercial regulations which British colonialists later tried to impose on China after their invasion of Canton [Kwangchow].[31]

The treaty also stipulated complete legal equality of Russian and Chinese subjects in the regulation of disputes arising between them. Both sides accepted the basic principle that incidents and disputes between their subjects should not complicate relations between the two states and should be judged by the authorities to whom the parties owed allegiance.[32] The treaty enjoined the governors of the border areas on both sides to punish all lawbreakers by 'putting them to death' for their crimes.

It is important to note that the treaty insisted upon a peaceful solution of all future disputes and excluded the use of violence; as stated in article 6: 'No such crimes

---

[31] The East India Company sent five vessels to China in 1637; these ships sailed up the Si Kiang River to the Canton forts without permission from the Chinese authorities, landed a detachment of troops and obliged the Chinese administration, by threatening to bombard the city, to authorize the entry of British merchants and the opening of a trading 'factory.' [The 'factory' (derived from factor) was the strip of land outside the city walls of Canton, facing the Pearl River, where foreigners were authorized to trade. They were forbidden to go beyond this area.]

[32] [It was this provision of the Treaty of Nerchinsk that established the precedent for extraterritoriality, subsequently adopted by all Western nations in agreements with China, and much resented by the Chinese.]

and excesses committed by private persons shall kindle war and bloodshed by either side. When cases of this kind occur they are to be reported by the side on which they occur to the sovereigns of both countries for amicable settlement by diplomatic negotiation.'

The Treaty of Nerchinsk played an important role in the development of relations between Russia and China. It regulated border clashes and excluded war as a means of solving conflicts. The treaty laid down legal norms providing for equality of commercial status, in which both governments were interested.

THE SINO-RUSSIAN AGREEMENT ON THE DISPATCH OF
RUSSIAN TRADE CARAVANS TO PEKING

Russian trade caravans began to visit Peking with increasing frequency after the conclusion of the Treaty of Nerchinsk. Father Gerbillon notes, on 25 May 1690, the arrival in Peking of a caravan consisting of 80 or 90 Moscow traders. A letter dispatched on 12 January 1692 by the Manchu nobleman Somgot to the Nerchinsk voivode, Fedor Skripitsin, also mentions the arrival in Peking of the trader Afanasii Safronov accompanied by 77 merchants. Somgot points out in this letter that although these merchants had reached Peking and were left to trade in complete freedom, 'he [Skripitsin] should not hope that this would henceforth become a regular practice.'

The dispatch of trade caravans through the nearly impassable desert steppes where hostile Mongol tribes roamed demanded considerable funds and large armed escorts. It still remained difficult to obtain Manchu authorization for the transit of caravans to Peking and the acquisition of camels and horses along the way, etc. The participation of the Russian authorities in the equipment of these caravans thus became a necessary prerequisite. The Russian government was interested in trading with China, since such commodities as rhubarb, tobacco, gold, silver and certain precious stones were a state monopoly and represented a large revenue for the Treasury.

While the Treaty of Nerchinsk was still being negotiated, the Russian ambassadors proposed that Chinese merchants be authorized by the Manchus to visit Russia for trade in certain commodities, such as silk, velvet, silver and precious stones, in exchange for Russian products. However, the Chinese merchants were not only prohibited from traveling to Russia, they were even prevented from going to the Russian border. The Manchu conquerors thought it dangerous to allow their Chinese subjects to come into contact with the outside world, since the struggle between Chinese detachments and Manchu troops in the south continued, and anti-Manchu secret societies were springing up throughout the country.

The imperial authorities made it a rule to authorize only Manchu merchants to trade along the Russian border, and these concentrated the greater part of this commerce, including that of Naun [Mergen or Nunkiang] into their own hands. Chinese merchants, who received no official assistance, had to be content with trading with the Russians at Peking, whenever the caravans reached the capital.

As affairs stood, it maybe said that the Russian side continued to take the initiative in the development of Sino-Russian trade. The Russian government, which possessed enormous reserves of furs collected by the Treasury as *yasak* or bought at a low price, was very much interested in opening up new markets in China.

Another embassy, headed by the veteran Danish merchant Izbrand Ides,[33] left Moscow for China in March 1692. Ides was to inform the Emperor that the Tsars Peter and Ivan wished to respect the Treaty of Nerchinsk; he was empowered to try to reach an agreement on the opening of government trade and the export from Peking of silver, medicinal herbs and rhubarb, which were in great demand in Russia. Ides was to suggest the opening of talks on the demarcation of the border in the Selenga River area, which had not been defined in the Treaty of Nerchinsk; the restitution of various fugitives and prisoners taken at Albazin was also to be discussed.

When Ides reached Peking in November 1693, the situation there was not conducive to talks on the subject of trade. A new campaign was in preparation by the Manchus against the Mongol khans in the west. The wars of conquest, which had so far been highly successful, were much more profitable to the Manchu dynasty than foreign trade. Valuable trophies and gifts from vassal populations reached the Emperor's court; his mandarins lived in great luxury and disdained commercial dealings, deeming trade to be the concern of 'beggars and servants' and not a fitting occupation for the Emperor's great noblemen.

The courtiers handed back the missive to Ides, invoking the pretext that in the letter brought by the Russian envoy the name of the Emperor appeared after that of the Tsars, without giving an answer to the proposals; by this means the mandarins hoped that the trade talks with the envoy would be broken off. Meanwhile Siberian furs continued to reach China in ever-increasing quantities and the demand for them grew steadily. The costly sables and marten pelts were in great vogue in China, where they were used for adorning the palaces and constituted part of the ceremonial dress of the Chinese nobility; furs were also highly sought after by the Chinese feudal lords. Despite the attitude of government officials, the Chinese merchants were very much interested in Russian wares and expressed dissatisfaction at the absence of regular trade with Russia. Eventually the court had to give way to this pressure and the Emperor announced to Izbrand Ides that he would permit the entry of Russian caravans, while continuing, however, to prohibit Chinese merchants from traveling to Russia.

ORGANIZATION OF STATE-OWNED TRADE CARAVANS AND
REGULATION OF SINO-RUSSIAN TRADE AT THE END OF
THE 17TH AND THE BEGINNING OF THE 18TH CENTURIES

The news that the dispatch of caravans to China had become possible elicited widespread interest in Russia, and the government of Peter the Great decided to take over the China trade. The costliest pelts (sable and silver fox) were declared a state

---

[33] Izbrand Ides, also known by the name of Elizar Elizar'evich Izbrand, had traded in Moscow since 1677.

monopoly, the Tsar's edict of 1697 stating that 'the collection and sale of sables shall henceforth depend entirely upon the will of His Majesty.' By this edict merchants were authorized to travel to China only in the entourage of state-owned caravans, and 'traders may trade in everything with the exception of sable and silver fox pelts.'

Owners of sables and silver fox pelts were forced to sell them to the Treasury at fixed prices. The edict of 1699 ruled that 'sable, the tails and underparts of sables and the costly silver fox pelts be given according to the edict to the voivode or to the heads of the customs; and money or wares shall be given out in exchange from the Treasury at the fixed prices, and there shall be no illicit trade in these forbidden wares.' The penalty for breaking this law under the edict was that 'a fine of as many rubles be paid as the value of those wares that were bought or sold.'

A Siberian Office was established in Moscow for the control of Sino-Russian trade; this administration was to organize and protect the state-owned caravans bound for China. The Siberian Office controlled a number of important warehouses in Moscow, to which furs collected for the *yasak* and the *desyatina* (tithe) were brought from all over Russia. Other commodities, such as broadcloth, leather, copper and pewter utensils, cotton fabric, tinsel, ceruse, pepper, and sal ammoniac, were also collected in these warehouses, from which they were dispatched to Siberia to be exchanged for furs or money; in the latter case the sums collected were used for buying furs at 'government' prices. When the amount of furs collected by the state was insufficient to equip fully a caravan, certain merchants, the 'pool traders,' were appealed to. These supplied the requisite furs on condition that they be paid twice the official price for their pelts on the caravan's return

Organization of the official caravans bound for China was a complicated affair. Each caravan was headed by a merchant, serving as agent, assisted by a government commissioner, four tax officers, and one Guards officer with 100 Cossacks under his command. With its administrative officials and escort, a state caravan numbered up to 200 persons. Its servants were paid in money and not in kind; they were forbidden to carry any wares, so that they should 'have no occasion to trade in them.'

It was decided that these caravans should be dispatched to China once a year; to ensure continuity, it was also decided that preparations for the dispatch of one caravan from Siberia should already begin while the preceding one was in Peking.

In their journey from Moscow to Peking government caravans covered a distance of 8,832 or 8,139 versts, depending on the route taken. Nerchinsk was the last Russian station along the route through Siberia. Here the merchandise was put into final lots, duties were paid on the privately-owned wares, which until 1706 were sent out with the government caravans, and final packing and sealing were performed under the supervision of the Nerchinsk voivode. The journey from Moscow to Peking and back took approximately two years. On their way to Siberia the caravans followed a route through Yaroslavl, Vologda, Ustyug, Solikamsk, Verkhoture, Turinsk, Tyumen and Tobolsk. Other routes through European Russia were also used by the caravan trade, i.e., an overland route through Murom and Nizhni Novgorod and a waterway comprising the Moskva, Oka, Volga and Kama rivers.

Before the discovery of the Siberian overland track, the caravans had followed three different routes from Tobolsk to the east: the first lay along the Irtysh River to the town of Tara and from there through Tomsk and Kuznetsk or through the Barabinsk steppe to Krasnoyarsk; the second followed the Irtysh to the Ob, went up the Ob to Narym and from there by portage to the Yenisei; the third descended the Irtysh and the Ob to the Ob Inlet and from there through Mangazeya by portage to the Yenisei.

Reaching the Yenisei by one of these three routes, the caravans could travel by water to the Russian-Mongolian border by using the Angara (Upper Tunguska) River, Lake Baikal and the Selenga. However, while Nerchinsk and not Kyakhta [Troitskosavsk] remained the main Russian trade center in the east, the merchandise was transported overland from Lake Baikal to the Shilka River and along this waterway to Nerchinsk. From there, and, later, from Kyakhta, the Russian caravans traveled through Mongolian territory at Urga and cut through the eastern part of the Gobi desert. This crossing was extremely hazardous; the Izbrand embassy, for example, lost 100 horses for lack of fodder (i.e., one-quarter of the caravan's pack animals) on the way to Peking, and on the return journey all the horses died, and the embassy was compelled to stop in Mongolia and dispatch riders to Nerchinsk to buy new ones.

When passing through Mongolia the caravans had to exchange part of their wares for cattle, camels and horses either to supplement their food supply or serve as pack animals. At Kalgan [Changkiakow], on the border between China and Mongolia, a halt had to be made to pay duties. In Peking special houses and stores were allotted to the travelers and the accompanying personnel lived as guests of the Chinese authorities. In their turn, the Russian administrators of the caravan were obliged to distribute a considerable part of the imported furs in the form of gifts to the Emperor's officals.

Sale of the Russian wares imported by the caravan and purchase of Chinese wares in Peking took several months. According to the regulations laid down by the Siberian Office, Treasury merchandise was to be sold before privately-owned commodities brought by the caravan could be marketed. These regulations, however, remained purely theoretical, and the merchants, by bribing the caravans' administrators, sold their furs before those of the Siberian Office. They thus obtained better prices at the expense of the Treasury.

In 1706, in order to eliminate all competition with the state-monopoly trade, Peter I prohibited the dispatch of privately-owned furs with the China caravans. The edict stated that 'merchants and vassals are forbidden to trade in pelts in Siberia,' and that 'traders shall not bring their wares into China without special permission on pain of death.' From that time caravans were to carry only Treasury furs to China and sell them for the Treasury's benefit. The Russian authorities informed the Manchu Emperor of the change in the regulations governing Russian trade and received his assent.

The Manchus preferred to deal with Russian caravans dispatched by the government since they found that such commerce could be more easily controlled and that duties were paid much more regularly, and the Manchu officials thus reaped greater profits. Private Russian traders were more troublesome: they often traveled to Peking without permission from the border officials, tried to avoid paying customs and did not always respect the regulations laid down by Peking to govern Sino-Russian trade.

The total value of Treasury merchandise exported from Russia by caravan sharply increased after 1706, when private trade had been prohibited. This is clearly shown by the following figures: the first state caravan dispatched to China in 1693 carried government wares of a value of 41,900 rubles, and private wares valued at 113,620 rubles; in 1710, each caravan carried state-owned merchandise only, valued at up to 200,000 rubles.

Although the Russian government had prohibited private merchants from trading at Peking, it could not arrest the development of private trade between Russia and China. As a result of the measures taken by Peter the Great for increasing the exports of the most important state monopolies, the private traders were obliged either to look for circuitous trade routes or to make shift with the restricted commercial procedure allowed by the state. Comparison of the caravan trade for 1702 (exports of government merchandise totaled a value of 47,000 rubles and private commodities, 566,400 rubles) with that of 1706 (184,000 rubles for exclusively government merchandise) clearly shows that the state caravan trade did not carry anything approaching the total amount of merchandise previously exported to China.

After private Russian trade had been prohibited in Peking it became concentrated at the Mongolian town of Urga, which was only 10 to 12 days' journey from Selenginsk, as compared to the journey of more than three months from Selenginsk to Peking. Russian merchants went to Urga ostensibly in order to trade in the commodities authorized by the Tsar's edict—Russian leather, linen, and similar items—although in fact they sold there 'large amounts of the best sables and other furs.'

Largescale private trade also continued at Peking under cover of the state caravans. According to the Peking archives, in the period from the conclusion of the treaty of Nerchinsk to 1730, more than 50 Russian envoys visited the Chinese capital, while according to Russian records only three official embassies (those of Izbrand Ides, Izmailov and Raguzinskii) and 14 government caravans were dispatched from Moscow in the same period. It may be assumed that the other 'envoys' were Russian merchants who were granted permission to trade by the Manchu authorities as genuine envoys. At the same time, of the furs conveyed by the official caravans, fewer were owned by the Treasury than by the caravan officials. The Russian envoy Raguzinskii complained that one-third of the wares transported by the state caravans were owned by the commissioners, the tax officials and other 'low-ranking officers.'

Another serious shortcoming of the state caravan trade was the narrow range of commodities in which it dealt. Russian exports usually consisted solely of furs, while gold, silver, pearls, precious stones, costly silks and other luxuries destined for the Tsar's palaces were imported from China. Russian manufactured products of excellent quality, curried leather, ironware, broadcloth, as well as such Chinese wares as cotton fabric and foodstuffs, which were in great demand in Siberia, were the exclusive province of private trade; the latter grew in volume, with the increase of the Siberian population. Private trading rapidly developed at Urga. According to a report of the Irkutsk voivode, Russian merchants used to travel there 'each as his own will dictated, and behave everywhere like men who do not bow to any authority.' At the same time the official caravan trade stagnated and even decreased. The value of Russian wares carried annually by caravan to Peking remained approximately the same from 1710 to 1716, while the number of caravans dispatched gradually dwindled.

Toward the end of the 1720's the Russian caravan trade suffered an interruption. The Manchus became highly suspicious of the caravans moving through Mongolian territory and of Russian trading in that region, fearing that commercial ties between Russians and Mongols would weaken Manchu influence in Mongolia. For this reason a Russian caravan was forbidden to sell its wares in Peking in 1717, and the regular caravan of 1718, not receiving permission to enter China, remained at Selenginsk.

At the same time, the policy of the Manchu court in respect to Chinese traders underwent a change. In the last decade of the 17th century and the first decades of the 18th, Chinese subjects had been forbidden to travel for the purposes of trade to Russia or to the outposts along the Russian border; this prohibition was now lifted. A letter sent in April 1719 from the Chinese Imperial Chancery to Gagarin, Governor of Siberia, stipulated: 'At present your stocks of wares along the border will not be bought by anyone, even if they are transported to the capital; and not only will your men suffer great loss as the days and months go by, but they will also ruin themselves in traveling to and fro; the same will happen to those who live along the border and supply cattle and fodder. This is why we shall not let your [men] through. But if some of your merchants wish to trade, let them remain in Selenginsk and dispatch their wares from there; we have made this known to our Chinese [merchants] who live not far from our borders, so that they may travel to Selenginsk with their wares and trade with your [merchants].'

The Russian caravan trade at Peking, and even the Urga trade (despite the greater freedom and variety it afforded), also did not suit Chinese merchants. The main Chinese exports at this time were tea, tobacco and silks; the Russian caravans, and more particularly the government caravans, bought these commodities only in small amounts. The main consumers of Chinese tea and tobacco among the northern and northwestern neighbors of China were the Mongols, the Kirghizes and the various other peoples inhabiting that territory which now constitutes the Mongolian People's Republic and Sinkiang province. Chinese traders carried their goods to these regions and Chinese trading settlements began to make their appearance along the Russian border.

The conveyance of Russian merchandise from Selenginsk to Peking cost Chinese merchants less than it did by Russian caravans. The Chinese exported a rich assortment of merchandise, such as tea, tobacco and millet from Peking, and sold them with profit to the Mongols or exchanged them for horses and fodder, whereas the returning Russian caravans from Peking carried mainly luxury products which were not sold along the way and could not, therefore, be used to defray the caravans' traveling expenses.

Peter the Great attempted to overcome these impediments. Only five years after he had prohibited Russian merchants from trading at Peking, he began to realize the weaknesses of the state monopoly system of trade; he decided to put the state caravans into the hands of private traders and thereby succeeded in adding considerably to the list of commodities exchanged between the two countries. Agents were instructed to compile a record of wares imported into China from other countries and Russian commodities other than furs that could be profitably marketed there. The Tsar also favored the opening of maritime trade with China through the port of Canton, an idea which was to be put into practice only over a hundred years later.

In 1719 Peter dispatched an embassy from St Petersburg to China in order to conduct a new series of talks on the renewal of the caravan trade and the regulation of border disputes; this embassy was headed by Lev Izmailov, a captain of the Preobrazhenskii Regiment of palace guards, who was elevated for the occasion to the rank of Envoy Extraordinary. Izmailov was instructed to reach agreement over the reopening of free trade between Russian and Chinese subjects, as established by the Treaty of Nerchinsk, and the free entry of Russian caravans into China. He was to inform the Emperor at the same time that Russia wished to meet in full the expenses entailed by the caravans' stay at Peking. Izmailov was also to obtain the Emperor's permission for the envoy's secretary, Lorenz Lange, to remain in Peking as first Russian counsul.

Considerable differences in the positions of both sides became apparent soon after the opening of Izmailov's talks, in November 1720,[34] with the Manchu ministers, and the Emperor himself, in Peking. The Manchus were mainly interested in political problems—the demarcation of the Russo-Mongolian border which would enable them to consolidate their influence in Mongolia, and the return of a large number of Mongolian fugitives. Izmailov had not been empowered to discuss these problems, and the main point raised by the Russian envoy, viz., the renewal of the caravan trade with China, was of no interest to the Manchu side.

The Izmailov talks, which lasted more than three months, did not lead to the conclusion of any agreements on commerce. The Manchu court, which had given verbal assent to Lange's establishment in Peking as agent of the Russian government and to the transit of caravans bound for the Chinese capital, insisted that the frontier between Russia and Mongolia be precisely determined and the fugitives from Mongolia (more than 700 in number) returned before the conclusion of trade agreement.

Lange's mission was also unsuccessful. The official caravan headed by commissioner Fedor Istopnikov, which arrived at Peking on 13 December 1721, encountered considerable difficulties in selling its wares. The mandarins prohibited Lange and

---

[34]   Izmailov left St Petersburg for Moscow on 16 July 1719 and Koscow on September 7; he reached
       Kazan on October of that year, Tobolsk on 16 December 1719, Irkutsk on 30 March 1720 and Peking
       on November 18 of the same year.

Istopnikov from selling their furs to Chinese merchants before the best lots had been made available at a low price to the imperial court.[35] On 8 May 1722 the Emperor's representative declared in the presence of the two Russian agents: 'The Emperor intends to interrupt all commerce and exchange of letters with Russia from now on and to prohibit Russian merchants from remaining inside China in the future; this is because the return of Chinese fugitives by Russia has been so long delayed and because no full satisfaction has yet been given regarding all [the points] on which the Emperor had enjoined the envoy Izmailov to report concerning the frontiers; no caravan whatsoever will be permitted to enter Peking; and for the same reasons they must prepare to leave on July 12. They shall be permitted to return when trade is reopened.'

The departure from Peking of Lange and Istopnikov marked a temporary interruption of the Russian caravan trade.

THE RUSSO-CHINESE TREATY OF KYAKHTA, 1727

The beginning of the 1715 Manchu-Chinese campaign against the Oirot-Dzungarian khanate and the continuing struggle to annex Tibet gave rise to considerable difficulties for the Manchu dynasty. In these circumstances strained relations with Russia could be of no advantage to the Manchu court. China's interest in the maintenance of a peaceful association with Russia was dictated by military, political and economic considerations. Trade with Russia was highly profitable, and large trading companies were being formed in the north of China to meet its requirements. The most important items of China's exports—tea, silks and tobacco—were finding a growing market among the Buriats, Tatars and Kalmucks settled in the outlying eastern regions of Russia, as well as among the Russian population of Siberia.

The death of the Manchu emperor Kang Hsi, after a reign of 55 years (1667-1722), marked a change of policy. He was succeeded on the Ch'ing throne by his son Yung Cheng, who pursued a consistent policy of good relations with Russia. In the second year of his reign, Yung Cheng took the iniative in reopening talks on border disputes and other points which had remained pending since the departure of Izmailov from Peking. Two high officials of the Manchu court, Privy Councilor Kung Olondoi[36] (who was also the Emperor's cousin), and Tkut, a counselor and President of the Mongolian Tribunal, reached Selenginsk on 16 July 1724 in order to meet Lange, the Russian consul who had remained at Selenginsk after his departure from Peking.

The Manchu representatives conveyed the Emperor's wish to maintain a permanent peace with Russia and forget all previous disputes. They declared that Yung Cheng was dissatisfied with the ministers who had terminated Russian trade in Peking and forced the Russian consul to leave the city. Olondoi and Tkut proposed that Lange should return to Peking and begin talks on the demarcation of the Mongolian border, which they had been empowered to discuss.

---

[35] Lange's report stated that the mandarins demanded that selected sables be sold to the Emperor at the rate of 3 *lan* each, whereas their current price in Peking reached 20 *lan*.

[36] [*Kung* is a title corresponding to duke.]

The Russian government continued to interest itself in the development of the China trade. The economic policy of Peter the Great aimed at promoting the development of Russian industry and commerce. His reign saw the establishment of 15 cloth and wool manufactories, 15 linen manufactories, 15 silk manufactories, 11 tanneries and five paper mills. The first Russian silver and lead mines were opened in the Nerchinsk area; iron foundries producing iron of high quality were set up in the Urals. There existed about 200 large enterprises in Russia at the end of Peter the Great's reign; in this period the export from Russia of ironware and broadcloth began. In 1712 a board for the supervision of trade was established which was later called the Board of Commerce.

The Russian government did all in its power to avoid difficulties in the establishment of good relations with China. In 1724, owing to complaints from the Manchu border authorities of unauthorized entry by Russian traders into Mongolia, the governor of Irkutsk recalled all Russian merchants living at Urga without passports to Selenginsk; they were henceforth forbidden to leave for Mongolia without a special permit from the Governor's Chancery. The Russian Ministry of Foreign Affairs instructed Lange to chart accurate maps of the Selenginsk area so that the position of the border between Russia and Mongolia in this region could be determined.

An embassy headed by Count Savva Lukich Vladislavich (Raguzinskii) was dispatched to China in June 1725, after the death of Peter the Great. The ensuing negotiations, which were begun in Peking and were concluded at the Sino-Russian frontier two years later, resulted in the Treaty of Burinsk, signed on 20 August 1727, which concerned the demarcation of the border in the vicinity of Kyakhta, and the Treaty of Kyakhta, signed on 21 October 1727, which regulated political and commercial relations between the two countries. Copies of the Treaty of Kyakhta, ratified by Tsar Peter II and the Emperor Yung Cheng, were exchanged by both sides at the Russian camp on the Kyakhta River on 14 June 1728.

The Treaty of Kyakhta is an important event in the history of Sino-Russian relations. It announced the establishment of everlasting peace between the two nations, and their aspiration to live in concord and friendship, stressing mutual respect for each other's laws and customs. In the words of article 1: 'This new agreement is purposely concluded in order to establish a firm and enduring peace between both empires; henceforth each state shall govern and restrain its subjects, and in its veneration of peace each shall strictly contain and strengthen its own [forces] so that the commission of hostile acts will be impossible.'[37]

The treaty devoted considerable space to commercial problems. Despite the negative aspects of the Peking caravan trade, and its failure to achieve economic viability, the Russian government persisted in its efforts to obtain China's agreement to the free transit of caravans. China conceded the renewal of this trade, and the treaty

---

[37] General agreement, concluded and exchanged at Kyakhta between the Russian Envoy Extraordinary Count Vladislavich and the Chinese ambassadors, Chabina, President of the Mandarin Tribunal, and the noblemen Tegut and Tulishen.

allowed the dispatch of goods to Peking once every three thears, the number of traders and other persons accompanying these caravans being limited, as before, to a maximum of 200.

The Russian side, in its turn, also made considerable concessions. It agreed to bring the private trading at the Mongolian town of Urga to an end and to transfer such Sino-Russian trade to the border outposts near Nipkov (Nerchinsk)[38] and along the Selenga Kyakhta River near Selenginsk, where 'houses shall be built and surrounded by fences or palisades as seems fit' (article 4).

The transfer of the trading posts to the border area met with the approval of the Russian merchant class, since it eliminated the necessity of sending out convoys for the merchandise through Mongolian territory and afforded greater latitude in the determination of wares to be marketed and the choice of market days.

The treaty enjoined a strict control of the border trade at Kyakhta and Nerchinsk on representatives of both sides. As stated in article 4: 'Whosoever wishes to travel to this trading post shall do so by a direct route; for if a person shall leave this route, either by error or in order to trade at other points, his wares shall be confiscated. An equal number of servants commanded by officers of equal rank shall be nominated by each side to cooperate in guarding the [trade] outpost and settling all disputes.'

Although the freedom of trade provided by the first Sino-Russian Treaty of Nerchinsk was ratified in principle in the new treaty, by this time China had already learned to regard the toleration of completely unrestricted trade with some misgivings because of its experience with Britain and other European states, which had imported through Canton large amounts of opium in flagrant contravention of the prohibition on its sale and consumption. In the Treaty of Kyakhta certain limitations on the merchandise which could be traded were introduced. Concerning this, article 4 stipulated: 'Any goods whatsoever may be bought and sold, except for those prohibited by the edicts of both empires.'

This limitation did not give rise to any practical difficulties in the pursuit of either official or private Sino-Russian trade. The Treaty of Kyakhta, which put Russian and Chinese trade relations on an equal footing, was concluded at a time when opposition to the British opium trade had flared up in the south of China. The activity of the Jesuit missionaries, whose influence on state affairs had been considerable during the reign of Kang Hsi and had promoted the opening up of Southern China to the European colonialists, provoked the indignation of the Chinese masses. In 1729, the pressure of public opinion forced Yung Cheng to prohibit the importation of opium into China and to expel the Jesuit missionaries from the country.

Meanwhile, the British adventurers representing the interests of the East India Company, whose infamous policy of brigandage in southeast Asia and particularly in India was notorious, continued their armed attacks on Chinese ports and organized the extensive illegal importation of opium. Under British military pressure the local Chinese authorities of Kwangtung province authorized the establishment of a British trading station at Canton in 1715. The central authorities refused, however, to con-

---

[38] [*Nipuchu* in Chinese.]

clude treaties or agreements with Britain or any other Western European state while these countries made unilateral and unequitable demands upon China.

Relations between China and Russia were based on the principle of equal rights and thus contrasted favorably with those existing between China and the nations of Western Europe.

FIRST CHINESE EMBASSIES TO RUSSIA

Relations between Russia and China continued to improve after the signature of the Treaty of Kyakhta. Both sides attempted to resolve peacefully all their disputes; these arose mainly because of incursions over the frontier by Mongols inhabiting the border areas on each side. During this period the Manchu-Chinese forces were combating the Dzungars, whose territories bordered on the Kalmuck khanates, themselves tributaries of Russia. The Dzungarian troops of Goldan Cheren defeated the Manchus in 1730-1731, destroying their army of 60,000 men. Fearing that the Kalmucks would join in league with the Dzungars, the Manchu court took steps to win over, or at least to neutralize the Kalmuck khans.

An embassy headed by Tulishen, who had previously visited the Volga region, passed through Selenginsk in February 1730 on its way to Moscow. The embassy also included five envoys, headed by Mandai, who were dispatched to the Kalmuck khan Cheren Danduki, a subject of Russia. They continued directly to Moscow in order to congratulate the new Russian Tsar[39] and ascertain Russia's position in the conflict in which China was engaged with Dzungaria. The first Chinese envoys were treated to a ceremonial reception along the route and upon their entrance to Moscow.[40]

In the course of the talks held at Moscow from 14 January to 18 March 1731, the Chinese envoys informed the Russian government of future movements of Manchu-Chinese troops near Russian territory, these forces being deployed in the war against the Dzungars, and begged 'the Russian court to entertain no suspicions.[41] The envoys asked permission to meet the khans of the Volga Kalmucks in order to win them over to the Chinese side in the Dzungarian conflict, and also requested Russia to forbid the passage of Dzungarian troops through her territory and to 'guard strictly

[39]   The Chinese embassy was to congratulate Peter II on the occasion of his accession to the throne; he was, however, already dead (18 January 1730) when the embassy entered Russia, and the envoys learned of Anna's accession to the throne while crossing Russia on their way to Moscow.

[40]   On 14 January 1731, a 31-gun salute greeted the arrival of the embassy, at the Red Gate of the Russian capital (Moscow again became the capital of Russia from 1728-1731), four regiments being drawn up, accompanied by a number of bands. When it departed, the embassy carried presents for the Chinese Emperor valued at 4,100 rubles: 3 pieces of gold and silver brocade, 4 lots of sables (of 40 pelts each) and 18 silver fox furs. The envoys were also presented with 22 batches of sable, 7 of fox and 14 of ermine (of 40 furs each), of a total value of 4,000 rubles.

[41]   In order to gain Russian support for the Chinese cause in the war against Dzungaria, the envoys declared that 'when the Chinese troops shall attack the Dzungarian people and take over their land, if any of this land should be required by Her Imperial Majesty because of its proximity to Her territory, this need should be declared and the land will be ceded to the Russian side.'

and instill fear into' any who might wish to remain in Russia. The Russians answered that in China's notification of its campaign against the Dzungars they saw an expression of sincere friendship on the part of a neighboring state.

Moscow authorized the Chinese envoys to meet the Kalmuck khans, but gave notice that this constituted an exception and that in the future communications with the Kalmucks, Russia's subjects, could be made only through Russian envoys.

In addition to discussing the political problems raised by the Chinese embassy, the Russian government complained of the nonobservance by the Manchu authorities of article 4 of the Kyakhta treaty. News had been received that in December 1727 the official caravan had met with difficulties at Peking and had returned to Russia with part of its merchandise unsold. Russia insisted that assistance should be forthcoming, not only to this caravan, which had again been dispatched (reaching Peking on 22 March 1732), but also to the caravan then in preparation.

Even before the return to Peking of the first Chinese embassy, the Manchu court dispatched a second embassy to Russia; its official mission was to extend the Emperor's greetings to the new Russian ruler, Empress Anne. This second Chinese embassy, consisting of two envoys, Deisin and Bayantai, reached Kyakhta on 21 April 1731 and entered St Petersburg on 27 April 1732. It reaffirmed, in the Emperor's name, China's desire for friendship with her neighbor. The envoys were received with the greatest pomp both in St Petersburg and along their route back to Moscow (27 July—2 August 1732). There they visited mills and factories and were shown the highlights of the city.

This visit promoted the development of friendly relations between the two neighboring states, as well as a closer acquaintance with the economic life and the nature of communications of both countries. These Chinese embassies to Russia were the first to be dispatched to a European state.

COMMERCIAL RELATIONS BETWEEN RUSSIA AND CHINA
AFTER THE CONCLUSION OF THE TREATY OF KYAKHTA

In the period preceding the conclusion of the Treaty of Kyakhta, Russian foreign trade policy had been influenced by the British doctrine of mercantilism. The Russian government considered the accumulation of *efimki* (term used to designate foreign currency), gold and silver, and the preservation of a favorable balance of trade to be the most important object of foreign trade.

Izbrand Ides had been instructed to obtain China's agreement to an annual export of 1,000 *poods* of silver. When dispatching Tret'yakov to China in 1719 as commissioner of a government caravan, the Board of Commerce instructed him in the following terms: 'All potentates strive to bring silver, both in ingots and in the form of money into their lands, and to abstain from exporting it...and we fully recognize that this must be the main concern of the European nations.' Tret'yakov was instructed to exchange all the wares of his caravan for gold and silver and to investigate 'whether the balance of Russo-Chinese trade is favorable or not.'

At this time China possessed considerable gold and silver reserves and was able to pay for the Russian (and in particular for Treasury furs) in bullion, the form of payment that the Russian commissioners required.

The Russian government considered the continuation of the state monopoly over most of the important items of Russia's trade with China essential for the achievement of its mercantilistic aims. After a short-lived change of policy in the reign of Peter II[42] the edicts of 1731 and 1734 reaffirmed the state monopoly of the fur trade and prohibited private merchants from selling furs on Chinese territory.

Russia continued to prefer trade by government caravans, although neither the scope of this commerce nor the range of products exchanged could satisfy the demands of either countries. The official prohibition of private trade on Chinese territory could not prevent its spontaneous increase at both Urga and Peking. The government caravan of 1735-1736 was faced with the competition of private wares, mostly furs, which had been brought to Peking during that year by private Russian traders and amounted in quantity to three times the number of those carried by the official caravan.

Opposition to the state monopoly of the caravan trade gradually increased even in official Russian circles. In 1730 Savva Vladislavich promoted a private trading company which was to have the monopoly of the entire China trade, including that of furs. Lange, the first Russian commercial agent, had been a staunch defender of the state monopoly of the caravan trade, but even he suggested in 1739 (not so much with the commercial interests of Russia in mind as those of the Western European countries), the organization of a trading company, modeled on the East India Company, with the participation of foreign capital.

Under the Treaty of Kyakhta the Manchu authorities had accepted the obligation to assist a trade caravan on its way to Peking once every three years; nevertheless, their hostility to the Russian caravans after the conclusion of the treaty continued as before. Governed more by political and military than by commercial considerations, the Manchus attempted to transfer the Sino-Russian trade to a number of outposts on the border and obstructed the sale of Russian wares in Peking. The maintenance of security served as a pretext to surround the Russian trading post in that city with a large guard, whose real function was to subject the Chinese merchants entering the post to a humiliating search (when they were even stripped to the point of undressing completely), to make precise note of all merchandise entering and leaving the post and to oblige the traders either to bribe the mandarins or to sell their best wares at a ruinous price.

The first Russian caravan to reach Peking after the signing of the Treaty of Kyakhta did not succeed in selling all its wares even after a stay of almost seven months (26 December 1727-13 July 1728), and was obliged to return to Selenginsk, having incurred considerable losses. The Manchu officials tried to justify their attitude toward this caravan by invoking the following excuse in their letter to the resident envoy at Selenginsk, Vladislavich; 'Soon after the caravan reached Peking we authorized

---

[42] On 26 June 1727 Peter II promulgated an edict which announced: 'The trade of sables and other commodities reserved for the benefit of the state is now free.'

Lange to open trade, as is customary and correct; however, only a small number of merchants came, because of the poor quality of the wares and the hot weather.'

Subsequent Russian caravans did not encounter better treatment. After magnificent ceremonial receptions in the Chinese capital for the caravans and the reading of imperial proclamations to the effect that complete liberty would be afforded to Chinese merchants to trade with the Russians, the Manchu authorities took secret measures to prohibit all trade in practice and forbade their subjects to buy Russian wares.

The official caravan trade thus became a costly and even prohibitive venture for the Russian Treasury. In 1740 the authorities took steps for the promotion of a private trading company to take over the state caravan trade. The Russian merchant class, however, proved hostile to this move and the attempt was unsuccessful. Traders found it far more profitable to travel to Peking with the government caravan, benefiting from the protection of its guards; they even made use of its wagons to carry their merchandise, and wrote off their losses at the expense of the Treasury with the tacit concurrence of the tsarist administration.

The Treaty of Kyakhta opened new prospects for private traders by permitting trade to develop along the border between the two countries. In this way the Russian merchants could house their merchandise on Russian territory and benefit from the protection of their own government, at the same time avoiding the considerable expense of transfering their wares from the Russo-Chinese border to Peking.

As soon as it lost the merchants' approval, trade by state caravans lost its importance; in 1756 it was brought to a close with the return of commissioner Vladykin's caravan. Border trade began to develop at the two outposts designated by the treaty—Kyakhta and Tsurukhaitui—and was to play an important role in the history of Sino-Russian commercial relations.

STRUCTURE OF THE RUSSIAN CARAVAN TRADE

The regular dispatch of official caravans to China had begun in the last decade of the 17th century. It may be inferred from a letter sent on 12 January 1692 by the Manchu nobleman Somgot to Fedor Skripitsyn, voivode of Nerchinsk, that the first Russian caravan to be dispatched after the conclusion of the Treaty of Nerchinsk apparently reached Peking in 1690. The dispatch of Russian state caravans to China later became a regular event, after the agreement reached between the Emperor and Izbrand Ides.

In the 60 years of the state monopoly of the caravan trade, 17 caravans were dispatched to China (excluding that of commissioner Yurinskii who was prevented by the Manchus from entering China in 1720), carrying merchandise valued at 2,036,497 rubles. As the sums obtained from the sale of these wares were used to buy Chinese products, it may be assumed that the value of Chinese commodities imported by Russia throughout the existence of the caravan trade also approximated two million rubles.

The state caravans from Russia mainly exported furs—Russian leather, diamonds, mirrors, watches, coral and various other wares—were brought only in small amounts. For long, sables constituted the bulk of the furs exported. In 1727, 51,920 sables, valued at 78,417 rubles, accounted for 28.8 percent of the total value of caravan exports for that year. As a result of unrestricted trapping of this valuable animal, the export of sables to China dropped in 1735 to 19,571 pelts, valued at 25,603 rubles;

MOVEMENT OF RUSSIAN CARAVANS TO CHINA

Date of departure	Date of return	Commissioner	Value of merchandise exported from Russia (in rubles)
1693	1696	—	41,900
1698	1700	Lyangusov	26,006
1700	1701	Bokov	47,000
1702	1704	Savateev	29,879
1706	1707	Sharin	184,000
1707	1708	Khudyakov	142,000
1710	1711	Savateev	200,000
1711	1713	Khudyakov	200,000
1716	1717	Gusyatnikov	200,000
1722	1723	Istopnikov	283,403
1724	1728	Tret'yakov	
1728	1729	Molokov	100,000
1731	1733	Molokov	104,390
1735	1736	Firsov	175,919
1740	1742	Firsov	100,000
1745	1746	Kartashev	100,000
1754	1756	Vladykin	100,000

it varied from 6,000 to 16,000 pelts yearly in the period from 1768-1785, although owing to the considerable rise in price the annual value of sables sold averaged 89,000 rubles. According to Lange's report, in 1717, a sable fetched only one ruble in Peking, while in the 1760's prices had already risen to 10 to 20 rubles per pelt.

Fox pelts were the second most valuable export to China, in particular of the red and cross fox. Fox furs, like sables, were in great demand there. The 1727 state caravan exported 5,948 pelts of silver fox, valued at 9,694 rubles, and 60,115 of red and cross fox, of a total value of 61,117 rubles; the data for 1735 are 925 furs valued at 1,523 rubles and 33,882 furs at 38,043 rubles, respectively. During this period prices reached approximately 1.5 rubles for a silver fox pelt and 1-1.25 rubles for red and cross fox.

Ermine and weasel also accounted for a considerable proportion of the Russian fur export to China by state caravan. In 1727 556,379 pelts of these two animals were exported, fetching 36,495 rubles, whereas in 1735 173,422 furs, valued at 12,594 rubles, were exported. Prices during this period reached 20-25 kopecks for ermine and 2 kopecks for weasel.

Beaver, otter, hare, marten, and squirrel pelts also constituted a considerable part of Russian fur exports to China. The export of squirrel pelts rapidly increased with with the decrease of other types of fur exports (sable, silver fox, beaver and ermine) in the 17th and the first half of the 18th centuries. While practically no squirrel furs had been exported up to the beginning of the 18th century, by 1728 commissioner Molokov's caravan was carrying 1,400,000 pelts of Siberian squirrel, sold at an average of 3 kopecks each.

Only very small amounts of Russian commodities other than furs were exported by the caravans. In 1727, the value of the Russian leather, cloth, mirrors, mammoth ivory, and whalebone carried by the caravan of that year amounted approximately to only 5,500 rubles. Since no state monopoly was imposed on these wares they were traded mainly by private merchants at the border posts of Kyakhta and Tsurukhaitui.

From China, the state caravans brought mainly silks (then known as *kamka*). In the 1650's Chinese silks were almost the only merchandise imported by private Russian traders. The silks brought back by the 1727 caravan were valued at 61,700 rubles, or 49 percent of the total value of the caravan.

The demand for Chinese silks in Russia was stimulated by the authorities. In order to promote the sale of imported Chinese silks, the government of Peter I decreed in 1717 that 'no spun or drawn gold and silver be worn, but only Chinese silks from Siberia.' In 1751 silks to the value of 103,000 rubles were imported from China, including the lots purchased at Kyakhta, and in 1759-1760 the amount of imported silks increased to a total of 173,000 rubles.

This demand led to the rapid development of a local silk industry. In 1761 Russia already posessed 40 silk mills with a total capital of 459,000 rubles. The development of this local industry should have stimulated the import of raw silk from China,[43] since Russia could produce the material only in limited amounts. However, owing to the great distance, with the resultant high cost of transport, and, above all, to the long interval between the arrival of caravans (approximately one year), Chinese raw silk could not compete with the European product; in consequence, silk import did not increase and in the 1750's amounted to approximately 200 *poods,* valued at 5,000 rubles.

At the end of Peter the Great's reign there was a considerable rise in the import of Chinese cotton fabric, particularly of the *kitaika* and *daba* grades, which were in great demand among the Siberian population. In 1727, 49,000 rubles worth of cotton fabric were imported from China, i.e., 39 percent of the total value of the wares carried by the caravan of that year; this included 64,651 pieces of *kitaika* cloth. This increase was somewhat impeded, however, since the state caravans were concerned mainly with supplying court needs, whereas cotton fabrics were sold almost exclusively in Siberia.

The import of Chinese cotton fabric increased only with the development of private trade at Kyakhta and Tsurukhaitui. It had already reached a total value of 250,000 rubles in the 1750's and accounted for more than 50 percent of Russian imports from China.[44]

---

[43] The first samples of Chinese raw silk were imported into Russia in 1670 by the Krasikov caravan (2 pounds).

[44] 257,000 rubles worth of cotton fabric were imported from China in 1751, this sum constituting 59.5 percent of the total value of Russian imports from China for that year.

Two other Chinese products—rhubarb and tobacco—which were a Russian state monopoly (these products, mainly rhubarb, also featured in the official Kyakhta trade) played an important role in the state caravan trade.

The state monopoly of rhubarb was established as early as 1649 as 'a monopoly of the secret rhubarb root.' For a long time it not only remained a highly profitable source of revenue but also furnished an important means of speculation for the Russian Treasury. The demand for this commodity was artificially stimulated by spreading false information about its extraordinary healing properties. Speculators could thus raise its price to 110 rubles per *pood* while buying it in China at 12-15 rubles; revenue from the sale of rhubarb reached up to 150,000 rubles a year.

The import of Chinese rhubarb by government caravans increased from 50 *poods* in 1701-1703 to 1,136 *poods* in 1738. Later effects of the contraband trade were felt and in 1753 official imports of rhubarb dropped to 500 *poods*. The tsarist authorities did all in their power to curtail the illegal import of rhubarb and its private sale by severely punishing transgressors of the state monopoly. An edict of 1735 stated: 'Although our previous edicts have strictly forbidden private persons from carrying the rhubarb root out of the country or overseas, many [lots] are being exported secretly, both from Siberia and by sea: because of this we have issued edicts throughout the country, bearing a seal, to affirm that no private person shall with impunity export from Siberia, or dispatch overseas, or carry out on his own person, one single pound of rhubarb, apart from rhubarb owned by the Treasury. If even one pound shall be found secreted on a person, all the belongings of that person shall be confiscated for our benefit without mercy and without taking into account explanations or pretexts.' Subsequent edicts decreed the death penalty for transgressors of the state monopoly of the rhubarb trade

A state monopoly of tobacco had also been imposed by Russia at the very beginning of the Sino-Russian trade. Traders in 1699 were obliged to hand over the imported tobacco (then known as *shar*) to the voivodes and customs authorities at previously determined prices. Throughout the duration of the caravan trade, tobacco remained a state monopoly, even during the short reign of Peter II (1727-1730) when the state monopoly of furs, rhubarb, silver and other commodities was repealed.

Other commodities imported by the government caravans were precious stones, porcelain, silverware and lacquer (wooden) utensils; the importation of tea developed only at the end of the 18th century.

With these commodities, the short list of Russian and Chinese products carried by the state caravan trade is about complete. The small volume of this trade, and the heavy expense incurred in conveyance of the merchandise through Russian and Chinese territory, restricted it to costly luxury articles or to state monopolies which were imported for purposes of speculation. The state caravan trade did not answer the needs of either Russia or China; this was particularly true of the border population of both countries, which required a wider scope for trade and a durable mutual economic relationship.

*   *

*

1. The Sino-Russian trade which began at the end of the 17th century was based on fair and equitable treaties concluded between the two countries in 1689 (Nerchinsk) and 1727 (Kyakhta); these set out reciprocal conditions of trade and defined the jurisdiction over the nationals of both countries.

2. In the initial period of commercial relations, the viewpoints of the Russian and Chinese authorities differed as to the importance of trade in the development of friendly relations. Russia attributed an extremely important role to this factor while the Manchu dynasty, which pursued an aggressive policy toward the Mongols and other nations, based its relations with Russia on military and political considerations.

During this period Russia, therefore, took the initiative in promoting Sino-Russian trade. On the other hand, the Manchus could not indefinitely prevent the natural development of trade with Russia, which corresponded with the basic interests of both nations and became an important source of revenue for both the Russian and Manchu governments.

3. While the political and economic centers of Russia and China were separated by territories with a low-density population, commercial ties could be strengthened only with the help and active participation of the authorities. No trading corporations wealthy enough to pay for the organization of the trading caravans and the expensive military escorts existed at that time either in Russia or in China.

Both Russian and Chinese governments participated in organization of the caravan trade; the former dispatched the caravans while the latter paid for their keep in Peking and assisted them en route through Chinese and Mongolian territory.

4. The Sino-Russian caravan trade gave an impetus to the development of the border areas and to certain industries in both countries.

The development by Russia of its Siberian communications begun in the middle of the 18th century, was undertaken partly in order to facilitate the passage of the official caravans from Moscow to the Chinese border.

The population of the Russian towns and agricultural settlements affected by this trade increased considerably, and in 1745 there were 17,133 inhabitants at Tomsk, 15,739 at Tobolsk, 12,341 at Yeniseisk, 11,374 at Kuznetsk, 10,384 at Irkutsk, 5,271 at Nerchinsk and 4,244 at Selenginsk.

The region on the Chinese side of the border also saw a gradual growth of commercial centers, an improvement of communications and an increase of population. The role played by the trading towns of Naun [Mergen, or Nunkiang] in Manchuria and Urga in Mongolia increased in importance toward the beginning of the 18th century. The increased export to Russia of silk and cotton fabrics, tobacco, porcelain, and later tea, stimulated China's industrial development.

5. However, as the bonds between Russia and China became closer and the border population of both countries grew, the initial form of commercial relations between the two states, viz., the dispatch of Russian government caravans to Peking, was found inadequate. These caravans became unprofitable for the Russian authorities as soon as the export of precious furs (silver fox, sable) to China decreased. Moreover, the requirements of the Siberian population could not be met by this form of

trade since the caravans mainly imported luxury articles from China for the court and did little to supply commodities for general consumption.

The attitude of the Manchu dynasty toward the caravan trade changed in the 1720's While the Manchus had previously prohibited traders from traveling through Mongolia or to the Russian border, after their subjugation of the Mongolian tribes they attempted to strengthen their hold over the territory by encouraging the migration of merchants to Outer Mongolia and the Russian border. At the same time the Peking authorities began to put obstacles in the way of the Russian caravans.

In the middle of the 18th century the Sino-Russian trade shifted to the border area between the two countries.

CHAPTER TWO

BORDER TRADE AND COMMERCIAL RELATIONS BETWEEN RUSSIA AND CHINA FROM THE MIDDLE OF THE 18th TO THE MIDDLE OF THE 19th CENTURIES

FROM the middle of the 18th to the middle of the 19th centuries, relations between Russia and China continued to develop, border trade assuming the new forms defined by the Russo-Chinese treaty of Kyakhta at the beginning of this period.

Almost until the middle of the last century, trade continued exclusively at a single point of the border, Kyakhta,[1] or Maimachin [Altan Bulak]; it was only toward the end of this period that commercial relations were initiated in another area, at the border between Russia and Sinkiang.

Russo-Chinese trade began to feel the effects of the maritime trade of Britain and other capitalist nations which had encroached upon the territory of South China; the consequences became serious once British capital had established colonial dominance in India.

DOMESTIC AFFAIRS AND INTERNATIONAL POSITION OF RUSSIA

In the middle of the 18th century the tsarist autocracy considerably reinforced the economic and political position of the governing landowning nobility. Estates which had previously been held by members of the aristocracy as service tenures were now bestowed in full; new tracts of land were also granted together with their 'black' (i.e., servile) peasant population, mainly in the Kama River basin, the Ural area and southern Russia. Landowners could sell their peasants and household serfs or dispatch them to the army as conscripts; the edict of 1760 authorized deportation of serfs in punishment for 'impudent acts.' This augmentation of the nobility's proprietary and judicial rights enabled landowners to increase considerably the volume of agricultural production through greater exploitation of the peasantry.

The nobility's growing influence was also felt on Russian foreign trade policy. The new customs tariff introduced by Empress Anne in 1732 abolished the protectionism instituted by Peter I, and with this the incentive to export finished and semi-finished products diminished. Import duties on luxury items, English cloths (following the Anglo-Russian trade agreement of 1734) and other industrial products were sharply reduced in the interests of the aristocracy; this inevitably decelerated

---

[1] [The town of Kyakhta was divided into two parts, Russian and Chinese (the latter situated on the tertory of Mongolia). When Mongolia became independent, the Russian part of the town continued to be called Kyakhta while the Chinese side, which had been known as Maimachin until 1920, was given the name Altan Bulak, or Kiachta. The Russian town was also divided into two parts, Kyakhta and Troitskosavk, which later amalgamated, the second name disappearing from the map.]

the rate of industrial production and affected the structure of foreign trade. The proportion of manufactured articles in Russian exports thus dropped from 55.5 percent in 1726 to 34 percent in 1760, while export of raw materials increased from 44.5 percent to 66 percent. Luxury items accounted for 67 percent of Russian imports from Europe in 1760. The main raw materials exported in 1760 included hemp, flax and oil-producing seeds (46 percent), leather (11 percent), and tallow (5 percent).

Russian industries continued to develop, albeit slowly. Entrepreneurs from both the nobility and the merchant class opened manufactories for linen, broadcloth, alcohol, leather and other articles. The growth of local industry was encouraged by a development of internal trade which followed the total abolition of internal customs in 1754 and an increase of duties on imported foreign industrial products.

With the development of industry, the political influence of the urban bourgeoisie, the merchant class, and that fraction of the nobility whose interests were linked with the country's industrial growth also increased. In 1757 these circles obtained the introduction of a new customs tariff which imposed relatively high duties on articles that could be manufactured in Russia. The accession of Catherine II in 1762 marked an intensification of protectionism. The tariffs of 1766 and 1782 successively raised import duties on manufactured products and luxury items while at the same time promoting import of such industrial raw materials (cottonwool, unrefined sugar) and fuel (coal) as could not be produced in amounts sufficient to meet the increasing requirements of Russia's industries.

Protectionism was accompanied by a number of measures intended to stimulate Russia's industrial production (freedom to organize industrial enterprises, increased banking credit facilities for industrialists, and in the establishment of private companies, repeal of some state monopolies, etc.). The number of enterprises increased from 984 in 1762 to 3,161 in 1796 (excluding mining industries, whose output was valued at 3.5 million rubles). Development of the metal industry was particularly rapid: the production of cast iron increased from 5 million *poods* in 1769 to 10 million in 1800. Russia became the foremost European producer of iron in the second half of the 18th century. Industry, however, was still unable to play an important role in the country's economy; at the end of the century, Russia remained a backward agricultural society in which the feudal element predominated.

The war of 1812, which had significant economic consequences and gave a new impetus to Russian capitalism, was followed by the rapid disintegration of feudalism in Russia. The number of enterprises (excluding mining industries, but including manufactories and artisan workshops) increased from 5,261 in 1825 to 9,994 in 1854. The number of industrial workers also grew during this period from 340,600 in 1825 to 860,000 in 1860; the proportion of free industrial workers[2] rose, particularly in the manufactories, reaching 87 percent in 1860.

Internal commerce advanced noticeably during this period. Almost a thousand fairs were held in Russia, among which the role of Makar'ev fair became increasingly important; in 1817 it was transferred to Nizhni Novgorod.

---

[2] [That is, in contrast to the forced labor of serfs.]

The volume of Russia's foreign trade increased by 120 percent during the first half of the 19th century, a favorable balance being maintained.

VOLUME OF RUSSIAN FOREIGN TRADE
(yearly averages in million gold rubles)

Year	Exports	Imports	Total volume of trade
1801-1805	75.10	52.76	127.86
1846-1850	151.75	131.52	283.27

Industrialization, the growth of cities and the increased internal and foreign trade also contributed to the development of communications. Russia's great rivers had remained the basic means of transport. The development of the internal market now gradually induced the tsarist authorities to begin railroad construction. The Warsaw-Vienna line was built in 1839, although mainly for strategic considerations; this was followed by the construction of the Moscow-St Petersburg railroad in 1842-1851.

Despite the growth in capitalist production, feudal relations still predominated in the 1860's, inhibiting the country's economy and perpetuating the lag behind the nations of Western Europe. The contradictions between the new, progressive capitalist mode of production and the backward, reactionary, feudal methods stimulated various social strata to protest against imperial absolutism and serfdom. The most important event in Russian social and political life in the first half of the 19th century was the Decembrist insurrection—overtly directed against absolutism and serfdom—considered by Lenin 'the first revolutionary movement against tsarism.'[3] Despite the absence of contact between the Decembrists and the masses, the uprising was to be of great significance for the revolutionary struggle of future generations against the regime, since it destroyed the prestige of absolutism. However, none of the forces existing at that time in Russian society were capable of heading a struggle against the landowning nobility or of leading it to a successful conclusion.

Russian influence on European affairs increased considerably after the Congress of Vienna; this circumstance provoked dissatisfaction in England, then the most advanced industrial nation and possessor of the largest mercantile fleet. Britain began to 'penetrate into Asia from two directions simultaneously: from India, and from the Black Sea.'[4] This advance was resisted by Russia in the Black Sea area and the Balkans.

Anglo-Russian relations continued to deteriorate in the 1830's, when Russia succeeded in improving relations with Turkey. Russia's growing influence in this country was preventing British and even, to a certain extent, French expansion in the Balkans and the Near East. However, Britain later succeeded not only in rekindling the Turko-Russian feud, but also in drawing Turkey into the anti-Russian camp. British

[3] Lenin, V. I. *Works,* 4th ed. Vol. 23, p. 234 [Russ.].
[4] Marx, K. and F. Engels. *Works.* Vol. 9, p. 383 [Russ.].

influence also became increasingly felt in Iran, Afghanistan and the Far East; she concluded an alliance with France and then with Austria in the 1850's.

DOMESTIC AFFAIRS AND INTERNATIONAL POSITION OF CHINA

In the second half of the 18th century the Manchu ruling dynasty succeeded in considerably extending China's territory and influence abroad. The resistance of the Dzungaro-Oirot khanate was broken in 1757 following a number of punitive campaigns, and Dzungaria was annexed to the Chinese Empire. A similar fate befell Kashgaria [Chinese Turkistan] in 1759. The Manchu forces of the Emperor Ch'ien Lung invaded Burma in 1765 and subjugated it after four years of struggle. Campaigns against Annam (Vietnam) were launched in 1788-1790 which again became a vassal of China. Nepal, invaded by Ch'ien Lung in 1792, suffered the same fate.

These military campaigns led to no economic gains of significance, since the exercise of Chinese suzerainty over Burma, Annam and Nepal was confined to the levying of a tribute by the Manchu emperor once a decade. These countries had in fact already been affected by British colonial expansion. However, the Manchu military successes served to strengthen their regime and intimidate their weaker neighbors.

Huge sums were required for the upkeep of the imperial court and bureaucracy and for maintenance of the large army.[5] Heavy taxes were levied on the Chinese population.[6] The Manchu authorities opposed all innovations, and prevented contact between Chinese merchants and foreigners; they prohibited, for example, the construction of large privately-owned factories and attempted to draw all existing sizable enterprises under the control or into the hands of the imperial court. The Kiangtachen potteries and the Kiangning [Nanking], Soochow and Changchow cotton and silk mills, as well as many other undertakings, were controlled by the court. These industries generally resorted to forced labor and extraeconomic forms of compulsion.

The Chinese authorities also limited the merchant fleet. In the Chihli [Hopeh] and Shantung provinces, for example, the building of ships and junks was absolutely forbidden; in Manchuria only single-masted vessels, not more than 32 ft long, without a deck, could be constructed; two-masted vessels up to 90 ft in length could be launched from the provinces of the southern seabord, but their arsenal was limited to two cannon, ten guns and not more than 30 *tzin* of gunpowder.

Mining, which had been consistently developed in China since antiquity, was not favored by the court and was severely hit by taxation.

The Imperial Treasury collected annual revenue taxes amounting to 44 million *lan* or approximately one million *poods* of silver, exclusive of excise duties, fines and other revenue.

The country's capital and other important cities were essentially administrative

---

[5] Yang Chung-p'ing (op. cit.) estimated that the army and the imperial court required even in the 17th century approximately 20 million bolts of cotton [about 810 million yards].

[6] Bichurin (Iakinf) states that at the beginning of the 19th century the Chinese imperial court collected a sum of 44 million *lan* or 88 million rubles in taxes and dues. *China's Civil and Moral Condition*, part 1. p. 99. Sankt Peterburg. 1848).

and commercial centers; the relatively small volume of handicraft production was mainly destined for the court nobility. The majority of these cities in no sense constituted economic centers, therefore, and were unable to assume the role played by the towns of Europe at the end of the feudal era. The enormous wealth accumulated by the Chinese ruling classes was used as private treasure or went into adornment of their palaces; it was not employed productively.

The economic dissociation between town and country fostered the existing alliance between agriculture and peasant craft production. In the words of Marx: 'Here [in India and China], the combination of agriculture on a small scale and domestic industry constitutes the broad basis of the mode of production; to this must be added, in India, the village community based on collective property of the soil, which community was likewise the original form of economic organization in China.'[7] At the beginning of the 19th century the Chinese village met its own manufactured requirements, mainly through peasant craft production. This stultified the development of urban-rural trade, and an autarky—the basis of the feudal system—continued predominant.

Internal trade remained localized. The activities of the city merchant guilds were limited to a certain territory beyond which they were not permitted to trade. Commercial capitalism and usury flourished in the countryside; land, which remained private property in China, became one of the greatest objects of speculation. Moneylenders either sold or leased land at high prices, having acquired it for a mere trifle from ruined peasants. Thus even within the framework of the feudal regime the private character of landed property was exploited, leading to further impoverishment and ruin of the peasantry.

The peasants, deprived of land and living, streamed to the cities; however, the limited scale of craft production constricted the labor market, and the newcomers merely swelled the ranks of the millions of urban poor; at the beginning of the 19th century Peking, Canton and other Chinese cities were teeming with beggars. These hardships elicited widespread discontent; popular uprisings flared up against the feudal regime and its mainstay, the foreign Manchu dynasty.

In 1796 a peasant uprising broke out under the leadership of the 'White Lotus' *(Pailienchiao)* secret society; its goal was the overthrow of the Manchus and restoration of the Ming dynasty. This revolt was not quelled until 1804. Another secret society, the 'Triad' *(Sunhohwei)* began activity in the same period. The southern maritime provinces witnessed the continuation of the perennial struggle against 'pirates' from the provinces of Kwangtung, Fukien and Chekiang. The Ch'ing [Manchu] administration proved incapable of grasping the situation and opposed all progressive remedies.

The Manchu court maintained its former supercilious attitude in relations with foreign nations: the latters' representatives were obliged to take part in a humiliating ceremonial before the Emperor; the 'Celestial Empire' was proclaimed the most powerful in the world, to which all other states should render obedience. No attempt

7 Marx, K. *Capital,* Vol. 3, p. 345.—Gospolitizdat. 1949 [Russ.].

was made to profit from European achievements. The splendor and arrogance of the Ch'ing dynasty could barely mask the country's backwardness, conservatism and inability to avert the imminent danger presented by the capitalist European nations.

At the beginning of the 19th century, however, the Ch'ing empire definitely abandoned its aggressive foreign policy, which had succeeded in isolating China from Western influences and preserving the feudal mode of production.

China's international position deteriorated rapidly. Great Britain and the United States were intensifying their efforts to penetrate into the south. China like India, which had already been conquered, seemed particularly tempting to the capitalist colonizers and clearly promised considerable gain. The great empire, with its population of approximately 400 million,[8] offered a large market for the developing European and American industries and a new source of cheap raw material and labor.

Commerce through the single port of Canton and through the medium of the monopolist Kung Hang[9] trading consortium, ceased to satisfy Britain's requirements. After the unsuccessful mission of the Earl of Macartney,[10] who had tried to obtain Peking's assent to a broadening of British trade, military pressure was brought to bear. At the same time the East India Company was conducting a large contraband opium trade in the south of China. In 1808 Britain attempted to seize Macao from the Portugese, alleging that France, which had occupied Portugal, was preparing to capture the island. However, this first attempt to establish a base near the Chinese coast was unsuccessful; the people of South China compelled the authorities to oppose this encroachment and the British squadron was forced to leave Macao.

A new British offensive began in the 1830's. In 1833 British merchants and manufacturers obtained the repeal by Parliament of the East India Company's monopoly in the East. This marked the beginning of repeated attempts on the part of British firms to establish themselves in China. In 1834 Lord Napier was dispatched to Canton as representative of the British government, without the approval of the Chinese authorities. In contravention of Chinese laws and customs, Napier attempted to abolish governmental control of foreign trade at Canton and to create favorable conditions for the free trade of opium. Interruption of the talks between Napier and the Chinese authorities was followed by the increased importation of contraband opium. The administration retaliated by confiscation. The now developing conflict served as justification for an attack on Canton by British warships. This marked the beginning of the first 'Opium War,' described by Marx as a 'predatory campaign.'

The defeat of the Ch'ing government forced China to conclude the first of several

---

[8] China's population in the 1840's was estimated at 400 million by the wellknown Russian orientalist Bichurin (Iakinf).

[9] [Ko Hong in Cantonese, as accepted in Western literature.]

[10] In 1792 a mission headed by the Earl of Macartney, governor of the Indian provinces of Madras and Bengal, was dispatched to China. Macartney reached his destination on 5 August 1793 and demanded in the name of the British government: 1) that a British ambassador be permitted to reside in Peking; 2) the opening to British trade of three ports (Tinghai, Ningpo and Tientsin) in addition to Canton; 3) the repeal of the Kung Hang monopoly; and 4) that British subjects be authorized to settle freely in and travel through China. (*Travels Inside China and Tataria of the Earl of Macartney in* 1792, 1793 *and* 1794, translated from the French. Moskva. 1804).

inequitable agreements, the Treaty of Nanking, which was to have serious consequences for the Chinese nation. Under the treaty, signed on 29 August 1842, five Chinese ports (Canton, Shanghai, Ningpo, Amoy and Foochow were 'opened' to British traders and China 'ceded' the island of Hong Kong to Great Britain; the British obtained the right of free trade in the treaty ports, the right to settle in them, and a number of other concessions which relegated China to an inferior and dependent position.

BEGINNING OF THE SINO-RUSSIAN BORDER TRADE

The 1727 Kyakhta Treaty initiated a border trade which was to play a most significant role in the development of trade relations between Russia and China. Private trade between Russian and Chinese merchants, which had previously flourished at Urga [Ulan Bator] in Mongolia and Nunkiang [Mergen] in Manchuria, was transferred by this agreement to the Kyakhta River[12] and the Nerchinsk area.

In April 1728 a group of Chinese merchants proposed to the Russian border authorities that trade should be opened along the Kyakhta River. The Russian administration agreed, and informed Russian merchants of the commencement of trade at Kyakhta and the impending arrival of Chinese traders. The first market was opened on 15 August 1728, only ten Russian and four Chinese traders having arrived by that date. Trade remained limited until the 1750's, despite steps taken by the Russian border authorities to attract both Russian and Chinese traders to the market. The report of the Russian commercial agent Lange, written on 23 March 1737 after passing through Kyakhta, states that 'Many merchants live at Kyakhta, just as before, and many Russian wares have been brought there; but there is no commerce because few Chinese merchants can be found at the border of Kyakhta while those who come do not bring the Chinese wares likely to be bought by the Russian traders; the latter lose all their money in consequence.'

In 1738 the Siberian Office enjoined the vice-governor of Irkutsk to ask the Chinese border authorities to send merchants to Kyakhta, 'for the lack of Chinese traders at Kyakhta causes the Russian merchants in the Kyakhta fort to remain there for long periods, and their wares spoil from being stocked.'[13]

The Russian state monopoly of furs, the main item exported to China, constituted the greatest stumbling block to the development of trade at Kyakhta. In their efforts to promote the caravan trade with Peking and ensure profits on this venture, the Russian authorities maintained and even intensified control of this state monopoly.

---

[12] Immediately after the conclusion of the treaty, building of the Russian trading settlement at Kyakhta was commenced at the border, at a distance of 4 versts from the Russian fort of Troitskosavsk. It was constructed on the initiative and under the direction of the Russian ambassador Savva Vladislavich, who had remained after the treaty's conclusion to carry out a topographical survey and organize trade. Construction of the settlement, which proceeded rapidly, was undertaken by 350 soldiers of the Tobolsk Regiment and by local inhabitants under the direction of Captain Knyaginkin. By 1728 there were already 32 *isbas* for the merchants and a market with 24 shops and warehouses.

[13] Sychevskii. *A Historical Note Concerning the Chinese Border*, p. 229. Moskva. 1875.

The Kyakhta trade became lively only after, for various reasons, the sale of furs was authorized by the Russians. In the first year of its existence, for instance, the highlight of the Kyakhta trade was the return to the state caravan from Peking. Furs to a value of 23,829 rubles were sold at Kyakhta throughout 1729 and 1730. The turnover at Kyakhta increased slightly at the end of 1730 because Treasury purchases of rhubarb were transferred there. An edict of 8 April 1731 stated: 'Rhubarb, the purchase and sale of which previously brought great profit to the Treasury and the Siberian Office and was then made public in 1727 by an edict of the Supreme Privy Council, is now designated state merchandise, to be as formerly exchanged for the Treasury's benefit.'

The monopoly for the purchase of rhubarb for the Treasury was conferred on a single merchant residing at Kyakhta. The merchant Svin'in enjoyed this right from 1737, and he was also authorized to purchase in Siberia 'squirrel, fox, ermine, polar fox, Kamchatka beaver and other furs which can be exchanged for rhubarb.'[14]

The prohibition on free trade in furs as well as the state monopolies imposed by Russia on the purchase of rhubarb and tobacco from China undermined private border commerce, since at that time precisely these wares constituted the main items of Russian trade and were in great demand.

Private commerce at Kyakhta was also much hampered by the complex and onerous Russian customs system. Merchants traveling from Moscow to Kyakhta and back had to pass a number of customs checks. High duties, reaching one-tenth of the value of all wares, including cash carried, had to be paid at the main Siberian customs house at Verkhotur'e by all traders importing merchandise from Russia-in-Europe into Siberia; additional dues, fines and legal or illegal exactions were levied upon traders in other Siberian towns by the tsarist officials.

Fixed prices, above which Chinese wares imported to Moscow could not be sold, were imposed by the Siberian Office, often involving the merchants in loss. The restrictions on private trade tempted Russian merchants to recourse to smuggling. Since in 1730-1740 Kyakhta thus became a center for contraband trade, state caravans suffered considerable losses. An edict of 1737 shows that, while there was a shortage of furs for the state caravans in Moscow, 'this Russian merchandise, brought to Peking by Russian traders, may be found there in amounts over three times greater than those brought by the state caravan; because of this, the last caravan to reach that city had great difficulty in trading and the price of Treasury merchandise dropped considerably.'

The state caravans proved unable to cope with the growing trade between Russia and China. This was due as much to their small turnover as to the limited number of wares carried. The caravans mainly supplied the towns of central Russia, and first and foremost, Moscow and St Petersburg; they only brought the costliest items because of the high cost of transport. On the other hand, the demand for Chinese wares was constantly increasing among the rapidly growing Siberian population

---

[14] *Polnoe sobranie zakonov* (Complete Collection of Russian Laws), Vol. 10, No. 7498; Cited from E. P. Silin, *Kyakhta in the 18th Century,* p. 53.—Irkutskoe oblastnoe izdatel'stvo. 1947 [Russ.].

(23 Siberian towns, including Yekaterinburg, had reached a population of approximately 185,000 in 1745). Aside from such costly Chinese products as silks, porcelain and precious stones, the Siberians required tea, tobacco, cheap cotton fabrics, sugar and other commodities. Siberia, on the other hand, could already offer for export, in addition to furs, the products of its various crafts; iron utensils, leather and coarse woolen broadcloth.

Private trade therefore developed despite all difficulties while the official trade decreased. In 1744 Chinese goods valued at 287,500 rubles were exchanged at Kyakhta, including furs and livestock worth 29,280 rubles. 'In eight months of the year 1746 Russian merchants bought and exchanged 177,106 rubles of Chinese wares at Kyakhta.'[15] A state-owned caravan which remained at Peking during the two years 1745-1746 succeeded in selling only 100,000 rubles of merchandise.

The heavy demand for such Chinese products as tea, tobacco and rhubarb encouraged Chinese merchants to expand trade with Russia. The construction of Maimachin (the 'Trading Town') was begun in 1730 on Mongolian territory opposite Kyakhta; this town became a center for Chinese merchants trading with Kyakhta.

The Kyakhta trade continued to expand in the years 1728-1750, despite four interruptions (in 1733, 1737, 1744, and 1747) due to minor incidents (skirmishes, thefts or infringements of the commercial regulations). The town's importance increased considerably after 1741 with the opening of a new route to Peking for the state caravans through Kyakhta. An edict of the Russian Senate in 1743 formulated the right of free settlement at Kyakhta 'for the enlargement of the merchant class' and allocated 'requisite land outside the town near the Kyakhta fort' for the construction of storehouses, industrial works and barns for livestock.

The second outpost (near Nerchinsk) to which private trade had been transferred under the Treaty of Kyakhta was destined to play only an insignificant role in the history of Sino-Russian commercial relations; this was the settlement at Tsurukhaitui, on the left bank of the Argun River, 300 versts from Nerchinsk. The Russians found Tsurukhaitui most inconvenient, and inadvantageous. The bulk of Sino-Russian trade was dependent on the area of Siberia west of Tsurukhaitui. The route from Kyakhta to Irkutsk (which in 1736 became the administrative center of the province)[16] was much shorter than that from Irkutsk to Tsurukhaitui. Kyakhta was connected by a convenient waterway (Angara—Lake Baikal—Selenga), while Tsurukhaitui was remote from the main Siberian towns, and wares dispatched there from Irkutsk had to be unloaded at least twice and transported overland. Finally, the location of the settlement had been badly chosen: it was situated on an open plain,

---

[15] Semenov [Izuchenie istoricheskikh svedenii o rossiiskoi vneshnei torgovle i promyshlennosti s poloviny XVII stoletiya po 1858 god] *Historical Information Concerning Russian Foreign Trade and Industry from the Middle of the 17th Century to 1858*, Part 3. p. 199. Sankt Peterburg. 1859 [Russ.].

[16] The previous administrative center of Siberia had been Tobolsk, residence of the vice-governor. In 1736 a decision of the Senate detached Irkutsk from Tobolsk and made it the independent administrative center of the newly created Irkutsk province. The vice-governor of Irkutsk was directly responsible to the Siberian Office.

50 versts from the nearest forest; even fuel had to be brought from the Chinese territory.

Since they were so far removed from the route taken by the state caravans from Selenginsk to Peking, the merchants of the Tsurukhaitui trading post did not enjoy the same advantages as those of Kyakhta in respect to the sale of furs and rhubarb.

On the Russian side, the Tsurukhaitui trade merely supplied the needs of the population of the Nerchinsk government, and traders from Irkutsk arrived there only occasionally. The Chinese traders were also lukewarm toward Tsurukhaitui since the Russians had little of interest to offer them there. No trading settlement was built near Tsurkhaitui on the Chinese side of the border; the trade was mainly carried on by the inhabitants of Naun [Nunkiang, or Mergen] who travelled there for this purpose.

The turnover at Tsurukhaitui was extremely small, reaching 4,170 rubles in 1722; 1,508 in 1733; 4,679 in 1734; and 7,748 in 1735. The increases noted for 1734 and 1735 were due, as in Kyakhta, to the sale of the batch of Treasury furs which had been sent back by Lange in 1733 after failure to sell them in Peking.

After the state caravan trade had been terminated in the 1850's, and with the shift of Sino-Russian trade to the border area, Kyakhta finally became the major center of this trade, maintaining its importance until the construction of the Trans-Siberian Railroad.

SINO-RUSSIAN BORDER COMMERCE AFTER TERMINATION OF THE STATE CARAVAN TRADE

In the 1740's and 1750's the state caravan trade became too expensive for the Russian Treasury to support. The authorities tried to induce private merchants to invest in the trade, or to transfer the caravan monopoly to a trading company specifically created for the purpose. Lange's unsuccessful effort to form in 1739 a 'company for trading with the nations bordering upon Siberia,' which would attract both Russian and foreign merchants, was followed by a further similarly vain attempt by Ostermann, a minister of the Cabinet, in 1741.

The abrogation of internal customs in 1754 and cancellation of duties previously levied on all currency exported to Siberia constituted highly important measures for the promotion of Russian internal commerce as well as the China trade. At the same time the Russian government established a bank which granted loans at a 6 percent interest; this also contributed to the development of Kyakhta, which stood badly in need of credit. Finally, after the opening of a 'Banking Credit Office' in Moscow in 1758, the merchants of central Russia trading at Kyakhta were permitted to pay customs duties with drafts payable up to six months; the merchants of Siberia received the same privilege in 1781. The repeated complaints against officials, who were accused of arbitrariness, embezzlement of public property, illegal requisitions, and exactions of customs duties above the legal rates, forced the authorities to take certain measures. In 1755 a representative of the merchants was delegated to assist at the Kyakhta customs house in the valuation of goods and customs duties.

An edict issued by the Irkutsk magistrate on 3 January 1757 proposed that the Selenginsk municipal authorities should elect from the merchants trading at Kyakhta 'good and reliable men for service at the Kyakhta border customs house, capable of evaluating the quality and price of Chinese and Russian wares, especially furs, knowing how to read and write...who would not be influenced by business and who would owe nothing to the customs. And after their election they should be speedily dispatched to the Kyakhta border customs to deal with customs matters.'

The increasing advantages bestowed upon private merchants could not but curtail the state China trade monopoly. The dispatch of state-owned caravans to China ceased in 1755[17] although the caravan trade was officially terminated only seven years later, in 1762. Its closure led to the concentration at Kyakhta of the bulk of Sino-Russian trade. Immediately afterwards the Kyakhta trade began to expand rapidly, despite repeated interruptions caused by border incidents.

The Chinese merchants displayed great interest in expanding trade with Russia. Russian historical studies furnish considerable data relating to the exceptional enterprise of the Chinese and their attempts to capture a leading place on the Russian market for their most important goods. A number of Chinese textile manufacturers began to produce the type of cloth in demand in Russia. Chinese merchants accepted Russian orders for goods destined for the Russian market, which were specially packed and marked for lengthy transportation and convenient handling.[18]

Even the Manchu ruling circles exhibited a growing interest in commercial dealings. Horses raised by Russians and Buriats in the territory lying beyond Lake Baikal were in great demand. In 1759-1761 alone, horses valued at 44,500 rubles were exported

SINO-RUSSIAN KYAKHTA TRADE IN 1755-1762

Year	Value of Russian wares (including re-export of foreign wares)	Value of Chinese wares	Total Volume of trade	Revenue from customs (to 1760 according to the tariffs of 1699 and later of 1761)
1755	606,084	230,981	837,065	193,173
1756	450,768	241,252	692,020	157,183
1757	421,878	418,811	840,689	147,215
1758	525,999	511,071	1,037,070	178,876
1759	718,145	698,985	1,417,130	230,481
1760	699,940	658,331	1,358,271	238,155
1761	391,469	619,598	1,011,067	230,840
1762	101,643	37,672	139,315	—

[17] In the second half of the 18th century Russia sent several lots of furs to Peking, the proceeds of sale to cover the expenses of the Russian church mission; these ventures cannot, however, be considered regular commerce.

[18] Senator Shuvalov, in a letter to the Siberian Office in 1759, proposed that an order be sent to Siberia 'stipulating that manufacturers in China should be enjoined through the merchants to ensure that state emblems be not stamped upside down, and that a sufficient amount of emblems be ordered, the state emblems in blue on white...'

through Kyakhta. In an effort to increase Russian imports, the Manchus demanded abolition of customs duties at Kyakhta, alleging that the high tariffs imposed on Russian wares raised the prices so excessively that buying from Russia became unprofitable.

Both turnover and revenue from customs at Kyakhta increased steeply as soon as the state caravan trade ceased.

In 1755 and 1756, before the Kyakhta customs had been properly organized, we find that the value of the Russian goods sold was much higher than that fetched by the Chinese merchandise, although equivalent amounts should have been exchanged since only barter was practiced at Kyakhta. As the Chinese would not have paid additional sums in cash, the difference must be attributed to excessively high valuations by the Russian customs. The officials based their valuation of Russian goods not only on the prices quoted by the merchants but also on the current prices obtaining in Russia proper; in addition, this estimate was made long before prices at Kyakhta had become stabilized.

Chinese goods, on the other hand, were valued at Kyakhta at the time of sale, and since many were specifically Chinese products (tea, tobacco, *kitaika* cloth, etc.) the merchants' declarations were accepted at face value. In order to pay less duty, the Chinese traders naturally tried to obtain the lowest possible estimate for their wares; this would seem to explain why the value of the Russian products exchanged at Kyakhta in 1755 and 1756 was so much higher than that of the Chinese. In the years 1757-1762 the total value of Russian wares exchanged at Kyakhta only exceeded that of Chinese merchandise exchanged during the same period by 130,000 rubles. The difference may be accounted for by Chinese liabilities, since the merchandise was paid for in promissory notes.

Sino-Russian trade decreased sharply in 1762 and was then interrupted for five years. This was due to infractions of the trade regulations and to illegal crossings of the frontier by the border population, as well as to the continuing hostilities between the Manchus and Dzungaria. An uprising of Oirot (Kalmuck) tribes, headed by Amursan, had broken out in 1756 on the territory of Dzungaria, which was already occupied by Manchu troops; a savage and bloody conflict then developed between the Oirots and the Manchu invaders. After the uprising had been repressed, Amursan fled to Russia. In 1758, Sheren, one of the Dzungar khans, also crossed the border to become a Russian subject. Russia asserted neutrality in the Sino-Dzungarian war. Requests for the return of Amursan and Sheren met with an unqualified refusal. Chinese emissaries were dispatched to St Petersburg to reach a settlement and restore mutual trade relations between the two countries. For the following ten years a series of diplomatic notes was exchanged concerning the return of the fugitives.

KYAKHTA TRADE AFTER ABROGATION OF THE RUSSIAN STATE
MONOPOLY ON FURS AND OTHER ITEMS

The Russian population of Siberia continued to be augmented by exiled and 'runaway' peasants in quest of land where they would no longer be serfs. According to the survey of 1762-1764, the Ob and Irtysh river basins already had a population of 200,000, while approximately 160,000 Russians lived east of the Yenisei. The flow of population to Siberia was still far from adequate to develop this great territory; nevertheless it helped to promote the expansion of the internal market.

In contrast to central Russia which at that time was passing through a phase of industrial expansion stimulated by the removal, proclaimed by Catherine II in 1775, of restrictions on the organization of industries, Siberian industries remained limited to a number of mining and ore-extraction enterprises in the Yekaterinburg [Sverdlovsk], Altai and Nerchinsk districts; other industries remained rudimentary. In the main, Siberia continued to attract commercial capital which drew its profits from the sale of central Russian industrial products and Chinese goods.

The Sino-Russian Kyakhta trade became an important consideration in the Russian budget. The revenue from customs levied on this trade in 1755-1761 reached a total value of 1,375,900 rubles. The Kyakhta trade in 1760 constituted 7.3 percent (1,358,000 rubles) of the total amount of Russia's foreign trade for that year (18.6 million rubles); in 1775 the proportion reached 8.3 percent (2,644,000 rubles of the total, despite an overall increase to 32.2 million rubles. However, commerce at Kyakhta could have developed much more rapidly if the restrictions on private trade had been abolished. The state caravan trade had been closed down because it failed to achieve its object, but the most important item of Russia's exports to China—furs —remained a state monopoly. Fur smuggling therefore, continued at Kyakhta with consequent heavy losses to the Russian treasury, despite stringent measures taken against the smugglers by the administration.

Growth of trade at Kyakhta depended, therefore, on removal of the artifical barriers imposed by the tsarist bureaucracy, whose officials regarded the state monopoly as a source of personal wealth.

The restrictions on private trade were lifted in 1762. On July 31 of that year, a government manifesto announced the cessation of the state caravan trade with Peking and affirmed the right 'of any person wishing to do so to trade on the border as well as in Peking, paying customs according to the tariff stipulated by the joint treaty between the Russian Empire and the Chinese State, and to dispatch his wares in the same manner as previously adopted by the state caravans...' [It continued]... 'And in order to conduct free trade with China, the previous prohibition imposed by the edicts of 1731, 1734, 1739 and 1752 on the exportation of furs, viz., Kamchatka beaver and lynx, Nerchinsk and Yakutsk squirrel, black and silver fox, grey fox, Kamchatka and Yakutsk sable, is repealed; these goods may also be traded abroad and their export is permitted to all persons after customs have been paid according to the tariff.'

In addition to the removal of restrictions on private trade, the Russian authorities took steps to initiate talks with China on the regulation of border conflicts and the reopening of trade at Kyakhta. On 28 August 1762 Catherine II announced to a meeting of the Board of Foreign Affairs her intention of dispatching to China a 'distinguished embassy' headed by Count Ivan Grigor'evich Chernyshov; the Chinese government was informed of this step by the diplomatic courier Kropotov, who had been previously appointed to journey to Peking. Kropotov was also ordered to organize a caravan of private traders destined for Peking when he arrived at Selenginsk, and to obtain the authorization of the Manchu court for its passage. However, his attempts to enlist Selenginsk and Irkutsk traders was unsuccessful. The merchants refused to take part in the venture, convinced that it would prove unprofitable and that the Manchus would maintain an unfavorable attitude. Kropotov was forced to load the caravan with furs owned by the Treasury; the proceeds of sale were allocated for the upkeep of the Russian Orthodox mission at Peking.[19]

In his answer to Catherine, handed to Kropotov at the border, the Manchu Emperor rejected the offer to dispatch an embassy to Peking to settle the issues in dispute and reopen trade; the letter was arrogant and rude in tone. The Manchus then evicted all the Chinese merchants from Maimachin, and their houses and stores were occupied by Manchu troops. The Russian authorities ordered the Selenginsk commander, Yakobii, to inform the Manchus that their insults would remain unanswered. He was also ordered to react favorably if the Manchus should propose renewal of the Kyakhta trade.

Both sides stood to lose by the interruption of the trade.[20] Clearly, such an interruption could not be of long duration, since the two countries were interested in renewal.

In February 1765 Yakobii informed the Russian Senate that five government officials had been sent from Peking to the border to reach a settlement. Kropotov, who had traveled in China and had knowledge of Sino-Russian trade problems was empowered by Catherine II to represent Russia in the talks with the representatives of the Manchu court. In addition to settlement of border disputes, he was ordered to reach an agreement on reopening of the Kyakhta trade. Kropotov's conversations with the *Askhan Amban,* Fulu,[21] culminated in the signing of the 'Supplementary Article to the Kyakhta Treaty of 1727,' on 18 October 1768.

This article reaffirmed the Kyakhta agreement, which had been concluded 'precisely in order to constitute a permanent peace treaty.' It was decided that the protracted controversy over the restitution of refugees should be 'brought to an end, and requests for the return of the fugitives shall cease.' Russia met the wishes of the Chinese merchants and all duties on merchandise at the Russian border were lifted. According to the agreement, 'no customs duty shall be collected at any time at the two trading points of Kyakhta and Tsurukhaitui'; it also modified the text of ar-

---

[19] In 1685 the Manchus had abducted 45 persons [Cossacks] (other sources put them at 25 or 50) from Albazin, among them the priest Maksim Leont'ev. These Russians, who made their home in Peking, became the nucleus of a Russian colony. After the death of Leont'ev in 1711, Russia requested permission for the dispatch of a Russian Orthodox mission to Peking to conduct the necessary rites for the Russian colony. The first church mission was authorized in 1711 by the Emperor Kang Hsi; it reached Peking in 1715 with the returning Chinese embassy headed by Tulishen.

[20] The diaries of Russian students of Chinese at the Orthodox mission in Peking, note that 'the disadvantage of the interruption of trade was felt in Peking itself (1763-1768) by ministers, courtiers and wealthy persons who used to buy Siberian furs and Kamchatka beaver.'

[21] [*Askhan Amban*—a Manchu appointment corresponding approximately to that of viceroy.]

ticle 10 of the 1727 treaty, which determined procedure for the arrest and trial of transgressors of the border regulations, as well as the penalties incurred.

The conclusion of the agreement was followed by the reopening of the Kyakhta and Tsurukhaitui trade, which showed a rapid increase in volume. In 1768 Kyakhta became the main outpost through which all legal Sino-Russian trade passed and it remained the only one after 1772. Its turnover increased 440 percent between 1757 and 1784.

VOLUME OF SINO-RUSSIAN TRADE AT
KYAKHTA IN 1757-1784
(in rubles of corresponding years)

Year	Total Volume	Annual Volume
1757-1761	5,664,227	1,132,845
1769-1773	11,257,086	2,251,417
1780-1784	30,416,744	6,083,348

The volume of trade at Tsurukhaitui remained very small (a value of 10,427 rubles in 1768; 3,463 rubles in 1769; 2,166 rubles in 1770; 2,245 rubles in 1771; and 1,788 rubles in 1772). When for some reason the Kyakhta trade suffered an interruption it showed a slight increase.

The rapid expansion of the Kyakhta trade was first due to abrogation of the state monopoly on the export of Russian furs, an item which accounted for 85 percent of the total value of Russian exports through Kyakhta in the years 1757-1784. Squirrel pelts[22] constituted the greater part of the furs exported; during this period (1757-1784, not including the years in which there were no commercial relations) from 2 to 4 million pelts were exported annually, reaching a maximum of 6,169,406 in 1781.

Other important items of fur export were (pelts a year): ermine[23] (140,000-400,000), sable[24] (6,000-16,000), polecat (20,000-50,000), fox (8,000-24,000), silver fox (300,000-1,200,000), and polar fox (10,000-15,000).

Colonization of Kamchatka, the Aleutian and other northern islands by Russian fur traders led to an increase in the amount of valuable furs brought to Kyakhta, in particular sea otter and beaver. The growing demand for furs in China stimulated the sale of both Russian and foreign furs at Kyakhta. The following amount of pelts were conveyed in transit across Russia on their way to Kyakhta between 1768 and 1785: beaver (30,000-50,000), otter (5,000-10,000), lynx, fox, corsak fox, rabbit, musquash and others.

---

[22] Yakutsk, Irkutsk, Barguzin and Nerchinsk squirrel were mostly traded at Kyakhta. The Chinese preferred Ob squirrel pelts. Pelts were priced in Russia as follows (prices per 1,000): Ob—30-35 rubles; Irkutsk—30 rubles; Nerchinsk and Barguzin—30-55 rubles; Yakutsk—20-22 rubles; Ilek river squirrel —40 rubles; Teleut squirrel—60-65 rubles.

[23] Ermine was sold at 10-15 rubles per 100 pelts in the towns of Siberia, and could be bought from the trappers at 6-8 rubles.

[24] Kamchatka sable was priced at 1-3 rubles per pelt.

The export through Kyakhta of merchandise other than furs also increased. 600,000-1,000,000 of lamb and sheepskins, 50,000-80,000 pieces of Russian leather, 3,000-15,000 arshin[25] of linen and 50,000-100,000 arshin of broadcloth, usually made from coarse wool, were exchanged between 1757 and 1784. The sale of foreign cloth, mainly from Germany, began to increase during this period and reached 100,000 arshin. Other goods, such as white sheet iron (1,000-1,500 sheets) and sai'ga horn[26] (up to 300,000 pieces) were also sold at Kyakhta. The main Chinese products exchanged were cotton cloth and silks, followed by raw silk, sugar candy, tobacco, tea, badian (Chinese anise), curtains and other minor items.

Among the cotton fabrics most in demand in Russia we find the *kitaika,*[27] of which up to 300,000 bales were imported yearly (each bale contained 10 bolts of $9\frac{1}{2}$ arshin each), and the *daba,*[28] of which 200-380 bolts (of 13-20 arshin each) were imported yearly. The proportion of cotton fabrics in Russian imports was so great that the most common of them, the *kitaika,* long remained the unit of exchange used in the Kyakhta trade.

Silks designated as *kamka*[29] were imported in an amount of 10,000-20,000 bolts, the import of other types of silks reaching 600-4,000 bolts. From 200 to 400 *poods* of raw silk and silk thread were imported in 1780-1785.

In the 1770's and 1780's tea was still a secondary item of Russian imports. Approximately 12,500 *poods* of [Paihuo] tea[30] and slightly more than 17,000 of bricktea were imported during this period. However, the consumption of tea by both the Asiatic and European population of Russia increased rapidly, and its import continued (by sea through England) even while the Kyakhta trade was closed down.

In the period 1770-1790 the range of goods exchanged at Kyakhta began to show a marked difference from that exchanged in the former Sino-Russian caravan trade. Furs, and sables in particular, had previously been the almost exclusive Russian export; in this period, however, although the export of furs through Kyakhta was six to seven times greater than during the state caravan period, it was insufficient to balance the increasing import of Chinese goods, and new products such as broadcloth and linen began to be exported. The type of furs exported by Russia also differed —squirrel pelts became the main item.

The range of imported Chinese goods changed to an even greater extent. Imports of precious stones, silver and gold, which had at first constituted the basis of the official caravan trade, either were brought in only in very small amounts or ceased entirely. The proportion of costly silks and velvet also decreased. Items of general use (*kitaika,* sugar, tobacco, and finally, tea) accounted for the greater part of the goods imported from China in the period under review.

[25] [One *arshin* = 28 inches]

[26] Sai'ga—species of antelope found in the steppes of Central Asia. Its horns are translucent and amber-colored; they are widely used in China as a medicinal drug of Tibet prescription.

[27] A light tissue, generally blue or black but sometimes cherry-colored, sold for 5-6 rubles per bale.

[28] A tissue for clothing generally blue, sold for 70-80 kopecks per bolt.

[29] *Kamka* designates a variety of Chinese silks, of which the best quality sold at three times the price of the *Kitaika.*

[30] From the Chinese *Pai Huo,* meaning 'wholesale.' This is a black tea sold in large consignments.

From time to time growth of the Kyakhta trade was hampered by measures taken by the border authorities when local conflicts occurred. Trade at Kyakhta was interrupted three times between 1768 and 1785. It was first cut off for three days in 1775, then for two years and 13 days (from 16 April 1778 to 29 April 1780) and was again interrupted from 1785-1792. This entailed losses to both sides and contributed to smuggling. The goods accumulated at Kyakhta and Maimachin were usually sold quite rapidly when trade was reopened; this subsequently led to an increased rate of commodity circulation, particularly after 1780. The Kyakhta trade continued to develop and played an important role in the Russian and Chinese economies.

SINO-RUSSIAN TRADE AT KYAKHTA IN 1768-1785
(in rubles of corresponding years)

Year	Value of Russian goods (including transit goods)	Value of Chinese goods	Total
1768	25,477	25,477	50,954
1769	1,074,651	928,984	2,003,635
1770	1,351,977	1,271,738	2,623,715
1771	1,246,410	1,142,510	2,388,920
1772	1,002,518	934,121	1,936,639
1773	1,140,185	1,153,992	2,294,177
1774	1,227,760	1,120,870	2,348,630
1775	1,365,825	1,278,584	2,644,409
1776	1,638,791	1,401,915	3,040,706
1777	1,440,546	1,342,127	2,782,673
1778	794,539	667,253	1,461,792
1780	2,700,187	2,700,187	5,400,374
1781	3,735,311	3,735,311	7,470,622
1782	3,520,342	3,520,342	7,040,684
1783	2,789,176	2,789,176	5,578,352
1784	2,413,356	2,413,356	4,826,712
1785	1,805,926	1,805,926	3,611,852

A large number of Russian and Chinese merchants took part in the Kyakhta trade. In 1768 Russia authorized formation of the following trading companies: 1) the Moscow company, for the export of beaver, otter, broadcloth, velveteen and other Russian and foreign goods through Kyakhta; 2) the Tula company, for the export of lambskins, pelts of various cats, etc...; 3) the Arkhangelsk and Vologda companies, exporting Russian furs, fox, fox paws, otter and goods produced in Moscow; 4) the Kazan company, for Russian and other types of leather; 5) the Tobolsk company, for Siberian furs and Russian leather; 6) the Irkutsk company, for Siberian furs.

Russian commercial capital was also drawn to Kamchatka. Trapping expeditions to the northern shores of Asia and America led to the formation of some quite important commercial artels in the newly opened region, both for trapping and for the export of the furs through Kyakhta. The wealthy Kyakhta traders, Andrei Tolstykh and Grigorii Volkov, were members of the Kamchatka trapping companies and supplied Kyakhta with beaver, otter, polar fox and other valuable furs. The Trapeznikov company, after almost 30 years of activity at Kamchatka and in the Pacific islands, in 1775 exported 54,929 sea otters, 29,108 sealskins, 31,658 polar fox, 150 ermine, 6,429 black fox, 7,055 gray fox, 3,670 red fox, 105 *poods* of walrus tusks and 60 of whalebone, and other goods, of a total value of 3.2 million rubles at Kamchatka prices. Approximately one-seventh of these furs was sold at Kyakhta to Chinese merchants at three times the Kamchatka price

The fair at Irbit, on the route from Verkhotur'e to Tobolsk, played an important role in the development of Russian trade with the East in the 17th and 18th centuries; in the last quarter of the 18th century the Nizhni Novgorod fair began to assume significance because of the increasing volume of the China trade and the growing number of merchants who participated. Nizhni Novgorod became an entrepot for furs from Arkhangelsk and Vologda, broadcloth from Moscow and Yaroslavl, and leather from the Volga towns brought there by merchants participating in the Kyakhta trade; it was there also that the greater part of Chinese goods was sold.[31]

Maimachin, the Chinese trading center on the border between Russia and Mongolia, also grew. At the end of the 18th century it housed almost 100 stores, 37 of which were quite large. Representatives from the most important cities of North China, and sometimes from other regions of the country, reached Maimachin through Kalgan Changkiakow and Urga. A fair was held at the small town of Maoch'eng, approximately 200 *li*[32] from Peking, where goods were purchased for dispatch to the Russian border and imported Russian wares were sold.

During the winter, goods were carried from China to Maimachin and back on camels bought for this purpose in Mongolia; in the spring, summer and early autumn the goods traveled on two-wheeled carts, drawn by horses or bullocks. The Chinese traders did not always bring the wares destined for sale directly to Maimachin; fearing that the accumulation of stocks at Maimachin would affect prices unfavorably, they usually stored their merchandise at Urga or in the various Mongolian villages between Urga and Maimachin, and transferred it to the final destination as required.

The Russian literature on the subject stresses the excellent organization of the Chinese merchants and their commercial ability. Chinese companies were frequently grouped into merchant guilds. The system of merchant organizations in China was relatively complex and well developed. Merchants were divided into three classes, according to capital. The first class included the 24 most important traders of the provincial towns, each with a capital of at least 6,000 rubles; the second class com-

---

[31] Chinese goods left Kyakhta in the spring by the Selenga River, Lake Baikal and the Angara to Yeniseisk; from there they were transported for 98 versts to the Moscow wharf on the Ket River. The wares then followed the Ket River, the Ob and the Irtysh up to Tobolsk, then along the Tobol and Tura rivers, by a portage to the Chusovaya River and from there to the Kama and the Volga. The voyage from Kyakhta to the Nizhni Novgorod fair took from one to three years.

[32] One *li* = approximately 640 yards.

prised 18 merchants of the provincial towns with a capital of 3,000 rubles; finally, 12 merchants of the provincial and district towns, possessing at least 500 rubles of capital, formed the third class. The merchants were organized into companies, usually four companies of each class for every town; these companies could operate a limited territory, prices were fixed by mutual consent for a period of not less than three years, and the percentage of permissible profit on the sale of Chinese (12 percent) and foreign (4 percent) goods was predetermined. The companies of the first and second classes enjoyed special governmental patronage. They received loans from the Treasury at a low rate of interest and were permitted to circulate promissory notes (of 300-1,000 rubles for companies of the first class and 100-300 rubles for companies of the second), and banking certificates payable at nominal value in four to 24 months.

Stability and discipline in the Chinese companies were ensured by their distinctive organization. Once he had become a member of a company, it was virtually impossible for a merchant to leave it or to withdraw the invested capital. Merchants of the first class bound themselves to invest their capital in the company for at least 100 years, those of the second class for 50, and of the third for 25. During this time, they were permitted to take only 20 percent of their profits, the other 80 percent being ploughed back into the company. Various institutions set up by these companies, including the so-called trustee banks, had wide powers of control over the behavior and private lives of the members.

The companies were directed by elected members who not only administered company affairs and the 'trustee' banks but also kept under observation the activities of other commercial and manufacturing enterprises (including foreign firms), initiated the construction of bridges, canals, public buildings and forts, kept a tally of the stocks of merchandise throughout the territory covered by the company, and so on.

The high degree of organization of the Chinese companies ensured them large profits in their dealings with Russian merchants. The latter were thus led in their turn to form close knit organizations and to agree to a set of rules for governing trade with Maimachin.

KYAKHTA TRADE AT THE END OF THE 18TH CENTURY

The Kyakhta trade was interrupted in 1785, and remained closed for six years and 11 months, following a dispute between the border administrations: Russia had refused to return to China a number of fugitives, the most prominent being Uladzai; another bone of contention was the attack on a Chinese caravan traveling through Mongolia to Maimachin by Buryats, who were Russian subjects.

Negotiations between the Governor of Irkutsk, Ludwig Nagel, and Sung Yung, *Askhan Amban* (Viceroy) of the Manchu Emperor at Urga, ended on 8 February 1792 with the signing of an agreement, in the form of an exchange of letters (protocol) in which both sides affirmed their desire 'to undertake no action in the future in contravention of the established treaty [of Kyakhta], not to commit breaches of that treaty, and to uphold it firmly...' The main point in this agreement concerned renewal of the Kyakhta trade. This time, not only Russia but the Manchu administration as well, showed interest in the speedy reorganization of the border trade, which had become an important source of revenue for the Manchu court.[32]*

The Kyakhta trade, which remained essentially a barter trade, excluded the possibility of payment in currency or by other monetary tokens. Nevertheless, the frequent interruptions, and absence of precise regulations by which the prices and volume of the trade could be determined, prevented enforcement of the original principle governing the Kyakhta trade—the balance of reciprocal deliveries. Merchants often resorted to the sale of merchandise for promissory notes or simple IOU's not underwritten by a banking or government institution; these practices led to claims and mutual recriminations which ended in interruptions of trade. The 1792 agreement bound the local border authorities to control the activity of their respective traders and prohibit the sale of goods on credit: 'As to the merchants of both sides, they shall be controlled by the authorities; all goods shall be paid for speedily at a fixed date; no extension shall be allowed; contraction of debts shall be prohibited...'

It must be stressed that the control exercised by the Chinese border authorities was quite thorough. The *Dzarguchei* (border commissioner) usually assembled the merchants every evening in order to fix prices and select the goods to be traded at Kyakhta. Each trader received from the *Dzarguchei* a 'ticket' authorizing the sale of certain goods; any violation of his orders was punished by a prohibition on trading for six days to two months, or expulsion from Maimachin, as well as by corporal punishment (up to 50 strokes with a bamboo cane). The coordinated activity of the Chinese merchants thus enabled them to acquire Russian goods at highly profitable prices.

After the renewal of commerce in 1792 the Russian merchants also took steps to regulate the Kyakhta trade. The merchant companies began to select trusted members whose function was to value the goods and fix the ratio between the unit of measure adopted for the barter trade—the *kitaika*—and Russian wares. The members formulated 'provisions' for the coming year to regulate the method for fixing prices and other conditions of the barter trade.

Shelekhov's American company[33] (which later merged with the Irkutsk commercial company) had a considerable influence on Russian trade at Kyakhta. The Russian-American company which was formed out of the merger of 1798 (four years after Shelekhov's death) received extensive privileges from the Russian government. It was granted a monopoly on lands along the northeastern coast of America from 55° N. Lat. to the Bering Straits, as well as on the Aleutian Islands, the Kuriles, and other Pacific islands. The company was also granted the right to annex newly discovered territory, to build settlements on these lands and to conduct completely unrestricted trade there. This reacted favorably on the Kyakhta trade, which showed

---

[32]* Duties collected by the Chinese customs at Kalgan and Kweichucheng amounted to more than 170,000 rubles at the beginning of the 19th century.

[33] The Siberian merchant Grigorii Shelekhov reached Kodiak Island off the Alaska coast in 1784 at the head of an expedition of three ships, and laid foundations for permanent Russian settlements.

a noticeable increase, while the Russian companies expanded and consolidated.

The exchange of Protocol and the strengthening of commercial organization on both sides of the border gave a considerable impetus to Sino-Russian trade at Kyakhta. Its turnover increased by almost 70 percent from 1792-1800, despite its irregular nature.

Furs continued to be the main items of Russian exports; they still accounted for 70 percent of the total value of exports through Kyakhta, i.e., a smaller proportion than previously. Siberian and Kamchatka squirrel were the most considerable, the export of pelts reaching 7 million. The export of cheap furs, such as cat skins, *corsac cat,* fox paws, rabbit pelts, etc. also grew. An increasing number of furs were brought to Kyakhta from the North Pacific islands and from America, where important trading stations had been established and extensive trappings of seal, beaver and otter was in progress.

KYAKHTA TRADE IN 1792-1800
(in rubles of corresponding years)

Year	Value of goods exchanged by each side[34]	Total commodity circulation
1792	2,467,279	4,934,558
1793	3,549,432	7,098,864
1794	2,522,941	5,045,882
1795	2,720,285	5,440,570
1796	2,551,764	5,103,528
1797	2,378,750	4,757,500
1798	2,783,942	5,567,884
1799	3,677,823	7,355,646
1800	4,191,923	8,383,846

Goods such as broadcloth, iron utensils, leather and livestock constituted 30 percent of Russia's exports instead of 15 percent as previously.

The structure of Russian imports from China also changed during this period, mainly in consequence of the increased demand for tea.

IMPORT OF CHINA TEA THROUGH KYAKHTA
(in poods)

Year	Black Paihuo tea	Green tea	Brick tea	Total
1798	14,398	6,704	25,875	46,977
1799	19,816	8,402	24,098	52,316
1800	30,017	8,387	31,450	69,854

[34] The goods exchanged by each side were of equal value.

Russia's multinational population consumed various kinds of China tea. The Siberian hunters and miners preferred the black brick tea[35] which was both cheapest and most convenient for prolonged storage. Inhabitants of the Central Asian regions of Russia consumed large quantities of green tea,[36] generally without sugar. Black Paihuo tea, particularly the better grade, was in demand throughout Russia.

REGULATION OF THE SINO-RUSSIAN TRADE AT KYAKHTA
AT THE BEGINNING OF THE 19TH CENTURY

The nature of the international situation in the first half of the 19th century was such as to increase the incentive of both Russia and China to maintain friendly relations. The ruling circles of the Ch'ing dynasty, under pressure from Britain, were convinced of the necessity for and expediency of peaceful, good-neighborly relations with Russia. Russia, also feeling that her interests in Europe and the Near East were endangered by the expansionist policies of Britain and her allies, was just as anxious to maintain friendly relations with China.

At the beginning of the 19th century the Russian government took a number of steps to consolidate Sino-Russian trade at Kyakhta. In 1800 the *Regulations Governing Trade at Kyakhta* (March 15), and an *Instruction to the Kyakhta Customs and the Members* (October 5), were issued. These regulations marked the government's decision to control the activity of the Russian companies; they introduced stringent rules to fix uniform prices for Russian and Chinese goods, since pricing was the origin of most of the disputes between Russian and Chinese merchants at Kyakhta. Russian merchants were forbidden to alter the prices determined by the merchant elders under threat of severe penalties.[37] When alteration became imperative (through increased or decreased demand, prolonged storage, etc.), the *Regulations Governing Trade at Kyakhta* made it mandatory to 'hand a formal written declaration to the elders, from not less than three merchants, commissioners, or stewards,' and 'to examine the necessity for, or inexpediency of, a new assessment at a general meeting of the elders and all the merchants, commissioners and stewards present at Kyakhta, in the presence of a member of the customs; this shall be on the same day as the handing over of the declaration, and no later than one day afterward.'

---

[35] Black brick tea is prepared from tea dust residue after selection of the better grades of tea. The dust is pressed into 'bricks' weighing approximately 2 kg.

[36] Green tea *(lücha)*, consisting of dark-green tea leaves, gives a weak greenish-yellow infusion and is very fragrant; the aroma is obtained by the addition of jasmine to the tea. Black tea (in Chinese *hungcha*, i.e., red tea) is made from the same leaves as green tea; their black color is obtained by special drying.

[37] Infringement of the *Regulations* entailed punishment as follows: a) sale of Russian goods below and of Chinese goods above the fixed price, or acquisition and sale of goods on credit—fine of 15 percent of the value of the goods; repeated offenders were expelled from Kyakhta and forbidden to trade there; b) insufficient control by the members and elders—their fine was fixed at twice the loss incurred by their fault, repeated offenders were expelled from Kyakhta; c) possession of gold, silver or opium—confiscation of the goods and expulsion of the offenders from the Transbaikal territory (the same punishment was meted out to those trading for money); d) failure to return goods taken from the storehouse (for exhibition to Chinese traders) in time—fine equaling five times the value of the given goods.

Control of observance of the regulations was entrusted to the members; they were given official status (being delegated by the authorities to the Kyakhta customs) and their instructions to the Russian merchants became mandatory.

The Russian government took steps to limit the competition of European merchants who by that time had become firmly entrenched at Kyakhta. The *Regulations* prohibited foreign traders who had not become Russian subjects from trading at Kyakhta on the Russian side. German, British, United States, Dutch, Norwegian and other European and American companies who had previously sold cloth and furs to China through Kyakhta were thus forced to sell at low prices to Russian firms at the Nizhni Novgorod fair or in the ports and towns of Russia-in-Europe.

The agreement reached between the Russian and Chinese border administrations concerned only the continuation of barter trade and excluded payment in money or drafts. Each side fixed its prices for the goods to be bought or sold, after which bargaining began. The value of the goods exchanged was not measured in monetary units but in units of the item most commonly exchanged. Up to 1800 this unit of exchange was the Chinese cotton *kitaika* fabric; at the beginning of the century it was replaced by China tea.

Nonobservance of this basic rule was severely punished by both sides, each having jurisdiction over its own subjects.

In 1800 Russia introduced a new tariff for the Kyakhta trade which stimulated export to China of manufactured products and protected Russian industry from foreign competition. This tariff set lower duties than the tariff of 1761 on all exported goods and most imported Chinese wares: the duty on tea, cotton and a number of other items was raised. The new tariff abolished the customs duty on broadcloth and considerably reduced that on dressed leather and furs. The transit trade in foreign wools was subject to a duty of 20 kopeck per arshin. The export of undressed leather, cloth for uniforms, flaxen thread, woolen felt, firearms, gunpowder, gold and silver bullion and foreign or Russian currency was prohibited. The import of dressed leather, wine, vodka, livestock, various metal wares and Russian currency (both coin and in bill) was also forbidden.

On the Chinese side trade regulations with the Russians at Maimachin—Kyakhta were established by an instruction[38] of the central authorities to the *Dzarguchei*. Its 16 points formulated rules for fixing prices, determined the fines and penalties to be imposed on transgressors of the instructions and gave detailed advice to the Chinese traders on the attitude to be adopted toward their Russian counterparts. No limitation was set upon the dispatch of goods to Maimachin from the most remote regions of China, but the Chinese merchants were to conduct themselves so that the Russians 'always hold our goods in high esteem and require our commerce, and the tie between both states should become closer.' When determining the amount of goods to be brought to the border, the Chinese merchants were to avoid accumulation of merchandise at Maimachin, observe closely the fluctuations of demand on the Russian

---

[38] A set of secret directions to the Chinese traders. It was published in Russia for the first time in the *Moskovskie Vedomosti* (Moscow Gazette) of 1852. No. 22.

side, and try to extract maximum profit from the exchange. As laid down by the instruction, they were to 'avoid both avidity in buying Russian goods and show of eagerness to trade, even though an item be greatly needed by some person, since private benefit should not come before the public welfare...'

In order to avoid the disputes frequently arising between Russian and Chinese traders, the latter were ordered to 'be courteous with the Russian merchants, and not to behave as formerly; it should not be forbidden for them to come to visit you or for you to invite them to feasts...' Violation of these rules by Chinese subjects entailed the following penalties:

a) 'Whosoever starts a quarrel of any kind with a Russian, even though he should later be found guilty, shall be placed under arrest for ten days, for any kind of dispute between merchants should be judged by the elders in a discreet and orderly manner so that minor enmities should not develop into serious disputes between states.'

b) 'Whosoever reveals these instructions or betrays the secret of the *Dzarguchei's* orders shall receive 50 strokes with a bamboo cane and be driven out of Kyakhta, and his business shall be handed over to another, as has been stated above.'

c) 'Whosoever shows cupidity in buying goods in contravention of the common ruling shall pay to the common fund a fine of ten times the value and be forbidden to trade: half a month for the first time, and double that period for a second offense, and he shall be driven out of Kyakhta for the third, as has been stated above.'

d) 'A merchant coming to Kyakhta for the first time is forbidden to trade in person for one year, even if he knows Russian, so that he should not in error disorder the general state of business.'

SINO-RUSSIAN COMMERCIAL RELATIONS AND THE KYAKHTA TRADE IN THE FIRST QUARTER OF THE 19TH CENTURY

At the beginning of the 19th century Sino-Russian trade continued to be concentrated mainly at Kyakhta—Maimachin, official relations between both states being maintained through the respective border administrations.

Maritime expeditions launched by a number of European nations—at first France (the expedition of La Pérouse in 1783) and later England (Broughton's expedition of 1793)—in the North Pacific not unreasonably aroused Russian apprehension as to the fate of her Far Eastern possessions.

The maritime trade of Western Europe and America with China increased considerably at this time. Shipping cargo from the Chinese ports to Europe and back cost less than its transportation through Siberia;[39] transport by sea was also twice to three times as fast. Additionally, it was more convenient for the large Russian settlements of fur trappers in Alaska, Kamchatka, Sakhalin and other North Pacific islands to trade with China by sea instead of through the remote and almost inaccessible Kyakhta.

---

[39] The price for shipping tea from China to England cost 30-40 kopecks per *pood*, while its transport from Kyakhta to Moscow cost 6 rubles or more per *pood*.

Progressive Russian circles were thus led to promote the idea of a maritime expedition to the Far East to investigate the conditions for navigation. An expedition launched by the navy, consisting of the vessels *Nadezhda* (450 tons) and *Neva* (370 tons), commanded by Kruzenshtern and Lisyanskii, sailed from St Petersburg in 1803 to reconnoiter the sea-lanes of the Pacific and Indian Oceans. It was financed by the Russian-American company and was to supply foodstuffs and other goods to the Russian settlements of America while loading there valuable furs for sale at Canton. The expedition reached Canton in December 1805 with a cargo of furs, after a voyage of more than two years.[40] Despite the strained relations existing between foreign merchants and the Chinese authorities, representatives of the Russian-American company traveling on the *Nadezhda* and *Neva* succeeded in selling their cargo at Canton and buying tea, chinaware and cloth.

This was the first step in the development of Sino-Russian maritime trade. However, there was to be no noticeable progress in the next fifty years.

In the same year Russia also dispatched a mission headed by Count Yu. A. Golovkin to Peking; it was instructed to reach an agreement with the Chinese government on the establishment of diplomatic relations between the two countries, the free entry of Russian ships into Canton harbor and navigation rights along the Amur River. Conditions, were not favorable for the opening of such talks however. The Manchus, alarmed at the unscrupulous activities of the British, were opposed to an increase of foreign trade at Canton and refused to accept foreign embassies in their capital. The Golovkin mission was halted at Urga and could not obtain permission to continue to Peking.

Despite the absence of cheap, convenient sea communications and its remoteness from the main commercial and manufacturing centers, Kyakhta's commerce continued, although slowly, to increase in volume. The value of the Kyakhta trade increased from 8.2 to 12.3 million rubles, viz., by 50.5 percent from 1801 to 1826.

VOLUME OF TRADE AT KYAKHTA IN 1801-1826
(in rubles, at exchange prices)

Year	Exports from Kyakhta to China			Imports to Kyakhta from China	Total Volume
	Russian goods	Foreign goods	Total		
1801	1,855,160	2,224,628	4,079,788	4,079,788	8,159,576
1805	2,376,959	3,365,369	5,742,328	5,742,328	11,484,656
1810	4,023,991	2,556,317	6,580,308	6,580,308	13,160,616
1812	2,397,524	538,489	2,936,013	2,936,013	5,872,026
1813	4,238,496	1,226,178	5,464,674	5,464,674	10,929,348
1826	4,073,179	2,069,190	6,142,369	6,142,369	12,284,738

[40] The expedition left St Petersburg on 7 August 1803. After crossing the Atlantic and rounding South America, the ships separated at the Hawaian Islands: the *Nadezhda* commanded by Kruzenshtern headed for the coast of Japan, Kamchatka and Sakhalin, while the *Neva* with Lisyanskii visited the Russian settlements of North America. They met again in December 1805 at Macao from where they sailed together for Canton.

The value of the goods exchanged at Kyakhta in 1810-1813 fluctuated considerably. The volume of trade increased rapidly up to 1810, i.e., before Napoleon's invasion of Russia, European goods in transit through Russia constituting a sizeable proportion of the exports to China. During the difficult years of Russia's struggle against invasion the value of exchanges at Kyakhta dropped to 5,872,000 rubles, thus decreasing by a factor of 2.2; the amount of foreign goods exported reached only one-fifth of its previous value. The end of the war saw a renewed growth of the Kyakhta trade, but the rate of increase remained below that noted for the first decade of the 19th century.

The proportion of Russian-produced goods in the exports through Kyakhta in-increased in the first quarter of the 19th century (particularly after 1810), while that of foreign (transit goods) showed a corresponding decrease. For example, while transit goods accounted for 54.5 percent of the total value of exports to China through Kyakhta in 1801, this had dropped to 33.7 percent by 1826.

The structure of Russian exports through Kyakhta also underwent considerable alteration in the same period. The importance of furs, which had constituted approximately 85 percent of the total value of exports in the 1780's began to decrease. In 1826 exports through Kyakhta totaled 6.1 million rubles, of which furs accounted for 2.9 million rubles, i.e., 47.5 percent. At the same time exports of broadcloth increased; in 1815 Kyakhta exported to China 533,930 *arshin* of cloth; this increased to 916,618 *arshin* in 1820, while the value of broadcloth imported through Canton in the same years by Britain, the United States and other countries totaled only 206,325 and 420,075 *arshin* respectively. It should be noted that the nations of Europe, and, primarily Prussia, at that time preferred to send their cloth to China via Siberia instead of by sea (a convention concluded in 1817 between Prussia and Russia gave to the former the right of transit for Silesian broadcloth and authorized its sale at Kyakhta through Russian merchants).

BROADCLOTH EXPORTS THROUGH KYAKHTA
(in million arshin)

Year	Russian manufacture	Prussian manufacture	Other origin
1818	313.1	446.9	41.6
1819	90.4	833.6	5.5
1820	66.6	841.5	8.5
1824	97.4	186.9	—

Exports of Silesian cloth dropped after 1820; this was due to increasing competition from English cloth imported through Canton as well as to the rapid development of Russian domestic production, particularly in Poland—at that time part of the Russian Empire.

Exports through Kyakhta of cotton fabrics produced in Russia and Western Europe also showed an increase in the 1820's. Cotton fabrics sold at Kyakhta in 1826 were valued at 667,000 rubles, 500,000 of which were paid for cloth produced in Western Europe. Other important items exchanged by Russian merchants at Kyakhta were Russian leather, morocco leather and calfskin, supplied mainly by the Volga towns and Siberian outposts.

Tea became the most important Chinese product exchanged at Kyakhta—Maimachin. Russia's tea imports through Kyakhta almost doubled from 1801-1830 and reached 143,200 *poods*.

AVERAGE ANNUAL IMPORT OF TEA FROM CHINA
(in poods)

1802-1810	75,076
1811-1820	96,145
1821-1830	143,196

Tea imports through Kyakhta were valued at 4.8 million rubles in 1825, 87.3 percent of the total value (5.5 million rubles) of Chinese goods imported there that year. The Kyakhta trade was thus becoming predominantly a tea trade where Russian imports were concerned. Such a rapid increase in tea imports created bottlenecks in the sale of this commodity in Russia. The government, which profited considerably from the tea trade (duties reached 69 kopecks per pound for the best green tea, 44 kopecks for ordinary green tea, 55 for black tea and 6 for brick tea), attempted to maintain imports at maximum prices, stabilization of prices on the Russian market being attained by encouraging the reexport of Chinese tea to Western Europe. With this in view a law of 1826 restored the import duties paid on Chinese tea reexported abroad, while merchants importing tea for sale within Russia were permitted to pay dues by installments every five months.

The development of Russia's cotton industry and the increased competition of fabrics produced in Western Europe considerably reduced Russian imports of Chinese cottons; this item, which had been the foremost Russian import from China in the second half of the 18th century, decreased in volume at the beginning of the 19th, dropping to approximately only 8 percent of total Russian imports.

IMPORTS OF COTTON FABRIC FROM CHINA
THROUGH KYAKHTA
(in thousand rubles)

1815	1,560
1817	1,462
1821	1,151
1823	633
1826	257

Other items imported by Russia included sugar candy, raw silk, and silk fabric. The amounts imported were, however, negligible, accounting merely for 2-5 percent of the total value of the Kyakhta imports.

Toward 1825 the volume of trade at Kyakhta ceased to expand, a slight decrease even being noted.

VOLUME OF SINO-RUSSIAN TRADE AT KYAKHTA
1824-1826
(in thousand rubles)

1824	14,860
1825	11,004
1826	12,284

This fluctuation can be explained not so much by a change in the state of Sino-Russian political relations, which remained amicable, as by the changing conditions of international trade. The rapid growth of merchant fleets, particularly those of advanced capitalist countries such as Britain, created serious competition for the primitive and lengthy Siberian trade routes.

The European nations then stopped sending their goods overland through Siberia to China, and the sale of European goods at Kyakhta ceased. Firms in central Russia also lost interest in Kyakhta, since Chinese goods transported by the cheaper sea routes could now be bought in the ports of Europe. Kyakhta ceased to be the sole trading outpost on the Sino-Russian border. The demarcation of the border in Central Asia necessitated the setting up of other stations.

Kyakhta then lost its previous importance and ceased to be the general Russian trading center for the Chinese border.

BEGINNINGS OF BORDER TRADE BETWEEN RUSSIA AND WEST CHINA (SINKIANG)

Commercial relations between the towns of West China and nearby Russian settlements go back to the end of the 18th century. A Russian edict of 1797 marked the 'Opening of Commercial Relations' between the Russian fort of Bukhtarma, situated on the upper course of the Irtysh River, and the Chinese towns of Chuguchak [Tahcheng, or Tarbagatai] and Kuldja [Ining, or Ili]. This trade, however, concerned only a limited number of items exchanged in very small amounts.

In 1811 the Lieutenant General of Siberia dispatched the interpreter Putimtsev to Dzungaria to investigate the possibility of developing trade with West China through the Bukhtarma fort. In the report which he wrote after his trip to Kuldja,[41] Putimtsev noted that at that time Russia was selling cloth and leather through Fort

---

[41] 'Diary of Interpreter Putimtsev on his Voyage from Fort Bukhtarma to the Chinese town of Kuldja and Return in 1811.' Published in the *Sibirskii vestnik* (Siberian Herald), of 1819.

Bukhtarma brought there by Kirghiz princelings who thereby avoided the Russian customs. Some of these goods were sold to the local garrison, others were exchanged with Chinese merchants who brought items needed by the Bukhtarma garrison for silver ingots (*yamby*,[42] used as currency in China). 'This limitation of the Russian trade,' wrote Putimtsev, 'also deprives China of many benefits, for undoubtedly the overt importation of high-quality goods from Russia would attract merchants from the surrounding trading towns.' Even the flow of Chinese silver to Bukhtarma, which in some years reached relatively important amounts, gradually decreased, and Sino-Russian trade at Bukhtarma ceased completely in the 1840's.

IMPORT OF CHINESE SILVER
THROUGH BUKHTARMA
(in silver rubles)

1826	21,037	1831	12,356
1827	60,395	1834	8,239
1828	148,302	1838	1,006
1829	84,323	1840	1,080
1830	80,681		

Trade with West China through other outposts—Semipalatinsk and Petropavlovsk —developed to a greater degree. It required the dispatch of trade caravans, as had been the custom in the Transbaikal region in the 17th and the first half of the 18th centuries. These caravans, which usually set out from Semipalatinsk and Petropavlovsk in July or August, reached Chuguchak or Kuldja in 50-60 days and returned to their original starting point in March of the following year.

The most important Chinese center for the Russian trade was Kuldja, a large commercial town which maintained close links with other cities of West China. Trade caravans traveled from Kuldja to distant Peking, passing through Urumchi [Tihwa] and Lanchow [Kaolan].

Before the middle of the 19th century development of trade at the Sinkiang border was hampered by stringent regulations imposed by the Manchu authorities. Caravans from the Russian towns had to stop either at the river before reaching the town of Kuldja or two versts from the townlet of Little Kuldja. The goods were unloaded at the trade warehouse in order to prevent sale to private buyers, and the caravans suite was lodged in a camp designated for the purpose until a special authorization to trade arrived from Peking. This usually took several months; merchants chosen from the caravan entourage, together with Manchu officials, then valued the goods in units of Chinese cotton (a length of *daba* 15-17$\frac{1}{2}$ *arshin* long cost the Russians approximately 2 paper rubles).

[42] [Russian mispronunciation of the Chinese word *Yüanpao*. *Yüan* was the name of the Mongol dynasty in China, *Pao* signifies money; *Yüanpao* thus means 'money of Yüan, i.e., silver ingots which circulated after the accession of the Mongol emperors. It should not be confused with the word *Yuan* designating a dollar, or a currency unit in general.]

In contrast to conditions at Kyakhta—Maimachin, where merchants of both sides paid no import or export duties (customs duties were collected far from the border in both cases), at the Sinkiang border the Russian caravans paid a 3 percent import duty on the price set for the exchange.

The Sino-Russian trade, which had developed spontaneously along the border of West China, remained unregulated up to 1851 by any agreed code and on the Russian side was limited to a small number of traders only, mainly from the border towns. The value of the goods exchanged in this region constituted only $\frac{1}{25}$ or $\frac{1}{30}$ of that exchanged at Kyakhta; this proportion increased, however, from year to year, particularly in the 1840's.

SINO-RUSSIAN TRADE AT THE SINKIANG BORDER
IN 1840-1851
(in thousand silver rubles)

Year	Russian exports	Russian imports	Total volume of trade
1840	194.2	173.1	367.3
1841	132.5	150.0	282.5
1842	143.6	151.3	294.9
1843	208.2	161.7	369.9
1844	192.4	148.3	340.7
1845	238.3	241.3	479.6
1846	209.4	304.9	514.3
1847	174.3	249.2	423.5
1848	118.6	134.5	253.1
1849	204.2	317.7	521.9
1850	211.5	530.5	742.0
1851	228.7	605.8	834.5

The value of Russian exports and imports from West China for the 12 years (1840-1851) preceding the commercial code regulating Sino-Russian trade at the border of Sinkiang Province was estimated at 2,255.9 million rubles and 3,168.3 million rubles, respectively. The disparity between these two figures, although barter trade only was conducted, is explained by the fact that the Russians paid for a certain part of the goods in silver coin or in gold. According to contemporary statements, the merchants of Troitsk could obtain credit in China.[43] Trade with Sinkiang thus differed from the Kyakhta trade not only in the method of levying customs duties but also in the method of exchange.

Main Russian exports were cotton fabric, linen, Russian leather and metal goods.

Tea was the main import from China. The value of tea imports increased from 59,588 rubles in 1842 to 579,848 rubles in 1851, i.e., its import had increased by almost

---

[43] *Rasskaz troitskogo kuptsa o puteshestvii Chuguchak* (History of a Voyage to Chuguchak by a Merchant of Troitsk), published by the Geograficheskoe Obshchestvo (Geographical Society) in 1850.

RUSSIAN EXPORTS TO WEST CHINA (SINKIANG) IN 1842 AND 1851

Goods	1842			1851		
	Amount	*Thousand rubles*	*% of total*	Amount	*Thousand rubles*	*% of total*
Cotton fabrics	—	71.2	49.5	—	118.2	51.7
Broadcloth	9,179*	12.0	8.5	32.351**	29.3	12.8
Woolen fabrics	—	0.3	0.2	—	2.4	1.1
Russian leather	4,804**	8.8	6.2	12,035**	27.8	12.1
Curried leather	—	0.2	0.1	—	1.7	0.7
Metal goods	—	41.4	28.8	—	30.8	13.5
Gold and silverware	—	—	—	—	0.4	0.2
Coral and nuggets	—	0.7	0.5	—	2.2	1.0
Furs	—	0.4	0.3	—	1.3	0.6
Other goods	—	8.6	6.0	—	14.5	6.3
TOTAL	—	143.6	100	—	228.7	100

* arshin   ** pieces

ten times by the latter date; during the same period the imports of Paihuo tea increased 23-fold from 21,209 rubles to 484,209 rubles. Imports of Chinese cotton and silks, which had played an important role at the beginning of Sino-Russian trade in this area, were considerably reduced by 1851: the value of cotton fabrics imported dropped from 18,869 rubles in 1842 to 5,870 rubles in 1851 and silks from 42,047 rubles to 11,570 rubles.

Despite the limited amount of trade between Russia and Sinkiang in the middle of the 19th century, the Russian merchant class showed a growing interest in this enterprise; traders from central Russia as well as from the Russian Central Asia also took part. The economic development of the latter region and the similarity between its population and that of West China, which had been linked by commercial ties

PROPORTION OF RUSSIAN IMPORTS FROM SINKIANG

Goods	1842			1851		
	Amount	*Thousand rubles*	*% of total*	Amount	*Thousand rubles*	*% of total*
Paihuo tea	449*	21.2	14.0	12,362*	484.2	79.9
Brick tea	3,151	38.4	25.4	7,394	95.6	15.8
Silks	—	42.0	27.8	—	11.6	1.9
Cotton fabrics	—	18.9	12.5	—	5.8	1.0
Woolen fabrics	—	0.07	—	—	1.5	0.2
Furs	—	—	—	—	0.4	0.1
Other goods	—	30.8	20.3	—	6.6	1.0
TOTAL	—	151.3	100	—	605.8	100

* poods

even before the arrival of the Russians and the Chinese assisted the course of commerce between Russia and China in this region.

KYAKHTA TRADE IN THE SECOND QUARTER OF THE 19TH CENTURY

Two factors essentially affected the development of Kyakhta trade in the second
quarter of the 19th century: the growing maritime trade with the southern coast of
China and strained Anglo-Chinese relations. The maritime trade of South China
with Europe and the United States developed to the detriment of the overland Sino-
Russian trade. After Napoleon's defeat and the subsequent reopening of the important sea routes, communications by sea from Europe to China became much
cheaper than the overland route through Siberia. The high cost of carriage through
Siberia first affected the transit trade: the transit of foreign goods to Kyakhta had
almost entirely ceased by the 1850's. The difference in carrier rates also had a noticeable
effect on prices in Russia: Chinese goods imported to European Russia by sea were
much cheaper than the same goods conveyed through Siberia. A. Korsak, who studied
Sino-Russian trade in the first half of the 19th century, notes that in the 1850's Paihuo
tea was sold at one ruble 50 kopecks per pound at St Petersburg, while its cost at
Irkutsk—745 km from Kyakhta—was one ruble 70 kopecks.

The maritime trade of China with Europe thus sapped the transit trade through
Siberia and considerably affected Sino-Russian trade at Kyakhta, particularly goods
originating in or destined for European Russia.

Maritime commerce, however, could not entirely replace the Kyakhta trade, for
the following two reasons: first, a large proportion of the Chinese goods bought at
Kyakhta was destined for Siberia and the Transbaikal area, while Russian goods from
these territories were exported in exchange; secondly, the Kyakhta trade was regulated by treaties signed by the two governments, while Canton, through which the
bulk of the maritime commerce with Europe passed, was the seat of constant unrest
resulting from Britain's aggressive policy, which culminated in the Opium Wars.

Despite the advantages of maritime commerce, the volume of trade at Kyakhta

VOLUME OF SINO-RUSSIAN TRADE AT KYAKHTA
IN 1827-1850
(in silver rubles)

Year	Exports to China	Imports from China	Total volume
1827	7,256,076	7,256,076	14,512,152
1828	7,349,184	7,349,184	14,698,368
1829	7,803,553	7,803,553	15,607,106
1830	6,398,597	6,398,597	12,797,194
1847	6,800,560	6,800,560	13,601,120
1848	5,349,918	5,349,918	10,699,836
1849	5,165,334	5,165,334	10,330,668
1850	6,916,071	6,916,071	13,832,142

decreased only slightly, and the greater part of Sino-Russian trade continued to pass through this town.

The increasing production of woolen and cotton fabrics by Russia not only compensated for the almost complete interruption of the transit of German and Polish cloth through Kyakhta and the decrease of cotton imports from Western Europe by more than 50 percent; it even became possible to expand considerably export of these items.

CLOTH EXPORTS FROM RUSSIA TO CHINA
THROUGH KYAKHTA
(in thousand *arshin*)

Year	Russian	Polish	Produced in Western Europe
1832	493.7	144.5	0.5
1834	555.9	247.3	—
1837	789.9	26.6	0.1
1840	1,241.1	—	—
1842	1,542.3	—	—
1845	1,525.1	—	—

In the 1830's and 1840's Russian cloth had gained a high reputation and was in demand not only in Manchuria and North China but in the remote southern Chinese provinces as well.[44] It was sold in all the important Chinese cities—Shanghai, Ningpo, Soochow, etc. Trade inspectors reported that the best Russian blue cloth was sold in Shanghai at 2 rubles 70 kopecks-2 rubles 80 kopecks per *arshin*, while the price of German cloth of the same quality was higher.

FUR EXPORTS FROM RUSSIA TO CHINA THROUGH KYAKHTA
(yearly average)

	1824-1828		1836-1840	
	Thousand rubles	*Proportion (in %)*	*Thousand rubles*	*Proportion (in %)*
Total exports	6,579.8	100	8,349.4	100
Furs	3,337.0	50.7	2,885.0	34.5

[44] The report of a contemporary French embassy to China contains the following information: 'One of the most curious aspects of the Canton trade is, of course, the sale of Russian cloth in the store of the Canton trader, Chan Ching, on Ta Chong street; for it is strange to find in the very south of China such merchandise, which is produced in Moscow, sold at the Nizhni Novgorod fair and exchanged by the Chinese at Kyakhta...The most important Canton high officials, states the Commercial Office, are the governor Kwang Chu-fu and his aide, Wang Fong, who both dress in ceremonial robes made of Russian cloth.'

Besides cloth, the main item exported by Russia through Kyakhta, furs also continued to play an important role.

The Russian-American company played a most active part in the exportation of Russian fur to China, especially sealskin, otter, beaver and polar fox. The proportion of Siberian furs decreased considerably. The wholesale trapping of sable, marten and silver fox in the Siberian forests depleted the reserves of these valuable fur-bearing animals, and their export to China dwindled. While an average of 4-6 million squirrel pelts, 2 million lambskins and 30,000 fox had been exported to China yearly in the 1820's, only one million squirrel pelts, 125,000 lambskins and 15,000 fox were exported in 1841-1843.

The third in rank in Russia's exports of this period after cloth and furs were leather goods—dressed Russian leather and goatskins. The nature of these exports also changed, however, in the 1840's. Leather, which had been supplied in large amounts by central Russia and the Volga region, was now used as a raw material or a semi-finished product by local industries. Kyakhta could thus obtain Russian leather and goatskins only from Siberia and Central Asia. The value of exports dropped from a yearly average of 969,000 rubles (paper) in 1824-1826 to an average of 677,000 rubles in 1839-1840.

In the 1830's grain products and livestock figured as important Russian exports through Kyakhta. In 1833 the inhabitants of the Transbaikal region were permitted by the Russian authorities to exchange large amounts of cereals, flour and livestock for brick tea, sugar candy, tussore, chinaware and other Chinese goods.

Among other Russian exports which were sent through Kyakhta may be noted antlers of the Transbaikal elk,[45] sai'ga horn and corals imported from Italy through Nizhni Novgorod.

RUSSIAN EXPORTS TO CHINA THROUGH KYAKHTA
IN 1825-1850
(in thousand silver rubles)

Goods	1825	1847	1848	1849	1850
Cloth and other manu-factured goods	1,566	4,367	3,484	3,625	4,514
Furs	2,905	1,840	1,342	1,047	1,640
Dressed and undressed leather	832	455	345	379	706
Alimentary products (flour, grain)	78	45	51	29	49
Livestock	52	15	12	14	15
TOTAL	5,501	6,800	5,350	5,165	6,916

---

[45] The antlers of young male elks are cut off from the live or dead specimens between May and August; this is before the antlers have hardened, when they consist of porous cartilage permeated with a thick blood mass. They were used in Tibetan medicine.

Tea was the greatest Chinese import. Toward the middle of the 19th century it accounted for approximately 95 percent of the total value of Chinese exports through Kyakhta.

The use of tea became widespread throughout Russia in the 19th century, and demand increased considerably.

The slight decrease of tea imports through Kyakhta in the years 1847-1850 may be explained by the increasing importation of Chinese tea via the Sinkiang border and other points not open to authorized trade. The competition created by importation of China tea by sea by British merchants made itself felt at that time. The only other Chinese commodity which played a relatively important role in the Kyakhta trade was sugar candy, the demand for which was rapidly increasing in Siberia. The importation through Kyakhta of raw silk, silks and cotton fabric, decreased steadily due to the development of Russian home production and increasing European competition. Other goods imported through Kyakhta, such as straw hats, artistic handicraft products, fans, paper and chinaware were secondary and their volume remained very small.

RUSSIAN TEA IMPORTS THROUGH
KYAKHTA
(in poods)

Year	Brick	Paihuo	Total
1802	23,451	21,581	45,032
1845	124,396	196,523	320,919
1846	109,695	227,452	337,147
1847	125,646	224,006	349,652
1848	116,249	253,746	369,995
1849	119,464	165,087	284,551
1850	85,440	212,178	297,618

Existing data on the Kyakhta trade show that its volume increased only with the growth of tea imports; at all other times the volume of trade dropped. The impact of

RUSSIAN IMPORTS FROM CHINA THROUGH KYAKHTA
IN 1825-1850
(in thousand silver rubles)

Goods	1825	1847	1848	1848	1850
Tea	4,796	6,648	5,172	4,598	6,543
Finished products	616.8	74.6	54.6	112.0	85.7
Sugar candy	40.2	62	84.3	125.3	93.3
Silk, paper and other goods	25.7	15.2	13.8	37.0	11.5
TOTAL	5,501	6,800	5,350	5,165	6,916

this decrease was felt particularly on finished products, mainly Chinese cotton fabrics and silks. One reason for the decrease was the development of Russia's textile industry; in the second quarter of the 19th century not only did its products reach the most remote Siberian outposts, but they were also exported to China. Russian printed cottons, velveteen, calico and other fabrics were in great demand in China, especially in Manchuria, Mongolia and the northern part of the country.

Another factor which arrested the development of Sino-Russian trade was its limitation to the single outpost of Kyakhta. The Russian and Chinese population of the extensive border area traded at settlements which had not been authorized by the official agreements. The volume of this illegal trade constantly increased.

According to A. Korsak, the population of the Transbaikal region met most of its needs in regard to Chinese tea and cotton fabrics by smuggling these items and exchanging them for furs, livestock, cereals, etc.

Finally, the regimen of trade instituted at Kyakhta—Maimachin was no longer appropriate for the changed conditions of international commerce. It continued as a barter trade, without the use of money or credit. The possession of either gold pieces or silver rubles was forbidden by Russia to the merchants at Kyakhta. Goods for the personal use of Kyakhta's small population were bought and sold with low denomination silver coins and paper money. The merchants were prohibited from the acceptance or giving of promissory notes or other bills to their Chinese counterparts and had to avoid the use of any form of credit. The low volume of the trade with China and its territorial limitations constituted severe handicaps for the North American Russian colonies of Kamchatka, the Okhotsk littoral and the North Pacific islands. Their settlers, who lived far from the Siberian centers, with which they could communicate only through the almost impassable forests and by use of the small rivers of the Yakutsk area, badly needed both the manufactured and alimentary products of Siberia. The Russian-American company and the traders and hunters of Kamchatka and the northern islands increasingly turned their backs on the Kyakhta trade, for it could supply them with only a limited number of Chinese goods (mainly tea) and the transport of these goods to the northeastern regions of Asiatic Russia, and to Alaska along the Lena River, or even through Yakutia and Okhotsk, was extremely expensive.

Once Shanghai had been 'opened' to foreign trade, representatives of the Russian-American company and other Russian commercial firms traveled there from Alaska to sell their furs and buy Chinese manufactured and alimentary products.[46] These visits remained irregular, however, for the British traders established at Shanghai kept putting obstacles in the way of the Russians.

The volume of Sino-Russian trade in the middle of the 19th century could no longer satisfy the needs of both countries. The necessity to establish more extensive commercial ties which would also involve maritime trade was then felt, but there were serious difficulties to overcome before a solution could be reached. The encroachments

---

[46]   In September 1848 the Russian vessel *Knyaz' Men'shikov* of New Archangel [Sitka] in Alaska anchored in Shanghai. It carried a cargo of 1,000 fox pelts, 4,100 sealskins, 235 otter pelts, 250 bearskins, 50 bobcat pelts and 40 barrels of flour.

of Britain into China, followed by those of the United States, France and a number of other capitalist countries, had changed the situation in the Far East. The Treaty of Nanking, imposed by England in 1842, as well as the subsequent inequitable treaties forced upon China by the United States (1844), France (1844) and other capitalists nations gave them the control of China's foreign trade. China lost the right to levy its own customs duties and regulate the commercial activities of foreigners in five of its most important cities, the so-called 'treaty' ports. Britain, the most powerful capitalist country of the time, controlled China's communications and its foreign maritime trade through the naval base set up on the island of Hong Kong. British vessels also appeared with increasing frequency in North Pacific waters, constituting a threat to Russia's possessions in that area.

*   *

*

1) Kyakhta—Maimachin remained for approximately 100 years (from the middle of the 18th to the middle of the 19th centuries) the most important, almost the sole, commercial center for Sino-Russian trade. The volume of commerce at the other outpost on the Transbaikal border—Tsurukhaitui—remained very small, and fell off entirely in the 1770's, while trade along the western border (with Sinkiang Province) began to develop only toward the middle of the 19th century.

Maritime commerce between Russia and China throughout this entire period was limited to the visits of two or three Russian vessels which put in at Canton and Shanghai.

2) Sino-Russian trade continued, as previously, to be regulated by the treaties of Nerchinsk and Kyakhta, which postulated equal rights for both sides. The volume of trade at Kyakhta increased by 1,550 percent between 1755 and 1850, from 837,000 to 13,832,000 rubles in value. This considerable growth served the interests of both Russia and China and demonstrated their mutual concern to develop commercial relations.

3) This century may be divided into two periods as regards the Sino-Russian Kyakhta trade, the first from the 1750's to the 1820's and the second from the 1820's to the middle of the 19th century. In the first period the Kyakhta trade remained unaffected by competition from the maritime commerce of the European nations, and its volume increased in value by 1,750 percent, from 800,000 to 15,000,000 rubles; in the second period the competition of European, and mainly British, maritime trade considerably affected turnover at Kyakhta, especially after Britain had succeeded in imposing upon China the inequitable (Nanking) treaty of 1842 which allowed her freedom to trade in the five 'treaty' ports (Canton, Shanghai, Amoy, Ningpo and Foochow). The volume of the Kyakhta trade decreased slightly during this period, dropping to 14 million rubles in value in the 1850's.

4) The structure of the Sino-Russian Kyakhta trade also underwent considerable modifications. In the middle of the 18th century furs were the main item of Russia's exports to China (85 percent of the total value of exports), while its most considerable imports were cotton fabrics and silks (85-90 percent of imports). Thus, at the be-

ginning of the Kyakhta trade, Russia mainly exported raw materials to China and imported finished products. This state of affairs had changed completely by the middle of the 19th century. Not only did Russia cease almost entirely to import cotton fabrics from China, but it began to export cloth to that country. Thus in 1850 cloth and other manufactured goods exported by Russia to China constituted 65.4 percent of Russian exports to that country while fur exports dropped to 23.7 percent of the total. As regards Chinese exports to Russia, they consisted mainly of tea: in 1850 tea accounted for 94.8 percent of the goods imported by Russia through Kyakhta. The structural changes of the Sino-Russian trade reflected the considerable economic changes taking place in both countries during the period under review.

5) Toward the middle of the 19th century, with the aggravation of the political situation in the Far East following the first European encroachments upon China headed by Britain and the increasing tension of Anglo-Russian relations in Asia, the development of commercial relations between Russia and China was retarded and no longer fulfilled the requirements warranted by the friendly relations between the two countries.

The tsarist government and the Manchu authorities perpetuated the backwardness of the border trade: until 1856 goods could only be exchanged at Kyakhta, without the use of money, promissory notes or other means of payment. This limited commodity circulation. Neither government was capable of organizing a steady flow of maritime traffic between their respective ports or of enlarging the volume of their overland trade.

CHAPTER THREE

COMMERCIAL RELATIONS BETWEEN RUSSIA AND CHINA ON THE EVE OF THE AGE OF IMPERIALISM (SECOND HALF OF THE 19th CENTURY)

THE international situation in the Far East became strained in the second half of the 19th century. Reinforced by its powerful Indian and South China (Hong Kong) bases, Britain began to exert pressure on the central and southern areas of China. France and the United States followed suit; Japan, well launched on the road of capitalist development by the 1868 revolution, also claimed 'rights' in Asia. At the beginning of the 1870's premonopolist capitalism, which had reached maximum development, intensified its colonial policies in the Far East as in other areas. Conditions were thereby created for transition to the highest and final stage of capitalism—imperialism. In the words of V. I. Lenin: '…just after this period an important "upsurge" in colonial annexation takes place and the struggle for the partition of the world becomes acute.'[1]

In these conditions commercial relations between Russia and China were more dependent on the international situation in the Far East and the means brought to bear by Western capitalism in its struggle for the annexation of east and southeast Asia, mainly of China, than on the interests and potentialities of both countries.

RUSSIA'S POSITION IN THE FAR EAST IN THE MIDDLE OF THE 19TH CENTURY

The defeat of the Russian Empire in the Crimean War (1853-1856) was a direct result of stagnation. 'The Crimean War,' wrote Lenin, 'revealed the rottenness and impotence of feudal Russia.'[2] In consequence Russia lost much of its political influence in Europe and tsarism was undermined by the growing revolutionary movement of the peasantry which followed that of the Russian proletariat. The disparity between the feudal relations of production which still predominated and the developing capitalist productive forces lay at the root of the internal contradictions in Russian society in the middle of the 19th century and determined the direction of the class struggle.

By the 1860's the majority of industrial workers no longer consisted of serfs but of free laborers (61.4 percent), and capitalist relations of production predominated in the cities. A surge of peasant risings, accompanied by protests of the revolutionary intelligentsia against feudal absolutism, forced the tsarist authorities to undertake

---

[1]   Lenin, V. I. *Works,* 4th ed. Vol. 22, p. 243 [Russ.].
[2]   Lenin, V. I. op. cit. Vol. 17. p. 95.

the 1861 land reform; thereafter, although a number of feudal institutions still survived, capitalist relations of production became the dominant factor in Russian agriculture.

The impotence of the Russian feudal autocracy in the Far East was also demonstrated in the course of the Crimean War. The lack of a navy or strong military bases in Kamchatka, Sakhalin Island, along the Okhotsk littoral, or at the Alaska trading stations, endangered Russia's Far Eastern possessions. Only the heroism of individual Russians saved Kamchatka and Sakhalin from seizure by Anglo-French forces. Foreign flotillas, which were exporting whaling products valued at millions of rubles, had already visited the Sea of Okhotsk and the Bering Sea in the 1840's. Not content with fishing in Russian territorial waters, these fleets repeatedly attacked and destroyed the Russian guard-posts at Kamchatka.

The tsarist autocracy displayed little interest in the fate of the Russian Far East; moreover, the government of Nicolas I even remained ignorant of the basic facts. Despite the discoveries of the Poyarkov expedition, which in 1643-1645 had followed the Amur River to the Okhotsk littoral, in the 1840's the Russian authorities were still giving credence to the inaccurate conclusions reached by the expeditions of La Pérouse (1783), Broughton (1793) and Kruzenshtern (1806) that the Amur estuary was clogged by sand and unfit for navigation and that Sakhalin was a peninsula. Communications with the Okhotsk littoral and Kamchatka continued along the Lena River through Yakutsk (separated from Okhotsk by 1,100 versts of forest, tundra and small rivers), while the sea route from St Petersburg still circumvented Africa and southeastern and eastern Asia (Russian warships reached the Far East after a voyage of three to four years).

However, despite the criminal neglect of the tsarist authorities, Russian progressive circles could not but display considerable interest in the fate of the Russian Far East. In 1847 N. N. Murav'ev was nominated Governor General of eastern Siberia. In the same year, G. I. Nevel'skii, commander of the troopship 'Baikal,' which sailed from Kronstadt to Kamchatka, achieved a certain notoriety. He enlisted the support of the new Governor General for the exploration of the Amur River estuary, although he had received no official authorization from Navy Headquarters.

Having sailed from Kronstadt on 21 August 1848, the 'Baikal' reached Petropavlovsk-Kamchatski on 12 May 1849 after a voyage of 8 months and 23 days (the trip usually took 14 months at that time). The 'Baikal' sailed for the eastern shore of Sakhalin Island on 30 May 1849, and Nevel'skii reported to Governor General Murav'ev on 3 September of the same year: 'Sakhalin is an island, seafaring ships can pass through the estuary and along the Amur River from the north and south. The ancient illusion has been dispelled. Truth has prevailed...'[3] On 1 August 1850 Nevel'skii hoisted the Russian ensign on the bank of the Lower Amur and organized the military outpost of Nikolaevsk.[4]

---

[3] *The Amur Region*, p. 45. Moskva. 1909 [Russ.]. See bibliography.

[4] Today Nikolaevsk-on-Amur. [This locality bears the ancient Chinese name of *Miaoerhcheng*. It is so designated on all maps published at Hong Kong and Peking.]

Nevel'skii's 'impudent deed' provoked the indignation of Chancellor Nesselrode.[5] Upon Nevel'skii's return to St Petersburg the report of his discoveries was examined by a special committee headed by the chancellor, on which Murav'ev also sat. Despite the latter's objections, the committee reached the following decision: 'To remove the outpost of Nikolaevsk; continue trade with the Giliaks from Petrovsk, without touching upon the Amur River, its basin, Sakhalin and the coasts of the Tatar strait,' and to degrade Nevel'skii to the rank of seaman for his 'highly impudent' deeds. He was saved from this infamy only by Murav'ev's intervention. A second examination of the Nevel'skii 'case' determined that his acts had been 'brave, noble and patriotic'; his rank was restored and he received the Order of Vladimir, 4th class. It was also decided to maintain the Nikolaevsk post, to dispatch an expedition to the Amur and to 'name Nevel'skii its commander in all respects.' Subsequently the courageous navigator of the Far East (1850-1854) explored Sakhalin Island and the Maritime Territory.

Events in the Far East attracted some attention during the Crimean War. In 1854 Anglo-French squadrons sailed along the Kamchatka coast and through the Sea of Okhotsk and the Sea of Japan, setting up a blockade of Kamchatka, the Okhotsk littoral, Sakhalin Island and the Maritime Territory. At Murav'ev's insistence the Russian authorities decided to dispatch military equipment and troops along the Amur to the Pacific coast to reinforce Russian outposts. This enabled the Russian defenders in the Far East to protect this region in 1855 from foreign occupation.

Chinese representatives of Heilungkiang Province reached the Mariinsk outpost on the Amur in 1855 to open talks with Murav'ev on demarcation of the Sino-Russian border. These conversations were curtailed, however, and were not renewed until 1858, at Aigun. At the same time the Russian government decided to open talks at Peking, dispatching in 1857 a mission headed by Putyatin, who was instructed to settle the border question and conclude a commercial agreement with China.

DOMESTIC AFFAIRS AND INTERNATIONAL POSITION OF CHINA IN THE 1850's AND 1860's

After the first Opium War China's independence in foreign affairs was whittled down and 'Chinese society began the transformation from a feudal society to a semicolonial and semifeudal one.'[6]

At this time Britain considerably increased exports to China, particularly cotton fabrics. Cloth manufactured in England was cheaper and its sale on the Chinese home market was a blow to China's handicraft and manufactured and domestic production.

Opium imports, which increased unchecked after the Opium War, also accounted for an important part of British trade. China was forced to pay with its best products, depleting its silver reserves. In addition to losses incurred by this trade China was

---

[5] Nesselrode's criminal neglect of the exploration of the Amur River led Murav'ev to accuse him of serving British interests to the detriment of Russia.

[6] Mao Tse-tung. *Selected Works,* Vol, 3. p. 207.

bound by the Treaty of Nanking to pay Britain a contribution of 21 million custom *liangs*,[7] which constituted a heavy burden on the budget. The Ch'ing dynasty did its best to shift the brunt of the consequences of the war onto the masses. A large number of new taxes were introduced, land rents were increased and millions of peasants were subjected to governmental labor impressment. The court made no effort to raise the country's agricultural productivity. The irrigation network, which played a vital role in China's economy, fell into disuse. Flooding and droughts ravaged the country-side and millions of unfortunate peasants were left to starve and perish. These large-scale disasters adversely affected the purchasing power of the peasants, and the domestic market contracted. The rural population was obliged to meet its clothing and household needs by resorting to home production and almost entirely ceased to rely on urban centers. Increasing foreign competition was another factor which hampered the development of urban handicrafts, and China's cities became choked with unemployed workers.

The stagnation of China's economy was severely felt by the laboring classes as well as by merchants and urban government workers. The majority of the population became hostile to both its native and foreign oppressors. These hardships were considered a consequence of feudal despotism; the 'Celestial Son' (the Emperor) was deemed incapable of resisting foreign invasion. In the 1840's urban revolts and peasant uprisings became increasingly frequent. The struggle of the population of Kwangtung Province against the British and other foreigners coalesced with the the widespread peasant unrest.

An uprising of coalminers against the local Manchu administration broke out on 11 January 1851 in the village of Chin'tien in Kwangsi Province.[8] The neighboring peasants also joined the movement, known as the Taiping rebellion, which swiftly spread through the southern provinces. It was headed by Hung Hsiu-ch'üan, who took the title of *Wang,* i.e., king of the Taiping. Antifeudal reforms undertaken by the Taiping in the south reinforced their authority and gained them the support of the peasants from the central provinces. In their victorious advance, the Taiping occupied Nanking on 29 March 1853 and proclaimed it the capital of their state (Taipingtienkuo).

Britain, the United States and France did not react immediately to the Taiping movement, for at first its nature was not entirely understood. The leading role played in it by the Christian *Shangti* society encouraged hopes in the British, French and American diplomats, who thought that foreign capital would be enabled to flow more freely into the Chinese economy. Although the declaration addressed by the

---

[7] [*Liang*—Chinese unit of silver currency; 1 *liang* = 1⅓ oz avoirdupois. The *liang* was not a coin, but a unit of weight. In treaty negotiations with China the foreign powers fixed the units of currency and weight for customs purposes, since there was no uniform currency or standard for weights and measures. A *liang* was usually designated as a *tael*—a word of Malay origin. The revenue from the Chinese Maritime Customs, headed by a British Inspector General (see below p. 85, note), was considered by foreigners the most stable source of indemnity and was accepted as security for foreign loans.]

[8] [Today Kwangsi Chuang Autonomous Region. Chuang designates one of the national minorities of China.]

Taiping to foreign governments[9] stated that foreign trade 'shall be free and no interdiction shall be imposed on it,' however, the import of opium—the most important British and U.S. export to China—was banned. This was a considerable blow to the interests of Anglo-American traders and threatened to deprive them of sizable profits.

The internal policies of the Taiping alarmed the British, American and French colonialists to an even greater extent. They eventually became convinced that the Taiping movement would strengthen China's position and prevent foreign capital from its untrammeled exploitation of the Chinese people and plunder of the country's resources.[10] The policy of the three great powers toward China became clearer in the Taiping government's second year of existence. They sided with the Ch'ing dynasty, but did not, of course, confine themselves to the same mid-19th century relationship. Profiting by the military and political difficulties confronting the imperial court, Britain, France and the United States decided on concerted action to bring the Ch'ing government to its knees and bend it to their requirements.

The representatives of the three powers demanded from the court a revision of existing commercial treaties. The British envoy received instructions to put forward the following new conditions:

1) Opening of the entire country and in particular all coastal towns to 'free' British trade; or, at least, the freedom of navigation along the Yangtze Kiang and the opening of Chenkiang, Nanking, Wenchow and Hangchow to 'free' trade.

2) Official recognition of the opium trade.

3) Abolition of internal Chinese duties on British goods.

4) Permission for foreign ambassadors to reside at Peking, or at least authorization of foreign envoys to conduct an official correspondence with ministers of the court and of foreign ambassadors to meet personally with provincial governors general.

After the conclusion of the Crimean War, Britain and France decided to enforce their demands by military means. At the end of 1856, using as a pretext the 'Arrow'[11] incident Britain, together with France, opened hostilities against China (second Opium War). In December 1857 Anglo-French troops occupied Canton, in May 1858 they took Fort Taku in the north, in the estuary of the Pai Ho River, and also occupied Tientsin. In June 1858 the Ch'ing authorities signed the Tientsin Treaties with Britain, France, the United States and Russia, whose troops had reached Tientsin with the Anglo-French forces.

---

[9] The declaration contained the following passages: 'Mutual trade shall be conducted between countries and order strictly maintained. In all future transactions, only opium imports into China shall be forbidden. Trade in all other items shall be free and no interdiction shall be imposed on it.' (Hwa Kang. *History of the Revolutionary War of the Taiping State,* p. 280. Moskva. 1952 [translated from Chinese to Russ.]).

[10] Land reform was considered by the Taiping the main economic problem of their state. In the 'Land law of the Celestial Empire,' land was to be reapportioned according to the number of mouths to feed in each household and large estates were to be divided up.

[11] [When sailing up the Pearl River to Canton in 1856 the 'Lorcha Arrow,' a ship flying the British flag, was boarded by Chinese officials in search of opium. The flag was hauled down and fourteen sailors were carried off, accused of piracy. The sailors were eventually returned, but no apology for the lowering of the flag was tendered.]

The British and French colonialists, however, remained dissatisfied with the outcome of the war. In 1860, their joint forces recommenced hostilities, penetrated inside the country and took Peking. The Peking Conventions mediated by the Russian envoy Ignat'ev, were concluded between Britain and France on the one hand and the Ch'ing government on the other; these conventions confirmed the Tientsin Treaties and added a number of new stipulations.[12]

Once the Ch'ings had capitulated, Britain, France and the United States decided to support them against the Taiping. On the territory of the foreign settlement the two European powers created at the beginning of 1862 a united force to oppose the Taiping regime. A special American detachment commanded by F. T. Ward was also formed. The intervention of this triple force on the side of the Ch'ings proved decisive. 'The objective causes of the defeat of the Taiping revolution,' wrote Hwa Kang, 'were mainly effected by the reactionary Manchu government, which shamelessly auctioned the nation's interests and concluded an agreement with the English, French, American and other foreign aggressors and the Chinese feudal-military class; this collusion aimed at suppression of the revolution and annihilation of the new authority   the Taiping government—by the most brutal methods.'[13]

COMMERCIAL RELATIONS BETWEEN RUSSIA AND CHINA IN THE 1850's AND 1860's

The state of Sino-Russian trade in the middle of the 19th century was far from representing the interests and economic possibilities of both parties.

The Russian market offered a great commercial potential to China, whose main item of export at that time was tea (in 1864, when the overall customs statistic returns for China were published for the first time, tea accounted for 31.3 million custom *liangs,* i.e., 58 percent of the country's total export which was valued at 54 million custom *liangs*). From 1800 to 1850 Russian imports of Chinese tea through Kyakhta rose from 69,850 *poods* to 297,618 *poods,* 19,070 *poods* being imported from West China (tea imports by sea were forbidden). However, the concentration of almost the entire volume of Sino-Russian trade at a single point—Kyakhta—and the limitations imposed (barter trade) hampered the development of the tea export which would have served China's interests.

The inadequacy and backwardness of the existing regimen of trade were felt even more on the Russian side. The commercial link with China through Kyakhta was most disadvantageous to the Russian settlers of the Okhotsk littoral, Kamtchatka, Sakhalin Island and the American continent (Alaska). The first voyage of a vessel of the Russian-American company carrying furs to Shanghai demonstrated the great advantages of maritime trade. In Shanghai Russian merchants could buy a large assortment of goods and deal with many traders, while Kyakhta was supplied by the Chinese mainly with tea, sold by agreement among a small number of companies.

---

[12] The Peking Conventions stipulated that the port of Tientsin also should be opened to foreign trade.
[13] Hwa Kang, op. cit., p. 287.

Maritime trade between Russia and China however, continued unregulated. Existing Sino-Russian treaties (Nerchinsk and Kyakhta) concerned only overland trade, authorizing it at Kyakhta and Tsurukhaitui exclusively although the border between the two states had already been defined in Central Asia also.

Sino-Russian commerce was thus confronted with the following three problems: 1) organization of trade at new points along the border; 2) opening of maritime trade; 3) transition from barter to commerce entailing currency exchange.

Treaty of Kuldja, 1851. Commerce between Russia and China along the common border in Central Asia had become stabilized toward the middle of the 19th century. The governments of both countries then decided to open discussions on trading procedure in this area. Conversations were initiated in 1851 between the Emperor's representative—I Shan, head of the Ili [Kuldja] District and other districts, and his deputy, Buyantai—and a Russian representative—Kovalevskii, colonel of the corps of mining engineers. The negotiations culminated in the signature of a commercial treaty at Kuldja on 25th July 1851.

The treaty permitted Sino-Russian trade at two points: Kuldja and Chuguchak [Tahcheng]. Many of its clauses resembled those of the Treaty of Kyakhta, which remained in force, but a number showed greater versatility. Although the treaty provided as the Treaty of Kyakhta, that trade at Kuldja and Chuguchak should take the form of barter and prohibited the handing over of goods on credit, it opened an avenue for credit exchange by authorizing it at the traders' risk. Article 12 states: 'If, in breach of the above article, a person shall hand over his goods for credit, the officials (both Russian and Chinese) shall refrain from interference in the matter, and shall not accept subsequent complaints.' Prices also became less rigid; traders of both countries were authorized to act freely in setting prices for barter. The affairs of Russian traders were to be supervized by a Russian consul, and those of the Chinese by an official of the Ili main office.

Customs duties, on goods traded at Kuldja and Chuguchak were abolished. In the wording of article 3: 'This trade is opened in the interest of mutual friendship between the two states, and no customs duties shall therefore be levied by either side.'

Russian traders were authorized by the treaty to enter Kuldja and Chuguchak between March 25 and December 10. If they had not finished sale of their wares at the end of this period, they could remain longer, and the Russian consul was to supervize their departure after their business had been transacted. Russian caravans passing through Chinese territory to the towns of Kuldja and Chuguchak were to travel under the protection of a Chinese guard along designated routes. Each caravan was to consist of less than 20 camels. When disposing of their livestock, Russian traders were to sell two heads out of ten to the Chinese administration in exchange for cotton cloth (at a rate of one piece of *daba* per sheep).

In accordance with the treaty, the Chinese administration opened trading stations at Kuldja and Chuguchak for the Russian traders. These were permitted to reside in the two towns after having obtained a certificate from the Russian consul. The treaty set up the following procedure for dealing with disputes and incidents involving

Russian and Chinese merchants: 'Minor affairs, i.e., disputes and quarrels between subjects of both sides, shall be resolved with due attention by the Russian Consul and the aforesaid Chinese official. If, however, a criminal case or other affair of consequence should unexpectedly arise, the relevant regulations in force at the Kyakhta border shall apply' (article 7).

The Treaty of Kuldja, as previous Sino-Russian treaties, may therefore be considered an equitable agreement. Its main difference from the Treaty of Kyakhta is the regulation of activities of traders of both sides on Chinese territory alone, while the previous treaty had established trade along the Transbaikal border on both Russian (Kyakhta) and Chinese (Maimachin) territory. This difference was not due to political considerations but related exclusively to local conditions. At that time trade could not be conducted along the border, since both sides remained unpopulated. On the Russian side there were no settlements in the entire border region.

The Treaty of Kuldja marked the beginning of regular Sino-Russian trade in Central Asia. Despite its remoteness from international commercial routes, this trade steadily developed.

Treaty of Aigun, 1858. Delimitation of the border between Russia and China was achieved in the 1850's, after the Crimean War, during which Anglo-French naval forces threatened Russia's Far Eastern possessions and the Pacific shores. The necessity to defend these territories revealed the importance of the Amur River, which could be used as a route from eastern Siberia to the Pacific.

Russia and China had at that time a common interest in the defense of their possessions against foreign encroachment. China, also at war with Britain and France, was opposed to the Anglo-French occupation in 1856 of the important towns of Canton in the south and Tientsin in the north. Russia's policy of nonintervention in the European aggression conducted against China in 1858-1860, and its position of arbitrator in the peace talks, enhanced its authority in the eyes of all Chinese social groups.[14]

The talks between Murav'ev, Governor General of Eastern Siberia, and the Chinese representative Prince I Shan, Commander-in-Chief of Heilungkiang, which were begun in 1855 and continued in 1858, ended in the signature of a treaty at Aigun on 16 May 1858.[15] Article 1 established the border between the two states as follows: 'The left bank of the Amur River from the Argun [Erhkuna Ho] River to the estuary of the Amur River shall be included in the Russian state, while the right bank downstream to the Ussuri River shall be included in the Taich'ing[16] state; the territories

---

[14]   The well-known 19th century Russian orientalist, Academician V.P. Vasil'ev, characterized the relations between Russia and China at this time in the following terms: 'After this it seems unnecessary to emphasize the friendliness of our relations with the Peking court. The Chinese are not known for ingratitude.' (V.P. Vasil'ev. *The Discovery of China,* collected articles published by the *Vestnik vsemirnoi istorii,* p.3. Sankt Peterburg. 1900.

[15]   The Treaty of Aigun was ratified by the Emperor of China (by an edict of the State Council) on 2 June 1858, and by the Russian Emperor on 6 July 1858.

[16]   [The official name of China under the Manchu dynasty. *Tai* = great.]

and lands extending from the Ussuri River to the sea shall remain as formerly the common possession of the Taich'ing and Russian states until the border between the two countries in this area shall be determined.'

Both governments also agreed to authorize navigation of exclusively Russian and Chinese vessels along the Amur, Sungari [Sunghwa Kiang] and Ussuri rivers, 'the ships of all other foreign states being forbidden to navigate these rivers' (article 1). Russian and Chinese subjects dewlling along the Ussuri, Amur and Sungari were permitted to conduct trade as along the other common borders, 'and the officials shall extend their protection on both banks to the traders of the two countries' (article 2)

The Treaty of Aigun was highly important for Russia both economically and strategically. It also helped to dispel uncertainty as to the exact border between the two neighboring states. The towns of Blagoveshchensk[17] and Khabarovsk[18] were founded on the Amur, and the growth of the Russian population in the Far East stimulated further development of commercial ties between Russia and China in this area.

Treaty of Tientsin, 1858 *and Supplementary Treaty of Peking,* 1860. While Murav'ev was conducting conversations at Aigun in 1858, a Russian mission headed by Admiral Putyatin reached Tientsin. Putyatin had received strict instructions to abstain from involvement in the military activities of France and Britain against China and to work for the conclusion of a maritime trade treaty with China, for at that time Russia was beginning to develop maritime connections in the Far East. The French and British military activities, however, retarded Putyatin's conversations. He was treated like other foreign diplomats by the Chinese authorities and forbidden to travel to Peking on the pretext that 'no serious subjects existed for conversations at Peking with a person of such importance.' Putyatin was thus obliged to conduct talks at Tientsin with representatives whom the Emperor had sent to meet the Anglo-French plenipotentiaries.

Conversations were concluded at the end of May and the Sino-Russian Treaty of Tientsin was signed on 1 June 1858. It regulated relations between the two governments, including the dispatch of regular (monthly) couriers through Kyakhta, affirmed Russia's rights to send envoys to Peking and authorized trade in the 'treaty' ports of China. Article 3 stated: 'Russian trade with China may in future be conducted not only overland at the former border points, but also by sea. Russian merchant vessels may enter the following ports for trading purposes: Shanghai, Ningpo, Foochow [Minhow], Szeming (Amoy), Kwangtung (Canton), Taiwanfu on Formosa Island, Kiungchow on Hainan Island and other localities open to foreign trade.'

This treaty was inequitable for China, since it afforded Russia the same facilities for maritime trade as those wrested from China by Britain and other European na-

---

[17] Blagoveshchensk [former Chinese name—*Hailanpao*] was the enlarged Ust-Zeiskaya Cossack village, founded in 1856.

[18] Khabarovsk [former Chinese name—*Poli*] was founded in 1858 as a garrison for a battalion of regular troops; it became the residence of the Governor General in 1884 and received urban status in 1893.

tions. Russia obtained the right to designate consuls in the treaty ports who would have—as did the consuls of Britain, France and the United States—jurisdiction over Russian subjects guilty of infringement of Chinese laws.

In accordance with Putyatin's instructions, the Treaty of Tientsin made no provision for border problems, which were being discussed by Murav'ev and were settled by the Treaty of Aigun. The Sino-Russian Treaty of Tientsin, together with the treaties signed almost simultaneously with Britain, France and the United States, remained pending, however, for the Emperor refused to ratify them. The treaties with Britain and France imposed onerous obligations on the Chinese people which raised a number of internal problems. China was to pay a tribute of 4 million *taels* to Britain and 2 million *taels* to France; foreign traders were to be given freedom of movement throughout China and British vessels allowed to navigate the Yangtze Kiang.

As previously stated, Anglo-French forces reopened hostilities in July 1860.

The Russian envoy, Ignat'ev, who reached Peking at the beginning of 1859, served as arbitrator in the peace talks between Britain, France and China. At the same time Ignat'ev signed with Prince Kung on 2 November 1860, a Supplementary Treaty to the Treaties of Aigun and Tientsin. The territory lying north of the Ussuri River to the sea which had been left in the common possession of China and Russia was now transferred to Russia alone (the border thus passed along the Ussuri and Sungacha Rivers, Lake Hanka [Hinka Omo], the Tur River, along the mountain range to the estuary of the Hubtu River and from there along the range to the River Tumen Kiang). Five articles concerned trade (articles 4,5,6,7 and 8). Article 7 bestowed on Russian subjects in China and Chinese subjects in Russia equal rights at all points open to trade, where they could 'freely conduct commerce, without intervention by local officials...'

In addition to the existing tax-free commerce at Kuldja and Chuguchak, article 4 of the Supplementary Treaty extended the same conditions to trade along the new border between Russia and China—the Amur, Ussuri and Tumen Kiang Rivers. China reconfirmed agreement to the passage of Russian traders to Peking (through Kyakhta), authorizing them to trade at Urga and Kalgan [Changkiakow] on their passage through Mongolia. In turn, Russia gave Chinese merchants the right to 'travel to Russia for trading purposes' (article 5). Article 6 of the treaty stated: 'As an experiment, trade shall be opened at Kashgar [Shufu] on the same basis as at Ili [Kuldja] and Tarbagatai [Chuguchak].'[19]

The 1858 Tientsin treaty and the 1860 Supplementary Treaty of Peking, therefore, conferred upon Russia all the rights which China had been forced to concede to Britain, France and the United States by the inequitable treaties of the 1840's and 1850's; Russia alone was unable to enjoy these concessions, for they concerned maritime trade and residence of foreigners in Chinese ports, while Russia conducted little maritime trade with China and there were no Russian colonies in Chinese ports.

---

[19] [Chuguchak—also Tarbagatai or Tahcheng: the latter name derives from *Tah*—the first syllable of Tarbagatai, and *cheng*—town.]

Attention was centered, as previously, on overland trade. The Treaty of Tientsin between Russia and China was augmented on 20 February 1862, with the signing of the 'Regulations for Overland Trade' (modified and completed in 1869). These regulations conferred upon Russian and Chinese traders the right of tax-free commerce in the entire border region and a number of other concessions, aimed mainly at stimulating Russian exports through Kyakhta.[20]

SINO-RUSSIAN COMMERCIAL RELATIONS FROM THE 1870's TO THE SINO-JAPANESE WAR, 1894-1895

Repression of the Taiping rebellion was followed by the growing dependence of the Ch'ing authorities on foreign governments, mainly on Britain. Robert Hart, an Englishman, was appointed Inspector General of Customs in 1863 and became the most important counselor to the imperial court.[21]

In the middle of the 1870's, Britain and its colonies controlled approximately 80 percent of China's foreign trade, and the British merchant fleet transported over 50 percent of Chinese exports and imports. With the assistance of Hart, Britain forced China to sign the Chefoo [Yentai] Agreement,[22] which opened four new seaports and six ports along the Yangtze Kiang to British trade. Britain also began to infiltrate into West China; utilizing Moslem anti-Manchu uprisings in Kashgaria [Chinese Turkistan] and Dzungaria, the British attempted to set foot in these areas and disrupt Sino-Russian trade.

China's resistance to foreign intervention thus decreased temporarily after the defeat of the Taiping rebellion and its dependence on foreign powers increased. However, the great Taiping movement had a considerable effect on the country's social and economic development.

The first repercussions of the use of modern weapons in China by Anglo-French-American forces were felt in the establishment of a number of arsenals: the Kiangnan arsenal in Shanghai was set up in 1865, and the Tientsin arsenal in 1870. Industrial enterprises began to make their appearance in China: a Chinese joint-stock company

---

[20] The 'Regulations for Overland Trade' consisted of the following main points: 1) No customs duties were to be imposed on trade along the Sino-Russian border for a distance of 100 Chinese *li* (approximately 50 versts) on both sides of the border. 2) Russian merchants were permitted to trade throughout the entire territory of Mongolia controlled by China, without payment of customs duties. 3) Russian goods traveling to Tientsin through Kalgan were to be taxed at a rate one-third below the general Chinese tariff on foreign goods. 4) Chinese goods bought at Kalgan by Russian merchants for export were to incur transit duties only. 5) If a Russian merchant bought in Tientsin for export overland Chinese goods originating in another port, for which customs duties had already been paid, no supplementary taxes were to be levied on this merchandise.

[21] Hart remained Inspector General of Customs in China until 1909, i.e., for 45 years. He also directed a number of port services, was responsible for sending Chinese students abroad, participated as negotiator in official Chinese talks with foreign governments, etc.

[22] In February 1875 A. R. Margary, a British intelligence agent, was killed, together with five Chinese companions, by unknown persons. Britain then demanded 'satisfaction' from China, consisting of greater trading privileges; those were embodied in the Chefoo Agreement of September 1876.

for exploitation of the Kaiping coal mines was created in 1881, the joint-stock company of the Shanghai spinning mills in 1882.

As China's dependence on Britain increased, a number of difficulties emerged to cloud Sino-Russian economic relations, caused by British hostility to the tsarist Empire. Russia's policy toward China also changed at this time: its intervention in Chinese affairs became more frequent as Russia increasingly participated in the general race of the capitalist states for foreign markets.

The main opposition that Russia had to encounter in China was that of Britain. British competition reduced Russian exports despite the existing favorable conditions for the development of Sino-Russian trade. Russian exports to China dropped from a value of 9.3 million rubles in 1851-1855 to 2.3 million in 1876-1880. British pressure on Sino-Russian trade was felt both in the maritime sphere and along the Sinkiang. In the 1860's rebellions against the Manchus flared up in Kashgaria and the Ili River valley. The insurgents united under the leadership of Yakub-Beg and proclaimed independence. Yakub-Beg, having come into contact with Britain, found it more than interested in the subjection of West China. Russian trade with Sinkiang was interrupted during this period and the trading posts destroyed. Britain attempted to set up a Moslem state on the territory lying between Russia and India which would be hostile to both Russia and China. In 1871 Russia reacted by occupying the town of Kuldja and the territory of the Ili River valley. The tsarist authorities then informed China that they would order retreat from the Ili [Kuldja] Territory as soon as China regained authority in the region.

In 1878 the Ch'ing authorities quelled the Sinkiang uprising and showed willingness to open talks with Russia concerning restitution of the Ili territory. Discussion of commercial problems revealed the unsatisfactory state of Sino-Russian trade. After the transition at Kyakhta from barter to currency payment and the authorization of imports of Chinese tea by sea through the Black Sea ports, the balance of Russian trade with China had become negative; Russia's main objective, therefore, was to increase exports to China. This could be achieved, as the Russian representatives emphasized, if Russian merchants were authorized to sell not only at the border posts, but in the towns of inner China. The Sino-Russian Treaty of St Petersburg, 1881, allowed Russian subjects to trade without payment of customs duties 'in the towns and other localities of the Ili, Tarbagatai, Kashgar, Urumchi, and other regions lying along the southern and northern slopes of the Tien Shan Range, to the Great Wall of China. This privilege shall be abrogated when the course of trade necessitates introduction of a tariff, concerning which both governments shall seek agreement' (article 12).

China was also interested in expanding tea exports to Russia. Britain, which had been a prominent customer for this item, was gradually shifting its tea purchases to India and Ceylon. Since tea would clearly remain for long the most important of China's exports, and since the Russian market seemed most promising, the Chinese authorities were prepared to grant concessions to encourage tea export overland. The Treaty of St Petersburg (according to the 'Regulations for Overland Trade' signed in conjunction with the treaty) fixed export duties payable on goods bought by Russian traders at Kalgan at 50 percent below the current general tariff. Modification of the scale of customs duties on tea was also of extreme importance for the Kyakhta tea trade: duty had previously been fixed by weight, without taking into account quality or price; according to the new treaty, the duty would depend on the value of the tea, and the cheaper variety (brick tea), the main Russian import through Kyakhta, was to attract only 30-25 percent of the previous rate.

The Treaty of St Petersburg reaffirmed the conditions of previous treaties (Tientsin and the Supplementary Treaty of Peking) concerning duty-free trade in Mongolia and along the Far Eastern border; it also regulated trade for Russian caravans traveling to Tientsin, Kalgan and Soochow.

Having obtained concessions for trade overland, Russia also attempted to expand its maritime trade with China. Subsequent events, however, demonstrated that neither the privileges conferred by the Treaty of St Petersburg nor the opening of a Russian shipping line from Odessa to Vladivostok could remove the impediments to the Russian export trade with China. Sino-Russian trade remained unilateral (except for the exchange along the Sinkiang border), and the Russian deficit grew.

The reasons for the crisis in Russian exports to China were more deep-seated. They were to be found in Russian economic backwardness and, primarily in the absence of industrial centers in Siberia or railroads to link Russian industrial centers to the Far Eastern border. The preponderance of Western (mainly British) capital in Chinese ports also constituted a considerable obstacle to Russian exports.

In the 1880's Russian businessmen and industrialists became insistent in their demands to the government as to the necessity of building a Siberian railroad to instil new life into the economy of Siberia and the Far East. Strategic considerations also became a factor. In 1882 Japan invaded Korea in an attempt to subjugate it and profit from China's impotence. Although Russian intervention enabled China to strengthen its position in this area temporarily and to force the Japenese to withdraw their troops, in 1885, in reality, Russia was not only far from being capable of containing Japan, a rapidly developing capitalist nation with British and United States backing, it was even unable to defend its own Far Eastern possessions.

The tsarist authorities were forced to concede the necessity of the Trans-Siberian railroad; the decision was taken by Alexander III on 22 May 1882 at a session of the Ministerial Committee; however, construction lagged behind schedule and by 1890 the line had not progressed beyond Ufa.

The Far Eastern situation became even more complicated at the beginning of the 1890's. Japan was preparing a second attack against Korea with the help of Britain and the United States. Britain, through its influence in the Ch'ing ruling circles, persuaded Li Hung-chang to speed up construction of a railroad from North China through Manchuria toward the Russian border. In 1890 Li Hung-chang entrusted Kinder, a British engineer, with the surveying of a line from Taku to Hunchun, passing through Shanhaikwan, Chinchow and Mukden [Shenyang].

In 1892, S. Yu. Witte, an advocate of the Siberian project, became Russian Minister of Finance. Witte reflected the opinion of the Russian commercial and industrial middle class on the prospects of trade with China when he wrote that by constructing the Siberian railway 'Russia may considerably increase the export of cotton fabric and woolens to China as well as of metal wares,' and that 'the Siberian railroad would support Chinese tea production by preventing a most dangerous rival of China (i.e., Britain) from acting as middleman in the export of Chinese tea to Europe.' He continued that, in view of this situation, 'not only Russia, but China also, is interested in transferring to Russia Britain's role in the export of tea and its trade in Europe; furthermore, Russia itself constitutes a large and ever-growing market for tea.' Witte thought that the Siberian railway would replace the sea route and inaugurate a new era in European relations with Asia. 'The Great Siberian Railway, by establishing unbroken communication by rail between Europe, the Pacific Ocean and the Asiatic East,' will open up 'new routes and new horizons not only for Russian trade but also for world commerce.' Witte also stressed the strategic importance of the Siberian railway for Russia and insisted upon its rapid completion.[23]

The importance of the Trans-Siberian Railroad to Siberia and the Far East was clear, and its construction was regarded favorably in Russia.

CHARACTER OF SINO-RUSSIAN TRADE IN 1850-1893
(TO THE SINO-JAPANESE WAR)

Sino-Russian trade underwent significant modifications in the second half of the 19th century. In this period commerce was carried on over a larger territory; new trading posts were built on the Amur and Ussuri rivers and along the Sinkiang border, and fairly regular maritime trade developed between Chinese and Russian Far Eastern (Vladivostok and Nikolaevsk-on-Amur) and Black Sea ports (Odessa).

In the 1850's, when the influence of Britain, France, the United States and Japan in North China and Korea—areas in the proximity of Russia's Far Eastern borders —was still relatively small, the structure and development of Sino-Russian trade were mainly determined by the policies of the Russian and Chinese governments. However, as Western influences gained ground and China's dependence on the capitalist nations increased, Sino-Russian trade largely began to depend not on the wishes and interests of the two countries but on the international situation in the Far East and the relative powers of the capitalist nations staking claim in this part of Asia.

Sino-Russian trade continued to be concentrated at Kyakhta to the end of the 1850's. Since it adhered to barter form until 1855, exports and imports were approximately balanced. The proportion of China's exports through Kyakhta began to increase after abrogation of the barter trade and in consequence of Russian authorization of payment for Chinese goods in currency, silver and gold. However, Russian exports rapidly decreased. The equilibrium of Sino-Russian trade became further disturbed after the repeal by the Russian government of the regulations prohibiting the import of tea through Odessa. Maritime trade between the Chinese ports (Canton,

---

[23] From S. Yu. Witte's report to the government, November 1892 (*Prologue to the Russo-Japanese War. Material from the Witte Archives,* Edited with an introduction by B. B. Glinskii. Petrograd. 1916).

Shanghai) and Odessa became unilateral. Russian merchants, who imported mainly Paihuo tea from Canton or Shanghai, were obliged to pay out currency, silver or gold to China, since Russian exports through European ports were almost eliminated by the severe competition and predominance of American and Western European firms at the Chinese end. Russia's Chinese trade deficit was also increased by the growing demand for Chinese goods, mainly foodstuffs, for the consumption of the Amur region and the Maritime Territory, where the Russian population was increasing too fast for local production to keep pace.

RUSSIAN TRADE WITH CHINA IN 1850-1893
(in thousand rubles)

Year	Exports to China	Imports from China	Total volume of trade	Balance of trade deficit
1850	7,127	7,446	15,192	319
1857	6,025	7,479	13,504	1,454
1881-				
1890*	2,156	25,400	27,556	23,244
1893	4,087	33,185	37,272	29,098

* Yearly average

If we disregard the Sinkiang border trade, where the exchange system continued and no noticeable competition was felt from a third party, Russian exports as a wdole continued to decline. Although the protectionist policy adopted by the tsarist authorities in 1877 to redress the general Russian foreign trade balance, achieved favorable results,[24] it remained without effect on the China trade. The reduction of Chinese customs duties on Russian goods stipulated by the Treaty of St Petersburg, and the dispatch of trade caravans bearing Russian wares to towns of central China, proved also of little consequence. The Russian trade deficit with China increased from year to year and reached a yearly average of over 23 million rubles in 1881-1890.

Russian exports to China did not diminish consistently along all trade routes. While the total exports to China dropped from a value of 7,127,000 rubles in 1850 to 4,087,000 rubles in 1893, exports to Sinkiang increased in the same period from 211,500 rubles to 3,036,000 rubles. The contraction of exports mainly affected broadcloth (from 1,328,000 *arshin* to 73,000 *arshin*) and furs (from 1,642,000 worth of rubles to 219,000 rubles) and was slightly mitigated by the increase of cotton fabric exports from 4,850,000 *arshin* to 6,580,000 *arshin*.

Chinese exports to Russia increased along all the routes in question, particularly the sea route to Odessa. From a value of 7,446,000 rubles in 1850 they reached

[24] In the five years from 1872-1876 Russia's foreign trade deficit reached 452.3 million credit rubles. In 1877 the authorities began to collect customs duties in gold, thereby raising them by 48 percent. An import duty of 40 kopecks per *pood* was levied on cotton. Duties were again raised by 10 percent in 1881 and by 10-20 percent in 1887. This reduced imports of luxury items and industrial raw materials and a favorable balance of trade was achieved, reaching 307.2 million rubles annually in 1887-1891.

33,185,000 rubles in 1893, i.e., an increase of almost 450 percent. This particularly applied to tea (7.027 million rubles—316,000 *poods*—to 28 million rubles, or 1,882,000 *poods*) and raw silk (from 57 to 1,342 *poods*), while exports of sugar candy decreased from 99,300 to 2,100 *poods*. New items of Russian imports from China were recorded in 1893: undressed leather (37,200 *poods*) and wool (107 *poods*).

Sino-Russian Trade at Kyakhta in 1850-1893. Trade continued to develop in the 1850's on the basis of the 'Regulations' of 1800, i.e., in the form of barter. The authorities on both sides strictly prohibited the use of credit and payments in currency, silver or gold. Russia meted out severe punishment to transgressors of the Kyakhta regulations. On 29 October 1851 the State Council ordered that a fine of 15 percent (of the transaction) be imposed on first offenders: a second offense incurred eviction from Kyakhta, the offender being prohibited from further participation in the Kyakhta trade. Merchants were also forbidden to diverge from official prices.

The importation of foreign goods to China, mainly British cottons and wools, considerably affected the Kyakhta trade. The conveyance of merchandise from Western Europe to Chinese ports was 5.5 times cheaper than its transfer overland from central Russia to Kyakhta. The Russian merchants, finding difficulty in selling their goods, constantly petitioned for the repeal of the barter trade, demanding the right to pay for Chinese tea and other wares in currency, silver or gold. The barter system prevented the flow of imports from China, including tea, since the Chinese were unwilling to trade their goods for Russian merchandise in view of the low prices on the Chinese market.

The tsarist policy at that time encouraged imports which afforded revenue to the Treasury. Tea imports came under this head and the Russian authorities agreed to mitigate the Kyakhta barter system. In 1854 Russian traders were permitted to pay in silver and gold, and on 1 August 1855 a governmental edict followed, modifying the Kyakhta trade regulations. It authorized Russian traders to pay for Chinese merchandise in gold to a value of one-third of the transaction where Chinese goods were exchanged for manufactured articles, or to a value of one-half of the transaction when exchanged for furs; Russian traders were also permitted to buy and sell at prices agreed with their Chinese counterparts.

This first step thoroughly overhauled trading procedure at Kyakhta. The new regulations resulted in a slight increase in the tempo of trade and in its volume. At the same time abrogation of the barter system completely altered the structure of commodity circulation. After 1854 the Kyakhta trade showed a deficit for Russia, which rapidly increased from year to year. Thus, the annual average of Russian exports through Kykahta totaled 4,825,000 rubles in 1854-1861, while yearly exports of gold and silverware and gold currency totaled 2,264,000 rubles.

In order to reduce this deficit, Russia tried to increase exports to China not only through Kyakhta, but also by sale of goods in the central areas of the country. In 1862 Russian trade caravans resumed the journeys to Peking and Tientsin, in accordance with the treaties concluded at these two cities. Even this step, however, proved inadequate to restore Russian exports to their former volume. The amount of goods thus carried gradually decreased and currency was increasingly substituted to pay for Chinese goods. The caravans dispatched in 1866, for example, exported from Russia goods valued at 305,000 rubles and took 440,000 rubles in currency while in 1869 they carried only 77,000 rubles worth of goods and 708,000 rubles in currency.

The difficulties encountered at Kyakhta did not affect the sale of Russian goods only. China's maritime trade with European Russia also undermined the Kyakhta tea trade. The transport of this product from the tea-producing areas to Kyakhta was much more expensive than dispatch to the nearest port. Conveyance from the tea plantations to Shanghai cost only one ruble 32 kopecks per *pood*, while the cost to Kyakhta was 10 rubles per *pood*; moreover, the first route took no more than 20 days, while the second over three months.

In order to counteract the slump at Kyakhta, in 1862 Russia lowered tea import duties there. Duty was fixed at 40 kopecks per lb. of green tea and 15 kopecks for black tea, duties levied in the European ports of Russia at this time reaching 65 and 35 kopecks per lb, respectively. In 1865 new preferential rates were fixed for Kyakhta: only 15 kopecks per lb for green and black tea and 2 kopecks for brick tea, while port duties were 55 kopecks per lb for green tea and 38 kopecks for black and brick tea.

A renewed attempt to protect and encourage the Kyakhta trade accompanied diplomatic conversations which preceded the 1881 Treaty of St Petersburg. Both sides acknowledged that the current Chinese export duties on tea could not but hinder development of the Kyakhta tea trade.

The future of tea export had then become an important consideration for the Chinese. Britain, the foremost customer for China tea, was successfully expanding Indian and Ceylonese tea plantations. In 1867 Britain was already importing 40,000 piculs[25] of Indian tea, and imports rapidly increased in the following years. Tea at

RUSSIAN OVERLAND TEA IMPORTS THROUGH THE TRANSBAIKAL BORDER (MAINLY VIA KYAKHTA) IN 1885-1893[26]
(in poods)

Year	Paihuo tea	Brick tea	Tile tea	Total
1885	369,540	579,683	—	949,223
1886	374,580	768,129	—	1,142,709
1887	497,869	974,978	—	1,472,847
1888	448,714	775,556	132	1,224,402
1889	423,857	726,807	10,203	1,160,867
1890	298,656	723,565	31,583	1,053,707
1891	260,728	593,806	32,610	887,144
1892	376,553	789,664	31,470	1,197,687
1893	377,502	831,935	32,780	1,242,217

[25] [One picul = 133.33 lb.]
[26] *Short Essay on the Opening, Development, and Present Position of Our Commercial Relations with China through Kyakhta*, ed. by the Kyakhta merchants. p. 83. Moskva. 1896.

the time constituted the main item of Chinese exports (in 1874, 55.3 percent of total exports).

Encouragement of tea export was considered a most important objective by the Chinese government; by the Treaty of St Petersburg a preferential duty on the export of the cheaper varieties of tea, the major item of the Kyakhta trade, was instituted. The new conditions reduced the difference in cost between maritime freight (from Canton to Odessa) and overland transport (from Kyakhta to Moscow) from 38 to 14.5 kopecks per lb, and encouraged export of brick tea through Kyakhta.

Despite some fluctuations, on the whole the Kyakhta tea trade expanded in 1885-1893, especially trade in brick tea. The increase in tea imports stabilized the value of Russia's total imports from China through Kyakhta at approximately 15 million rubles. Tea became the main, almost the sole, Russian import via the Siberian border.[27]

RUSSIAN IMPORTS THROUGH KYAKHTA
IN 1850-1893[28]
(in thousand rubles)

	1850	1875	1885	1893
Total imports	6,916	13,133	15,296	14,903
Imports of tea	6,523	12,030	14,439	13,977

On the other hand, Russian exports through Kyakhta continued to dwindle, despite the concessions conferred upon overland trade by the treaties of Tientsin and St Petersburg. The value of exports through Kyakhta dropped from 7 million to 0.9 million rubles from 1850 to 1893.

In 1893 Russia's exports through Kyakhta were valued at only 1,031,000 rubles, while Chinese exports reached 14,903,000 rubles; Russia's deficit, paid for in gold and silver currency, thus amounted to 13.7 million rubles. Kyakhta had ceased to be an important center for the sale of Russian goods, and many Chinese firms established there closed down. Only eight firms, mainly dealing in the sale of Chinese goods, remained in 1870 of the 120 firms and stores in business before 1862. The Kyakhta trade had almost entirely petered out by 1870 and thereafter the town became merely a transit station.

The Kyakhta trade, which had continued as barter up to 1854-1855 and had ensured an equivalent exchange of products, thus incurred a deficit in 1850-1893 entailing large yearly payments in currency and gold. It must be added that the Kyakhta

[27] The Kyakhta tea trade was closely tied to the main tea-producing areas of China. Large Russian wholesalers opened offices at Hankow: the Brothers K. & S. Popov, Molchanov, Pechatnov & Co., Tokmakov, Molotkov & Co., Chirkov, Panov & Co.

[28] Data for 1850 are taken from A. Korsak, op.cit., p.278., and the following period from *Short Essay on the Opening, Development and Present Position of Our Commercial Relations with China through Kyakhta, op.cit.*, (Appendix), pp. 2-11. Data for 1875, 1885 and 1893 include goods imported through other points of the Far Eastern border, of a value of 1.3-1.8 million rubles.

tea trade proved unprofitable for the Russian Treasury, since approximately 1-1.5 million rubles were lost yearly because of preferential duty.

RUSSIAN EXPORTS THROUGH KYAKHTA IN 1850-1893[29]
(in thousand rubles, excluding gold, silver and other currency)

Goods	1850	1875	1885	1893
Cloth and other manufactured articles	4,515	1,865	1,246	718
Raw materials for industrial purposes	706	138	98	18
Furs	1,640	474	456	189
Alimentary products	63	30	56	11
TOTAL	6,916	2,554	2,077	1,031

Sino-Russian Maritime Trade. Before 1880 Russian vessels visited Chinese harbors sporadically; there had been Russian scientific expeditions or merchant ships sailing from Russia's European ports to her Far Eastern and North American possessions. A few commercial voyages were made to Shanghai by vessels of the Russian-American Company for the sale of furs and acquisition of foodstuffs.[30] The Crimean War and the subsequent sale of Alaska by the Russian government prevented the company from developing this trade to a noticeable extent.

A regular sea route was opened in 1880 from Odessa to Vladivostok by the Russian Volunteer Fleet. At first these vessels were used for internal transport, and only from the mid-1880's did they begin regular sailings to Canton and Shanghai, loading there tea and other products for export to European Russia.

TEA IMPORTS FROM CHINA BY SEA
THROUGH ODESSA[31]
(in thousand poods)

1885	246,193	1890	661,709
1886	380,511	1891	721,988
1887	370,323	1892	471,660
1888	495,524	1893	640,676
1889	511,579		

[29] Data for 1850 are taken from A. Korsak, op. cit., pp. 264-265, and for the following period from the *Short Essay on the Opening, Development and Present Position of Our Commercial Relations with China through Kyakhta,* (Appendix), pp. 13-17.

[30] The last voyage on behalf of the Russian-American Company was made in 1853; furs from Alaska were exchanged for foodstuffs and tea.

[31] *Short Essay on the Opening, Development and Present Position of Our Commercial Relations with China through Kyakhta,* p. 83. (Russian customs data indicate that 637,000 *poods* of tea were imported through Odessa in 1893).

Raw silk, undressed leather and silk fabrics were also imported through Odessa in addition to tea. Total imports from China through Odessa reached a value of 13-14 million rubles at the beginning of the 1890's, i.e., approximately the value of Russian imports through Kyakhta.

On the other hand, Russian exports to China through the same port were almost nonexistent and consisted of chance lots of paper, cotton cloth and metal goods. Exports through Odessa totaled only 34,500 rubles in 1893.

The maritime trade between the two countries thus showed an even greater Russian deficit than incurred by the Kyakhta trade. The cheaper freight rates by sea could not change the position of Sino-Russian trade, although the entire history of past commercial relations convincingly demonstrated the economic advantages of mutual trade for both nations.

Maritime trade between Chinese ports and the Russian Amur region (the Amur and Maritime Territories) was still rudimentary in the 1890's, mainly because these areas were sparsely populated.[32]

The duty-free trade conducted within a 50 verst-wide strip on both sides of the border mainly supplied local needs and was not recorded in the Russian customs statistics. The trade of Nikolaevsk-on-Amur and Vladivostok with Chinese ports in 1893 was confined to the importation of foodstuffs, valued at 102,000 rubles, and certain Chinese industrial products and handicrafts, at 4,600 rubles.

The Russian Far East, cut off from Russia's industrial centers and unproductive locally, in the 1890's could only be an importer of Chinese goods. Its rich resources were insufficiently utilized, even for local needs, and were certainly not exported, although precisely these resources could have been the means of furnishing a stable basis for maritime trade between Russia and China.

Sino-Russian Trade along the Sinkiang Border. Commerce in this area developed under more favorable conditions than both the Kyakhta and the maritime trade. Russian goods did not encounter sizable competition from a third party and were in

SINO-RUSSIAN TRADE ALONG CHINA'S WESTERN BORDER
(in thousands of rubles)

Year	Russian exports to Sinkiang		Russian imports from Sinkiang		Total volume of trade		Excess of exports (+) or of imports (−)
	value	%	value	%	value	%	
1850	211.5	100	530.5	100	742.0	100	−319.0
1853	675.7	319.5	688.6	129.8	1,364.3	183.8	− 12.9
1893	3,036.4	1,435.4	2,792.2	526.3	5,828.6	785.5	+224,2

[32] In 1859-1882 a total of 14,414 peasants were transplanted to the Amur region (8,709 to the Amur Territory and 5,705 to the Maritime Territory); this excludes Cossack settlements along the Amur and Ussuri rivers. The latter population reached 18,500 in 1869; only 11,550 soldiers were stationed in the Amur region in 1880, including Cossacks.

great demand in West China, an area remote from the foreign-controlled ports and bordered on the south by the backward regions of India.

Immediately after the conclusion of the Treaty of Kuldja (1851), the volume of Sino-Russian trade grew noticeably, and the value almost doubled from 1850-1853. Later the agitation of the 1860's and 1870's in Sinkiang repeatedly interrupted commerce. The volume of trade through the Sinkiang border, however, increased by more than 680 percent from 1850-1893, Russian exports multiplying by 14.3 and imports by 5.3. The value of goods exchanged was approximately the same for both sides, since generally barter was employed.

Russia's main item of export throughout the second half of the 19th century remained cotton fabrics; their value increased from 117,600 rubles in 1850 to 2,037,500 rubles in 1893, i.e., by 1620 percent.

In addition to the goods listed in the following table, corals and *korol'ki* constituted important items of Russian exports in the 1850's (a value of 600 rubles in 1850

RUSSIAN EXPORTS TO SINKIANG IN 1850-1893[33]

Goods	Unit	1850		1853		1893	
		volume	thous. rubles	volume	thous. rubles	volume	thous. rubles
Cotton fabrics	thous. arshins	...	117.6	...	288.6	5,832	2,037.5
Wool cloth	arshins	...	6.4	...	7.7	2,350	2.2
Broadcloth	arshins	30,900	30.3	91,500	158.4	7,160	9.0
Silks	arshins	...	...	...	...	23,240	30.6
Sugar	poods	—	—	—	—	9,508	84.6
Tobacco	poods	—	—	—	—	2,284	6.9
Cigarettes	thous. units	—	—	—	—	848.6	1.5
Leather (curried, including Russian leather)	poods	...	27.1	...	53.4	5,403	157.8
Shoes	poods	—	—	—	—	249	8.7
Paper	poods	—	—	—	—	1,453	10.6
Matches	poods	—	—	—	—	1,726	18.1
Candles	poods	—	—	—	—	3,799	40.4
Window glass	poods	—	—	—	—	177	0.7
Porcelain	poods	—	—	—	—	441	6.4
Mirrors	poods	—	—	—	—	235	3.4
Cast iron, iron, steel	poods	—	—	—	—	40,060	90.4
Cast iron, iron and steel products	poods	...	21.6	...	44.2	17,983	97.5
Furs	poods	...	2.0	—	53.8	—	—
TOTAL	—	—	211.5	—	675.7	—	3,036.4

[33] Data for 1850 and 1853 are taken from A. Korsak, *op.cit.*, pp. 436-437, and for 1893 from the *Review of Russia's Foreign Trade for 1895 along her European and Asiatic Borders. (Poods* may be converted to *arshin;* one *pood* of woolen cloth = 50 *arshin;* one *pood* of broadcloth = 40 *arshin;* and one *pood* of silk = 70 *arshin*).

and 22,400 rubles in 1853), as well as silverware and gold (a value of 2,100 rubles in 1850 and 2,900 rubles in 1853).

Russian exports increased in variety in the 1890's. New items were introduced, such as sugar, tobacco, cigarettes, shoes, matches, candles, window glass, porcelain and mirrors. Exports of cast iron, iron, steel and auxiliary products, as well as curried leather, increased considerably. At the same time broadcloth and wool exports decreased sharply, while the export of furs—which at this period had reversed, becoming a Russian import from Sinkiang—ceased entirely.

Russian exports to Sinkiang in 1893 passed through two customs districts, Semipalatinsk (totaling 2,191,000 rubles, i.e., 72 percent of total exports) and Turkistan (845,000 rubles, or 28 percent of the total).

Trade with Sinkiang in the 1890's was not only limited to inhabitants of Central Asia; merchants from Moscow, Nizhni Novgorod and Kazan also participated. The Russian cotton industry found there a potential market. The sale of Russian goods gradually shifted from the border outposts to all important towns in Sinkiang.

The structure of Chinese exports from Sinkiang changed even more in the period 1850-1893. As at Kyakhta, imports from China in the 1850's consisted essentially of tea. Tea accounted for 95 percent of the imports for 1850 (a value of 502,100 rubles out of a total of 530,500) and 97 percent in 1853 (a value of 671,100 rubles out of a

RUSSIAN IMPORTS FROM SINKIANG IN 1850-1893[34]

Goods	1850		1853		1893	
	amount (poods)	thous. rubles	amount (poods)	thous. rubles	amount (poods)	thous. rubles
Tea	17,470	502.1	21,093	671.1	3,143	57.7
Wool	—	—	—	—	107,138	422.4
Woolen cloth	—	0.6	—	1.2	25,810	137.3
Cotton fabrics	—	6.6	—	4.5	—	—
Undressed leather	—	—	—	—	36,882	179.4
Raw silk	—	—	—	—	225	19.1
Silks	—	14.3	—	4.1	199	67.5
Dried fruits	—	—	—	—	4,023	11.7
Fresh fruits	—	—	—	—	2,132	3.9
Walnuts	—	—	—	—	2,069	3.6
Tobacco	—	—	—	—	576	1.7
Furs	—	—	—	1.1	23,916	324.6
Raw cotton	—	—	—	—	3,617	23.3
Livestock	—	—	—	—	...	406.9
Animal fat	—	—	—	—	6,683	25.9
Porcelain	—	—	—	—	1,935	41.0
Other goods	6.97	—	—	6.6	—	—
TOTAL	—	530.5	—	688.6	—	2,792

[34] Data for 1850 and 1853 are taken from A. Korsak, op.cit., p.438, and for 1893 from the *Review of Russia's Foreign Trade for* 1895 *along her European and Asiatic Borders.*

total 688,600). In 1893, however, tea imports from Sinkiang amounted to a value of only 57,700 rubles, which constituted 2.6 percent of total imports. It decreased in volume from 17,470 *poods* in 1850 and 21,093 *poods* in 1853 to 3,143 *poods* in 1893. As a result of the construction of the Siberian railroad to the Transbaikal region (the line from the Urals to Omsk was completed in 1894), the transport of tea from Sinkiang to central Russia was no cheaper than conveyance from Kyakhta or by sea to Odessa. On the other hand, tea prices in Sinkiang were almost twice the Kyakhta prices, owing to the distance from China's tea-producing areas.

Products of local stock-raising became the main items of Sinkiang exports to Russia in the 1890's. Wool, livestock, leather and animal fat accounted for 37 percent (a value of 1,034,600 rubles) of Sinkiang exports. They were followed by furs (11.6 percent), silks and woolen cloth (7.3 percent—204,800 rubles), etc. Small amounts or raw cotton, dried fruits, tobacco, walnuts, and a number of other goods, began to be exported to Russia. Exports of cotton fabrics ceased, their production in Sinkiang being insufficient even for local needs.

Sinkiang traded almost exclusively with Russia in the 1890's. More than 90 percent of its exports consisted of raw materials, while Russian exports to Sinkiang were almost entirely finished and semifinished articles. Sinkiang was thus a supplier of raw materials for Russian industries and a buyer of the latter's industrial products.

*   *
*

1) In the second half of the 19th century Sino-Russian commerce expanded over a broader territory. Kyakhta ceased to monopolize this trade and gradually lost importance. After the conclusion of the Treaties of Kuldja (1851) and Aigun (1858), Sino-Russian trade along the border of West China (Sinkiang) was regularly maintained (the 1860's and 1870's excepted, during the Moslem rising of Yakub-Beg in Kashgaria [Chinese Turkistan] and Dzungaria), and commerce was initiated along the Amur and Ussuri rivers. The Treaty of Tientsin (1858) and the supplementary Treaty of Peking (1860) conferred upon tsarist Russia the same concessions as those wrested from China by the Western European powers and the United States; Russia then embarked on maritime trade between the Russian Far East ports (Vladivostok, Nikolaevsk-on-Amur) and the Black Sea (Odessa) and the Chinese treaty ports.

2) The structure of Sino-Russian trade underwent considerable changes in the second half of the 19th century. Abrogation in 1854 of barter trade at Kyakhta (then the main trading post) by the Russian government, and authorization of tea imports from China by sea to the Russian Far Eastern and Black Sea ports, resulted in a considerable deficit in Russia's trade with China, except for trade along the Sinkiang border.

The tsarist authorities, who encouraged tea imports mainly out of fiscal considerations did not succeed in competing with European and American products on the Chinese market, and Russian exports to that country decreased rapidly. The growing deficit of Russia's foreign trade balance with China was to a certain extent also caused by the increasing demand for Chinese products among the Russian population of the Amur region and the Maritime Territory, emigrants from central Russia who had come to settle virgin land. In the 1890's Russia's negative balance of trade with China reached an annual average of 25 million gold rubles. The decrease of Russia's average annual exports to China from a value of 9,272,000 rubles in 1851-1853 to 2,186,000 rubles in 1880-1890 was caused by underdevelopment of the Russian territories near the Chinese border and the absence of modern communications (railroads) between the Russian industrial centers and the eastern frontier; it was also a consequence of China's increasing dependence on Britain, France and other capitalist states, which had established strongholds in the treaty ports.

3) The construction of the Trans-Siberian Railroad was a major Russian undertaking in the 1880's and 1890's. It was designed to connect the Russian Far East with the country's industrial centers and was expected to remedy Russia's economic and military deficiencies and create conditions for further development of Sino-Russian trade. Russian governmental circles were also motivated by aggression. They had no objection to joining the general capitalist melee over the partition of China or to extracting new profits by exploitation of Russian and Chinese workers, to the detriment of the national interests of the Russian Far East.

CHAPTER FOUR

ECONOMIC RELATIONS OF TSARIST RUSSIA WITH CHINA IN THE AGE OF IMPERIALISM

DETERIORATION OF THE FAR EASTERN SITUATION

AT THE beginning of the 1890's, conditions in the Far East became more complex. The inequitable treaties forced upon China by foreign powers had opened up 23 treaty towns (ports and border railroad stations) to foreign trade by 1894, and there were foreign settlements in ten ports by that date.

While Britain and France took the most prominent role in the foreign aggression against China, Japan also began activity on the Far Eastern stage. Following the overthrow of the *shogunate*[1] in 1868 and the first constitutional changes, Japan began to conduct a policy of aggression against her neighbors. The Ryukyu Islands, which at that time were subject to China, were occupied in 1872, and Japan then directed her efforts at Korea, also at the end of the 1880's and the beginning of the 1890's, the goal of American expansionist ambitions. Since Britain considered Russia her main rival in the Far East, the British attempted to induce the reactionary circles of the Ch'ing dynasty to initiate hostilities against the tsarist government.

This policy did not meet with success. Both Russia and China realized that a strained relationship on their part could benefit the mercenary aims of Britain, the United States and Japan. The tension which developed between China and Russia in 1884-1885 was terminated by the agreement signed at Hunchun in the summer of 1886 confirming the frontiers established in 1860.

Having failed in the attempt to provoke a clash between Russia and China, Britain, forced to change her tactics, then tried to enlist the help of the rising capitalistic Japanese state in maintaining the British monopoly of the China trade: the intention of British ruling circles was that Japan should engage Russia on China's northern frontier. In order to persuade the Japanese in 1890 Britain agreed to abandon the rights of extraterritoriality which she had wrested from Japan by an inequitable treaty in 1858 and encouraged Japanese aggression against Russia and China in every way. This policy was also adopted by the United States.

Japan in turn received these overtures willingly, being convinced that her aggressive program could not be implemented without foreign aid. The 'equal rights' thus obtained were taken to imply a tacit agreement by the Anglo-Saxon nations to Japanese interference in China's affairs similar to the European; these 'rights' were soon employed to initiate hostilities against China.[2]

---

[1] The hereditary commander-in-chief of the army; until 1868 the virtual ruler of the country.

[2] A popular rising in Korea against feudal oppression and Japanese aggression, headed by the *Ton Hak* (oriental teaching) sect, served as a pretext for the Sino-Japanese war. The Emperor of Korea, who was

The backward feudal Ch'ing Empire was not prepared for war against Japan, who had been supplied weapons by Britain and the United States and had at her disposal powerful naval forces. After the loss of the greater part of her navy as a result of Japan's unexpected aggression, China soon capitulated. This defeat had important consequences. Japan not only demanded that China renounce her suzerainty in Korea, but also the payment of an indemnity of 200 million *taels,* the transfer of Formosa, the Pescadores (Penghu Liehtao), and the southern part of Manchuria, including the Liaotung Peninsula, as well as a number of other concessions.

Russia, France and Germany were opposed to these demands. On 23 April 1895, after the conclusion of the peace treaty of Shimonoseki between China and Japan in which the Japanese requirements were met, diplomatic intervention of the three powers induced Japan to waive a number of her conditions; the claim to South Manchuria was abandoned, but China's indemnity was raised to 230 million *taels* (a Sino-Japanese convention relinquishing the Liaotung Peninsula to China was signed on 8 November 1895).

The Treaty of Shimonoseki not only included the cession of Chinese territory and the payment of a substantial indemnity; another important concession to Japan, and to the other powers which already enjoyed the status of 'most-favored nation' by previous treaties, was included in paragraph 4 of article 6 of the treaty. This conferred trading privileges as well as the right to establish industrial enterprises in the treaty ports; it entailed the setting up of a number of companies, the construction of railroads throughout China, etc. China was therefore opened not only to foreign trade but also to foreign capital. In other words, the treaty created a legal basis for one of the objectives of the imperialist powers—unlimited investment in China with a view to controlling the country's economy.

After the Sino-Japanese war the struggle among the European powers, Japan and the United States, for dismemberment of China flared up anew. At that point Britain began to lose her monopoly over Chinese affairs.

TSARIST PENETRATION OF MANCHURIA

The payment of the 230 million *taels* indemnity to Japan which China had assumed by the Treaty of Shimonoseki constituted a heavy burden on the Chinese budget, which was already showing an unfavorable balance. The sum could not be found without foreign cooperation.

Chinese relations with the United States and Britain were strained; on the eve of the Sino-Japanese conflict, America had prohibited Chinese immigration (Sino-Ameri-

incapable of suppressing the insurrection, turned to China for assistance. After the dispatch of Chinese troops, Japan also sent a force to Korea. The rebellion once suppressed, Japan refused to recall her men and demanded that the Korean authorities should undertake a number of 'reforms' which would ensure 'special privileges.' The palace was occupied on 23 July 1894, and an aged regent installed as head of state; Korea was obliged to declare war on China and appeal to Japan for help. Even before the declaration of war, the Japanese fleet attacked and sank a British troopship carrying Chinese soldiers to Korea. War on China was officially declared by Japan on 1 August 1894.

can Washington Convention of 17 March 1894 on immigration), a measure which was received unfavorably by China. Alleging neutrality, the United States refused both the Chinese request for American participation in the peace treaty that terminated the Sino-Japanese conflict and the Russian proposal for joint diplomatic intervention against the stringent clauses of the treaty. The British had also displayed their support of Japan throughout the war.

Russia was viewed in an entirely different light. Her reputation as China's ally could be attributed to the long duration of friendly relations between the two nations as well as to the amicable attitude adopted during and after the Sino-Japanese war. The Chinese government, therefore, turned to Russia for financial assistance.

On 24 June (6 July) 1895 representatives of the Russian and Chinese govenments signed an agreement in St Petersburg for a 4 percent Chinese Government loan of 400 million gold francs, guaranteed by the Russian government to Russian and French banks. The conditions of the loan were much more favorable than those customary for international loans of the time (all British, German and French loans to China carried an annual interest of 5-6 percent; only one, the Anglo-German loan of 1898, stood at $4\frac{1}{2}$ percent). The loan was to be defrayed by customs revenue, and the declaration, which substituted for a contract, stated: '…the Chinese government affirms its decision to refrain from conferring upon a foreign power any right or privilege enabling supervision or control of the Chinese Imperial revenue' (article 4).

Following this step Russia proposed an alliance directed against renewed Japanese aggression against China or Russia's Far Eastern possessions. Such an alliance was undoubtedly in the interests of both parties. Japan had demonstrated her aggressive intentions only too well and had shown her contempt of the obligations assumed under the various treaties and of the traditions of her neighbors. The speeches of Japanese politicians revealed the expansionist aims of Japanese imperialism against Russia, while the occupation of Formosa and the efforts of Japan to dominate South Manchuria confirmed that her intentions toward China were no less aggressive.

The Russian proposals for a defensive alliance against Japan were favorably received by China. Conversations were opened in Peking with the Russian ambassador and continued in the Russian capital, where Li Hung-chang[3] had been dispatched by the Chinese on the occasion of the coronation of Nicolas II.

It became clear, however, in the course of the talks that the Russian autocracy intended to expand a future treaty to include, in addition to the defensive alliance, privileges for Russian investment in the construction of a Manchurian railroad. In the discussions of the 1880's as to the best choice of route for a Trans-Siberian Railroad, Rear-Admiral Kopytov had put forward a project entitled 'On the Most Advantageous Route for the Main and Continuous All Russian Great Eastern Rail-

---

[3] Li Hung-chang entered politics during the repression of the Taiping rebellion and was a prominent member of the Ch'ing ruling clique up to his death in 1902. He became governor of Kiangsu Province in 1862; from 1864 to 1870 he was Viceroy of Nanking, the southern capital, and Governor General of the Kiangsu and Chekiang provinces; from 1870 he served as Governor General of the metropolitan Chihli [Hopeh] Province and practically directed imperial foreign policy.

road,'[4] which recommended the construction of a line from Irkutsk to Kyakhta and from thence to Chinese territory, through Abagaitui, Tsitsihar, Kirin and Ninguta [Ningan] to the village of Nikolskoe[5] in Ussuri Territory, i.e., through Manchuria.

In 1890, the tsarist government became concerned at the news that a survey had been made by Kinder, a British engineer, for construction of a railroad from the port of Taku to Hunchun, i.e., to the Russian border, through Shanhaikwan, Chinchow [Chinhsien], Mukden [Shenyang], and Ninguta.

In view of the strategic importance of Manchuria for the defense of the Far East, and its extensive resources, Russia made an effort to outstrip the other powers and obtain China's agreement to the construction of a Russian railroad on Manchurian territory. This project was not unfavorably received by the Chinese government. Ever since the repression of the Taiping uprising, the ruling circles of the Ch'ing dynasty found it quite natural to seek the support of a foreign power, so long as this support did not undermine the feudal system which they maintained. In making the necessary concessions to Russia, they counted on the latter's power to counteract the growing pressure from Japan, Britain and others.

On 22 May 1896 Li Hung-chang signed a secret Sino-Russian defensive alliance in Moscow. The preamble to the treaty stated that 'His Majesty the Emperor of All Russia and His Majesty the Chinese Emperor, desiring to strengthen the peace happily concluded in the Far East and to protect the continent of Asia from new foreign invasion, have decided to conclude a defensive alliance...' The treaty provided that, in the event of Japanese aggression either against Russian territory in Eastern Asia or against China or Korea, both parties should cooperate with all their land and maritime forces and contribute to the provisioning of the armies (article 1). Article 3 states 'During military operations all Chinese ports shall in case of need be open to Russian warships, which may seek from the Chinese authorities any cooperation required.'

China also agreed to the construction of a railroad to Vladivostok through the Heilungkiang and Kirin provinces, to be undertaken by the Russo-Chinese Bank.[6] The treaty did not determine the conditions under which the railroad was to be built (these were to be agreed upon by the Chinese envoy to St Petersburg and the Russo-Chinese Bank) but stipulated that this venture should not serve as a 'pretext for any seizure of Chinese territory or encroachment upon the sovereign rights of His Majesty the Chinese Emperor.'

---

[4] 'O naivygodneishem napravlenii magistral'noi i nepreryvnoi vserossiiskoi velikoi vostochnoi zheleznoi dorogi,' in *Istoricheskii obzor KVZhD, 1896-1923* (Historical Essay on the Chinese Eastern Railroad, 1896-1923). p. 5. (Izdanie) Pravleniya KVZhD. Harbin. 1923.

[5] [Formerly *Shwangchentze* in Chinese, today the city of Ussuriisk.]

[6] The Russo-Chinese Bank was founded at the end of 1895. Prince Ukhtomskii was elected director. The board of directors included Rotshtein, Neitslin (the Bank's representatives in St Petersburg and Paris), Bark, Chabrier, Shipov, Davydov, Ettinger, Krupp and Pokotilov. Its capital first stood at 6 million rubles and was raised by the shareholders to 11.5 million rubles in 1897; the Chinese government also added a sum of 4.5 million rubles; the bank's total capital thus reached 16 million rubles. In 1910 the Russo-Chinese Bank was reorganized into the Russo-Asiatic Bank by a merger of the joint-stock company of the Russo-Chinese Bank with the Russian Northern Bank.

The conversations held at Moscow for the conclusion of the alliance were accompanied by talks on the construction of the future railroad in Manchuria. Although the treaty stated that the discussions surrounding the contract were to be led on the Russian side by the Russo-Chinese Bank, they were in fact conducted by the Ministry of Finance. Russia's initial proposals were that the Chinese government should grant a permanent concession to the Russo-Chinese Bank for the construction of the railroad, that the gauge should be similar to the Russian gauge and that the railroad should be used freely for the transport of Russian troops.

The contract between the Russo-Chinese Bank and the Chinese government, by Li Hung-chang in May 1895, contained the following clauses:

1) The Chinese government granted to the Russo-Chinese Bank an 80-year concession which was to commence on completion of the line and its operation.

2) After this 80-year period the railway and all related property were to become the property of the Chinese government without compensation; 36 years after the completion and inauguration of the line, China should have the right to buy it if 'full restitution of the entire capital spent for the line as well as of all debts and interests incurred for the line's construction' were made.

3) The Russo-Chinese Bank was to create a company for the construction and maintenance of the railroad, to be called the 'Chinese Eastern Railroad Company' (C.E.R.).

4) The President of the C.E.R. was to be a Chinese subject designated by his own government; acquisition of shares was to be limited to Chinese and Russian subjects.

5) The C.E.R. was to commence work within 12 months of the contract's ratification by the Emperor of China and complete construction work with six years.

6) The gauge was to be the same as that of Russian railroads.

7) Government land required for the construction of the railroad and its operation, as well as for the extraction of building materials (sand, stones, lime, etc.), was to be handed over by China free of charge to the C.E.R., while private land was either to be paid for immediately or compensated for by payment of a yearly rent.

8) Duty on goods exported or imported by Russia through the C.E.R. was to be one third below that levied in Chinese ports.

9) The C.E.R. was to be held responsible for the 'direct transport of all Russian troops and military material in transit along the line from one Russian station to the other, and no intermediate stops could be made under any pretext whatsoever.'

10) The Chinese government contributed 5 million *taels* to the Russo-Chinese Bank and was to participate proportionately in all gains and losses of the bank.

After Li Hung-chang's departure from Moscow, the final version of the contract was negotiated by the Chinese envoy at St Petersburg, Hsü Ching-ch'eng, who signed the agreement for the construction and operation of the C.E.R. with the Russo-Chinese Bank on 3 September (27 August) 1896; the exchange of contracts took place later at Peking, on September 20 of the same year.

According to the provisions of the joint alliance and the contract, the C.E.R. was thus established as a commercial venture without direct official Russian participation. Several articles of the contract, however (article 6, giving the company exclusive rights over the management of the land received and the construction of buildings on this land; article 12, by which China conceded to the company full rights of management of the railroad, etc.), revealed the true intentions of the tsarist government and the financial monopolies, i.e., of the Russo-Chinese Bank, whose functions were far from commercial. The participation of the bank on the Russian side in the talks demonstrates not only the efforts of the Tsarist and Ch'ing authorities to conceal the true nature of the agreement, and the participation of the Russian government in the construction and management of the C. E. R., but also the increasing role of monopolistic capital in tsarist policy.

Tsarist Russia's participation in the aggression of the capitalist powers against China at the end of the 19th century. Toward the end of the 19th century the struggle for the partition of the world and the establishment of monopolies in semicolonial territories became a constant factor in the imperialist policies of the capitalist countries; this was seen most distinctly in nations which had previously lagged behind in economic development but at the beginning of the 20th century could be classed among the most advanced capitalist states.

At the end of the 19th century the struggle of the imperialist countries centered upon China.

For several historical reasons Germany counted as one of the aggressor nations in China in 1897-1898. An incident, created by the killing of two German missionaries in Shantung Province, served as a pretext for a German squadron under Admiral von Diedrichs to effect a landing and occupy the port of Tsingtao at the end of 1897. Germany then demanded a long-term lease on Kiaochow Bay. In its efforts to avoid complications, the Chinese government instructed the local authorities not to oppose the German forces; but at the same time the alliance concluded with Russia was invoked, and China turned to her for assistance. However, even before the Shantung incident Nicolas II had given Wilhelm II his assent to the seizure of Kiaochow Bay by Germany. The tsarist authorities therefore avoided taking effective measures to support China and took advantage of the latter's difficulties to wrest a concession in the Liaotung Peninsula, sending the navy into Port Arthur [Lüshunkow].

Three weeks after the signature of a Sino-German treaty ceding Kiaochow (6 March-22 February 1898), Russia signed a convention with China for a 25-year lease of Port Arthur, Dalny [Talienwan, Dairen in Japanese] and the adjacent waters. Throughout this area 'all military command of land and sea forces as well as the higher civil authority shall be entirely in the hands of the Russian authorities and will be assumed by one person, who shall not, however, have the title of Governor or Governor General' (article 4). Port Arthur became an exclusively military harbor open only to Russian and Chinese naval units. According to the same convention Dalny was declared 'open to foreign trade,' except for one bay reserved for military purposes, and merchant vessels of all nations could enter the port freely (article 6).

In addition to the lease of Port Arthur and Dalny, China agreed to extend the C. E. R. concession of the Russo-Chinese Bank 'to a branch line from a main-line station to Talienwan (Dalny) and also, if necessary, from the same main line to another more convenient point on the littoral of the Liaotung Peninsula between the town of Yingkow [Newchang] and the estuary of the Yalu River' (article 8). In concession it was stipulated that China should grant no other concessions to subjects of a third party in the area of the projected railroad, apart from the agreement to the construction of a line from Shanhaikwan to the closest point of the C.E.R.

After the conclusion of the 1898 convention Russia therefore owned a concession for the construction and operation of a railroad through Manchuria, from its western border across to Nikolsk-Ussuriiski [today Voroshilovsk-Ussuriiski, or Ussuriisk] and Dalny, as well as a naval base at Port Arthur.

IMPERIALIST 'SPHERES OF INFLUENCE' IN CHINA

In her efforts to reinforce her positions in China, Britain forced China to sign on 7 July 1898 an agreement to the lease of Weihaiwei [Weihai], opposite Port Arthur on the Gulf of Chihli [Gulf of Po Hai] 'for the better protection of British trade in the adjacent waters...' Britain did not even attempt to conceal that her policies in North China were directed against Russia. Imperialist British circles also reinforced their positions by concluding agreements with financial groups of other countries. At the end of 1898 and the beginning of 1899 British banks signed agreements with German banks (2 September 1898) to delimit the spheres of interests of railroad construction, and with American banking firms (1 February 1899) on a joint venture to participate in Chinese railroad construction. An exchange of notes took place on 16/28 April 1899 between the governments of Russia and Britain on spheres of railroad interests in China.

The main imperialist powers thus divided China's economic regions into spheres of influence in 1898-1899. The participation of imperialist monopolies in railroad construction lay at the root of this division; it was considered a most profitable capitalist venture ensuring certain benefits as well as large orders for the metropolitan steel industries, and expanding the internal market of semicolonial China. A feature of these agreements was that they were concluded without China's participation, as it were behind her back, although China was directly concerned.

However, the division of China into spheres of influence could not satisfy all the imperialist competitors. Despite the participation of British banks, many British monopolies remained outside the deal, and there was no consensus of British public opinion on the policy of the spheres of influence, a policy which might limit the scope of British imperialism. This policy was combatted by a number of British monopolies that had interests in the various provinces of China.

The United States was also opposed to spheres of influence. Having wrested the Philippines from Spain in 1898, America was in a position to build powerful naval bases close to the Chinese littoral; U.S. policy toward China could thus become more active. American imperialist circles were far from satisfied with the role left to them in China after the delimitation of the British, Russian, French and German spheres of influence. The U.S. government thus demanded the establishment of an 'open door' policy. The financial power of the American monopolies led them to hope that the 'equal possibilities' conferred by the 'open door' would enable them to eliminate competition and obtain a monopoly of the Chinese market.

Participation of tsarist Russia in the imperialist intervention of eight nations in China. The capitulation of the Ch'ing ruling circles to imperialism did not signify that China had ceased to resist aggression. In the words of Mao Tse-tung, 'The history of China's transformation by imperialism in league with Chinese feudalism into a semi-colonial or colonial country is at the same time the history of the Chinese people's fight against imperialism and its toadies.'[7]

Uprisings against the feudal despotism of the Ch'ings broke out in China in 1898-1899, as a result of the continuing pauperization of the masses. In the north of the country, where the destructive effects of foreign intervention were particularly severe, these uprisings were of both an anti-feudal and an anti-imperialist nature. Members of the secret *I Ho Ch'üan* [*I Ho T'uan*] (Righteous Harmony Fists) usually designated by the name of Boxers, frequently headed the revolts. In order to manoeuver in this dangerous political situation the Ch'ing authorities declared their support of the insurgents.

The imperialist governments intervened in China in the name of the West's 'civilizing' mission against Chinese 'barbarism.' In his article 'The China War,' which unmasked the imperialist nature of foreign intervention, V. I. Lenin wrote: 'What caused these Chinese attacks against the Europeans, this rebellion put down with such zeal by the British, French, Germans, Russians, Japanese and others? "The animosity of the yellow race against white," "Chinese hate of European culture and civilization," are the arguments used by the instigators of the war. Yes, the Chinese really hate Europeans, but which Europeans do they hate, and why? It is not the people of Europe that are hated by the Chinese—no conflict ever existed with them— but the European capitalists and the European governments subservient to their interests.'[8]

These lines penned by the revolutionary leader reflected the attitude of the progressive class of Russian society—the working class—toward events in China. Only the working class, which had borne the yoke of Russian tsarism and exploitation by the country's capitalists could appreciate the historical significance of the Chinese people's struggle against the foreign invaders or perceive the community of interests between workers of all nations. Capitalist chauvinism did not succeed in poisoning the conscience of the Russian revolutionary working class, which consistently demonstrated the friendly attitude of the Russian people toward the Chinese masses, oppressed by feudal despots and world imperialism. Revolutionary Russia rejected the policies of tsarism; in Lenin's words: 'The policy of tsarism in China is a criminal policy which intensifies the oppression and exploitation of the masses.'[9]

The imperialist governments attempted to suppress the voice of the workers' parties and opposed the popular risings by force, thereby supporting the interests of

[7] Mao Tse-tung. *Selected Works.* Vol. 3, p.151.
[8] Lenin, V. I. *Works.* Vol. 4. p. 348, 4th ed.
[9] *Ibid*, p. 351.

monopolistic capitalism. When the rebellion had been suppressed, China was forced to pay a huge indemnity. On 7 September (25 August) 1901 China was not only forced to sign the so-called Peace Protocol with the eight imperialist governments, which invoked severe measures against Chinese public leaders 'considered guilty by the foreign powers,' but also obliged to pay a sum of 450 million custom *taels*. Since China did not possess such a sum (annual Chinese exports for the period 1896-1900 were valued at only 176 million custom *taels*), the imperialist powers transformed this indemnity into a debt which China was to pay from 1 January 1902 to the end of 1940, a 4 percent interest being added to the unpaid amount (percentages were calculated from 1 July 1901). The Boxer indemnity was to be paid out of customs revenue over and above the amounts which China had already signed away to foreign powers for loans previously contracted, as well as out of the internal customs revenue and the salt tax.

The importation of arms was forbidden for two years (this period could be prolonged by the foreign powers at will), the Chinese forts at port Taku were to be destroyed, and foreign powers were to have the right to garrison troops at Peking for the protection of the legation quarter. Foreign troops remained quartered on Chinese territory at points that had not been specified by the various treaties and agreements. Each of the rivals attempted to delay the recall of troops in order to exert pressure on the Chinese government and exact further concessions.

The common front that had united the imperialists to repress the popular uprisings did not reflect their general intention to exploit China's resources. The occupation of Manchuria by tsarist Russia and the conclusion of an agreement between Admiral Alekseev, Commander-in-Chief of the Liaotung region, General Grodekov and the Governor of Mukden, according to which Russia retained virtual control of Manchuria, was opposed by Britain, the United States and Japan. Conversations were held between Britain and Japan in April 1901, i.e., before the signature of the Boxer Protocol, to discuss an alliance directed against Russia; this Anglo-Japanese alliance was signed on 30 January 1902. Incited by Britain and the United States, Japan began to prepare for war against Russia.

CONSTRUCTION OF THE CHINESE EASTERN RAILROAD

Russia's defenses in the Far East remained inadequate. The vast expanses of her Far Eastern possessions, with their rich resources, were sparsely populated and were not linked with the country's industrial centers. Lack of roads and an outmoded Russian fleet made these areas dependent on the nearest foreign markets and thus encouraged the predatory aims of Japan, Britain and the United States.

In this state of affairs the construction of a railroad connecting the Russian Far East to Eastern Siberia, which was already linked by railroad to the Urals and the cities of central Russia, constituted an important step which would serve Russian economic and strategic interest in the Far East at the end of the 19th century. The Far Eastern railroad was to speed up the flow of settlers to the Amur and Maritime territories and promote the development of the Russian economy.

The tsarist government, however, displayed a criminal neglect of the country's interests by continuing to disregard its Far Eastern territories. At the same time it was prepared to invest on a large scale in Manchuria in order to keep up with the race for the partition of China. The Russian official circles and middle class tried to prove that a railroad tract passing through Manchuria would be much shorter, and therefore much cheaper, that it would traverse populated areas where manpower would be easier to obtain, and would afford a junction to Port Arthur—a harbor on the Yellow Sea which could be used all the year round. In reality the Manchurian railroad was to shorten the distance from Chita to Vladivostok by no more than 600 versts; as to the cost of construction, it subsequently became clear that each verst of the Chinese Eastern Railroad cost 80 percent more than the Siberian Railroad— 150,000 rubles instead of 83,000.

Manchuria also afforded no distinct advantages in the supply of manpower. At the beginning of the construction of the track the population of North Manchuria was less than 2 million; furthermore, the area west of Tsitsihar was populated mainly by Mongol nomads and a small number of Chinese, primarily gold miners and fur trappers whom the Russian administration did not succeed in mobilizing even for the construction of the earthworks. The trained personnel were brought in from Russia and other European countries. For the heavy work Chinese workers were usually recruited from Shantung Province and other northern Chinese provinses, which were also reservoirs of manpower for the construction of harbors, coal mines and other industries of the Russian Far East.

The Russian builders of the C. E. R. suffered great hardship from the unimaginable climatic conditions, particularly in South Manchuria, and lack of the most elementary sanitation and medical facilities. In the summer of 1899 plague broke out in Yingkow (Newchwang), spreading swiftly to the southern towns of Manchuria. An epidemic of cholera in 1902 caused even greater losses to C.E.R. workers. According to official data, which are far from comprehensive, there were 1,050 cases of cholera among the Russian colony of 30,000 in Manchuria, including 647 deaths.

By deciding in favor of the Manchurian project of a track to Vladivostok and rejecting the Amur scheme, Russian autocracy set back the development of the Russian Far East by almost 15 years. This was to have serious consequences. At the beginning of the 20th century Russia's Far Eastern territories still remained economically underdeveloped and sparsely settled, [10] while the neighboring areas of Manchuria saw the development of towns and of modern railroad, river and maritime communications by Russian investment and manpower.

The imperialist policies of the tsarist authorities in China injured the age-old friendship between the two nations. Despite the Russian undertakings in the treaty of alliance of 22 May 1896 to avoid 'any seizure of Chinese territory or any encroachment upon the sovereign rights of His Majesty the Emperor of China,' the tsarist

---

[10] In 1900 there were only 32,798 Russian peasants of both sexes, in the Amur Territory and 50,901 in the Maritime territory; the Amur Cossacks at that date numbered 11,300 and the Ussuri Cossacks 7,300 (data from 'Priamure' [The Amur Region] pp. 90-95).

administration attempted to turn Manchuria into a vassal of the Russian crown, in disregard of the sovereign rights of the Chinese people.

Although a director designated by the Chinese government was put at the head of the C. E. R., his functions were limited to seeing that the company's obligations to the Chinese government and local authorities were fulfilled. The real head of the company was the deputy director, nominated by the Russian Ministry of Finance. The executive functions were delegated by the director to the chief engineer for the period of construction and to the manager of the railroad, also appointed by the Russian Ministry of Finance, during the operation of the line.

The C. E. R. whose profits were guaranteed by the Russian government independently of actual profit or loss, undertook in turn the following obligations:

a) upkeep of the line and all its appurtenances and rolling stock to ensure the safe, convenient and uninterrupted flow of passengers and goods;

b) insurance of movement along the line to correspond with the volume of transport on neighboring Russian lines;

c) maintenance of direct connections with Russian railroads;

d) modifications of the rates for the transit of goods and telegraphic communication to be introduced only with the agreement of the Russian government;

e) carriage of Russian postal matter free of charge (paragraph 3 of the C. E. R. statute).

These obligations were to extend over the entire 80-year period of the concession, irrespective of whether the line remained in the hands of the C. E. R. or was bought out by the Chinese side.

The Russian Ministry of Finance obtained the right to designate not only the deputy director of the Board, the chief engineer and the manager of the railroad, but also the heads of certain departments and other engineers; it could also recommend the appointment of members to the Committee of Inspection. The distribution and use of the company's capital were also controlled by the Ministry of Finance (paragraph 27 of the statute).

Russian and Chinese subjects enjoyed special privileges inside the Concession Zone of the Chinese Eastern Railroad (C. E. R. Zone). Russian subjects had the extraterritorial rights defined by the 1860 Sino-Russian Treaty of Peking, the only difference being that the jurisdiction over such subjects was to be exercised not by a Russian consul but by the engineer-in-chief of the works, and later (when the line commenced operation), by the manager of the railroad.

Agreements concluded between the chief engineer and the provincial Manchu administration[11] created a 'Chief Bureau of Foreign and Railway Affairs,' at Harbin with branch offices along the line for dealing with disputes and litigation throughout the C. E. R. Zone. The director and deputy director of this bureau were designated

[11] Agreement between the Construction Office of the C. E. R. and the military Governor General of Kirin Province, signed on 5 July 1901 (the first agreement was signed on 19 May 1899), and agreement between the Construction Office of the C. E. R. and the military Governor of Heilungkiang Province, signed on 1 January 1902

by the Chinese provincial administration after consultation with the engineer-in-chief (in the period of construction) or the manager of the C. E. R. (during operation). Examination by the bureau of the affairs of Chinese subjects living in the C. E. R. Zone also required the participation of Russian administrative officials. In other words, both Russian and Chinese subjects living in the C. E. R. Zone were to be under the jurisdiction not of the Chinese civil courts, but of mixed courts similar to those functioning in the foreign concessions of China's treaty ports.

The tsarist government made an effort to speed up the construction of the C. E. R. as much as possible. Following the visit of the Finance Minister, Witte, to Manchuria in the autumn of 1902 and of Kuropatkin, the Minister of War in spring of 1903, the tsarist authorities decided to operate the line, which was still unfinished. On 1 July 1903 the C. E. R. was officially handed over by the Construction Office to the Management. A main line and branch lines totaling a length of 2,373.27 versts were thus opened; the total value of the buildings and property was estimated at 374,955,598 rubles, including repairs carried out after the Boxer uprising, amounting to 71,745,878 rubles. The transfer also listed a number of unfinished projects, valued at 57,569,255 rubles.[12]

In addition to the investment in the C. E. R. proper, the railroad Board had invested 17,571,250 rubles in Dalny [Talienwan] harbor, and 10,418,843 rubles in the town itself, and had purchased ships for a Pacific line to Dalny, valued at 11,925,769 rubles.[13]

By the middle of 1903 Russia had successfully completed the construction of railroad and harbor facilities in Manchuria;[14] these were to have an important effect on the economic development of Northeast China[15] and to sow discord among the imperialist powers in the Far East.

ECONOMIC CONSEQUENCES OF THE RUSSO-JAPANESE WAR
ON SINO-RUSSIAN RELATIONS

In 1903 Britain and the United States began to incite Japan to an attack on Russia. Favorable circumstances having arisen, in the night of 8 February 1904 Japan attacked the Russian fleet anchored near Port Arthur and destroyed three major vessels without declaring war. At the same time Japanese armies entered Korea, crossed the Yalu River (29 April-1 May) into South Manchuria and landed on the Liaotung Peninsula. The Russian troops put up a heroic defense at Port Arthur (which continued until 2 January 1905) and inflicted heavy losses upon the Japanese at Liaotung (29 August-3 September) and Mukden [Shenyang] (Febroary-10 March 1905); one year after the beginning of hostilities Japan was already looking for a way to end the conflict.

[12] *Historical Essay on the Chinese Eastern Railway,* p. 123.
[13] *The Amur Region,* p. 166.
[14] The construction of the C. E. R. is considered to have begun officially on 16 (28) August 1897.
[15] This term today designates the previous territory of Manchuria, minus the western Mongol areas which in 1945 were transferred to the Inner Mongolian Autonomous Region.

The tsarist government which had been shaken by the first [1905] Russian Revolution also wished to terminate hostilities. It was ready to accept an unfavorable and dishonorable peace if only to ward off the wave of revolutionary activity threatening to submerge it. As Lenin wrote after the fall of Port Arthur: 'It is not the Russian people but autocracy which has suffered a disgraceful defeat.'[16] By the Treaty of Portsmouth Russia recognized Korea to be within the Japanese sphere of influence, the Russian lease of the Liaotung Peninsula, including Port Arthur and Dalny, was transferred to Japan, the southern part of the C. E. R. (from Dalny to Kwanchentze [Changchun] station), and the southern part of Sakhalin Island (south of the 50th parallel) were handed over, and fishing rights in Russian Far Eastern waters were conceded. The Treaty of Portsmouth was to have a negative effect on both the development of Sino-Russian relations and China's general situation.

Russia's war expenditure, excluding the value of property handed over to Japan in Manchuria, reached 2,282,800,000 rubles.[17] In addition to this, Russia transferred to Japan 715 versts of the southern section of the C. E. R., the harbor of Dalny with its equipment and numerous auxiliary railway and commercial enterprises, including shipbuilding and locomotive works at Dalny, coal mines at Fushun, Shihpeiling, Taokiatun, etc. The total property received by Japan was valued at 123,000,000 rubles.[18]

In addition to the heavy expenditure and losses incurred by the war, the interruption of the routes to China through Manchuria was a severe blow for Russia. Japan controlled all the communications from the Sino-Russian frontier to the Yellow Sea and North China through Mukden [Shenyang]—Shanhaikwan [Linyü] and was therefore able to control all Sino-Russian trade through Manchuria. Its position in Korea and the Liaotung Peninsula also afforded Japan an advantage in the maritime trade with China's northern and central ports.

One of the most significant consequences of the Russo-Japanese war was an increase in the imperialist conflicts over China and a shift in the balance of power. The struggle for the partition of China between Russia on the one hand and Britain, Japan and the United States on the other then became secondary, while that between Japan and the United States assumed major importance.

SINO-RUSSIAN ECONOMIC TIES AFTER THE RUSSO-JAPANESE WAR

The Russian Revolution of 1905 considerably affected the development of revolutionary movements in Asia. Lenin called the revolutionary wave in this area of the world after 1905 'the awakening of Asia.' World capitalism and the Russian movement of 1905 have definitely awakened Asia. The hundreds of millions of downtrodden people sunk in medieval barbarism have come to life and begun the struggle

---

[16] Lenin, V. I. *Collected Works*, 4th ed., Vol. 8, p. 37.

[17] *The Amur Region*, p. 166.

[18] According to the estimate of the C. E. R. Economic Bureau (statistical yearbook of the C. E. R. for 1923), the railroad stock transferred to Japan was worth 81 million rubles. To this must be added the Russian capital investments at Dalny and Port Arthur, valued at approximately 42 million rubles.

for the most elementary rights of man, for democracy.'[19] China was one of the countries in which a popular liberation movement developed. A series of mass uprisings broke out in 1906-1908 in South and Southwest China, headed by the *Tungmenghui* society led by Sun Yat-sen. The most important of these was the first uprising of Chinese workers at Pingsiang (Kiangsi Province) in 1906. This was followed, in 1907, by mutiny at Wuhan[20] and peasant revolts in the Lienhsien and Ch'inhsien districts of Kwangtung Province. In 1906 the *Tungmenghui* society began to distribute the 'People's Paper' *(Min Pao),* which disseminated a republican ideology. The revolutionary theories of the *Tungmenghui* and its leader, the great democrat and patriot Sun Yat-sen, became increasingly popular among the laboring masses and progressive intelligentsia.

These popular liberation movements in China had the heartfelt support of the Russian working class, which had begun its struggle against tsarism, and of its revolutionary vanguard—the Bolsheviks. Their leader, V. I. Lenin, who closely followed all the developments in the Chinese revolutionary movement, was convinced that these first uprisings and popular revolts of the Chinese people would necessarily become a 'conscious democratic movement.'[21] Lenin saw in the young democratic forces of Asia a useful ally for the European proletariat in its struggle for the liberation of humanity from the fetters of capitalism and the building of a new classless society.

The friendship between the Russian and Chinese peoples, represented by the revolutionary vanguard of Russia and by Chinese progressive circles fighting for independence and democracy, thus developed behind the backs of the ruling cliques, while relations between the Ch'ing authorities and the tsarist government deteriorated from year to year.

Ch'ing independence in foreign affairs became increasingly restricted after the suppression of the Boxer uprising.

On 13 February (31 January) 1907 a convention was concluded between Russia and Japan on the delimitation of their 'interests' in Manchuria. The separation between North and South Manchuria was additionally assisted by the fact that immediately after the southern part of the C. E. R. had been transferred to Japan the gauge was narrowed and direct communication by rail from North Manchuria to the Liaotung Peninsula and port Dalny (renamed Dairen by the Japanese) was prevented.

The interruption of the direct railroad from North to South Manchuria considerably raised the cost of freight from North Manchuria to port Dalny. In addition, the tariffs imposed by the administration of the South Manchuria Railway (S. M. R.) and Dalny harbor were higher for Russian, Chinese and other firms than for Japanese enterprises. The line to Vladivostok, 740 versts from Harbin, was shorter by 147 versts than to Dalny and naturally became the cheapest freight route for North Manchuria.

---

[19] Lenin, V. I. *Collected Works,* 4th ed. Vol. 19, p. 66.
[20] [Wuhan is today a group of three cities, the Han Cities—Hankow, Hanyang and Wuchang—at the junction of the Han and Yangtze Kiang rivers.]
[21] Lenin, V. I. *Collected Works,* 4th ed. Vol. 15, p. 162.

The Russian government's decision to unify the management of the Chinese Eastern Railroad and the Ussuri Railroad was an important step toward strengthening the ties between North Manchuria and Vladivostok. On 22 September 1906 the government ratified an agreement between the two companies temporarily transferring the Ussuri Railroad to the C. E. R. up to 1 January 1931, Russia retaining the right 'to demand at any time the restitution of the railway before the end of the period, undertaking only to advise the company one year in advance.'[22]

The agreement therefore transferred an 836-verst line connecting Khabarovsk to Vladivostok, to the C.E.R., with branches from Nikolsk-Ussuriiski [Ussuriisk] to the Manchurian frontier. The C. E. R., was also to manage the Suchan[23] branch line (74 verst), and wharfs on the Amur River at Khabarovsk and on the Ussuri River at Iman; in addition, it was entitled to use a strip of the Golden Horn Bay in Vladivostok harbor— the Egersheld warf.[24]

The merger of the C. E. R. and the Ussuri Railroad and the utilisation of Vladivostok harbor by the C. E. R. strengthened the ties between North Manchuria and the Russian Far East. Vladivostok began to play an important role in Manchuria's trade, particularly in the export of Manchurian soybean, oilcake and other foodstuffs in transit to Europe.

VOLUME OF GOODS CARRIED BY C.E.R. COMMERCIAL
AGENCY VIA VLADIVOSTOK HARBOR
(in thousands of poods)

1909	21,560
1910	24,268
1911	34,089
1912	30,722

After the Russo-Japanese war the C. E. R. concluded a number of supplementary agreements with the Chinese administration. An agreement signed with the authorities of Heilungkiang Province on 30 August 1907 authorized the company to work coal mines throughout the province and in a strip of 30 *li* on both sides of the railroad. In 1907 the company concluded two agreements for the exploitation of forest areas in the Kirin and Heilunkiang provinces, an agreement on telegraphic communications and another on postal services and the dispatch of postal correspondence.

The C. E. A. thus became the main rail artery of North Manchuria and the Russian Maritime Territory and was an important factor in the economy of the region.

[22] Agreement between the Chinese Eastern Railroad and the Ussuri Railroad, ratified by the Russian government on 22 September 1906 and published by the edict of 4 October 1906 ('Historical Essay on the Chinese Eastern Railroad,' pp. 364-366).

[23] [Formerly *Sucheng* in Chinese.]

[24] Temporary use of the Egersheld wharf by the C. E. R. had already been considered at the beginning of the railroad's construction. This wharf, situated in the southern part of Vladivostok harbor, was 400 sajenes [2,134 meters] long and 50 sajenes wide. Its transfer to the company was considered after Russia had lost Dalny and came into effect on 25 August 1906; Egersheld wharf was then declared open, i.e., goods in transit there to be free of customs duty.

Participation of tsarist Russia in the international banking consortium in China. Wishing to extract new colonial profits, British, French, and German banks created a united consortium [25] in 1909 which forced the Chinese government to sign a new 5 percent loan, the so-called Hukwang[26] loan of £5.5 million for the construction of railroads to traverse China from north to south and passing through the rich provinces of Hupeh and Hunan. The creation of this powerful group of banks worried American financial cirlces. With the help of the State Department these magnates therefore set up a powerful banking group[27] which also competed for a Chinese loan in order to finance railroad construction and industry.

At the same time the United States developed a program to put American capital into Manchuria. On 6 November 1909 the Secretary of State, Knox sent a memorandum to Britain, followed up by memoranda to other governments, proposing an international loan to China for the acquisition of the C.E.R. and S.M.R. for 'internationalization' of the companies; the memorandum also stated that if Japan and Russia refused the proposal a new railroad should be built from South Manchuria (the town of Chinchow) to the Russian-Manchurian frontier (Aigun). On 27 October 1910 American banks headed by Morgan concluded an agreement with the Chinese government on a $50 million loan which was to 'strengthen' the economic position of the Imperial Court and finance industrial and railroad construction in Manchuria. American financial circles demanded admission to the existing banking consortium on the strength of this agreement.

The admission of American banks to the consortium constituted a threat to the interests of tsarist Russia and Japan, since the main purpose of these banks was to gain ground in Manchuria; both countries therefore protested against the American expansion. On 4 July 1910 a Russo-Japanese agreement was signed stating that both sides would 'support and respect the *status quo* in Manchuria as determined by the treaties, conventions and other agreements previously signed between Russia and Japan as well as between these two powers and China.'[28] The two governments agreed that whenever new circumstances tending to change the existing situation in Manchuria arose, they would 'immediately open bilateral talks to agree upon measures found necessary for the preservation of the said *status quo*.'[29]

Russia and Japan also demanded admission to the international banking consortium and that the activities of its British, French, German and American members be

---

[25] The consortium included the following banks and companies: Britain—Hong Kong and Shanghai Banking Corporation, British-China Corporation, Central Railway Company; France—Banque d'Indochine, representing eight important French banks; Germany—Deutsch-Chinesische Eisenbahngesellschaft, a syndicate of German banks.

[26] [Hukwang was an administrative area at the time of the Yuan (Mongol) dynasty (1277-1368) which included the four provinces of Hupeh, Hunan, Kwangtung, and Kwangsi. It was divided into provinces under Kang Hsi (1662-1722). The name designates in the modern period the two provinces of Hupeh and Hunan.]

[27] The U.S. banking group comprised Morgan, Harriman, Kohn, Loeb & Co., the First National Bank and the National City Bank.

[28] Article 2 of the Russo-Japanese Agreement of 4 July 1910 (Izvolskii-Motono Agreement).

[29] *Ibid.,* article 3.

limited to China proper, leaving Manchuria as a sphere of 'special' Russian and Japanese interest. Britain and France accepted the Russian and Japanese banks despite the American opposition, since, in view of the deteriorating situation in Europe, they wished to draw closer to these two countries. The consortium was thus expanded to include six imperialist powers.

The admission of Russia and Japan to the consortium was a setback to American policy in China. The American banks would have lost their independence and have been obliged to share the profits with their poorer rivals. American ruling cirlces thus found it unprofitable to remain in the consortium and the U.S. banks withdrew from it.

SINO-RUSSIAN ECONOMIC RELATIONS DURING THE CHINESE REVOLUTION (1911-1913)

China's international position did not improve in 1911. The imperialist powers continued to manoeuver for the retention and expansion of their territorial and other privileges in China, thereby weakening Chinese autonomy.

China's internal situation also took a turn for the worse. The pauperization and dispossession of the peasantry continued. According to sample data, over 70 percent of the peasants were either tenants or half-tenants. In Kwangtung province the percentage was 78 percent, in Kiangsi Province 71 percent, in Hunan Province 71 percent, and in Szechwan province 70 percent. The national average was no less than 50 percent even including the underdeveloped provinces of the northeast and northwest.

The dominance of foreign capital in the main branches of China's industries and in transport impeded their development and narrowed the sphere of activity of Chinese capital. Both the domestic and foreign policies of the Ch'ing government gave rise to discontent not only among the working population but also among the Chinese middle classes. The desire for democratic change was gaining a stronger foothold throughout the country while the Chinese authorities tried to delay the promised democratic reforms and increase the power of the Imperial Court by the transfer of all higher officials.[30]

The reactionary Ch'ing regime did not succeed, however, in allaying the general discontent. Mass peasant movements were gaining momentum throughout China in 1910-1911. The disaffection also spread to the urban poor, particularly in the large commercial and industrial centers of Shanghai, Canton, Nanking, Changsha and Lanchow [Kaolan] and continually included new strata of the population. Extensive revolutionary propaganda in the army was disseminated by the *Tungmenghui* Society led by Sun Yat-Sen. In the south military groups formed to oppose foreign intervention and became the mainstay of the anti-Manchu movements.

A new cause of dissatisfaction was the signing on 20 May 1911 of an agreement between China and the four-power international banking consortium (Britain,

---

[30] Following the deaths of Emperor Kwang Hsu (14 November 1908) and Empress Tz'u Hsi (15 November 1908), Pu I, the two-year-old son of prince Chun (brother of the late Emperor) was put on the throne.

France, Germany and the United States) for a new £6 million loan for railroad con-struction that had followed the Imperial edict of 9 May 1911 nationalizing China's railways. These measures, which strengthened the position of the imperialist powers in China, were viewed as high treason by the public and evoked widespread indig-nation.

On 10 October 1911 an insurrection of the military garrison of Wuchang, prompted by the *Tungmenghui* society, initiated the revolution of 1911-1913. The revolution rapidly spread among the workers of Shanghai, Canton, Wuhan and other industrial centers, as well as to the peasants of the southern provinces. The provincial author-ities were soon ousted and revolutionary governments created in their stead. A pro-visional revolutionary government was formed in Wuhan on 20 October 1911, headed by Hwa Hsin, a leader of the *Tungmenghui;* on November 3 a similar government was set up in Shanghai led by Ch'en Ch'i-mei, a member of the society's right wing. Finally a conference of provincial representatives was convened at Canton in Dec-ember; it proclaimed the creation of a Republic and the formation of a revolutionary government temporarily headed by President Sun Yat-sen (December 29).

These popular risings were more than a mere anti-Manchu rebellion. The partic-ipation of the peasant masses lent an antifeudal complexion to the revolution and endangered the very existence of the feudal basis of Chinese society. V. I. Lenin des-cribed the revolutionary situation in China as follows: 'China's liberty has been achieved by an alliance of peasant democracy and the liberal bourgeoisie. It will be shown in the near future whether the peasants will be able to maintain their dem-ocratic position without the leadership of the party of the proletariat *against* the liberals, who are only waiting for a convenient moment to shift to the right.'[31]

The revolution perplexed and frightened Chinese reactionary classes. The Ch'ing authorities, in their attempts to win over the upper bourgeoisie, the landowners and the high military officials, published an edict on 22 October 1911 announcing the opening of the second session of the Constitutional Assembly; this was followed by the appointment of Yuan Shi-kai as military Commander-in-Chief of the Yangtze Kiang river basin (on October 27); at the beginning of November he was nominated Prime Minister.

The bourgeoisie throughout the world was also disturbed by the revolutionary events. The ruling circles of a number of countries began to plan military intervention against the Chinese revolutionary forces. The imperialist powers, who clearly under-stood the futility of maintaining the imperial Manchu regime,[32] counted on the help of the bourgeoisie and landowners to curb the revolution and protect their interests in China. Yüan Shih-kai's nomination was supported by the imperialist powers. The French Minister of Foreign Affairs, Poincaré, addressed a note to all the powers on 13 January 1912 suggesting that they uphold the candidacy of Yüan Shih-kai for the

---

[31] Lenin, V. I., *Collected Works,* 4th ed. Vol. 18, p. 372.
[32] In the initial stage of the Chinese revolution, the Japanese government urged the Russian authorities to organize an armed intervention in support of the Chinese monarchy. However, the swift breakdown of the Manchu regime convinced the tsarist government of the futility of such a step and the Japanese proposal was rejected.

Chinese presidency. This proposal was accepted by Britain and the United States, and later by Russia, Japan and Germany. Strengthened by this support the Chinese counterrevolution under the leadership of Yüan Shih-kai passed to attack. The revolutionary forces grouped in the south around Sun Yat-sen did not succeed in gaining the support of the antifeudal peasant movement or the rising working class and were thus unsuccessful in their opposition to the reactionaries. A part of the bourgeoisie and the military-feudal clique, scared by the role taken by the working masses, joined the counter revolutionaries. Yüan Shih-kai came into power.[33]

The imperialist powers soon took measures to ensure a counter revolutionary victory. The international banking consortium agreed to the so-called Reorganization Loan of £25 million to the Yüan Shih-kai government. The conditions were stringent: payment was ensured by transfer of the most important item of China's revenue—the salt tax—to foreign control. Yüan Shih-kai's agreement to this condition, given without the knowledge of the senate, caused widespread disatisfaction. Lenin wrote at that time: 'The new Chinese loan is concluded *against* Chinese democracy: "Europe" stands up for Yüan Shih-kai, who is preparing a military dictatorship. Why is she supporting him? Because the deal is an excellent one. The loan is for a sum of approximately 250 million rubles at 84 percent. This means that the bourgeoisie of "Europe" *pays* China 210 million rubles while taking 225 million from the public.' The tsarist government participated in the 'Reorganization Loan,' directed against the Chinese people's interest, with a sum of 26.3 million rubles.

In order to give satisfaction to the imperialist powers, Yüan Shih-kai made the following declaration: 'I proclaim herewith that all treaties, agreements and other obligations assumed and concluded by the previous Ch'ing government as well as by the Republic of China with all foreign governments shall be strictly respected and likewise all contracts signed by the previous government with foreign companies and individuals. At the same time the present document acknowledges all the rights, privileges and advantages conferred by China upon foreign subjects as provided in international agreements, the jurisdiction of their nationals, and all existing precedents and customs, in order to maintain friendly relations and to preserve peace.'[35]

Attempting to profit from the civil war between the reactionary north and the revolutionary south, the tsarist government decided to prolong the term of the Sino-Russian commercial treaty of 1881. On 24 August 1912 before the conclusion of the talks between the representatives of both countries, which had been opened in 1911, at the expiration of the 1881 Treaty of St Petersburg, the Russian embassy at Peking informed the Chinese Ministry of Foreign Affairs of Russia's decision 'to consider the

---

[33] On 14 February 1912 Sun Yat-sen published a declaration to the National Assembly (constituted by representatives of the provinces) announcing his decision to refuse the nomination for the presidency and proposing the candidacy of Yüan Shih-kai in order to unite the nation. The latter was elected Provisional President of the Republic on 16 February by the National Assembly.

[34] Lenin, V. I. *Collected Works,* 4th ed. Vol. 19, p. 78.

[35] Declaration by the President of the Republic of China, Yuan Shih-kai, on 10 October 1913 concerning the relations between the Republic of China and foreign powers.

1881 Treaty of St Petersburg extended for another ten years, i.e., to 7/20 August 1921.'[36]

Russia attempted to justify this unilateral decision by article 15 of the Treaty of St Petersburg, which provided for the automatic renewal of the treaty if neither of the contracting parties states its desire to modify it. This argument had no factual basis, for China had initiated the conversations of 1911; on 1 January 1913 the tsarist government itself also modified the treaty's clauses by insisting that goods in transit through a 50-verst strip along the frontier should be free of customs duty. This inequitable measure showed Russia's attitude to the obligations assumed under the treaty and to the sovereign rights of the Chinese people. The latter's struggle for land and democracy terrified the Russian bourgeoisie and landowners, who clearly understood that the victory of the revolution would be a blow to their imperialist 'interests' in China.

The Bolshevik party, the vanguard of the revolutionary working class, had a different attitude toward the fight of the Chinese people for their liberation. Lenin warmly greeted the Chinese revolution. In January 1912 the Prague conference of the Russian Social-Democratic Workers' Party adopted a resolution proposed by Lenin on the Chinese revolution which expressed the admiration of the Russian working class for the heroic struggle of the Chinese people. This resolution stated: 'In view of the campaign in the official and liberal ("Reck") press which supports, in the interests of the Russian capitalists, the seizure of Chinese territories bordering upon Russia, the conference takes note of the international significance of the Chinese people's revolutionary struggle which announces the liberation of Asia and undermines the supremacy of the European bourgeoisie, greets the Chinese revolutionary republicans, bears witness to the heartfelt sympathy with which the Russian proletariat follows the successes of the revolutionary masses in China and condemns the attitude of Russian liberalism which supports the tsarist policy of usurpation.'[37]

From the very beginning of the Chinese revolution Lenin foresaw the possible turn of events in that country. He pointed out that the imperialist governments would take all steps to throttle Chinese democracy and 'plunder China, initiate its partition and rend its territories from it,'[38] while the Chinese liberal bourgeoisie 'whose politicians, such as Yüan Shih-kai, have the greatest capacity for treason…shall betray the democrats tomorrow in order to make a deal with any old or new "constitutional" emperor.'[39]

The Chinese revolution was defeated by the united efforts of the Chinese reactionary classes and the international imperialist bourgeoisie, without having solved the most important problems of Chinese society. Nevertheless it had far-reaching significance. It greatly influenced the development of China and the entire Asiatic continent.

---

[36] Note sent by the Russian envoy in Peking on 24 August 1912 to the head of the Chinese Ministry of Foreign Affairs concerning the prolongation of the 1881 Treaty of St Petersburg.
[37] Lenin, V.I. *Collected Works*, 4th ed. Vol. 17, pp. 434-435.
[38] Lenin, V.I. *Collected Works*, 2nd ed. Vol. XVI, p. 354.
[39] *Ibid.*, p. 28.

In its struggle the Chinese people had enjoyed the constant sympathy and moral support of 'a trustworthy ally, the proletariat of all the civilized nations.'[40]

RUSSIAN INVESTMENTS IN CHINA ON THE EVE OF THE
FIRST WORLD WAR

Capital exports played an important role in the activity of capitalist monopolies in the age of imperialism. In his classic work, *Imperialism, the Highest Stage of Capitalism*, V. I. Lenin subjected modern capitalism to a detailed analysis. He stressed that: 'Commodity exports were typical of the old capitalism, based on the predominance of free competition. Capital exports have become typical of the new type of capitalism in which monopolies predominate.'[41]

This conclusion was also corroborated by tsarist Russia's relations with semi-colonial China. Russian capital exports for 1895-1914 amounted to considerably more than the value of goods exported to China in that period, and showed a distinct increase in 1895-1904 when the entire territory of Manchuria was within the Russian sphere of influence. Thus, the value of Russian commodity exports during this period reached 101.9 million rubles, while Russian capital investments in China totaled 563.5 million rubles.

Tsarist Russia had been the first state to offer a significant loan to China in 1895, when the Chinese government had been made to pay an indemnity to Japan. Four Russian banks (the St Petersburg International Commercial Bank, Russian Foreign Trade Bank, St Petersburg Discount-Loan Bank, Volga-Kama Commercial Bank) and a number of French banks floated a Chinese loan of 400 million francs guaranteed by the Russian government; the Russian participation in this loan amounted to 150 million francs, or approximately 56.5 million rubles.

After the signature of the contract for the construction of the C.E.R., Russian capital chose the most profitable and secure type of investment—railway construction. From the beginning of its construction to the completion of the C.E.R. (including works unfinished at the inauguration of the line on 1 July 1903) Russian investment in Manchurian railway construction reached 441 million rubles (at the end of 1904), which included 71,745,878 rubles for reconstruction after the Boxer uprising. During the same period Russian investment in the construction of Dalny and Port Arthur harbors and of ships owned by the C.E.R. were valued at 51.9 million rubles; the investments of private Russian commercial firms at Harbin and other Manchurian cities reached approximately 15 million rubles.

In addition to their Manchurian investments, Russian commercial firms invested smaller amounts in the construction of private and commercial buildings, warehouses and tea-processing factories on the concessions received by tsarist Russia at Hankow (1896) and Tientsin (1903). These investments totalled approximately 5 million rubles.

---

[40] *Ibid.*, p. 396.
[41] Lenin, V. I. *Collected Works*, 4th ed. Vol. 22, p. 228.

The sphere of Russian investment in Manchuria contracted after the Russo-Japanese war of 1904-1905. The transfer to Japan by the Treaty of Portsmouth of the southern part of the C.E.R., Dalny and Port Arthur entailed the loss by Russia of railroad and harbor installations, coal mines, industries and buildings valued at 123 million rubles. The scope of Russian capital in China was then limited to North Manchuria and Sinkiang Province.

RUSSIAN INVESTMENTS IN CHINA AT THE END OF 1904[42]

Type of Investment	Million rubles
C.E.R. construction	441
Construction of Dalny Harbor	17.6
Construction of the city of Dalny	10.4
Construction of Port Arthur	12
C.E.R. maritime and river fleet	11.9
Private investments in Manchuria	15
Private investments in rest of China	5
Loan of 1895 (unpaid balance)	50.6
TOTAL	563.5

Further Russian investments in the C.E.R. took the form of hidden investment. By guaranteeing profits to the C.E.R. the tsarist government assumed a considerable part of the company's expenses for the current functioning of the railway and assigned large annual sums to cover the line's 'deficit.'

The official investments of the C.E.R. remained insignificant, reaching only 3 million rubles for 1906-1913.

This relationship between the C.E.R. and the tsarist government made the former a source of large benefits for the Russian industrialists and bankers, who constructed and supplied and advanced credit for, the railroad. Private Russian industrial and commercial firms as well as towns and villages sprung up in the vicinity of the C.E.R. The Russian population of North Manchuria passed the 100,000 mark after the Russo-Japanese war.

In addition to the forest concessions which the C.E.R. had obtained through agreements concluded with the Chinese administration of Heilungkiang and Kirin provinces in 1907 (930 km² in the area of Shihtowhotze [Liangtzeling] station, 115 km² around the stations Kaolingtze—Hengtaohotze, etc.), Russian enterprises received important forest concessions in North Manchuria: the firm of Skidel'skii received 2,000 km² around the stations of Maoerhshan and Wukimiho [Shangchih], 2,200 km² around Weishaho [Weiho], 640 km² near Taimakow, 750 km² near Silinho

---

[42] The cost of construction of the C.E.R. to 1 July 1903 were valued at 374,955,598 rubles (*Historical Essay on the Chinese Eastern Railway*, 1896-1923, p. 123) and supplementary investments for the second half of 1903 and for 1904 reached 66 million rubles (*Statistical Yearbook of the C.E.R.*, Harbin, 1923 p. 324).

and 445 km² near Makiaoho—a total of 6,035 km²; the Koval'skii enterprises were granted 510 km² near the station of Imienpo, 2,765 km² near Yabuloni [Yabuli],[44] 740 km² near Hailin, 430 km² near Hengtaohotze and 1,710 km² near Muling[45]—

RUSSIAN GOVERNMENT INVESTMENT COVERING
THE 'DEFICIT' OF THE C.E.R.[43] (IN THOUSAND
RUBLES)

1903 (second half)	4,517
1904-1906	86,321
1907	21,252
1908	15,607
1909	12,653
1910	10,329
1911	9,470
1912	7,984
1913	5,934
1914	4,513
TOTAL	178,580

a total of 6,155 km²; [46] a number of smaller concessions were also obtained (Northeastern Forestry Company, Shevchenko etc.). These private Russian forest concessions had access railroads as well as macadam roads; they owned mills and were not only important suppliers of wood for the railroads, industries and towns of Manchuria but also the main exporters of wood for the region. Russian forestry investments in Manchuria totalled approximately 5 million rubles.[47]

Russian capital also participated in the exploitation of Manchuria's mineral resources. During the preliminary survey for the C.E.R. (1896-1899 and 1901) the Russian Geographical Society discovered considerable deposits of coal and other useful minerals. The largest coal deposit, discovered by the Russian mining engineer N. Bronnikov in 1901, was that at Chalainoerh,[48] stretching from the northwest shore of Lake Dalai Nor to the Argun Erhkuna Ho River. The coal mines opened by the C.E.R. on this site, which in 1910 passed into the hands of the contractors Skidel'skii and Bocharov, were the main source of coal for the western lines of the C.E.R.

---

[43] *Statistical Yearbook of the C.E.R.*, Harbin, 1923.

[44] [The Chinese transcription of the Russian name. In the English literature on the subject the station is also sometimes called Yablonia.]

[45] [Named after the Muling Ho River; Muling is the Manchurian name for the Muren River, a tributary of the Ussuri.]

[46] *Jubilee Collection of the Harbin Stock Exchange* 1907-1932, pp. 132-133. Harbin, 1933.

[47] According to data published by the committee of the Harbin stock exchange, the investments for Koval'skii's concessions were valued at 2 million gold rubles. If the size of all the other Russian concessions is considered, their investments may be estimated at approximately 3 million rubles.

[48] [The Chalainoerh coal mines were named after the C.E.R. station of Chalainoerh, the Chinese version of the Mongol name for a lake not far from the railroad—the Dalai Nor.]

as well as for the settlements and industries of this region. Investments in the Chalainoerh coal mines for 1902-1927 were valued at more than 14 million gold rubles,[49] and amounted to approximately 10 million rubles by 1914.

Russian gold prospectors were granted the first concessions for gold mining by the Chinese authorities in 1901, in the northwestern part of Manchuria, the territory of the former 'Zheltuga Republic.'[50] The prospected areas gradually expanded in the direction of the middle course of the Amur. Most of the gold extraction in these areas of Manchuria was carried out by Russians and Chinese in cooperation. Capital investment remained inconsiderable and did not pass the million ruble mark.

Of the manufacturing industries, the largest amount of Russian investment went into flour mills. The first modern mills were built in Manchuria by Russian industrialists during the construction of the C.E.R. Their number increased considerably as a result of the Russo-Japanese war and of the growth of the Russian population in both Manchuria and the Russian Far East. In 1910 there were already 14 such mills in North Manchuria, owned by Koval'skii, the Russian Flour Mills Company, Borodin and Tetyukov, the Sungari Mills Co., Ltd., and other Russian firms.

Russian capitalists also laid the foundations for Manchuria's sugar industry. The first sugar beet plant was built in 1909 at the Ashiho [Acheng] railroad station;[51] its daily yield reached 24,000 *poods* of sugar beet. A second plant processing 36,000 *poods*[52] daily was built three years later at Hulan Ho.[53] Russian enterprises also included oil mills (Borodin's refinery for vegetable oils), alcohol stills (Borodin's) soap plants and other industries at Harbin and at various stations of the C.E.R.

According to the data of the C.E.R. Economic Bureau, the Chamber of Commerce and Industry and the Harbin Stock Exchange[54] Committee, Russian investments in the manufacturing industries of North Manchuria up to the beginning of the first world war may be estimated at approximately 35 million rubles.

Russian investments in public and private urban construction as well as in Manchurian banking and commerce were no less important. They may be extrapolated

---

[49] *Jubilee Collection of the Harbin Stock Exchange*, p. 74.

[50] Gold prospecting on the Manchurian territory of the upper Amur was begun in the middle of the 19th century, after gold had been first prospected along the Russian shores of the Amur. The Russian and Chinese prospectors created joint syndicates and formed settlements. The prospecting reached its peak in the 1880's in the territories around the Argun. The Sino-Russian settlements in this area were called the 'Zheltuga Republic' *(Jubilee Collection of the Harbin Stock Exchange*, p. 30). [Zheltuga is the old Russian name for the Mo Ho, in northwestern Manchuria; this small river 15 versts long falls into another river, a tributary of the Emuerh Ho, itself a right tributary of the Amur. Large gold lodes were discovered there in 1883. More than 6,000 Russian and Manchurian prospectors flocked to the site and founded independent settlements there. In 1886 the town of Zheltuga was occupied by a Chinese force; the Manchurians were ruined, and some were punished; the Russians left without opposition. Moho (the former Zheltuga) is today a district town of the northernmost district of Heilunkiang Province.]

[51] [*Ashiho*—the Chinese name for the Manchurian Alchuka Bira River.]

[52] *Jubilee Collection of the Harbin Stock Exchange*, p. 208.

[53] [*Hulan Ho* is the name of a tributary of the Sungari River on which the town of Hulan stands. The text should read *Hulan*.]

[54] *North Manchuria and the C.E.R.*, published by the Economic Bureau of the C.E.R., Harbin, 1922.

from the data for a single large Russian commercial firm, I. I. Tschurin & Co., Ltd,[55] which owned large stores, warehouses and living quarters, valued at approximately 3 million rubles, in Manchuria; if to this, data published by the Harbin Stock Exchange Committee on the holdings of a number of important Russian firms in North Manchuria and the volume of their business are added, the total private Russian investment in public and private buildings, banking and commerce in North Manchuria may be estimated to have amounted to no less than 40 million rubles in 1914. According to the well-known orientalist S. F. Remer, Russian private investment in other areas of China—Hankow, Tientsin, Shanghai and Sinkiang province—reached 9 million rubles in 1914, in addition to which the Russian church mission owned possessions in China valued at 1.5 million rubles.

As already noted, the tsarist government participated in the financing of two loans to China: the 4 percent loan of 1895 and the Reorganization Loan of 1913. China's obligations to Russia at the end of 1913 for the 1895 loan amounted to 37.6 million rubles, and the Russian share in the Reorganization Loan was 26.3 million rubles.

TSARIST RUSSIA'S INVESTMENTS IN CHINA IN 1914

Type of investment	Million rubles	Million $
C. E. R. (including the cost of the southern line Kwanchengtze [Changchun]—Port Arthur and Russian subsidies covering the railroad's deficit	708.5	363.5
Privately-owned houses, public buildings, banks and commercial enterprises in Manchuria	40	20.5
Installations at Dalny and Port Arthur	51.9	26.6
Manufacturing industries	35	17.8
Mining industries	11	5.6
Private property in other areas of China	9	4.6
Private forest concessions	5	2.6
Property of the Russian church mission	1.5	0.8
1895 loan (unpaid balance at end of 1913)	37.6	19.3
Reorganization Loan of 1913 (Russian share)	26.3	13.5
TOTAL	925.8	474.8

[55] In 1868 the merchants of the second guild I. I. Tschurin and the brothers Nikolai and Vasilii Babintsev organized at Irkutsk an unlimited liability company under the name of I. I. Tschurin & Co. This company later extended its activities to the entire Russian Far East; in 1899, during the construction of the C. E. R., the company opened a branch in Harbin, and in 1900 expanded to Yingkow [Newchwang] and Port Arthur. These two branches closed down in 1905. In 1917 the firm existed throughout Russia as an unlimited liability company under the name of 'A. V. Kas'yanov—Successor to I. I. Tschurin & Co.' However, the Harbin branch, then one of the firm's most important branches with a wide network of industrial and commercial interests in Manchuria, took advantage of the situation in 1917 and did not join the reorganized company in Russia; it continued as a branch of the former I. I. Tschurin & Co.

Russian investment in China on the eve of the first world war may thus be estimated at 925 million rubles. Tsarist Russia therefore, despite its financial difficulties, occupied second place in China as an investor, after Britain ($607.6 million).

RUSSIAN TRADE WITH CHINA BETWEEN THE
SINO-JAPANESE WAR AND THE FIRST WORLD WAR

The penetration of foreign capital into China intensified after the defeat of the Ch'ing Empire by the Japanese in 1894-1895. The increase of foreign investment, the formation of 'spheres of influence,' and the construction of powerful military bases enabled the imperialist powers to infiltrate all branches of China's economy and to transform the country's foreign trade into an instrument for the enslavement of the Chinese people.

The volume of China's foreign trade increased from a value of 315 to 925.5 million custom *taels,* i.e., a growth of 290 percent, from 1895 to 1914. Trade with Russia expanded fairly rapidly, although it developed at a slower rate than China's other foreign trade. From 1895 to 1914 the volume of Sino-Russian trade increased from

RUSSIA'S FOREIGN TRADE WITH CHINA IN 1895-1914[56]
(in thousand rubles)

Year	Russian exports to China	Russian imports from China	Total volume
1895	5,047	41,567	46,614
1896	5,501	41,457	46,958
1897	6,430	39,274	45,704
1898	6,256	40,293	46,549
1899	7,525	43,515	51,040
1900	6,702	45,945	52,647
1901	9,711	46,903	56,614
1902	9,315	52,177	61,492
1903	22,441	56,498	78,939
1904	22,972	52,455	75,427
1905	31,588	60,549	92,137
1906	57,530	97,427	154,957
1907	26,440	89,742	116,182
1908	23,285	93,344	116,629
1909	21,782	74,607	96,389
1910	20,158	78,813	98,971
1911	25,598	82,311	107,909
1912	30,688	76,254	106,942
1913	28,801	75,650	104,451
1914	28,765	89,558	118,451

[56] *Reviews of Russia's Foreign Trade along her European and Asiatic Borders for* 1895, 1904 *and* 1914. The data up to 1913 include trade with Mongolia.

a value of 46.6 to 118.3 million rubles, i.e., by over 250 percent. This rate of increase was far from regular and registered a number of fluctuations.

Commodity circulation between Russia and China did not increase in the first few years following the Sino-Japanese war owing to the lack of modern overland communication and the inadequacy of the Russian merchant fleet. A noticeable expansion of Sino-Russian trade began when the Siberian Railroad track approached the Chinese border and the construction of the C. E. R. was begun; the increase became particularly apparent once the C. E. R. was put into operation.

The Russo-Japanese war gave a new impetus to the development of Sino-Russian trade. The presence of Russian troops in Manchuria during the war and for the first year following the end of hostilities made it imperative for Russia to increase her exports to this area. This was accompanied by an extension of harbor installations as well as increased road and urban construction in Russia's Far Eastern territories; the flow of immigrants to the Amur and Maritime territories was accelerated, stimulating exports of Chinese goods, mainly foodstuffs, to these Russian areas.

The volume of Sino-Russian trade decreased after the withdrawal of Russian troops from Manchuria and the transfer to Japan of the southern part of the C. E. R. and Port Dalny. Trade began to expand again from 1910. The population of the Russian Far East grew rapidly (particularly in Vladivostok, Khabarovsk, Blagoveshchensk, Chita), while the construction of the Amur railroad, the enlargement of Vladivostok harbor, and finally the unification of the C. E. R. and the Ussuri Railway, accompanied by the opening of Egersheld wharf to free trade at Vladivostok, contributed to the expansion of Sino-Russian trade.

Throughout this entire period Sino-Russian trade showed as before, a large deficit for Russia. For the 20-year period 1895-1914 the value of Russia's imports outstripped exports by 887 million rubles, i.e., an average annual deficit of 44.4 million rubles. Despite this general trend, however, the rate of expansion of Russian exports remained considerable. Thus, while the volume of Russian imports from China increased by 210 percent from 1895 to 1914, her exports to China increased by 575 percent. In 1895 the volume of Russian exports attained a value of only 5 million rubles, 3.5 million rubles or 70 percent of which consisted of cotton fabrics. Other exports for this year, valued at 1.5 million rubles, were Russian leather (341,000 rubles), furs (135,000 rubles), metal (139,000 rubles), metal wares (123,000 rubles), and other goods (829,000 rubles).

The structure of Russian exports changed considerably by 1914. Despite the increasing export of cotton fabrics, which rose from a value of 3.5 million rubles in 1895 to 5.3 million in 1904 and 12.1 million in 1914, the proportion of this item in the volume of total exports dropped noticeably, from 70 percent in 1895 to 42 percent in 1914. This was accompanied by a marked increase in the export of such items as metal wares (1,848,000 rubles), metals (593,000 rubles), sugar (793,000 rubles), tobacco and products (1,289,000 rubles), spirits (606,000 rubles), fish (612,000 rubles) and linen and clothing (496,000 rubles).

By 1914 Russia had begun to re-export China tea in considerable amounts to Sinkiang province as well as to the border areas of Manchuria. These exports reached

15,734 *poods,* a value of 204,000 rubles, in 1904 and increased to 64,883 *poods,* or 534,000 rubles, in 1914.

The export of Russian oil products to Manchuria increased sharply in 1904, total export to China for this year rising to 3,900,510 *poods,* valued at 2,812,000 rubles. These exports subsequently decreased after the withdrawal of Russian troops from Manchuria, and only 83,293 *poods,* or a value of 162,000 rubles, were exported in 1914.

RUSSIAN EXPORTS TO CHINA IN 1895, 1904, AND 1914[57]

Goods	Units	1895		1904		1914	
		amount	thous. rubles	amount	thous. rubles	amount	thous. rubles
Cotton fabrics	thous. arshin	8,362	3,480	12,976	5,294	29,171	12,086
Woolen articles	,,	62	55	522	161	715	711
Metal wares	poods	...	123	...	940	...	1,848
Metal	,,	46,871	139	197,137	560	373,997	593
Russian leather	,,	13,611	341	23,983	357	4,134	121
Furs	,,	2,155	135	2,737	54	7,201	72
Horn	,,	1,805	107	402	99	1,518	288
Livestock	head	24,567	86	3,091	14	2,481	68
Paints and dyes	poods	2,324	26	9,455	122	4,477	34
Matches	,,	2,680	52	9,571	62	20,672	93
Stearin candles	,,	2,594	31	26,093	256	5,332	59
Sugar	,,	6,989	65	301,843	1,609	219,176	793
Tobacco	,,	2,713	12	34,189	472	32,913	631
Cigarettes	thous.	170	1.2	539,000	1,108	284	658
Alcohol	—	—	—	—	763	—	492
Wines	—	—	1.5	—	1,743	—	90
Liqueurs, vodka and brandy	—	—	2.0	—	162	—	24
Tea	poods	159	2.1	15,734	204	64,883	534
Butter	,,	399	3.8	21,091	321	848	12.7
Fish	,,	1,611	3.6	99,676	429	335,250	612
Oil and oil products	,,	571	2.3	3,900,510	2,812	83,293	162
Linen clothing	,,	422	15.3	22,829	533	6,143	496
TOTAL	—	—	5,047	—	22,972	—	28,765

Fur exports during the 20-year period preceding the first world war dropped from a value of 135,000 rubles in 1895 to 72,000 rubles in 1914, although the total weight increased from 2,155 *poods* to 7,201 *poods;* this was because mainly cheap furs were exported officially through the customs, while the most valuable pelts (sable, beaver, marten, polar fox) were smuggled into Manchuria.

---

[57] *Reviews of Russia's Foreign Trade along her European and Asiatic Borders for* 1895, 1904 and 1914. (*poods* are converted into *arshin* according to the following scale: 1 *pood* of cotton fabric = 100 *arshin,* 1 *pood* of woolen fabric = 50 *arshin*).

The routes for Russian exports also changed noticeably in the period 1895-1914. Of the total exports to China in 1895 (valued at 5,047,000 rubles) the greater part went to Sinkiang (74.5 percent, or 3,724,000 rubles) and through Kyakhta (19.3 percent, or 967,000 rubles); in 1914 the main bulk of exports reached China through the Transbaikal and Amur borders by rail, along the Amur and Ussuri rivers, and by sea through Vladivostok.

The proportion of Russian exports through Sinkiang decreased from 74.5 percent in 1895 to 38.4 percent in 1914, despite an increase of exports to this province by almost 300 percent (from 3,724,000 to 11,056,000 rubles). The export of oil products, sugar, metal wares, cotton and woolen fabriss and the re-export of China tea to Sinkiang greatly expanded.

The completion of the Amur railroad and the establishment of tobacco and metal industries in the Russian Far East created the neceesary conditions for an expansion of Russian exports from her industrial centers as well as from her Far Eastern possessions. In contrast to the 1890's when most of the overland Sino-Russian trade in the Far East went through Kyakhta, by the eve of the first world war the number of trading outposts had increased. The large commercial centers of Blagoveshchensk and Khabarovsk, connected by rail to Siberia and Vladivostok, were built on the Amur. Important river steamer lines maintaining regular communication between Harbin, Fuchin [Fugdin], Kirin, Sansing [Ilan Hala, or Ilan] and the Russian towns were operated on the Amur and its tributary the Sungari.

In such conditions the volume of trade along the Sino-Russian Far Eastern border had multiplied by a factor of almost 1,500 percent by 1914 and reached a value of 16,146,000 rubles, or 56 percent of Russia's total exports to China. It should be noted in this context that customs statistics do not indicate the real volume of Russian goods exported from the Transbaikal and the Amur Region to China. In addition to furs, as already mentioned, amounts of such valuable goods as ginseng, deer antlers, deer musk, trepang, sea kale, etc., were also smuggled from the Far East to Manchuria and exchanged by Chinese merchants for Chinese goods at the border outposts and at points inside the Amur Region.

Fish, sea kale, tobacco products and furs were exported to China by sea from Vladivostok. Sugar and cotton fabrics mainly reached China by sea from Odessa or other European ports. The Chinese customs statistics estimated the value of Chinese imports from the ports of European Russia in 1914 at 1,068,000 *taels,*[58] or approximately 360,000 rubles.

Imports from China rose from 41,567,000 to 89,558,000 rubles between 1895 and 1914.

The proportion of tea in Russia's imports from China decreased from 85 percent in 1895 to 44.2 percent in 1914, but tea remained the main item of Russian imports from China. Russia was also the destination for most of China's tea exports.

Russian tea imports reached a maximum in 1915; this was followed by a decrease due to the world war.

---

[58] Huo Tsing-ying. *China's Foreign Trade* (in English). p. 340.—Shanghai, 1935.

Among Russian imports from China, tea was followed in order of importance by the products of stockraising: livestock (from 722,000 rubles in 1895 to 7,770,000 rubles in 1914), wool (136,000 *poods* in 1895, 622,000 *poods* in 1914), raw leather (from 80,900 to 136,900 *poods*). The value of imported furs more than trebled, increasing from 1,119,000 rubles in 1895 to 3,626,000 rubles in 1914; imports of raw silk multiplied during this period by 530 percent (from 350 to 2,223 *poods*). Considerably more foodstuffs, mainly destined for the Russian Far East, were imported.

GEOGRAPHIC DISTRIBUTION OF RUSSIAN EXPORTS TO CHINA IN 1895 AND 1914[59]

Goods	Units	1895				1914			
		total	*Sinkiang*	*Kyakhta*	*other areas*	*total*	*Sinkiang*	*Kyakhta*	*other areas*
Cotton fabrics	thous. arshin	8,362	7,222	766	374	29,171	15,564	11,838	1,770
Woolen articles	"	62	27	26	9	715	155	560	—
Metal wares	thous. rubles	123	105	3	15	1,848	544	1,278	26
Metals	poods	46,871	45,787	650	434	373,997	65,831	254,076	54,090
Russian leather	"	13,611	2,192	10,018	1,401	4,134	2,209	1,925	—
Furs	"	2,155	310	1,697	148	7,201	4,442	2,674	85
Sugar	"	6,989	6,389	470	130	219,176	80,439	75,887	62,850
Tobacco	"	2,713	2,052	—	661	32,913	8,171	20,519	4,223
Cigarettes	million	170	70	—	100	284	5	279	—
Tea	poods	159	33	—	126	64,883	10,242	54,638	3
Fish	"	1,611	1,358	178	75	335,250	1,369	150,437	183,444
Oil products	"	571	558	—	13	85,293	29,545	55,748	—
TOTAL	in thous.	5,047	3,724	967	356	28,765	11,056	16,146	1,563

In 1895, 32,000 *poods* of grain and groats were imported from China, while there were no meat imports; in 1914 the volume of imports of grain, soya beans and groats reached 9,614,000 *poods* and 691,000 *poods* of meat were also imported. At the same time communications between the Russian Far East and Russia's industrial centers improved; the demand for cotton fabrics and silks was thus met by Russian production, and importation of these goods from China decreased.

The establishment of direct railroad communications between Russia and China considerably altered the geographical pattern of Russian imports. China tea began to be imported mainly by sea from Vladivostok, and the ancient tea route through Kyakhta lost its importance. Tea imports through Sinkiang also ceased almost entirely. Russia began to re-export China tea to Sinkiang and the border areas of Manchuria, since the transport of tea by Russian railroads from central China to these areas was much cheaper than along internal Chinese routes.

[59] *Reviews of Russia's Foreign Trade along her European and Asiatic Borders for* 1895 *and* 1914.

Livestock, fresh meat imported through the ports of South Manchuria (Dalny, Port Arthur), and raw silk mainly originating in Shanghai were also imported from China by sea.

RUSSIAN IMPORTS FROM CHINA IN 1895, 1904 AND 1914[60]

Goods	Units	1895		1904		1914	
		amount	thous. rubles	amount	thous. rubles	amount	thous. rubles
Tea	thous. poods	2,285	35,350	2,550	33,164	3,374	39,774
Livestock		—	722	—	1,756	—	7,770
Cattle	head	...	...	...	...	106,585	5,502
Others	,,	...	...	...	...	226,503	1,312
Raw leather	poods	80,930	488	90,001	801	136,907	1,163
Furs	,,	54,491	1,119	84,826	1,211	274,064	3,626
Wool	,,	135,879	582	310,500	1,920	622,236	6,700
Raw silk	,,	350	37	1,544	308	2,223	530
Cotton fabrics	thous. arshin	6,076	1,160	9,687	1,560	5,063	913
Silks	,,	464	1,028	433	1,013	254	735
Eggs	poods	—	—	9,546	45	380,904	1,091
Meat	,,	—	—	42,569	173	691,402	3,597
Wheat	,,			2,750,376	2,637	6,815,078	7,264
Corn	,,			4,266	4	253,890	212
Oats	,,	32,211	7.1	30,325	17	350,828	303
Barley	,,			490,113	477	649,102	554
Millet	,,			196,031	122	845,766	764
Buckwheat	,,	—	—	—	—	217,609	210
Beans	,,	—	—	—	—	481,136	548
TOTAL		—	41,567	—	52,455	—	89,558

CHINA'S TEA EXPORTS[61]

Year	Total exports (in tons)	Exports to Russia (in tons	Russia's part in China's total tea exports (in %)
1890	100,678	35,386	35.15
1900	83,687	40,243	48,09
1910	94,355	58,899	62.42
1915	107,749	70,297	65.24

[60] *Reviews of Russia's Foreign Trade along her European and Asiatic Borders for* 1895, 1904 *and* 1914.
[61] Huo Tsing-ying, *op.cit.*, p. 368 (piculs are converted into metric tons according to the scale 1 picul = 60.45 kg).

The volume of imports from Sinkiang Province expanded rapidly. From 1895 to 1914 Russian imports from this province grew by 270 percent; livestock imports rose from a value of 565,000 rubles to 1,697,000 rubles, and the volume of wool from 1,467 to 6,087 tons; fur imports increased from a total of 621 to 2,475 tons.

Sino-Russian trade along the Far Eastern border felt the competition of the imperialist powers which considerably affected both structure and geographical distribution; the development of trade along the Sinkiang border was much more regular. The number of items carried remained more or less stable and the greater part of the trade consisted in an exchange of goods.

SOURCES OF RUSSIA'S IMPORTS FROM CHINA[62]

Goods	Units	1895				1914			
		total	Sinkiang	Trans-baikal border (Irkutsk customs)	Amur border and by sea	total	Sinkiang	Trans-haikal border and Amur border	by sea
Tea	thous. poods	2,285	3.2	1,500	781.8	3,374	3.8	184	3,186.2
Livestock	thous. rub.	722	565	—	157	7,770	1,697	5,073	1,000
Raw leather	thous. poods	80.9	71.2	—	9.7	136.9	54.2	77.5	5.2
Furs	thous. poods	54.5	37.9	3.6	13	274.1	151.2	121.9	1
Wool	thous. poods	135.9	89.5	0.5	45.9	622.2	371.3	217.1	33.8
Raw silk	poods	350	43	—	307	2,223	1,830	—	393
Cotton fabric	thous. arshin	6,076	2,850	640	2,586	5,063	4,790	273	—
Silks	thous. arshin	464	16	—	448	254	254	—	—
Meat	poods	—	—	—	—	691	6.4	372	312.6
Grain & groats	"	32.2	32.2	—	—	9.132	62.2	9,008	61.8
Beans	"					482	1	470	11
TOTAL	thous. poods	41,567	3,869	20,908	16,790	89,558	14,202	30,273	45,083

ECONOMIC RELATIONS OF TSARIST RUSSIA WITH CHINA
DURING THE FIRST WORLD WAR

The European war which broke out in August 1914 obliged the tsarist government to concentrate its forces along Russia's European borders and reduce its activities in the Far East.

[62] *Reviews of Russian Foreign Trade along her European and Asiatic Borders for 1895 and 1914.*

The war considerably altered the nature of Sino-Russian trade. The industries of central Russia, geared to the war effort, could no longer produce goods for export to China in the necessary amounts or maintain a sufficient supply for the country's eastern regions. The export of Russian goods to China proper ceased almost entirely; Russian exports in the war years mainly consisted of commodities produced in the Russian territories along the Chinese border.

On the other hand, wartime conditions created a greater demand for Chinese alimentary products and raw materials in the Far Eastern possessions as well as in central Russia. The value of Russia's imports from China had increased considerably by 1916 and reached 65.5 million *taels,* compared to 43.3 million *taels* in 1914; imports of Chinese goods through the Pacific ports, the Transbaikal area and the Sinkiang border increased in particular.

The volume of Russian exports in 1916 was slightly greater than in 1914 (a value of 25.7 million *taels* as against 22.1 million), but the products of Russia's Far Eastern possessions (fish, wood, furs, sea kale, deer antlers, ginseng, etc.) accounted for almost two-thirds of this sum while the export of such articles as cotton fabrics, sugar, oil products, and metal wares produced in European Russia contracted sharply.

The war also affected China's internal situation. By reducing the pressure exerted by the imperialist powers on China, it provided a good opportunity for the Chinese middle classes to develop local industries. However, economic and political backwardness prevented China from taking advantage of these favorable circumstances.

Two imperialist powers, the United States and Japan, which did not directly take part in the European war, remained in the Far East and had sufficient means at their disposal to maintain China in an inferior position. However, conditions were not identical for the two. Despite the enormous financial and commercial resources of the United States, Americans were not as yet sufficiently prepared for direct military aggression in the Far East; they possessed no bases on Chinese territory and their investments mainly centered around trade, while China's industries and transport were controlled by other imperialist powers.

American imperialist circles thus had to play for time in order to reinforce their position in China either by the creation of reliable bases or by increasing their control over the Chinese government. As in the previous period, the United States tried to disguise her imperialist policies in the name of 'internationalization.' A treaty was concluded between America and China on 15 September 1914 which stated the wish to 'pursue peace throughout the world,' but in fact deprived the Chinese government of its independence and subordinated it to an 'international commission.'

The United States, however, did not succeed in putting their plans for China into effect in this way for they had to cope with another contender for supremacy—Japan. The latter decided to take advantage of her geographical position and strong military bases in South Manchuria and Korea to oppose America by military force. Using the pretext of war against Germany, a considerable Japanese force occupied Shantung province. This was followed by the so-called 'twenty-one demands' made upon the Chinese government, which exposed the aspirations of Japanese imperialism to attain a position of political and economic dominance in China.

SINO-RUSSIAN TRADE ROUTES DURING THE FIRST WORLD WAR[63]
(in thousands of Chinese custom liangs)

Year	Overland trade			Pacific ports			Amur ports			European ports			Total		
	Russian Exports	Russian Imports	Total Volume	Russian Exports	Russian Imports	Total Volume	Russian Exports	Russian Imports	Total Volume	Russian Exports	Russian Imports	Total Volume	Russian Exports	Russian Imports	Total Volume
1914	11,298	3,965	15,263	9,267	26,784	36,051	460	8,349	8,809	1,068	4,238	5,306	22,093	43,336	65,429
1915	6,790	6,246	13,036	9,751	42,348	52,099	453	6,252	6,705	29	4,550	4,579	17,023	59,396	76,419
1916	6,735	20,444	27,179	18,588	37,056	55,644	314	3,790	4,104	56	4,222	4,278	25,693	65,512	91,205
1917	2,933	13,438	16,371	8,094	28,748	36,842	154	7,085	7,239	35	477	512	11,216	49,748	60,964

[63] Huo Tsing-ying, *op.cit.*, p. 340 (no Russian customs records were published for the war years).

Aquiescence to the Japanese demands, although in a slightly modified form by Yüan Shih-kai threatened to transform China into a Japanese colony. The Chinese people clearly opposed the predatory plans of Japan, and named the date when the Yüan Shih-kai government signed the agreement with Japan, May 25, the 'day of national shame.' Japanese goods, banks and commercial organizations were boycotted throughout the country. Japanese imperialism during this period constituted the most important problem confronting the Chinese people.

Not only did the tsarist government refrain from any opposition to the imperialist policies of Japan in her attempt to subjugate the great Chinese nation, bound by age-long ties of friendship with Russia, but it clearly tried to protect Japan and regarded her plans favorably. The Russian bourgeoisie and landowners saw a powerful ally of international reaction in the Japanese Empire. According to their calculations Japan was capable of protecting the positions which Russia had acquired in China and if necessary of sustaining the failing antidemocratic regime in Russia itself. Contrary to the real foreign and domestic interests of Russia the tsarist government allied itself to Japanese imperialism, which planned to subject not only China but the Russian Far East and Siberia as well.

A secret treaty was signed between the tsarist government and Japan on 3 July 1916 (new style) which augmented and concluded the secret conventions of 13 February 1907 and 4 July 1910: Japan and tsarist Russia were to 'protect' China from the encroachments of other states and 'reach an agreement concerning the measures to be taken to avoid such a situation,'[64] By assuming this obligation, tsarist Russia accepted the existing *de facto* situation in China where Japan had seized key economic positions and ensured her predominance throughout the country. The treaty also provided that in the event of hostilities by China 'each party will come to the assistance of the other at the latter's demand, and in such an eventuality each of the high contracting parties assumes the obligation not to conclude peace without the previous agreement of the other contracting party.'[65]

The tsarist government kept knowledge about the Russo-Japanese alliance secret from its own public, knowing that the news would give rise to discontent. This treaty was additional proof of the antinational policies of Russian autocracy, which had lost all contact with its subjects. The Russian people rejected the treasonable policy of tsarism. New revolutionary forces were developing which gathered for the final struggle against the monarchy, against all predatory imperialist wars, for the freedom and equality of all nations.

The imperialist war which broke out in Europe in 1914 could not deflect the Russian working class from its revolutionary aims. The vanguard of the Russian proletariat, the Bolshevik Party, raised high the banner of proletarian internationalism and constantly castigated the imperialist policies of Russian tsarism.

The Bolsheviks headed the growing revolutionary movement and led the nations of Russia to their historic victory, which opened a new era in the relations between

---

[64] Secret Russo-Japanese Treaty (Alliance) of 3 July 1916, from article 1.
[65] *Ibid.*, from article 2.

the nations of the world. Through its leader the Russian people expressed their firm conviction of the final victory of the Chinese people. Lenin wrote on the eve of the first world war: 'Whatever the fate of the great Chinese Republic, which is now the prey of various "civilized" hyenas, there is no power in the whole world which can restore the ancient servile regime of Asia or sweep out of existence the heroic democratism of the masses of the Asiatic or semi-Asiatic countries.'[66]

*   *
*

1) The struggle between the capitalist countries of Europe, the United States and Japan for the partition of semicolonial China reached an acute stage at the end of the 19th century. The capitalist governments, including that of tsarist Russia, used the 'right' of free investment to occupy key positions in Chinese industry and railway construction, forcibly countered the resistance of the Chinese people and strengthened their control of the reactionary Ch'ing government.

2) The tsarist government obtained concessions for the construction of a railroad in Manchuria and a military naval base at Port Arthur.

Tsarist Russia's activities, like those of the other capitalist countries in the age of imperialism, were characterized not so much by the export of commodities to China as by capital investment. The volume of Russia's commodity exports to China for 1895-1904 thus reached a value of 101.9 million rubles, while her total investments in China for the same period equaled 563.5 million rubles. Russia's total investments in China at the beginning of the 20th century almost equaled those of Britain (246.5 million dollars in 1902 compared to 260.3 million dollars).

3) The expansion of tsarist Russia in China was opposed by the other imperialist powers who also attempted to enforce their domination. The increasing conflict of interest between tsarist Russia on the one hand and Britain and Japan, supported by the United States, on the other, led to the Japanese aggression against Russia. As a result of her military defeat, one of the most important Russian trade routes to China—through South Manchuria—was completely blocked.

However, despite the defeat of Russian autocracy in the Far East and the accompanying blow to the development of Sino-Russian economic relations, on the eve of the First World War Russia continued to occupy the second position after Britain as an investor and her share in China's foreign trade was almost as great as that of the United States (7.5 percent—United States and 7 percent—Russia in 1913).

The outbreak of the First World War altered conditions in the Far East. The European nations, and Russia also, were obliged to loosen their economic ties with China.

4) The deterioration of Sino-Russian relations in the age of imperialism was a consequence of tsarist Russia's adventurist policies, and of the increasing dependence of China's reactionary ruling circles on the imperialist powers.

[66]   Lenin, V. I. *Collected Works,* 2nd ed. Vol. 16, p. 333.

The Russian working class and its revolutionary vanguard, the Bolshevik party led by the great Lenin, warmly greeted the struggle of the Chinese people against imperialism and denounced the predatory policy of tsarism. The Bolsheviks blazed the way for new relations between nations based on equality and respect for the rights and interests of both great and small nations.

CHAPTER FIVE

ECONOMIC RELATIONS BETWEEN SOVIET RUSSIA AND CHINA IN 1917-1924 (FROM THE OCTOBER REVOLUTION TO THE ESTABLISHMENT OF DIPLOMATIC RELATIONS BETWEEN THE TWO COUNTRIES)

THE October Revolution in Russia opened a new era in the history of mankind. The young socialist Soviet state which it created proclaimed by its very first decrees and declarations[1] the principles of freedom and equality of all nations and its attachment to the respect of independence and sovereignty in the relations between large and small states. Soviet Russia stood out as the friend and protector of colonial and dependent nations oppressed by the imperialist bourgeoisie. The Soviet of People's Commissars announced: 'We carry freedom on our banners to all oppressed nations of the world.'[2]

The Soviet Government rejected the tsarist practice of secret diplomacy and ceclared void all the inequitable treaties obtaining special rights and privileges which the tsarist authorities had made with colonial and semicolonial eastern countries. It proposed holding talks with these countries in order to conclude equitable treaties which would respect the interests of both parties and exclude any intervention into domestic affairs by either party.

The victory of the revolution and the foundation of a socialist system in Russia thus opened up new vistas for the development of friendly relations between the peoples of Russia and other nations, including China.

However, events were to show that serious difficulties would hinder Soviet foreign policy. The imperialist bourgeoisie considered the very existence of the Soviet Socialist Republic as a direct threat to their supremacy and therefore opened hostilities against the newly established state and blockaded its borders.

China also found herself in a difficult position at that time. After the end of the European war, the imperialist powers turned their attention to the East. China became the focus of imperialist conflicts. The imperialist bourgeoisie and internal reactionary forces attempted to isolate China from the Soviet Union having deprived the Chinese people of their sovereign rights and prevented them from developing relations with other nations to accord with their own interests.

---

[1] Decree on Peace, adopted by the 2nd All-Russian Congress of Soviets on 26 October (8 November) 1917; 'Declaration of Rights of the Peoples of Russia,' 15 November 1917.

[2] Address of 3 December 1917 'To all Moslem Workers of Russia and the East.'

THE OCTOBER REVOLUTION IN RUSSIA AND THE POSITION OF
RUSSIA'S FAR EASTERN TERRITORIES IN THE FIRST YEARS
OF THE SOVIET REPUBLIC

Plans for armed intervention against Soviet Russia were discussed in November-December 1917 by the Allied powers. Britain was to act in Transcaucasia, Central Asia, the Northern Caucasus and the north of Russia from Murmansk to the Urals; the Ukraine, Bessarabia and Crimea were left to France; the United States and Japan 'received' Siberia and the Far East as their 'share.'

On 12 January 1918 Japan dispatched the battleship *Iwami,* followed by the cruiser *Asahi,* to Vladivostok. Despite the existing agreement, from the very beginning Japan attempted to outstrip her rivals and seize Siberia and the Russian Far East. In a note to the United States the Japanese government declared that if American troops were to invade the latter territory 'the Japanese people would be offended that others were interfering in affairs that by rights pertained to them.'[3]

Having provoked the assassination of two Japanese subjects in Vladivostok Japan used this as a pretext for landing troops there, on 5 April 1918. The American monopolies, which were interested in maintaining commerce with Russia and planned to seize the rich resources of Siberia, feared that Japan's activities in Siberia and the Russian Far East would increase the latter's power and hinder their own expansionist policy. These considerations, therefore, prompted President Wilson to insist on the participation of American troops in the intervention against Russia; but this, of course, met with opposition from Japan.

Before risking open invasion of Siberia and the Far East, the imperialist governments embarked on a number of measures calculated to weaken the revolutionary regime. In May 1918 the Allies organized a rebellion of the Czech army corps in Siberia. On 29 June the White Russian forces succeeded, with foreign support, in overthrowing the authorities at Vladivostok. On 17 July the United States published a memorandum announcing her intention of intervening against Soviet Russia in the Far East, deceitfully declaring that these operations were to be of 'limited scope' and were merely destined to 'assist' the movements of the Czech corps from Siberia to the Far East.

Japanese, American, French, British and Canadian troops began to land at Vladivostok in August 1918[4] and moved into Russian territory.

The reactionary Peking government of Tuan Chi-jui signed under Japanese pressure a military convention with Japan on 16 May 1918 agreeing that Japanese and Chinese troops would be dispatched to Siberia under Japanese command 'against the Germans.' On August 30 the Tuan Chi-jui government declared that 'Chinese troops have been dispatched to Russia in order to join the Allies and for joint

---

[3] *Foreign Relations,* Vol. 2, p. 30, New York. 1920.
[4] The British troops landed on August 3, the French on August 10 and the Americans on the 16th; Canadian troops disembarked around August 10. There were already 28,000 Japanese soldiers in Vladivostok by the middle of August.

operations.'[5] These troops did not take an independent part in the Allied intervention and were used by the Japanese as auxiliaries. Such were the beginnings of the war launched by the imperialist forces in the Far East against the young Soviet Republic with a view to destroying the Soviet regime, preventing the spread of the revolution's influence among the oppressed nations of the East and seizing the Soviet Far East and Siberia.

A counter revolutionary coup succeeded at Omsk in November 1918 helped by the Allied powers, Admiral Kolchak being proclaimed 'Supreme Ruler of Russia.' Kolchak's army, however, was defeated by the end of 1919 through the heroic efforts of the Siberian and Far Eastern partisans, the revolutionary activities of the urban proletariat and the successful advance of the Red Army from the Urals. The forces led by the White generals Denikin and Yudenich were also defeated in the autumn of 1919. The young Soviet state had thus bravely faced an unfavorable military situation and demonstrated the vitality of a socialist government representing the interests of the working masses.

In January 1920 the Allied powers were forced to acknowledge the failure of their interventionist policy. The Supreme Allied Council decided on 16 January 1920 to lift the blockade imposed on Soviet Russia and withdraw all foreign troops from Siberia. American forces were evacuated in the spring of the same year. After Kolchak's defeat in Siberia the partisans and workers' detachments in the Far East destroyed the counter revolutionary machinery. A Maritime Democratic Government which united all the revolutionary forces against the White forces and the foreign occupation army was set up in Vladivostok.

Japan, however, continued to occupy the Transbaikal and Maritime territories (including Khabarovsk) as well as Northern Sakhalin, although her hopes for easy gains had been lost. Despite the savage regime which Japan imposed on the occupied territories, the forces fighting for the liberation of the Far East from the interventionists grew constantly. The Red Army's power increased, the partisan movement grew and their opposition to the Japanese and counter revolutionary hetmans became decisive.

Because of the country's severe domestic and international situation and the remoteness of the Far Eastern territories from Central Russia, the Soviet Government found it inexpedient to allow a crisis in its relations with Japan. It was therefore decided to organize the territory lying between the Selenga River and the Pacific shore into a Far Eastern Republic. In taking this step, the Communist Party led by Lenin had confidence in the revolutionary political consciousness of the Russian people and their unshakable devotion to their land. In his speech to the RCP(b) faction of the VIIIth All-Russian Congress of Soviets on 21 December 1920, Lenin explained his position: '...circumstances have thus obliged us to set up a buffer state—the Far Eastern Republic—for we know quite well the calamities inflicted on the Siberian peasants by Japanese imperialism, the unprecedented barbarity of the Japanese in Siberia... Nevertheless we cannot wage war against Japan and must do

---

[5] *Declaration of the Chinese Government*, 30 August 1918.

all in our power not only to postpone this war but even to avoid it altogether, if possible...'[6]

On 6 April 1920 the congress of workers of the Baikal Region announced to the governments of the world the formation of the independent democratic Far Eastern Republic (FER) which included the regions of the Amur, the Maritime and Transbaikal territories, Sakhalin and Kamchatka, as well as the concession zone of the Chinese Eastern Railway. The Constituent Assembly of the FER, which voted on a constitution and elected a government, was convened in February 1921.

The FER, nominally an independent republic, naturally maintained the most friendly relations with Soviet Russia. These relations were later defined by the treaty of 'economic union' signed on 17 February 1922.

The Far Eastern Republic swiftly merged all the detachments of partisans and workers into a revolutionary army which successfully advanced through the Transbaikal region. The Japanese were forced to open negotiations with the FER which resulted in a treaty to end hostilities on the Transbaikal front and stipulating the evacuation of Japanese troops from the area. This clause was put into effect between July and October 1920 and the counter revolutionary armed gangs led by hetman Semenov had no alternative other than to follow the Japanese to Manchuria.

These first successes of the FER's revolutionary forces, however, were not adequate to re-unite the entire territory of the young republic and establish peace in the Far East. In March 1921 the Japanese military clique organized a meeting at Mukden between hetman Semenov and Japan's henchman in Manchuria, Chang Tso-lin: Japan promised to aid Semenov and the remnants of Kolchak's forces against the FER and Soviet Russia. On 26 May 1921 the Japanese disarmed the militia of Vladivostok, gave their assistance to a counter revolutionary coup and set up with the support of the United States, Britain and France a 'government' headed by the Merkulov brothers, important local merchants.

Baron Ungern, who had during this time occupied Outer Mongolia (the territory of the present Mongolian People's Republic), published a manifesto at Urga (Ulan-Bator) declaring that hetman Semenov, supported by Japanese troops, was advancing upon the FER in the Maritime Territory, while his own forces would support Semenov from Urga. These plans came to naught; Red Army detachments, with the FER revolutionary forces led by Suhe Bator and Choibalsan of the Mongolian revolutionary army, defeated Ungern's forces and assisted the Mongolian people in their fight for liberation and independence. Partisan detachments successfully combated the counter revolutionary regime of the Maritime Territory.

The difficulties encountered in Russia, the post-war crisis of 1921 which hit Japan severely, and her imperialist conflicts with the United States, led Japan to agree to the FER's proposition to open negotiations.

The Conference between Japan and the FER opened at Dairen (Dalny) on 26 August 1921. The terms proposed by Japan were quite unacceptable and predatory (the 'seventeen demands,' and three accompanying secret articles): the FER was to

---

[6] Lenin, V.I. *Collected Works,* 4th ed. Vol. 31, p. 435, [Russ.].

agree that 'Vladivostok become a purely commercial harbor placed under foreign control' (article 1) and undertake 'never to maintain a navy in Pacific waters and to destroy its existing naval forces' (article 14). The Japanese demanded that 'official agreement be given to the presence of resident Japanese military missions and Japanese officers with the right to travel therein throughout the territory' of the Far Eastern Republic (article 14). In the economic field Japan's priority demands were a reconsideration of the Russo-Japanese fishery convention favoring the rights of Japanese fishers (article 2) and the application of Japanese commercial and hunting laws to Japanese traders and trappers on FER territory on the basis of 'reciprocal rights' (article 7).

The FER government was to 'confer upon Japanese subjects rights of free navigation of the Amur River under the Japanese flag and declare to the Chinese government its readiness to allow navigation along the Sungari River to Japanese subjects under the Japanese flag'; these advantages should be given 'to Japanese subjects only, and the rights defined by this article cannot be conferred upon other nationals' (article 11). Article 13 required that 'both parties recognize all the rights acquired by subjects of both governments prior to the conclusion of the present agreement and maintain them without change.' In other words, Japan wished to strengthen the colonial regime which she had set up in Northern Sakhalin and maintain possession of the fishing industries and other property seized from Russia. Finally, the FER government was to 'lease the northern part of Sakhalin Island to the Japanese government for a period of 80 years' (article 15).

The secret articles accompanying these demands required that 'the Japanese government shall evacuate its troops from the Maritime Region at its own discretion and whenever it shall find it necessary and convenient' (secret article 2) and that 'the Sakhalin region shall be evacuated after the actual lease of the northern part of Sakhalin Island shall have been effected under the conditions stipulated by article 15 of the treaty' (secret article 3). Japan accompanied these insolent claims by renewed military pressure on the FER by supporting a White Russian attack on Khabarovsk from the Maritime Territory.

The FER delegation rejected the Japanese demands, and on 12 February 1922 the Republic's revolutionary forces inflicted a decisive defeat on the invaders by overcoming the Whites at Volochaevka. Khabarovsk was thus liberated on February 14. The revolutionary forces of the FER continued their advance toward Vladivostok, mopping up all vestiges of opposition. A wave of public feeling swept Japan against her protracted intervention in Russia, and the country's international position became more difficult after the Washington Conference. These circumstances led Japan to agree to a withdrawal of troops from the Maritime Territory before 1 November 1922 and to accept the Russian proposals to negotiate with representatives of the FER and the RSFSR.

The conference opened at Changchun on 4 September 1922. The RSFSR and FER delegations demanded the evacuation of Japanese troops both from the Maritime Territory and from Northern Sakhalin. These requirements were rejected by the Japanese, who proposed that the demands put forward at the Dairen conference serve as a basis for negotiations. This condition being quite unacceptable, the Russo-Japanese talks were broken off on 26 September 1922. Japan's renewed attempts to delay the evacuation of her forces from the Maritime Territory with the help of White Russian groups led by Diterikhs, one of Kolchak's generals, also failed.

The revolutionary forces of the FER occupied Vladivostok on 25 October 1922. On 15 November 1922 the People's Congress of the FER announced its own dissolution, the establishment of Soviet authority throughout the Far Eastern territory and the adherence of the Far Eastern Republic to Soviet Russia.

CHINA'S SITUATION TOWARD THE END OF THE FIRST WORLD WAR

The end of the First World War did not alleviate the situation of the Chinese people. China continued to suffer under the heavy yoke of imperialism, particularly of Japan and the United States whose influence had increased during the war years; exploitation by the feudal rulers and the military clique continued to reach untold dimensions, and the country was prevented from pursuing an independent policy based on equal rights with other nations which could have served its domestic and foreign interests.

Before the end of the war the imperialist powers started negotiations for the partition of China. Japan's main goal at this time was to maintain her hold over Germany's previous possessions which she had taken over.

Conversations on this subject between Britain and Japan, begun at the end of January 1917, were concluded by an exchange of notes. The note sent by the British ambassador in Tokyo on February 16 to the Japanese Ministry of Foreign Affairs stated: 'His Majesty's government gladly responds to the desire of the Japanese government in declaring that in the peace conference Britain shall uphold Japan's claims to Germany's rights in Shantung and the latter's island possessions north of the equator; it is understood that at the peace conference the Japanese government shall regard as favorable the claims of Great Britain to the German islands south of the equator.' The answering note dispatched by the Japanese Foreign Minister on February 21 declared that 'the Japanese government values highly the friendly tone' of the British note and that it considered Britain's agreement to the transfer of Germany's Shantung possessions to Japan as 'proof of the close ties binding the two allied powers.'

Having enlisted the support of Britain, Japan also laid its claim to Germany's Far Eastern possessions before France and tsarist Russia. Exhausted by the war against Germany, France approved these demands, merely asking Japan to 'cooperate in order to make China break off her diplomatic relations with Germany.'[7]

The Tuan Chi-jui government severed its diplomatic relations with Germany and Austro-Hungary on 14 March 1917. The Chinese Parliament's debate on this occasion revealed, however, that public opinion looked askance upon any participation of China in the European war while the imperialist hold on the country was tighten-

---

[7] Memorandum of the French ambassador to the Japanese Foreign Minister, 1 March 1917.

ing and the democratic movement forcibly suppressed. On 10 May 1917 the Chinese Parliament refused to vote for China's participation in the war and demanded Tuan Chi-jui's resignation. President Li Yuan-hung was compelled by parliamentary opposition to dismiss Tuan Chi-jui and place the Peking garrison under his own command.

Supported by the imperialist 'allies,' a northern military party clique opposed the president and obliged him to dissolve parliament. In their desire to reinforce the reactionary elements, a number of warlords attempted to restore the Ch'ing dynasty by proclaiming, on 1 July 1917, the accession of the nine-year-old Pu I, the last Emperor, who had been dethroned by the 1911 revolution. Pu I only remained in power for a few days; after the monarchists had been chased from Peking, Tuan Chi-jui resumed his previous functions.

Widespread agitation began simultaneously in Shanghai and the south of the country against the reactionary forces and for the restoration of democratic liberty and the summoning of Parliament. The members of the dissolved House, meeting in Shanghai under the leadership of Sun Yat-sen, published a manifesto declaring the dissolution of the House illegal and demanding its convocation. Parliament convened at Canton and in August 1917 elected a Provisional Government headed by Sun Yat-sen.

The Chinese reactionaries, however, succeeded with Japan's support in repressing the democratic movement in the south and overthrowing the new government. The Tuan Chi-jui government, following Japan's instructions, declared war on Germany and Austro-Hungary on 14 August 1917. Certain nationalist circles which supported this step hoped that China's participation in the war on the side of the Allies would help to reinforce her sovereign rights and admit her to equal rank in her relations with the imperialist powers.

The two main imperialist rivals in the Far East—Japan and the United States— were at the same time continuing to wrangle behind China's back. On 28 July 1917 Japan dispatched the Ishii mission to the United States; its official purpose was to represent Japan at a ceremony in which the United States marked their gratitude to their 'allies' for their fight against Germany, but the mission was charged with the task of 'reaching an agreement with the United States by an open exchange of views with American public figures concerning Chinese problems.'

After two months of negotiations an agreement was reached, the United States recognizing Japan's 'special rights' in China. The note sent by Secretary of State Lansing to the Japanese Ambassador Extraordinary, Viscount Ishii, stated: 'The governments of the United States and Japan acknowledge that territorial proximity creates special bonds between nations and as a consequence of this the United States government recognizes Japan's special interests in China, particularly in the part to which her possessions are contiguous.'

Japan agreed at the same time to promote America's notorious 'open door and equal opportunity' policy, calculated to encourage the 'free' penetration of American capital into China where it could supplant the lesser Japanese monopolies. Japan was attempting to appear a reliable partner for repressing the growing Chinese opposition to the imperialist domination and protecting China from the 'bane' of Russian revolutionary influence.

Britain and France, whose hands were tied in Europe by the war against Germany and had no effective forces stationed in the Far East, had no objection to use of the Japanese army against Soviet Russia for protecting their possessions in China.

In 1918 Japan concluded a number of agreements with Tuan Chi-jui (exchange of notes on military cooperation on March 25, military treaty of May 16, naval treaty of May 19 and supplementary military Treaty of September 6) which tightened her control over the Peking government.[8] The Japanese occupied the whole of Manchuria, seized all Manchurian railroads, including the C.E.R., and transformed this region into a powerful base for eventual attack against the Soviet Far East.

In addition to these military and political steps, in 1918 Japanese monopolies began to put into effect their mining and railroad construction projects. Nishihara, a financial agent of the Japanese government, arrived in Peking in the spring of 1918. To avoid the accusation of separatist activities that might be leveled by Britain, France and the United States at Japanese government banks of the 'International Banking Consortium,' Nishihara passed himself off as a private representative of the Bank of Chosen [*Chosen Ginko*] and Bank of Taiwan [*Taiwan Ginko*].[9] He succeeded in concluding agreements between the Japanese and Chinese governments concerning Japanese loans to China.

A declaration published by the Japanese government on 2 October 1918 stated in this context that before its resignation the Terauchi cabinet had advanced a number of loans to the Chinese government allegedly for the construction of five railroad tracks in Manchuria and Inner Mongolia, and two in Shantung Province, and one important metallurgical plant. The Terauchi cabinet had also allegedly granted a loan to the Chinese bank of communications, loans for the construction of telegraph lines and of a railroad between Kirin and Hweining as well as for the exploitation of forests and gold mines in the provinces of Kirin and Heilungkiang. In fact the 'Nishihara' loans were used for military purposes, bribing Peking officials, etc.

The United States also showed intensive activity in China. The most important U.S. banks created a new banking consortium in China in the summer of 1918, hoping by this to oust Japan, with the assistance of Britain, from the positions acquired during the war years.

The discussions on China held at the Paris peace conference (January-April 1919) revealed an irreconcilable conflict between the American and Japanese imperialist rivals and again demonstrated to the Chinese people that the 'great powers' participating in the conference intended to maintain China's semicolonial status by every means and to deprive her of the most elementary sovereign rights. The imperialist powers—Britain, France, Japan, the United States and Italy—ignored China's applications for reestablishment of her legal right to possessions acquired by Ger-

---

[8] Reinschithen, the U.S. ambassador to China, complained that foreign missions were obliged to obtain Japanese agreement before being admitted to an audience with the Tuan Chi-jui government.

[9] [*Chosen*—Korea; *Taiwan*—Formosa.]

many through a number of inequitable treaties. The Treaty of Versailles assigned important 'rights' to the Japanese, who received the German possessions in Shantung Province; Japan thus acquired strategic vantages in China making possible control of both Manchuria and North China.

This new partition by the imperialist powers roused indignation throughout the country, the Chinese bourgeoisie joining its protests to those of the working masses. Peking students organized a demonstration on 4 May 1919 against recognition of the articles of the Versailles Treaty applying to China. An extensive boycott of Japanese goods was conducted throughout the country. The workers of the largest industrial centers—Shanghai, Tangshan and other cities—gave their enthusiastic support to the patriotic attitude adopted by progressive circles of the intelligentsia and there were political strikes against the imperialist powers. The *Fourth of May Movement* constituted a turning point in the development of the Chinese democratic revolution. The democratic movement was encouraged by the victory of the socialist revolution in Russia.

In the words of Mao Tse-tung: 'The gun salvos of the October Revolution have brought Marxism-Leninism to us. The October Revolution has helped the progressive circles of the world and China to shape their country's fate and reexamine their own problems in the light of proletarian ideology. To follow the Russians—this was the conclusion.'[10]

SOVIET-CHINESE ECONOMIC RELATIONS IN 1917-1924

Immediately after it was established, the Soviet Republic offered to negotiate, in concordance with China's wishes, the cancellation of the Sino-Russian treaty of 1896, the Peking (Boxer) Protocol of 1901 and all the treaties concluded between tsarist Russia and China in 1907-1916, as well as the conclusion of new treaties based on the recognition of equal rights for both parties and mutual respect of sovereignty. However, the Peking authorities concealed this offer from the Chinese population. The negotiations between the People's Commissariat of Foreign Affairs and the Chinese embassy in Russia were broken off in March 1918 through the direct pressure of international imperialist circles.

The Peking Prime Minister, Tuan Chi-jui, and Chang Tso-lin, governor of the 'three eastern provinces' (Manchuria) acquiesced to Japanese militarism and succeeded in maintaining China in isolation from the Soviet Union for the benefit of their masters. Russian government property in Manchuria—the concession zone of the C.E.R.—was in danger of being seized by the imperialist powers and constituted a focus for the White Russian forces; the latter endeavored to retain the railroad in the hands of the tsarist administration and protect the privileges of the Russian bourgeoisie conferred by the treaties which had been cancelled by the Soviet government.

Meanwhile the peals of the October Revolution had also reached remote Manchuria. The 100,000 workers and employees of the C.E.R. and Russian industries in

---

[10] Mao Tse-tung. *The Dictatorship of the People's Democracy*, pp. 5-6. Moskva-Gospolitizdat. 1949.

Manchuria greeted the establishment of the Soviet Government with enthusiasm and stood united in their determination to protect Russian government property until an agreement was reached between the Soviet and Chinese governments and to prevent its depredation by the tsarist administration. The C.E.R. workers and employees abolished the 'Special Council' and the 'Special Committee' of the C.E.R. directorate which embodied the supreme administrative authority of the tsarist government.[11] The Russian colony elected a Harbin Soviet of Workers' and Soldiers' Deputies to control the operation of the C.E.R. and protect the rights of Russian citizens in Manchuria; the Soviet expressed its solidarity with the revolutionary Russian people and recognized the authority of the central Soviet government. On 21 November 1917 Soviet Russia empowered the Harbin Soviet to represent Russia on Manchurian territory and placed Russian citizens under its protection.

On 31 January 1918 the People's Commissariat of Communications for Soviet Russia informed Lieutenant-General Horvath, the exdirector of the C.E.R., that the railroad constituted Russian government property and was being transferred from the direction of the C.E.R. joint stock company (whose officers were in Petrograd) to the People's Commissariat of Communications; Horvath was also recalled to Petrograd.

Invested with the legal authority of the Soviet of People's Commissars, the Harbin Soviet addressed the following memorandum to the local Chinese administration: 'To the *Taotai*.[12] The Russian people have achieved a second revolution in October. New people representing new ideas now stand at the head of the government. The Harbin Soviet of Workers' and Soldiers' Deputies, on the order of the Petrograd government, has proclaimed itself an official body. No representatives of the previous government have any right to speak in the name of the Russian people, since the Russian people has no trust in them. Taking advantage of the international situation, local officials have refused to leave their posts peacefully, using China's protests as a pretext. These men are using all means to remain in power against the

---

[11] The 'Special Council' of the C.E.R. directorate was created in 1910 by the tsarist government and consisted of the director of the railroad (president), his aide for civil affairs, the Russian consul-general at Harbin and the president and attorney-general of the Russian border territory tribunal. The 'Special Council' dealt with:

  1) relations with foreign consulates in the concession zone of the C.E.R.;   2) complaints and claims of foreigners against the C.E.R.;   3) problems of jurisdiction and determination of the authority of administrative and consular bodies over Chinese and foreign subjects within the concession zone;   4) acquisition of long-term concessions from the Chinese authorities by Russian subjects;   5) eviction from the concession zone of persons considered harmful to law and order;   6) other administrative affairs. A 'Special Committee' of the directorate was created in the concession zone in 1905 having no connection with the 'Special Council'; it was responsible for protecting the railroad and ensuring that all nontechnical rulings were respected by workers and employees. The 'Special Committee' included the railroad director, his aide for civil affairs, the chief of the C.E.R. police detachment, the head of the Transamur Military District and a staff officer delegated by the chief of the Transamur Railroad Brigade.

[12] [Under the Manchu regime the *Taotai* was a provincial official administering grain stocks, the salt monopoly, posts, the armed forces and customs. The office continued to exist for some time after the end of the Manchu reign in 1912. It corresponds approximately to that of governor.]

will of Russian democracy—they are intimidating the Chinese population and authorities by predicting massacres and plunder. This is untrue. We assure you and your citizens living in the Concession Zone of the Chinese Eastern Railroad that you have nothing to fear from the Russian inhabitants. The Soviet of Workers' and Soldiers' Deputies has taken in the past and will continue to take the most stringent measures for the preservation of order and for the personal protection of all the citizens of Harbin and of their property. At the same time we hereby notify you that General Horvath has no authority in administrative and diplomatic affairs. These functions are temporarily entrusted to citizen Boris Slavin, President of the Soviet of Workers' and Soldiers' Deputies. If in the past difficulties have arisen between the Chinese and Russian empires there can be no misunderstandings between the great Republics of China and Russia, and our freedom-loving people have no cause for quarrel.'[13]

However, Chang Tso-lin's administration, which maintained close ties with Japanese imperialism, did not establish relations with the new Soviet administration, which was inspired by a socialist policy and was prepared to develop its relations with the Chinese people on the basis of equal rights and mutual respect of sovereignty. Heedless of China's interests, the venal Chang Tso-lin authorities reinstated the tsarist administration (which of course directed the railroad only nominally. The C.E.R. in fact was run by the Interallied Technical Council headed by Stevenson, an American).

In 1919 the Whites set up in Peking with the support of France and the United States, an illicit 'Joint Stock Chinese Eastern Company.' Its creation was made possible because a member of the board of directors of the Russo-Asiatic Bank, who had fled from Petrograd after nationalization of the bank by the Soviet Government, had taken an illegal power of attorney for a small amount of C.E.R. stock previously owned by the Russo-Asiatic Bank. The company 'elected' a board which included Kolchak, Horvath and other leaders of the White Russian forces. Behind the screen of the 'C.E.R. Board' the United States, France, Japan and the other allies established their control of the railroad.

The allied command freely used the C.E.R. to transport interventionist troops to the Soviet Far East and Siberia. The revenue was employed for maintaining and forming counter revolutionary groups which were to fight the Soviet Union. The White Russians and the Japanese military clique openly stole C.E.R. property causing considerable material damage to Soviet government property.

As a step in their attack against the Far Eastern Republic, the allies compelled the Chinese administration to close the Manchouli [Lupin] station on 3 December 1920 in order to sever the connections with the Transbaikal railroad. This paralyzed all traffic on the eastern branch of the C.E.R. Traffic continued on the western branch leading to the Ussuri Railroad since the Maritime Territory and Vladivostok harbor remained in Japanese and White Russian hands, but its volume decreased considerably. Data published by the C.E.R. Economic Bureau show that grain exports

---

[13] *Historical Essay on the C.E.R.,* 1898-1923, pp. 594-595.

from North Manchuria to Vladivostok fell to a volume of 6.1 million *poods* in 1920 compared to 11.5 million *poods* in 1919 and 32 million *poods* in 1917, respectively. Japan, whose troops continued to occupy the C.E.R., routed North Manchuria's main exports (88 percent) and imports (90 percent) through Dalny (Dairen); as a result only the small southern section of the C.E.R., from Harbin to Kwanchengtze [Changchun],[14] was carrying Manchuria's foreign trade.

The isolation of the C.E.R. from the Russian railroads and its transformation into an artery for allied military traffic in Manchuria put it in an extremely precarious financial situation. The disorganization of the C.E.R. furnished the proof the allies needed to demonstrate that the railroad could not exist without allied aid, i.e., without foreign loans. The U.S. and French ruling circles who had advanced claims to Russian property in Manchuria tried to involve the C.E.R. in debt and thus gain control of it by using their 'rights' as creditors. The result of this financial manoeuvering was that by the end of 1921 the Interallied Technical Council found the C.E.R. to owe debts, mainly to the United States, amounting to 1,495,535 gold rubles and 3,931,169 yen.

The danger that the C.E.R. would fall into the hands of the United States, then Japan's main rival in the Far East alarmed Japanese ruling circles. Japan was even prepared to make concessions to the Far Eastern Republic, which was considered less dangerous as Japanese troops and White forces were still stationed in the Far East; Japan also used the Chang Tso-lin administration as a screen for its activities. Japan certainly had no intention of allowing the United States to reinforce its position in Manchuria.

Led by these considerations the Japanese government endeavored, in addition to its participation in the general so-called Interallied Technical Council, to put the Russian railroad in debt to the Chinese administration, which was under Japanese influence. A 2 million silver dollar loan was thus 'allocated' by the Peking government to the C.E.R. Japan also prevented the United States from controlling the C.E.R. in technical matters. Although the Interallied Technical Council was presided over by Americans, in fact Japan controlled all aspects of the railroad's operation by means of special railroad detachments of her army of occupation.

At the Washington Conference (November 1921-February 1922), which took place without the participation of the RSFSR and the FER, the United States decided to push its advantages as concerned the C.E.R. and for the 'internationalization' of the railroad. The Soviet government protested vigorously to the members of the conference 'against any resolution that might be adopted by the Washington Conference in violation of Russia's rights.'[15] This firm stand and the conflicts among the imperialist powers themselves prevented the conference from arriving at a joint decision.

---

[14] [When Russia ceded the southern part of the C.E.R. to Japan, the 240-kilometer section from Harbin to Kwanchengtze was retained. Kwanchengtze, the last Russian station, was three kilometers from Changchun, the first station of the Japanese South Manchurian Railroad.]

[15] *Foreign Policy of the U.S.S.R., 1917-1944,* Vol. 2. p. 209. Moskva. 1944.

However, despite the sharp conflict of interests between the United States and Japan their views coincided on one point—both feared an agreement between China and Soviet Russia and tried to prevent it. They thus took all possible measures to ensure that the C.E.R., which had considerable economic importance for Manchuria and was not less valuable to China and Russia from the strategic standpoint, should not remain in Russian or Chinese hands.

This consensus inspired the American and Japanese ruling circles to support the White Russian administration of the C.E.R. and prevent Soviet representatives from taking over. The Whites were considered temporarily capable of balancing the conflicting interests of the two rivals, while China's inequitable status could be maintained in the name of Russia.

The fear of the revolutionary influence that Soviet Russia might wield on the Chinese people and the desire to maintain China's reactionary semifeudal regime forged strong bonds between the Chinese feudal lords and bourgeoisie on the one hand and American, Japanese, British and French imperialist circles on the other. The Chinese reactionaries sacrificed the real interests of their country to their own class interests; they rejected the Soviet proposal to establish relations based on friendship and equal rights and kept secret both the Soviet declaration of 25 July 1919 proposing negotiations for the establishment of diplomatic relations, and reaffirming the Soviet government's decision to renounce all inequitable treaties concluded by tsarist Russia with China and the repeated Soviet proposals of October 1920.[16]

Despite the Soviet declarations the Chinese militarists betrayed their own nation by authorizing the White Russians remaining in the C.E.R. concession zone to maintain an armed guard as well as their tribunals and other attributes of power granted by the inequitable treaties signed with tsarist Russia. However, it became increasingly difficult for the White Russians and the Chinese to maintain control of the C.E.R. as the territory of the Far East was gradually liberated from the interventionist and White forces. After the evacuation of Japanese troops from the con-

---

[16] The Soviet government's appeal on 25 July 1919 to the Chinese people and the governments of South and North China reads as follows: 'After two years of war in which no effort has been spared, Soviet Russia and the Soviet Red Army are advancing eastward through the Urals, but not for purposes of coercion, enslavement or conquest. This has already become clear to every Siberian peasant and every Siberian worker. We bring to the people liberation from the yoke of foreign bayonets and the foreign gold which throttles the enslaved nations of the East and the Chinese people first and foremost. We bring aid not only to our own laboring classes but also to the Chinese people and repeat our declaration made at the time of the Great October Revolution of 1917 which may have been concealed from the Chinese people by the corrupt American-European-Japanese press... No single Russian official, priest or missionary shall venture to interfere in Chinese affairs and if he were to commit a crime he would be judged by a local court. In China there should be no other authority or justice than the authority and justice of the Chinese people.'

The Soviet government's appeal of October 1920 stated: 'The government of the Russian Soviet Federative Socialist Republic denounces all the treaties concluded with China by the previous tsarist government of Russia, rejects any encroachment upon Chinese territory, abandons all the Russian concessions in China and gives back to China without any compensation and for all time all the possessions rapaciously seized by the tsarist government and the Russian bourgeoisie.'

cession zone and the dissolution of the Interallied Technical Council in October 1922, the White Russian and Chang Tso-lin administration could no longer ignore the insistent demands of Manchurian commercial circles for the reestablishment of the junction between the C.E.R. and the Transbaikal and Ussuri Railroads.

By the beginning of 1921, after the Japanese interventionists and Semenov's armed gangs had been chased from the Transbaikal territory, the C.E.R. administration had already been compelled to seek an agreement with the Transbaikal Railroad. Negotiations took place in 1921 and 1922 and on 1 October 1922 an agreement was reached between the boards of the C.E.R. and the Transbaikal Railroad on the establishment of a direct link between the two railroads, on the mode of payments for freight and on the use of rolling stock.

The eviction of interventionists and Whites from Vladivostok considerably reinforced Soviet Russia's position in the Far East. The administrative organs of Soviet power, over which was a single central authority, were then reestablished throughout the territory of the Soviet Far East, except for North Sakhalin.

The removal of the interventionists from the Soviet Far East and the subsequent evacuation of Japanese troops from the concession zone of the C.E.R. reduced imperialist pressure on China. Conditions for contacts between the U.S.S.R.[17] and China thus improved. The reactionary Peking government continued however, to boycott the friendly Soviet proposals, blindly taking orders from their imperialist masters.

The southern government[18] headed by Sun Yat-sen adopted a friendly attitude to the Soviet Republic from its very beginnings and endeavored to establish relations with Soviet Russia. In 1918, while the Soviets were being attacked by the imperialist powers and the corrupt capitalist press misinformed world opinion as to the real state of affairs in Russia, the great Chinese revolutionary and democrat Sun Yat-sen sent a dispatch to Lenin applauding the successes achieved by the Soviets and expressing his warmest sympathy for the Soviet people.

Relations between the governments of the RSFSR and the southern China government proved difficult to establish however. The occupation of the Soviet Far East by the interventionists severed Soviet Russia from China; moreover, the southern government's position was an extremely difficult one, for the militarists had set up a blockade of Sun Yat-sen in Canton (which lasted until 16 June 1922). The Soviet appeals of July 1919 and October 1920 came to the knowledge of the southern government only in the middle of 1921.

[17] On 26 December 1922 the 10th All-Russian Congress of Soviets decided on the merger of the RSFSR, the Ukrainian SSR, the Transcaucasian SSR and the Belorussian SSR into a Union of Soviet Socialist Republics. On 30 December 1922 the 1st Congress of Soviets of the Union proclaimed the formation of the Union of Soviet Socialist Republics.

[18] Sun Yat-sen formed a government in Canton on 6 September 1917. A conference of representatives of the southern provinces convened in May 1918 and elected a southern Chinese government; however, since the Kwangsi warlord group led the cabinet, Sun Yat-sen was compelled to leave for Shanghai, returning to Canton in November 1920. In June 1922 the Kwangtung warlord Chen Kiu-ming brought about a coup in Canton and Sun Yat-sen was again forced to leave for Shanghai; he again returned to Canton on 21 February 1923 after Chan Kiu-ming's defeat and organized a new southern government.

Notes were exchanged for the first time between Sun Yat-sen, President of the southern government, and the People's Commissariat of Foreign Affairs of the RSFSR only in June 1921; they stated the joint views of the Chinese and Soviet people as to the necessity for waging a resolute struggle against the oppressors of the laboring classes and of colonial nations.

As soon as Soviet policy concerning China became general knowledge, Chinese public opinion showed great interest in Soviet Russia. In his answer to a letter sent by the People's Commissar of Foreign Affairs of the RSFSR Dr. Sun Yat-sen wrote: 'I wish to meet you and other friends in Moscow. I am extremely interested in your activities, particularly in the organization of your Soviets, your army and your educational system. I should like to receive any information that you and others can give me on these matters, particularly in regard to education. Similarly to Moscow, I should like to lay the groundwork for the Chinese Republic in the minds of the young generation—the toilers of tomorrow. My best wishes to you and to my friend Lenin as well as to all the others who have achieved so much for human freedom.'[19]

The southern government made the Soviet proposals widely known. These glad tidings which heralded a new era in China's history spread swiftly throughout the country. Popular agitation developed in both the south and the north for the recognition of the Soviet government and the establishment of friendly relations. It was understood by progressive Chinese circles that the establishment of relations with the Soviet Union on the basis of the Soviet proposals would be a severe blow to the imperialist system of inequitable treaties and would further the Chinese people's struggle for restoration of the Republic's sovereign rights.

This growing popular movement in favor of friendly relations with Soviet Russia constituted a threat to the colonial powers. Friendship and cooperation between the Chinese people and the Soviet Union would, in their view, bring their domination of China, which had lasted for almost a century, to an end; they therefore opposed it by all available means.

The results of the Washington Conference did not satisfy a number of the Chinese intellectuals and that part of the middle class which had hoped to gain the support of the United States. Not only did the treaties concluded at the conference maintain China's semicolonial status, but they even increased the servility of the country's position. China's lawful demands concerning her sovereignty were unanimously rejected by the imperialist powers. In rejecting China's proposals, the so-called 'ten points,'[20] the United States, Britain, Japan and the other members of the conference declared that China was 'not yet ready' to enjoy equal rights with other nations. They informed China of their readiness to 'relinquish the right to extraterritoriality once

---

[19] *Bol'shevik* (The Bolshevik), No. 19, p. 48. 1950.

[20] The ten points demanded the respect of China's sovereignty by the imperialist powers, rejected the conclusion of treaties concerning it without it's knowledge and denied extraterritorial rights within China. As a concession to the powers the Peking government agreed to recognize the principle of 'open doors and equal opportunities' for foreign trade and investments in China. The propositions also expressed the desire to reduce the term of China's obligations to foreign governments, etc...

they were convinced that China's laws, administration and other concerns could meet their requirements satisfactorily.'[21]

The Nine Power Treaty adopted by the Washington Conference on 6 February 1922 regarding the Chinese customs tariff not only disregarded the Chinese people's minimum demands for an independent customs but restated China's complete dependence on the imperialist powers.

The Washington Conference again demonstrated to the Chinese people that no sympathy or support for the independence and freedom of oppressed nations could be expected from an imperialist state, whatever its disguise; it was also evident that the conflict between the imperialist powers over China could only lead to the substitution of one power for another.

In contrast to this, the treaties concluded between Soviet Russia and Persia (concerning the establishment of diplomatic relations, 26 February 1921), Afghanistan (concerning the establishment of diplomatic relations, 28 February 1921) and Turkey (Treaty of Friendship and Brotherhood, 16 March 1921) clearly demonstrated the socialist policies pursued by the Soviet government based on recognition of the complete equality and sovereignty of all nations. These documents gave the lie to the capitalist propaganda which was sowing doubt throughout the world as to the sincerity of Soviet foreign policy.

Soviet Russia's influence and authority gained rapid ground among the oppressed nations of the East, including China. Mass meetings and discussions were held in Canton, Shanghai and Peking calling for the immediate establishment of diplomatic relations with Soviet Russia. The number of Russia's friends in China constantly increased.[22] These circumstances compelled the reactionary Peking government to accept the Soviet proposals for negotiations on the establishment of diplomatic and economic relations. Talks were opened in Peking in 1921 with delegates of the Far Eastern Republic and continued in 1922 with representatives of the RSFSR. At the very beginning of these negotiations France, the United States and Japan tried to force Peking to reject any agreement with the Soviets on one of the main points—the status of the C.E.R. as Russian government property—by making unfounded financial claims.

France seized the branches of the Russo-Asiatic Bank in China and attempted to 'prove' her right to the bank's property, including the C.E.R., contrary to the widely known facts. The Russo-Asiatic Bank, created in 1895 on the initiative of the Russian Finance Ministry with the official backing of the Russian government, was indubitably Russian property; moreover, the bank had almost no share in the fixed capital of the C.E.R. or in subsequent loans to the railroad.

American and Japanese claims to the C.E.R. 'rested' on debts incurred by the railroad in 1918-1922, i.e., when the C.E.R. had been forcibly seized by the inter-

---

[21] Resolution of the Washington Conference concerning extraterritoriality in China, 10 December 1921.

[22] During the festivities marking the 25th anniversary of the Peking National University in 1923 the students made a survey among those present; in answering the question: 'Who is China's friend, the United States or Soviet Russia?' 497 persons chose the latter and 107 the former (A. Ivin 'Sovremennyi Kitai' (Contemporary China).—*Novyi Vostok*. No. 5. 1924).

ventionists and used as a base for their activities against Soviet Russia. These claims were naturally repudiated by the Soviet government, and the Peking authorities had no alternative but to recognize Soviet Russia as the sole legal owner of the C.E.R. Their representatives clearly understood that any other solution to the issue could lead not only to the railroad being controlled by the imperialist powers, but to the loss of North Manchuria as well.

The White Russians also interfered in the Sino-Soviet talks. The ex-officials of the tsarist embassy and consulates in China continued to occupy the premises, to administer Russian government property and even to maintain official relations with the representatives of foreign states. Although after the dissolution of the Interallied Technical Council and the withdrawal of Japanese troops from the concession zone of the C.E.R. the railroad was administered by the autonomous government of the Three Eastern Provinces (Manchuria),[23] the White Russian police and other tsarist administrative organs continued their illegal control of the railway.

The use of the Russian share of the 'Boxer indemnity' also gave rise to protracted discussions. In refusing, for the benefit of the Chinese people, its share of the 'Boxer indemnity,' the Soviet government insisted that it be used for education.

The various delays in the Sino-Soviet negotiations and the final rejection by the Peking government of the treaty which had been already agreed upon and initialed on 14 March 1924 caused widespread dissatisfaction in China. Trade unions and other public bodies, student federations and professors expressed their alarm at the interruption of the negotiations in public meetings as well as by petitions and telegrams sent to the Peking authorities and demanded the immediate conclusion of an agreement with the Soviet Union.

Despite pressure from the United States, France and other imperialist powers, the Peking authorities had no choice but to defer to Chinese public opinion. They also could not disregard the fact that the Soviet Union had established diplomatic relations with Britain and Italy in February 1924 and with Sweden, Norway and Greece in March of the same year.

The Sino-Soviet conversations ended on 31 May 1924 by the signature of an 'Agreement of General Principles for the Settlement of Issues between the Union of Soviet Socialist Republics and the Chinese Republic.'

THE SINO-SOVIET TREATY OF 1924—CHINA'S FIRST EQUITABLE TREATY

The Sino-Soviet agreement concerned a number of issues between the Soviet Union and China and the Soviet government's declarations of 1919 and 1920.

Reestablishment of China's sovereignty. The clauses of the Sino-Soviet treaty gave equal rights to China in its foreign affairs for the first time since the 'opium wars'

---

[23] Chinese jurisdiction over the C.E.R. was implemented by the President of the C.E.R. Board (who was at the same time the Chinese government's representative on the board), General Pao Kwei-ching, on 14 March 1920.

and permitted enjoyment of all the rights of a sovereign state. Article 4 stated: 'The government of the Union of Soviet Socialist Republics, in accordance with its policy and with the declarations of 1919 and 1920, declares null and void all treaties, agreements, etc., concerning the sovereign rights or interests of the Republic of China concluded by the previous tsarist government and any third party or parties.' Both governments bound themselves to avoid in future the conclusion of any treaties or agreements to the detriment of the sovereign rights or interests of either contracting party.

The abrogation of the tsarist treaties and the renuciation of 'special rights and privileges on all the concessions' (article 10) dissolved all previous consular courts, concessions and autonomous bodies in the concession zone of the C.E.R., and Soviet citizens living in China and their property were henceforth within the jurisdiction of the courts of the Chinese Republic.

The renunciation of extraterritorial rights by the Soviet Union constituted a most important step for China in principle. The Sino-Soviet treaty furthered China's struggle for independence. It gave strength and confidence to the Chinese democratic forces and negated the 'arguments' of imperialist circles on China's 'unfitness' to exercise her sovereign rights. The treaty was concluded at a time when the imperialists were demanding more rights for foreigners.

Renunciation of Russia's share in the Boxer indemnity. The treaty took note that 'the government of the Union of Socialist Soviet Republics agrees to renounce Russia's share in the Boxer indemnity' (article 11). This was accompanied by the statement of Soviet Russia's wish that this sum be used 'wholly and exclusively to create a fund to raise the level of education of the Chinese people' (excerpt from the declaration).

Basic principles of the management of the C.E.R., property of the Soviet Union. In regard to the C.E.R., both parties agreed to abolish the special rights acquired by tsarist Russia in the railroad concession zone but concluded[24] that the Chinese Eastern Railroad remained the legal property of the Union of Soviet Socialist Republics since it had been built at the expense of the Russian people. At the same time the Soviet government agreed that 'the government of the Chinese Republic could exercise the option to buy back the Chinese Eastern Railroad and all its property with Chinese capital and that all assets and liabilities of the railroad would then be handed over to China' (article 9, point 2). It was also agreed that 'the future of the Chinese Eastern Railroad shall be determined by the Union of Soviet Socialist Republics and the Chinese Republic, without the participation of any other party or parties' (article 9, point 5).

As a number of technical matters concerning the management and operation of the C.E.R. remained pending, the treaty provided that 'the rights of both governments issuing from the contract of 27 August (8 September) 1896, for the construction and

---

[24] The Sino-Soviet agreement on general principles for the settlement of issues was accompanied by a separate 'Agreement Concerning the Temporary Management of the C.E.R.'

management of the Chinese Eastern Railroad, remain valid insofar as they are not contrary to the present treaty and the treaty concerning the temporary management of the said railroad and do not prejudice the sovereign rights of China' (article 9, point 7).

The Sino-Soviet treaty thwarted the plans of the imperialist powers as regards the C.E.R.

Prohibition of the existence or activity of organizations or groups hostile to the contracting parties. The treaty stated (article 6) the obligations of both governments to 'forbid on their territories affiliation to or the existence and activity of any organization or group the purpose of which is to oppose by force the government of either of the contracting parties.'

At the time China was sheltering many White Russian armed gangs led by Semenov, Kalmykov, Nechaev and other exiled tsarist generals, which were conducting hostile activities against the Soviet Union; both contracting parties thus agreed to forbid the activities of such organizations against either side. A note of the Chinese government to the Soviet Union declared that the relevant authorities would be instructed 'to discontinue the service of all ex-subjects of the Russian Empire at present in the ranks of the Chinese army and police who either personally or by their actions constitute a threat to the security of the Union of Socialist Soviet Republics.'

Outstanding issues not settled by the treaty. The negotiations preceding the treaty left many issues outstanding, which were to be discussed at a special Sino-Soviet conference. This conference, to be held within one month of the signature of the treaty, was to work out detailed supplementary agreements on various points (article 2), such as:

1) a survey of the Soviet-Chinese border (article 7);

2) rights of navigation on the 'rivers, lakes and other expanses of water along the common border, on the basis of equal rights and reciprocity' (article 8);

3) the amount required from and mode of payment for the Chinese government's purchase of the C.E.R. (article 9, point 3);

4) a treaty of commerce between the Soviet Union and China (article 13);

5) a tariff 'for both contracting parties based on the principles of equity and reciprocity' (article 13).

The Sino-Soviet treaty was a most important factor in helping to strengthen the international position of both governments. For China it was the first equitable treaty to be concluded with a foreign government since the 'opium wars' and gave legal force to a new type of relationship between nations based on equal rights, respect of the sovereignty of both large and small nations and the preservation of mutual interests.

The consequence of the Soviet government's abrogation of the inequitable tsarist treaties was that approximately half of all the foreigners residing in China—who were Russian subjects—were henceforth within the Chinese jurisdiction. Those demanding the continuation of the special rights and privileges accorded to foreigners thus found themselves in a difficult position. The renewal of diplomatic relations with the Soviet Union secured the long territorial border at China's rear.

The Sino-Soviet treaty was also important to the Soviet Union. In addition to the reestablishment of normal diplomatic relations with a neighboring country and settlement of the main economic and political issues, the treaty increased the prestige of the Soviet Union among the peoples of Asia and thwarted the expansionist plans of the imperialist powers in the Far East.

The imperialists were forced to acknowledge that their plans for armed intervention against the Soviet Union had failed both in the West and in the East. The expulsion of interventionist troops from the C.E.R., and the transfer of this railroad, of great importance to the Soviet Far East, to joint Sino-Soviet management strengthened the Soviet Union's position in the Pacific and created favorable conditions for negotiations with Japan, whose troops continued to occupy the northern part of Sakhalin.

SINO-SOVIET TRADE IN 1917-1924

The initial period: 1917-1922 *(up to the evacuation of foreign interventionists from the Soviet Far East).* The blockade of Soviet Russia by the allies, followed by their intervention in Siberia and the Soviet Far East, disrupted the normal trade routes between Russia and China. On 24 December 1917 the reactionary Peking government, joining the anti-Soviet front, prohibited all exports from China to Soviet Russia. However, this measure did not succeed in severing completely the commercial ties between the Russian and Chinese population of the border area, in existence for over 250 years.

The isolation of the Soviet territories in the Far East and Central Asia from Russia's vital supply centers led to an increased demand for Chinese goods in these areas, including manufactured articles previously supplied by European Russia. The border trade was also encouraged by the many Russian and Chinese firms with branches throughout Manchuria and the Soviet Far East.

Enterprises such as the Russian I.I.Tschurin & Co., Ltd., or the German firm Kunst und Albers, owning large general stores in Vladivostok, Khabarovsk, Blagoveshchensk, Chita and other cities of the Soviet Far East, also took an important part in the retail and wholesale trade of North Manchuria. The Chinese firms I Tai Hang, Sung Tai Hang and Shih I Tang, possessing large warehouses for pharmaceutical products in Manchuria and other areas of China, were the main vendors of ginseng, reindeer antlers and trepang, and retained agents in Vladivostok and other localities of the Soviet Maritime Territory for the purchase of these goods. The Chinese flour mills of Manchuria—Son Ho Shing *(Shwang Ho Sheng)*, Wang Fu Chwan, Kwang Hsing Kung Ssu, An Yü and I Chang Tai—were the main flour suppliers to Siberia and the Soviet Far East.

These and many other industrial and commercial enterprises were interested in maintaining their ties between China and the Soviet Union and used all possible means, both legal and illegal, for the continuation of trade.

The lax supervision along the Sino-Russian border and the lack of an organized customs service on either side gave rise to extensive smuggling. Before the liberation of the Soviet Far East by the Red Army, smuggling accounted for most of the trade between the Russian and Chinese border territories. It was also promoted by the free interchange of Russian and Chinese currency throughout the border territories of both states. The ruble, which had remained until 1917 the basic monetary unit in the concession zone of the C.E.R., continued to circulate until 1922. The Manchurian market was flooded with *Romanovkis, Kerenkis, Kolchakovkis, bufferkis* (issued by the Far Eastern buffer republic) and other local currencies: *Horvathki* (issued by the C.E.R. and the Russo-Asiatic Bank), etc. Chinese currency—silver and paper *tayangs*—circulated throughout the Russian border areas.

A considerable part of the smuggling consisted of an exchange of goods. Chinese merchants would travel to remote Russian gold fields, fur-trapping areas, regions rich in medicinal herbs and reindeer farms where they traded their manufactured articles and foodstuffs for gold, valuable furs, ginseng and reindeer antlers.

The rapid increase of population and the growth of commercial towns on the Chinese banks of the Amur, Argun and Ussuri rivers, as well as in other border areas, was indirect proof of the extent of smuggling along the frontier. Many commercial firms, warehouses and industrial enterprises were established during this period in the Chinese towns of Heiho [Sahalien], Hulin, Fuchin [Fugdin], and Lahasusu[25] [Tungkiang] at the Manchouli and Pogranichnaia [Suifenho] stations of the C.E.R., as well as in the border settlements of Sanchakow [Tungning], Hunchun and Mishan.

In the first few years after the October Revolution official Chinese trade was conducted through the Manchurian border only with the areas of Siberia and the Soviet Far East occupied by the Whites. The structure of Sino-Soviet trade now changed radically.

Cotton fabrics, clothing, groceries, drugs, writing materials, fish, haberdashery, ores, chandlery, and cement had been the main Russian exports to Manchuria in 1913; Russia lost the Manchurian market for these products in the postwar years and began to export mainly coal, timber and furs. Imports from Manchuria to Siberia and the Far East mainly consisted of foodstuffs. Russia's exports of cotton fabrics and clothing to Manchuria which had reached a volume of almost 2.5 thousand tons in 1913, dropped to 43 tons in 1917. In the same period, Manchurian grain exports to Siberia and the Far East increased from 3 to 68 thousand tons. For certain years in the post-war period, Manchuria was not only an important source of foodstuffs and other goods for Siberia and the Far East but also a transit area.

The volume of transit goods from Vladivostok through Manchuria increased almost threefold from 1913 to 1917 and reached 17.2 million *poods*; this was due to increasing American military aid, first to the tsarist government and later to the provisional government. A marked contraction of the transit trade in 1918 was followed

---

[25] [Lahasusu—the Manchurian name for the town lying at the junction of the Sungari and Amur rivers. In the course of the Sinicization of Manchuria during the last 20 years many Chinese names have been substituted for Manchurian designations; Lahasusu was changed to Tungkiang.]

by a renewed increase in 1919 when Kolchak's troops were at liberty in Siberia. The transit trade through Manchuria and Chinese exports to Russia along the Manchurian route ceased almost entirely in 1920, i.e., after Kolchak's defeat and the occupation by the C.E.R. by the Whites and the Allies. Most commercial dealings with China were then conducted via Vladivostok and the border towns along the Amur (Vladivostok-Khabarovsk), which were in the hands of the occupation forces.

MANCHURIAN TRADE WITH THE TRANSBAIKAL AND MARITIME TERRITORIES
THROUGH MANCHOULI AND POGRANICHNAIA STATIONS
(in poods)

	1913	1917	1918	1919	1920
Manchurian imports from the Transbaikal territory	2,023,640	772,039	75,362	572,128	75,513
Goods in transit from the Transbaikal to the Maritime Territory through Manchuria	1,649,133	1,345,303	100,457	449,568	9,832
Manchurian exports to the Transbaikal territory	1,117,050	6,296,232	656,236	2,940,286	556,111
Goods in transit from the Maritime Territory to the Transbaikal through Manchuria	6,037,176	17,176,604	545,562	4,225,347	117,170

The counterrevolutionary defeat in Siberia was followed, in accordance with Soviet law, by the establishment of governmental trade organizations.[26] The *Sibdal'vneshtorg* (Siberia Far Eastern Trade Bureau), entrusted by the Soviet government with all foreign trade with China and Mongolia, was established on Siberian territory in 1920.

A number of important Chinese firms established in Manchuria which in the past had maintained strong commercial links with Russia also militated in favor of reestablishment of Sino-Russian trade. The foreign trade of China, and particularly of Manchuria, was severely hit by the general postwar depression of 1921 as well as by increasing foreign competition. In 1922, 1,675 Chinese and 1,387 foreign commercial enterprises went bankrupt in Harbin alone.

The Chinese firms hoped to find an extensive market for their products in Soviet Russia and to purchase there such goods as furs, timber, coal, petroleum products and others. An office of the *Sibdal'vneshtorg,* Soviet Russia's first governmental commercial organization in Manchuria,[27] opened in Harbin in 1922 with the assistance of Chinese business circles. It was followed by the opening of a transport

---

[26] The People's Commissariat of Foreign Trade *(Narkomvneshtorg)* was created on 11 June 1920, and opened local branches shortly afterwards.

[27] Prior to the opening of the office of the *Sibdal'vneshtorg* representatives of the All-Russian Central Union of Consumers' Societies—the *Tsentrosoyuz*—who were responsible for the sale of furs and Siberian stag antlers in Manchuria, and the purchase of a number of Chinese products there, had been active in Harbin since 1918.

office of the *Dobroflot* (Volunteers' Fleet) (which later merged with a department of the joint stock company *Sovtorgflot* [Soviet Commercial Fleet]) and in June 1923 the Chinese administration authorized the opening of the Soviet joint stock Far Eastern Bank.

After Semenov's defeat in 1921 (the expulsion of his armed gangs from Chita and the reunification of Siberia with the Far Eastern Territory), trade between Manchuria, Siberia and the Transbaikal territory, began to expand considerably, mainly through Manchouli station. Exports from the Transbaikal territory to China through the station grew in 1921 to a volume of 25 thousand tons of freight, mainly coal, timber, building materials, firewood, furs and Siberian stag antlers. China's exports to the Transbaikal Territory also increased in 1921, reaching a volume of 27.4 thousand tons, mainly flour, meat, eggs, animal fats, vegetable oils, sugar, fish.

The Soviet organizations succeeded in establishing a commercial link through the Sinkiang border earlier than in other areas. At the end of 1919 the Russian territories in Central Asia had already been liberated from the Whites and reunited with the central areas of Soviet Russia. The traditional flow of trade between the populations of both sides of the Sinkiang border was thus renewed.

The interruption of commercial relations between Russia and Sinkiang in 1917-1919 had led to an economic decline in this province. Prices for raw materials produced in Sinkiang (leather, wool, cotton) dropped in 1917 to 50 to 70 percent of their 1916 level, although those manufactured articles (cotton fabrics, ironware, matches, etc.) increased by 200-300 percent.[28]

The possibilities for speculation which thus developed in Sinkiang attracted many agents of German, American and British firms[30] who sent their goods to Tientsin and thence by pack horse through Kansu Province, purchasing in Sinkiang local wares at low prices. These foreign enterprises, which tried to shift the payment of the high cost of transport over expensive routes to the Sinkiang population, could not constitute a firms basis for the foreign trade of the province. Moreover, they were interested in a limited number of products only and usually confined their purchases in Sinkiang to animal gut, furs and gold, neglecting the main economy of the province—animal husbandry and farming. The quantity of products imported from Western Europe, the United States and Japan was also quite limited, mainly luxury items which did not meet the requirements of the majority.

Consequently, during the civil war Sinkiang commercial circles worked for the establishment of official relations with Soviet-Russia and the renewal of Sino-

---

[28] Data for 1917-1920 are taken from *The China Year-Book*, 1921-1922, p. 1,020 and for 1921-1922 from *The China Year-Book*, 1928, pp. 134-135.

[30] Beginning in 1918, domestic industries for processing animal casings producing more than 400,000 bundles annually were created by American firms in 22 Sinkiang towns. German animal-casing factories (for sausage skins) also later opened in Sinkiang. The Russo-Asiatic Bank, whose branches in Shanghai and other Chinese cities were at that time in the hands of the Whites and French banks, played an important role in furthering the penetration of American and West European firms into Sinkiang province. In 1921 the bank imported 600,000 rubles worth of various foreign goods from Shanghai to Urumchi [Tihwa], including Japanese manufactured articles, American footwear and sugar, and exported to Central China large amounts of furs and animal casings.

CHINA'S FOREIGN TRADE WITH RUSSIA IN 1917-1922[29]
(per Russian area, in thousand U.S. $)

	1917	1918	1919	1920	1921	1922
1. Exports by sea to European Russia	492.1	0.1	47.8	5.7	156.9	0.6
Imports by sea from European Russia	36.7	16.0	18.3	0.3	–	28.9
Total value	528.8	16.1	66.1	6.0	156.9	29.5
2. Overland exports to Soviet Russia	13,841.4	2,485.2	7,667.9	5,281.7	2,795.3	6,305.6
Overland imports from Soviet Russia	3,021.5	1,807.0	2,397.2	4,354.6	1,316.1	5,902.9
Total value	16,862.9	4,292.2	10,065.1	9,636.3	4,111.4	12,208.5
3. Exports to the Soviet Far East along the Amur	7,298.5	2,007.4	4,308.0	3,912.4	1,618.5	2,244.3
Imports from the Soviet Far East along the Amur	158.8	333.9	132.5	471.9	395.7	895.5
Total value	7,457.3	2,341.3	4,440.5	4,384.3	2,014.2	3,139.8
4. Exports to Soviet Pacific ports	29,611.1	13,907.5	17,613.1	8,757.0	12,807.0	24,022.2
Imports from Soviet Pacific ports	8,337.1	5,892.8	16,997.3	7,108.5	4,945.5	5,021.9
Total value	37,948.2	19,800.3	34,610.4	15,865.5	17,752.5	29,044.1
5. China's total exports to Russia	51,243.1	18,400.2	29,636.8	17,956.9	17,377.7	32,572.7
China's total imports from Russia	11,554.3	8,049.7	19,545.3	11,935.4	6,657.3	11,849.2
TOTAL VALUE	62,797.4	26,449.9	49,182.1	29,892.3	24,035.0	44,421.9

[29] Afanas'ev-Kazanskii. 'Ekonomicheskoe polozhenie Zapadnogo Kitaya' (The Economic Situation of West China). *Novyi Vostok.* No. 3. 1923.

Russian trade. Through the mediation of Kuldja merchants negotiations opened at the beginning of 1920 between the Chinese administration of the Ili (Kuldja) territory and local Soviet governmental bodies. They were concluded on 27 May 1920 by the signing of a protocol (the Ili Protocol) which regulated border trade between the Ili territory and neighboring Soviet areas.

The Ili Protocol authorized the Soviet side to 'open in Kuldja a Soviet government agency to deal with diplomatic and commercial problems.' The Chinese authorities of the Ili territory could in their turn open an agency for the same purpose in Vernyi [Alma-Ata]. The protocol stipulated that commercial dealings between the two neighboring territories would be transacted at Hocheng [Hoerkwosze].

Trade between Sinkiang and the Soviet territories of Central Asia began to develop again after the signing of the protocol. At first, however, it remained limited in scope while only private firms and local governmental organs were concerned, and included only a small number of items.

According to data published by the People's Commissariat of Foreign Trade of the Russian Soviet Federative Socialist Republic the trade of Soviet Central Asia with Sinkiang province reached a volume of approximately 300 tons in 1920, compared to 50,000 tons before the war; although it doubled by 1922, it then equaled only 600 tons. Sino-Soviet trade developed further in this area only after the central Soviet departments, which carried a great number of items needed by the Sinkiang population, began their activities.

The second period: 1923-1924. After the eviction of the interventionists and White Russians from the Maritime Territory, the legislation of the Russian Soviet Federative Socialist Republic became effective in the Soviet Far East; foreign trade became a monopoly of a single governmental body, the People's Commissariat of Foreign Trade. A commission of this body toured the Far East at the end of 1922 and Soviet foreign trade organizations were set up there at the beginning of the following year. However, the unified tariff of the Russian Soviet Federative Socialist Republic was modified for the Far Eastern territory, and a number of special exceptions were introduced. In view of the remoteness of the territory from Russia's central industrial areas and of postwar conditions, the Soviet government authorized duty-free imports to the Soviet Far East and the Pacific coast north of the Amur estuary.[31]

Trade between the Far Eastern Territory and China developed at this time on both Russian and Chinese gound. Many representatives of important Chinese firms (Sung Tai Hang, Shih I Tang, I Tai Hang) resided in Vladivostok and other cities of the territory (Khabarovsk, Blagoveshchensk, Chita, etc.); these agents not only dealt in imports and exports but also purchased the items in which they were interested throughout the Far Eastern Territory. Their extensive contacts with hunters, ginseng gatherers and fishermen enabled them to bypass the governmental economic organizations, which were then only beginning their activity, and purchase directly

---

[31] Ruling of the Far Eastern Revolutionary Committee, 16-17 January 1923.

furs, ginseng, trepang, reindeer antlers and other goods which they themselves exported to China, licensed by the Soviet foreign trade organizations.

Export-import operations with China were also carried out under government license by the Russian private firm I. I. Tschurin & Co., Ltd., the German firm Kunst und Albers and others, which possessed agencies and enterprises on Soviet Far Eastern territory for processing raw materials.

However, as the Soviet foreign trade organizations became firmly established, Soviet export-import operations were gradually concentrated in the hands of governmental bodies, mainly *Dal'gostorg,* (Far Eastern Trade Bureau), which in 1923 took over from the *Sibdal'vneshtorg* office the Soviet commercial representation in Manchuria. *Dal'gostorg* and other Soviet governmental bodies strengthened their commercial bonds not only with Manchuria but also with cities of Central China (Tientsin, Shanghai).

The establishment of commercial relations between the Soviet Union and the central areas of China was warmly supported by Chinese business circles. Despite the absence of normal diplomatic relations, Chinese firms exported more than 6,000 tons of tea to the U.S.S.R. in the first years after the liberation of Vladivostok from the Whites and the occupation forces; China then encountered great difficulties in marketing this product owing to Japanese and Indian competition. On the other hand, Russian timber, salted fish (Siberian salmon, humpback salmon) reindeer antlers, ginseng, trepang, sea kale and other Far Eastern products for which there was great demand in China began to reach the Shanghai and Tientsin markets.

Sino-Soviet trade along the Sinkiang border also increased considerably at this time. Commercial operations were carried out by Chinese traders, who were authorized by the 1920 Ili Protocol to enter Soviet territory, and by Soviet governmental bodies which were established in Sinkiang province.

SINO-SOVIET TRADE (EXCEPT FOR SINKIANG PROVINCE)
IN 1923-1924[32]

Russian Imports from China			*Russian Exports to China*		
Goods	*tons*	*thous. rubles*	*Goods*	*tons*	*thous. rubles*
Tea	6,153	5,736	Timber & lumber	96,218	2,364
Animal fat	21	736	Coal & coke	65,198	795
Shoes & leather wares	—	214	Fish	3,993	482
Woolen, hemp, linen fabrics & products	235	254	Petroleum products	1,125	53
Paper & paper products	235	185	Furs	4	46
			Caviar	24	38
Wheat & other grain	2,809	171	Scrap iron	609	34
Leather	358	141			
TOTAL	15,140	8,951	TOTAL	170,339	4,255

[32] *Foreign Trade of the U.S.S.R for* 1918-1927/8. Statistical survey. Leningrad-Moskva. 1931. [Russ.].

Animal casings were the only product still purchased in Sinkiang by American and West European firms and transported for export to Chinese ports over the Hami [Qomul]-Lanchow [Kaolan] route. All other products, of vital importance for the economic prosperity of the province (wool, cattle, undressed leather), were exported to the Soviet Union.

SINO-SOVIET TRADE IN 1923/24 ALONG THE SOVIET-SINKIANG BORDER[33]

Sinkiang Exports to the USSR				USSR Exports to Sinkiang		
Goods	*units*	*amount*	*thous. rubles*	*Goods*	*amount (in tons)*	*thous. rubles*
Wool	tons	2,548	1,121	Cotton fabric	66	149
Horses	head	8,141	407	Sugar	105	21
	tons	2,639		Electrometallurgical wares	83	21
Small livestock	head	50,694	314	Matches	23	9
	tons	4,068	267	Porcelain, pottery, glass	21	9
Cattle	head	6,292				
	tons	2,053	35			
Undressed leather	tons	89				
TOTAL	tons	11,544	2,198	TOTAL	830	413

The appearance of Soviet products on the Sinkiang market undermined the speculation of America, German and other foreign firms. Sinkiang's trade with the United States and Western Europe, which had developed when the province had been cut off from the Soviet Union during the Civil war, began a swift decline.

In contrast to trade with Western Europe, the United States and Japan, which led to an unfavorable balance of payments and undermined industry, Sino-Soviet trade offered China distinct advantages.

While the capitalist countries used China as a market for their products and capital investments, the Soviet Union's trade with China was bilateral and mutually beneficial. Soviet purchases in China were then much greater than sales. The removal of all artificial barriers between the Soviet Union and China by the treaty of 31 May 1924 opened extensive possibilities for the development of Sino-Soviet economic relations. Both parties were interested in establishing their trade on a legal basis, since this accorded with the basic interests of both Soviet and Chinese peoples.

1) The Russian October Revolution laid the foundations for a new era in the relations between the Chinese and Soviet peoples. The Soviet government renounced all the inequitable treaties which concerned China concluded by tsarist Russia with China or with other states. The new Soviet policy received the warmest sympathy

---

[33] Foreign Trade of the U.S.S.R. for 1918-1927/8.

of the Chinese people. Chinese progressive circles saw in Soviet Russia a reliable friend and a protector of national independence.

The establishment of friendly relations between Soviet Russia and China encountered, however, serious difficulties; the imperialist intervention against Soviet Russia led to the temporary occupation of the Soviet Far East and to Russia being isolated from China; moreover, the continued imperialist domination of China deprived the Chinese people of sovereignty in international relations.

2) Relations between Soviet Russia and China gradually improved as Soviet territories were liberated from the White Russians and foreign occupation forces. Widespread popular agitation for the recognition of the Soviet government developed in spite of countermeasures taken by international imperialism and sabotage by Chinese reactionaries. Commercial relations between the border areas of both states were restored along the entire Sino-Soviet land frontier. Governmental commercial organizations were set up in Soviet Russia for handling the Chinese trade, and Chinese business circles became increasingly interested in trading with the Soviet Union. Favorable conditions for the establishment of normal relations between China and the Soviet Union developed in 1924; the Soviet government's international position had improved and the Chinese revolutionary movement against imperialism and domestic reaction had grown stronger.

3) The Sino-Soviet 'Agreement on General Principles for Settling Issues between the U.S.S.R. and the Chinese Republic,' signed in Peking on 31 May 1924, was China's first equitable treaty based on equal rights and mutual respect of sovereignty. This agreement laid a firm basis for the development of economic relations between the U.S.S.R. and the Chinese Republic. It broke the chain of inequitable treaties which bound China to the imperialist powers.

The Sino-Soviet treaty aroused the ire of the imperialists, who saw it as a menace to their supremacy in China.

CHAPTER SIX

ECONOMIC RELATIONS BETWEEN THE SOVIET UNION
AND CHINA IN 1925-1936

BY 1925 the domestic situation and the international position of the Soviet Union had improved. The national economy, which had been destroyed by the war, was being successfully rebuilt. The gross volume of agricultural production in 1924-1925 was valued at 9,031.3 million rubles in prewar prices, reaching 71 percent of the 1913 level; the gross volume of industrial production reached 5,333 million rubles compared to 7,000 million in 1913, also approximately 71 percent.

Lenin's electrification project had been particularly successful. The plan elaborated in 1921 by the State Commission for the Electrification of Russia advocated the construction of 30 power stations with a total output of 1,500,000 kw within 10 to 15 years; a total power of 152,350 kw had already been reached by the end of 1925 and an additional output of 326,000 kw was envisaged for 1926.

By this time diplomatic relations had been established with almost all the important capitalist states, except the United States. An understanding had been reached with Japan on main issues; in accordance with the 'Convention Concerning the Basic Principles Defining the Relationship of the Union of Socialist Soviet Republics with Japan,' signed in Peking on 20 January 1925, the Japanese occupation forces were withdrawn from North Sakhalin on 15 May 1925 and the sovereign rights of the Soviet Union were thus restored throughout the Soviet Far East.

Until then Japan had been one of the main instigators of armed intervention against the Soviet Union by her support of the White Russian forces of hetman Semenov and other tsarist generals who had taken refuge in Japan or in South Manchuria after their defeat by the Soviet Army; the Japanese government now undertook the reciprocal obligation to prohibit throughout the territory under its jurisdiction the existence of organizations or groups 'claiming to constitute the government of any part of the other party's territory.'

The Soviet Union consolidated its domestic situation and international position while increasing conflicts were developing within the imperialist camp. The Washington Nine-Power Treaty, which forced Japan to make concessions in favor of the United States and Britain in the spheres of influence which she had acquired during the war years, established only a temporary balance of power. New conflicts were developing in the Far East between the main imperialist rivals—Japan and the United States. The strengthening of the economy and international position of the Soviet Union was reflected in the expansion of her foreign trade.

The Soviet Union's exports amounted to 579 million rubles in 1924/25 compared to 373 million rubles for the previous year; imports increased from 233 million to 723 million rubles in the same period. This expansion of foreign trade was consistent with the structure of the Soviet economy. Economic reconstruction and planned industrialization demanded increasing importation of machinery and certain raw materials; this led in turn to an increase of exports to cover payments and foreign currency reserves.

At the same time capitalist countries which found some difficulty in selling their commodities were highly interested in the Russian market. In 1926 a number of capitalist governments abandoned the financial boycott and, to promote their exports, began to guarantee commercial transactions concluded with the Soviet Union (Germany took this step in 1926, Austria in 1927 and Britain in 1929).

Neighboring Asiatic countries were particularly interested in expanding their trade with the Soviet Union. Geographical proximity, combined with the remoteness of the European and American industrial markets, gave evident economic advantages to such trade. The Soviet Union's new commercial policy, based on Leninist policies toward the oppressed nations of the East, was also an important factor.

On the basis of the Sino-Soviet treaty of 31 May 1924, the Soviet government extended considerable assistance to China for the restoration of her sovereign rights in North Manchuria. The interventionist troops and interallied administration were compelled to withdraw from this region, and the authority of the Chinese officials was thus reinstated. The North Manchurian economy benefited from the C.E.R.'s return to normal commercial activity once the railroad became jointly administered by the Soviet Union and China. While Manchuria's main harbor, Dairen (Dalny), was controlled by Japan, and Japanese firms used their dominant position in Dairen and on the South Manchurian Railroad to dictate conditions for North Manchuria's exports, the Soviet government granted favorable terms to Chinese firms for the transit of their goods through the Soviet harbor of Vladivostok which was connected to Manchuria by a direct railroad line.

Chinese merchants were authorized to buy Soviet goods in Vladivostok and reexport them to other countries through the free port on Egersheld wharf. Extensive border trade also developed at Lake Hanka [Hinka Omo] (Turii Rog), along the Ussuri river (Iman-Hulin [Linkiang]), at Sanchakow [Tungning], in the towns of Blagoveshchensk and Heiho [Sahalien] and in other localities. The Chinese border population of these areas, which found it extremely difficult to export local produce (mainly soybean) over several hundred miles, to remote railroad stations, was offered the possibility of selling them along the border to the Soviet *Dal'gostorg,* and of purchasing (at the same time) essential industrial products (kerosene, cotton fabrics, salt, matches, agricultural implements and other goods).

The Soviet government opened the Sinkiang border to the unlicensed importation of Chinese goods, and Chinese firms were authorized to participate in a number of fairs held in Central Asia (the Kuyandy fair in Semipalatinsk Province and the Karkara fair in the region of Semireche [Dzhetysu] as well as in the Nizhni Novgorod fair. Chinese and other Asiatic firms were permitted to open agencies on Soviet territory and effect commercial transactions through the Moscow Commodity Exchange.

The commercial ties established by Soviet foreign trade organizations on Chinese territory also expanded considerably in 1924-1925. A Soviet Trade Delegation opened in 1925 in Tientsin, with branches in Shanghai and Harbin and commercial agencies in Urumchi [Tihwa], Kuldja, Kashgar [Shufu] and Chuguchak [Tahcheng]; the network of Soviet economic organizations also widened.

The following Soviet organizations carried out commercial activities on the territory of China proper (behind the Great Wall) in 1925-1926:

1) *Dal'gostorg,* for the export and import of soybean, furs, sea products reindeer antlers, ginseng and other secondary items;

2) *Neftesindikat* (Oil Syndicate), exporting Soviet petroleum products;

3) *Tekstil'sindikat* (Textile Syndicate), exporting Russian cotton fabrics and other textiles;

4) *Chaeypravlenie* (Tea Bureau), importing tea from China;

5) *Sovtorgflot,* for shipping and forwarding operations.

Agencies of *Dal'les* (Far Eastern Timber Bureau), *Dal'ugol'* (Far Eastern Coal Bureau) and the *Transport* company operated in China for a short period. Sino-Soviet trade also passed through branch offices of *Tsentrosoyuz* (the All-Russian Central Union of Consumers' Societies, which had a branch in England registered as a British firm), while most financial operations passed through *Dal'bank* (Far Eastern Bank).

The Soviet side was represented during this period in Sinkiang Province by the following organizations: 1) the *Sherst* joint-stock company, which purchased mainly wool; agencies of *Kazgostorg* (Kazakh Governmental Trade Bureau), which imported undressed leather, animal casings, livestock as well as other goods, and exported Soviet products; 2) an agency of *Glavkhlopok* (Main Cotton Bureau), which imported raw cotton; 3) branch offices of *Sovtorgflot* and of the *Transport* company, for shipping and forwarding operations.

Other representatives handling transactions for Soviet organizations in Sinkiang included the *Kazgosmedtorgprom* (Kazakh Governmental Medical Trade and Production Bureau) agency in Kuldja, which provided drugs and medical supplies; *Neftesindikat,* which imported petroleum products to Sinkiang; and *Rossredaz* (the Russian Central Asian Commercial Company), which purchased coarse undressed leather.

Payments were made through special accounts of the commercial agencies or through the local branches of Chinese banks.

The signing of the Sino-Soviet treaty of 31 May 1924 was thus followed by mutual efforts of Soviet organizations and Chinese business circles to expand trade; the organizations created for this purpose served the interests of both the Soviet Union and China and promoted commercial development.

SINO-SOVIET ECONOMIC RELATIONS DURING THE FIRST CHINESE
REVOLUTIONARY CIVIL WAR (1925-1927)

A mighty wave of agitation swept China at the beginning of 1925. At that time China's working class, led by the newly created Communist Party, began to play a leading role in the nationwide revolutionary struggle. The revolutionary stronghold in the south—the Canton government—gained strength with Communist support. In February-March 1925 the revolutionary Canton forces launched their Eastern Campaign, defeating the southern warlord Chen Kiung-ming, whose forces menaced Canton from the east.

The second All-Chinese Trade Union Congress, representing more than 500,000 workers, convened in Canton on 1 May 1925 and summoned China's working class to active participation in the nationwide struggle against imperialism and against the warlords, the main support for the Chinese feudal rulers.

Industrial city workers of Central and North China demanded from their employers a shortening of the working day and the recognition of their political rights. Strikes which broke out at the beginning of May 1925 in one textile plant in Shanghai and several plants in Tsingtao were supported by workers in other industries.

The peasant movement also intensified. Insurgent peasants of Kwangtung and other South China provinces created peasant unions and vigilance committees, opposed the authority of the *tuhao* and *liehshen*,[1] disarmed and dispersed the *Mintuan* detachments[2] and joined the ranks of the nationwide revolutionary movement. In November 1925 the peasant vigilance committees supported the National-Revolutionary Army's Second Eastern Campaign which defeated the Chen Kiung-ming forces and actively cooperated in strengthening the Canton government.

The struggle against feudalism merged with the opposition to the imperialists, who held commanding positions in the Chinese economy; this determined the nature of the developing bourgeois-democratic revolution in China.

The imperialists and the Chinese reactionary circles gathered their forces against the revolution and attempted to terrorize the Chinese people. Following the massacre of Chinese workers by the Japanese in Shanghai and Tsingtao, the British police of the international settlement opened fire on demonstrating students and workers on 30 May 1925. The 'Thirtieth of May' events roused widespread indignation among Chinese workers, intellectuals, and middle classes, and consolidated the revolutionary popular front. Mass demonstrations were held in Peking, Hankow, Changsha, Tsingtao, Tientsin, Nanking, Amoy, Foochow, Kaifeng, Hangchow and other cities against the regime of feudal and imperialist domination.

The spearhead of the anti-imperialist struggle was directed at this stage against Britain, which bore the responsibility for the 'Thirtieth of May' events. A boycott by the Chinese population caused the volume of British trade to decrease rapidly, while a 16-month strike of Hongkong dockers paralysed a substantial part of British commercial shipping operating in Chinese waters. In the face of determined popular opposition, the imperialist powers changed their tactics. In addition to raising their military potential in Chinese waters and in the various foreign concessions, they strove to consolidate the political influence of the Chinese reactionary circles.

---

[1] The *tuhao* (local despots) and *liehshen* (malicious notables) were the most cruel oppressors of the Chinese peasantry.
[2] The *mintuan* were armed detachments maintained by the landowners to protect their interests and repress peasant agitation.

For this purpose the members of the 1922 Washington Conference called a conference on customs in Peking in August 1925; commissions dealing with the cancellation of extraterritorial rights in China met a few months later, in January 1926 (the Washington Conference had resolved that these issues were to be examined within three months of its conclusion). The foreign and Chinese reactionary press tried to describe these meetings as important political events, which took place supposedly to satisfy the Chinese people's anti-imperialistic demands.

The imperialists also attempted to isolate and discredit the Chinese revolutionary movement by asserting that 'Moscow's hand' was at work in China, that the Chinese revolutionaries were 'Russian agents,' etc.

British Foreign Secretary Chamberlain and Lord Birkenhead, Secretary for Indian Affairs, accused the Soviet Union of 'undermining British policy in China' and demanded severance of diplomatic relations. Imperialist agents in the Chinese reactionary circles organized provocations against Soviet organizations in China in order to undermine the relations between China and the Soviet Union established by the treaty of 31 May 1924, and thus isolate China from the Soviet Union.

Trouble began at an early stage on the C.E.R. The restoration of Chinese sovereignty in the railroad concession zone, and the equitable participation of Chinese citizens in the railway administration was viewed very unfavorably by British, French and American ruling circles, for it set up an undesirable precedent to imperialist property in China and strengthened the arguments of progressive circles for the repeal of the special rights and privileges enjoyed by foreigners. The C.E.R.'s profitability had improved considerably, its freight turnover expanded, the training of Chinese personnel had progressed satisfactorily and the railroad was technologically among the best in the world.

Two reactionary generals—Pao Kuei-ching, President of the C.E.R. board of directors, and Chang Hwan-hsiang, chief of staff of the military guard of the C.E.R.—served the imperialist interests in Manchuria; before the reinstatement of the Soviet officials on the C.E.R., these two men had profited from the lack of any tight control and used the railroad to derive personal gain. The financial control to which the C.E.R. was now subjected again excluded any possibility of extracting personal profit from an official position.

Local military authorities attempted to disrupt the operation of the C.E.R. by paralyzing first the Kwanchengtze terminus, and later the entire southern section of the railroad. Ivanov, the Soviet C.E.R. director, was arrested in Harbin, on 21 January 1926, and a series of measures against railroad workers followed—arrests, searches and the suppression of unions.

These provocations by the local warlord clique were directed against both Chinese and Soviet interests. Imperialist circles, which were inciting China to clash with the Soviet Union and violate the Sino-Soviet treaty, exploited the repercussions of the conflict to demonstrate that the Chinese administration was incapable of fulfilling the international obligations it had assumed and of preserving law and order throughout the country. They tried to discredit the very idea of equal rights in their relations with China and to justify the need to maintain extraterritoriality.

Chinese public figures, business circles, and even official representatives of the Peking government, appreciating the danger and disadvantage to China in severing relations with the Soviet Union, severely condemned the illegal acts committed by local warlords and did everything in their power to settle the conflict developing over the C.E.R. A note from the Peking Foreign Minister to the People's Commissar of the U.S.S.R. stated on this issue: 'Since the Chinese Eastern Railroad serves the mutual interests of your government and ours, I hope that if the employees of the C.E.R., both your nationals and ours, shall adopt a spirit of mutual sincerity and equity, in order to smooth out issues in complete agreement and for the best, without striving to obtain merely temporary and unilateral benefits, both parties will then get along together splendidly and there will be no cause for misunderstandings.'[3]

Negotiations which opened on 24 January 1926 between the Soviet consul in Mukden and the chief of the central diplomatic department of the three eastern provinces were concluded by the signing of 'Basic Points for an Agreement,' which provided for the release of the C.E.R. director and the renewed operation of the railroad on the basis of the 1924 agreement.

Despite this first setback, international reactionary circles did not abandon their plans for wrecking Sino-Soviet relations. These circles were alarmed not only by Sino-Soviet cooperation on the C.E.R., but also by the development of Sino-Soviet trade. The imperialist press waged a violent campaign against the presence of Soviet representatives in China.

These anti-Soviet press attacks became particularly violent after the Southern Revolutionary Army launched its 'Northern Campaign' *(Peifachün)*.[4] The Chinese reactionaries, supported by the Peking authorities, who were then considered to be the official Chinese government, obediently enacted the anti-Soviet policy of imperialist circles. Prior to the 'Northern Campaign' the various anti-Soviet provocations in the north of the country had remained purely local and had not been supported by the Peking authorities; after the campaign, however, the Peking government itself unleashed anti-Soviet press attacks.

At the beginning of September 1926, Chinese reactionary officials, acting on orders of Chang Tso-lin, Prime Minister of the three northeastern provinces,[5] seized a number of C.E.R. ships on the Sungari river, and occupied and closed the building housing the railroad's registration department. The Peking authorities, completely ignoring the Soviet proposal to 'examine carefully all issues arising as a result of existing agreements between the two states,' continued their open violation of the treaty of 31 May 1924.

The height of Peking's perfidious anti-Soviet policy was the raid on the Soviet Embassy in Peking by Chang Tso-lin's soldiers on 6 April 1927. Without having

---

[3] *Foreign Policy of the U.S.S.R. for* 1917-1944, Vol. 3, p. 43. Moskva. 1944. [Russ.].

[4] The National-Revolutionary Army created in Kwangtung province cleared the province of counter-revolutionaries at the beginning of 1926 and in July of that year launched a campaign to the north against the feudal-warlord ruling circles; this was called the 'Northern Campaign.'

[5] [This is the same as the 'three eastern provinces,' i.e., Heilungkiang, Kirin and Mukden—as Manchuria was designated before 1932.]

made any preliminary claims, an armed detachment of policemen and soldiers of the *Ankuochün*[6] forcibly entered the embassy grounds, arrested a number of Soviet and Chinese members of the staff and ransacked several buildings, including that of the military attaché.

The police and soldiers of the *Ankuochün,* wanting no impartial witnesses to their activities, refused to admit the Soviet chargé d'affaires to the premises. As is evident from the declaration of the Peking Minister of Foreign Affairs, these actions took place with the full knowledge and support of the diplomatic corps, and thus the true instigators of this disgraceful use of force and violation in international practice are clearly revealed.

The Soviet government demanded the release of the staff members and restitution of confiscated property; in protest it was forced to recall from Peking the charge d'affaires and the entire embassy, leaving only consular staff.

A note dispatched by the deputy of the People's Commissar of the U.S.S.R., Litvinov, stated: 'The Soviet government fully understands that irresponsible foreign imperialist circles are provoking the Soviet Union to war. The Soviet government fully understands that the Peking cabinet has become a pawn in the game played by foreign imperialist circles. But the Soviet government's policy is, has been, and shall be, based on the interests of the laboring masses of the world, including those of the Chinese people and the working classes of all nations.'[7]

The progressive circles grouped around Sun Yat-sen had an entirely different attitude toward the Soviet Union. Sun Yat-sen's new government, which was established in Canton at the beginning of 1924, steadfastly endeavored to establish friendly political and economic relations with the Soviet Union.

The business and commercial circles in South China which had made efforts to establish connections with Soviet foreign trade organizations after the conclusion of the 1924 Sino-Soviet treaty were warmly supported by the head of the Canton government. A group of Chinese merchants representing the Chinese United Petroleum Corporation of Shanghai opened negotiations in the middle of August 1924 with representatives of *Dal'gostorg* for the purchase of petroleum products from the Soviet *Neftesindikat.* Representatives of Canton commercial organizations joined these negotiations in the middle of November, and an agreement was concluded with *Neftesindikat* on 27 February 1925 for the sale of Soviet petroleum products in South China. The first shipment of benzine, kerosene, oil and fuel oil soon left Vladivostok for Canton on the Soviet steamship *Indigirka,* and the sale of these products began in May 1925.

The arrival of Soviet petroleum products in South China, while the Canton government was subjected to a *de facto* blockade by Britain and the United States, helped the Chinese authorities to combat speculation, lower the artificially soaring market prices on kerosene and benzine, and supply local demands for petroleum products.

---

[6] [In December 1927 Chang Tso-lin created an army which was to oppose the Kuomintang's national-revolutionary forces, and named it *Ankuochün*—governmental pacification forces.]
[7] *Foreign Policy of the U.S.S.R. in 1917-1944*, Vol. 3, p. 110. Moskva. 1944.

Trade with Soviet organizations was highly profitable for the Chinese. Participation of foreign intermediaries was avoided, since the goods were delivered directly to the governmental distributors; petroleum products could thus be sold at fixed prices despite the rise of their market price.

This trade was hindered, however, by certain factors. Transport was the first problem. The small number of Soviet and Chinese vessels traveling between Canton and the closest Soviet port, Vladivostok, (a distance of 1,700 nautical miles) excluded any possibility of regular passenger and freight services. Since the Soviet petroleum products from Vladivostok reached the warehouses specially opened by the Chinese in Canton and Swatow [Shantow] quite irregularly, sales were necessarily affected. Secondly, the Chinese organizations trading with the Soviet Union encountered numerous difficulties in Canton. Right-wing Kuomintang circles, in control of the commercial and financial affairs of the Canton government, tried to sever the existing commercial ties with the Soviet Union. The well-known right-wing leader, Sung Tzu-wen,[8] who managed the sale of petroleum products throughout the zone controlled by the Canton government, had close ties with American Standard Oil and Texas Oil, and with their cooperation undermined the sale of Soviet petroleum products. A strict licensing system was imposed for the marketing of Soviet petroleum products, while American benzine and kerosene were sold through third parties without limitation.

In spite of all these difficulties, trade with the Soviet Union continued to interest Chinese merchants and progressive circles. The policy of better relations with the Soviet Union, the first socialist state, which had laid the foundation for new bonds between nations based on complete equality and mutual respect, became increasingly popular among the Chinese masses.

The great revolutionary and democrat, Sun Yat-sen, actively advocated the establishment of friendly relations with the Soviet Union. In the message sent just before his death to the members of the Central Executive Committee of the Soviet Union Sun Yat-sen enjoined the Kuomintang to maintain unbroken contact with the Soviet Union, and expressed confidence that the Soviet Union would soon find a staunch friend in a liberated China and that 'in the great struggle for the liberation of oppressed nations of the world both allies will march hand in hand to victory.'

SINO-SOVIET TRADE IN 1925-1927

The volume of trade between the two countries began to increase noticeably after the establishment of diplomatic relations and the arrival in China of Soviet governmental trade delegations. It expanded from 61.4 to 99.8 million *taels,* i.e., by 62 percent from 1925 to 1927. Trade between Soviet Far Eastern ports and Chinese ports developed particularly swiftly, increasing in the same period from 55,991,000 *taels*

---

[8] In 1924 Sung Tzu-wen was president of the Central Bank of Canton. During the Kuomintang dictatorship he served as Finance Minister, Minister of Foreign Affairs, and President of the Executive *Yuan* [Council]. He fled to Formosa after Chang Kai-shek's defeat.

to 91,108,000 *taels*. China's maritime trade with European Russia, which had been interrupted by the Russian civil war, also increased from 405,900 *taels* to 3,103,000 *taels*.

The rapid increase of the export-import value was caused to a certain extent by the depreciation of the Chinese *tael* (which dropped from 84 cents in 1925 to 69 cents in 1927), insofar as prices were calculated in Chinese currency. However, even if American currency is used for calculations (its exchange rate remained constant during this period), the Sino-Soviet volume of trade is found to have increased constantly from US $51,598,000 in 1925 to US $68,849,000 in 1927. This increase in the volume of trade was due mainly to an increase in the value of Chinese exports.

The Sino-Soviet commercial operations continued, as before, to fall into two main categories—Soviet trade with Manchuria and China proper, and trade with Sinkiang Province.

Russian trade with China proper and Manchuria. The value of Soviet imports from China proper and Manchuria was more than twice that of exports to these areas. Tea was the main Soviet import from China proper.

Tea accounted for 80 percent of the value of Soviet imports from China (not including Sinkiang); this was approximately one third of China's total exports of this item. Other items imported by the Soviet Union from China proper and Manchuria in relatively constant quantities were animal fats, undressed leather and vegetable oils.

In addition to importing Chinese goods for domestic consumption, in the autumn of 1925 Soviet trade organizations began to purchase considerable amounts of soybean, oilcake and vegetable oil in Manchuria for re-export to Western Europe. In the autumn and winter of 1925-26 *Dal'gostorg* shipped over the C.E.R. 5,823,384 *poods* of various goods to Vladivostok for re-export, including 3,982,635 *poods* of soybean, 1,410,252 *poods* of oilcake and 430,497 *poods* of vegetable oil. *Dal'gostorg* also purchased one million *poods* of soybean in the Manchurian border areas—Mishan, Hulinhsien, Sanchakow [Tungning], and Fuchin [Fugdin]—which it shipped directly to the nearest stations of the Ussuri railroad.

Many North Manchurian firms, such as the Eastern Asiatic Co., the Siberian Co. and others also re-exported Manchurian soybean and soybean products through Vladivostok.

Chinese soybean, oilcake and soybean oil re-exported through Vladivostok were purchased almost entirely by Britain and Japan in 1925-1927; at the same time the Soviet Union began to re-export these products also to Germany, Holland and Denmark.

In view of China's mounting difficulties with her exports as a result of the severe competition for markets among capitalist countries, Soviet purchases in China were welcomed by extensive Chinese business and commercial circles. This particularly applied to tea, which China encountered serious difficulties in marketing. Not only did Britain and Japan buy no China tea whatsoever, but they endeavored to prevent its exportation, since it competed on the world market with the Japanese and the Indian tea.

The development of Soviet exports to China was also undermined by the imperialist powers in control of Chinese foreign trade, despite the geographical proximity between the two countries and the convenient transport facilities.

VOLUME OF USSR TRADE WITH CHINA IN 1925-1927 ALONG VARIOUS ROUTES[9]

Type of trade	1925		1926		1927	
	thous. taels	*thous. US $*	*thous. taels*	*thous. US $*	*thous. taels*	*thous. US $*
Trade between European ports and China:						
Imports to China	73.6	61.8	84.2	64.0	36.2	25.0
Exports from China	332.3	279.1	1,382.7	1,050.9	3,066.8	2,116.1
TOTAL	405.9	340.9	1,466.9	1,114.9	3,103.0	2,141.1
USSR trade with China through Amur ports:						
Imports to China	10.4	8.7	137.9	104.8	109.7	75.7
Exports from China	21.3	17.9	3.4	2.6	0.2	75.8
TOTAL	31.7	26.6	141.3	107.4	109.9	75.8
USSR trade with China through Far Eastern ports						
Imports to China	8,557.4	7,188.2	16,919.3	12,858.7	17,787.1	12,273.1
Exports from China	47,433.7	39,844.3	62,159.2	47,241.0	73,320.8	50,591.4
TOTAL	55,991.1	47,032.5	79,078.4	60,099.7	91,107.9	62,864.5
USSR trade with China over the Siberian land border						
Imports to China	4,823.6	4,051.8	5,570.7	4,233.7	4,674.3	3,225.3
Exports from China	174.4	146.5	575.0	437.0	786.4	542.6
TOTAL	4,998.0	4,198.3	6,145.7	4,670.7	5,460.7	3,767.9
Total volume of trade:						
Imports to China	13,465.0	11,310.5	22,712.1	17,261.2	22,607.3	15,599.1
Exports from China	47,961.7	40,287.8	64,120.3	48,731.5	77,174.2	53,250.2
TOTAL	61,426.7	51,598.3	86,832.4	65,992.7	99,781.5	68,849.3

Although Soviet exports to China proper and Manchuria increased from 1925 to 1927, their value still remained less than half that of the corresponding imports.

The British, American and Japanese imperialist monopolies, which controlled China's major banks and ports and also the customs, dominating other foreign firms and Chinese enterprises. Obviously, despite the interest in Soviet products among Chinese merchants, the foreign monopolies could obstruct and check the expansion of Soviet exports to China.

[9] *The China Year-Book*, Tientsin, 1929-1930. pp. 162-173.

Despite these unfavorable conditions, considerable amounts of some Soviet export items did reach the Chinese market. Suchan coal, Ussuri timber, Kamchatka fish, as well as furs, sea products and textiles found a large market there. Soviet cotton and linen fabrics were in demand even in important textile centers such as Shanghai.

MAIM ITEMS OF USSR IMPORTS FROM CHINA PROPER AND MANCHURIA[10]

Goods	1924/25		1925/26		1926/27	
	tons	thous. rubles	tons	thous. rubles	tons	thous. rubles
Tea	7,103	8,389	16,740	17,613	15,113	15,826
Wheat	17,924	2,124	334	40	—	—
Animal fats	1,889	833	1,857	782	2,016	913
Coarse undressed leather	372	178	898	578	214	141
Fine undressed leather	...	...	1,052	1,337	1,214	1,198
Vegetable oil	372	113	522	128	563	134
Cotton fabrics	19	48	43	135	43	102
TOTAL	31,215	12,509	28,742	23,033	21,798	19,690

Chinese firms opened special stores in Harbin and other cities of North Manchuria dealing in Soviet products such as furs, fishery products, sea products, fabrics and other goods.

RE-EXPORTS FROM NORTH MANCHURIA TO BRITAIN AND JAPAN THROUGH VLADIVOSTOK[11] (in tons)

Goods	1924/25	1925/26	1926/27
Soybean	590,003	602,140	737,371
Oilcake	108,165	373,406	489,639
Soybean oil	31,386	33,717	45,966

Many Chinese firms increased their purchases from *Dal'gostorg* wholesale stores in Vladivostok. The activities in Vladivostok of large Chinese enterprises such as Shih I Tang, Sung Tai Hang, I Tai Hang and others expanded; their representatives usually worked through a single commercial organization, directed from 1925-1930 by the merchant Wang Fu-chin.

The entire stock of such export items as reindeer antler, ginseng, bear gall, and musk, most of the sea-kale and trepang, and some types of furs exported to China were sold in 1925-1927 by *Dal'gostorg* in Vladivostok.

[10] *Foreign Trade of the U.S.S.R. in 1918-1927/28*, pp. 592-594.
[11] *Foreign Trade of the U.S.S.R. in 1918-1927/28*, pp. 783-784.

Soviet trade with Sinkiang Province. Conditions for Sino-Soviet trade across the Sinkiang border were more favorable for both parties. Since Sinkiang was situated far from the powerful British, Japanese, American and French naval and economic bases in the ofreign concessions and treaty ports, the imperialist powers did not interfere in this region to the same extent as in Manchuria and China proper. The provincial Chinese administration and merchants were thus better able to protect their foreign trade interests.

MAIN ITEMS OF SOVIET EXPORTS TO CHINA PROPER AND MANCHURIA[12]

Goods	1924/25		1925/26		1926/27	
	tons	thous. rubles	tons	thous. rubles	tons	thous. rubles
Timber	93,451	1,608	38,337	727	25,128	603
Coal	116,005	1,038	161,767	1,482	140,247	1,267
Petroleum products	6,076	673	12,907	1,750	7,333	1,100
Fish	5,314	481	4,527	629	2,384	428
Cotton and linen fabrics	—	—	578	2,710	364	1,717
Electrometallurgical products	946	266	17,207	2,218	19,242	1,865
Furs	3	245	8	305	7	42
Red and black caviar	16	18	30	53	38	52
TOTAL	231,567	6,426	239,196	11,134	198,160	8,512

The first few years of trade with Soviet Russia had a favorable effect on the Sinkiang economy. Commercial operations with Soviet organizations, based on mutually advantageous prices, helped stabilize the Sinkiang market. This undermined speculation in scarce European and American industrial products imported by British, American and German firms along the costly Tientsin (or Shanghai)—Lanchow [Kaolan]— Urumchi [Tihwa] route. Sinkiang's main products found a profitable market in the Soviet Union.

Wool, undressed leather and cotton imported from Sinkiang were important for the development of Soviet industry, while beef and other alimentary products were in demand among the population of the Soviet border towns.

Soviet fairs helped to increase the volume of trade with Sinkiang. In order to encourage the participation of Sinkiang merchants, the Soviet government authorized unlicensed and duty-free importation from Sinkiang to these fairs and extended the same conditions to the exportation of products purchased in the U.S.S.R.

Sinkiang merchants were active in three Soviet fairs: the Kuyandy fair (Semipalatinsk Province), the Karkara fair (region of Semirechensky) and the Nizhni Novgorod fair. The first two of these, situated near the Sino-Soviet border, were visited in 1925-1927 mainly by the nomadic population of Soviet Central Asia and the Sinkiang

[12] *Foreign Trade of the U.S.S.R. in* 1918-1927/28, pp. 241-242.

border area. The annual volume of trade carried on by Sinkiang merchants reached one million rubles at the Kuyandy fair and approximately one and a half million in Karkara. Cattle was the main item, followed by wool and undressed leather. Trade with Sinkiang merchants at the Nizhni Novgorod fair was even more important.

SOVIET IMPORTS FROM SINKIANG PROVINCE IN 1924/25-1926/27[13]

Goods	Units	1924/25		1925/26		1926/27	
		amount	thous. rubles	amount	thous. rubles	amount	thous. rubles
Wool	tons	3,428	1,909	4,365	3,412	5,261	5,626
Horses	head	8,141	407	7,792	556	6,265	511
Cattle	head	12,933	609	10,611	563	13,073	756
	tons	4,237		3,475		4,269	
Small livestock	head	84,919	751	111,480	1,201	84,478	1,047
	tons	6,982		9,290		6,995	
Undressed leather	tons	427	240	532	502	85	104
Raw cotton	tons	181	137	2,004	1,574	2,676	2,453
TOTAL	tons	18,215	4,357	22,342	7,971	20,457	10,294

It attracted 71 Sinkiang firms in 1926 and 73 in 1927, and the volume of trade reached 6,228,000 and 7,044,000 rubles, respectively. The main items imported from Sinkiang to the Nizhni Novgorod fair were wool (approximately 30,000 *poods*), cotton (30,000-40,000 *poods*), fine undressed leather (approximately 500,000 pieces), coarse undressed leather (12,000-20,000 pieces), goat's wool (approximately 1,000 *poods*), as well as horsehair, raw silk and furs. The Sinkiang merchants used receipts from the sale of their goods to purchase Soviet cotton fabrics, sugar, plates, ironware and other products at the fairs.

In view of the great distance between the Nizhni Novgorod fair and the Sinkiang border, the Soviet organizations permitted the Sinkiang merchants to turn their goods in at the Sino-Soviet border or at the nearest border areas.[14]

Despite these excellent conditions, not all Sinkiang merchants could participate in the fairs. Many found it too costly to travel for several months to the Soviet Union, stock their unsold goods, and bear the necessary expenses until transactions were completed. This promoted the activity of Soviet organizations in Sinkiang Province, a particularly convenient arrangement for small and medium Sinkiang merchants

---

[13] *Foreign Trade of the U.S.S.R.* in 1918-1927/28, pp. 594-595.

[14] According to the Nizhni Novgorod fair regulations, a Sinkiang merchant offering a certain product had to present to the fair authorities a bill of lading of *Sovtorgflot* or *Transport*, proving that the goods in question had really been imported to the fair committee. After each sale the vendor either dispatched the goods to the buyer or turned them in at the border. Sinkiang goods which remained unsold at the end of the fair could either be shipped back free of duty and license or sold through the Moscow Commodity Exchange.

and producers of raw materials, since they could sell their goods on the spot to the Soviet trade body without using middlemen, who were generally large merchants.

In the period which followed the reopening of Sino-Soviet trade these fairs offered representatives of both parties the important opportunity of exchanging a large variety of items. The direct contact between vendor and buyer promoted the development of Sino-Soviet trade and particularly of Soviet exports, which increased from year to year: exports to Sinkiang in 1924/25 accounted for only 38.3 percent of the total volume of trade (2,683,000 rubles for exports and 4,357,000 for imports). This percentage increased to 43.5 in 1925/26 (exports for that year were valued at 6,096,000 rubles and imports at 7,971,000); in 1926/27 Soviet exports almost balanced imports, reaching 49.9 percent of the total volume of trade (exports, 10,232,000 rubles, and imports, 10,294,000 rubles).

SOVIET EXPORTS TO SINKIANG PROVINCE IN 1924/25-1926/27[15]

Goods	1924/25		1925/26		1926/27	
	tons	thous. rubles	tons	thous. rubles	tons	thous. rubles
Cotton fabrics	124	1,269	822	3,935	1,581	6,545
Sugar	404	307	978	642	1,649	851
Electrometallurgical products	211	100	441	273	919	580
Pottery, porcelain, glass	72	44	215	178	510	429
Kerosene	209	37	584	134	281	59
Matches	40	13	53	33	409	211
Tobacco products	6	31	5	15	60	222
Confectionery	11	14	10	16	28	28
Rubber products	9	46	2	8	34	98
TOTAL	3,010	2,683	4,676	6,096	7,302	10,232

The relative importance and value of the main Soviet export to Sinkiang (cotton fabrics) increased yearly. Textile exports increased by more than 400 percent between 1924-25 and 1926-27, and by the end of the period constituted 64.1 percent of the total value of Soviet exports to Sinkiang. Exports of sugar, electrometallurgical products, tobacco and rubber products, confectionery and other goods also increased noticeably. Soviet exports became the main source of supply for the Sinkiang population.

CONDITIONS IN CHINA AFTER THE DEFEAT OF THE
REVOLUTIONARY FORCES IN THE FIRST REVOLUTIONARY WAR

The year 1927 was significant in the development of the Chinese revolutionary movement. At the end of 1926 and the beginning of 1927 the national revolutionary forces

---

[15] *Foreign Trade of the U.S.S.R. for 1918-1927/28*, p. 243.

reached the Yangtze Kiang along its middle and lower reaches. The victory against the armies of Wu Pei-fu, Sun Chuan-fang, Chen Kiung-ming and other warlords stirred the urban and peasant masses into a revolutionary fervor. A powerful peasant movement developed along the route of the National Revolutionary Army, from south to north, and peasant leagues were created in many localities. Mao Tse-tung wrote: 'Fearing the peasant leagues, the most important *tuhao* [local despots] and *liehshen* [malicious notables] fled to Shanghai, less important ones escaped to Hankow, even lesser ones to Changsha, others to the district centers, while the small fry who remained in the villages threw themselves on the mercy of the peasant leagues.'[16]

Revolutionary agitation was also growing in the Chinese cities. At the beginning of 1927, 2,800,000 workers were registered in trade unions, and the Communist Party membership had grown to 57,900.

The Chinese Revolution was led by the working class under the banner of the Communist Party. In the cities liberated by the National Revolutionary Army, the workers began resolutely to implement the Chinese people's demands concerning the imperialist powers' 'rights' and 'possessions.' At the beginning of January 1927 local revolutionary organizations occupied the British concessions in Hankow and Kiukiang, leaving Britain no choice but to conclude an agreement with the Minister of Foreign Affairs of the national government, according to which these concessions were handed over to Chinese administration. As the National Revolutionary Army approached Shanghai the workers of this important industrial center organized combat groups and prepared for an armed struggle for democratic freedom and the independence of their homeland.

The urban and rural revolutionary movement undermined the semicolonial and semifeudal Chinese regime. The Chinese feudal rulers and bourgeoisie feared that the scope and goals of the Chinese Revolution were extending beyond a mere bourgeois revolution. This fear was manifested in the position adopted by the Kuomintang, which betrayed the national interests and endeavored to suppress the Chinese Revolution with the help of American, British, French and Japanese imperialist circles. Having taken over the military command, the Kuomintang members, led by Chang Kai-shek, openly betrayed the revolution. Their arrival in Shanghai was followed by the massacre and mass execution of Chinese communists and prominent progressive figures of workers' organizations.

At this time the imperialists openly opposed the Chinese Revolution. On 24 March 1927 American and British warships bombarded Nanking, bringing death to hundreds of innocent victims. Chang Kai-shek's butchery in Shanghai and the Anglo-American bombardment of Nanking were further attempts to suppress the Chinese Revolution.

A right-wing Kuomintang government was set up in Nanking in September 1927 under the leadership of Chang Kai-shek.

The rovolutionary forces grouped around the Communist Party were relatively small and were compelled to abandon the major industrial and commercial centers, where the united front of the Chinese reactionary classes and the imperialist powers clearly

---

[16] Mao Tse-tung. *Selected Works*, Vol. 1, p. 39. [Russ.].

had the upper hand; they withdrew to rural areas where they could lead the struggle of the peasant masses, who had been the mainstay of the bourgeois-democratic revolution. Individual detachments led by communists set up revolutionary strong-holds in the provinces of Hunan and Shansi, the centers of the anti-feudal peasant movements.

The Workers and Peasants Revolutionary Army was organized in the autumn of 1927; it deployed in the easily defended mountain area of Chinganchang, where the first workers' and peasants' government was set up.

As conflicts developed between the imperialist powers at the end of the 1920's, Japan's position in China began to deteriorate. Even in Manchuria, Chang Hsüe-liang[17] in the face of Japanese opposition raised the Kuomintang flag and recognized the Nanking Kuomintang government as the official authority throughout China.

The decline of Japanese political influence was accompanied by increasing Kuomintang dependence on the United States. With Chang Kai-shek's support the Americans undermined the 'rights and privileges' of their rivals in China. Behind a smoke screen of democratic proclamations ('protection of the integrity' of Chinese territory, reestablishment of customs autonomy, etc.), the United States maneuvered for the reexamination of all existing agreements between China and other states and attempted to present this as a manifestation of 'friendly feelings' toward China in her struggle for national independence. The real goal was to deprive Japan and Britain of their spheres of influence in China and of all the privileges derived from their land bases, settlements and important industrial property; thus, with the support of the obedient Chang Kai-shek clique,[18] the United States began to clear the way for American capital.

IMPAIRMENT OF SINO-SOVIET RELATIONS AFTER THE ADVENT OF THE KUOMINTANG REACTIONARIES TO POWER

The advent to power of the reactionary Kuomintang government further undermined China's international status. Conflicts among the imperialist powers over China developed with renewed vigor, while the Chinese people's resistance to foreign domination declined. Instead of trying to rebuild the national economy and abolish foreign domination, the Nanking authorities directed their efforts toward suppressing the forces which were struggling for freedom and independence.

The Chang Kai-shek ruling clique disregarded the equitable 1924 Sino-Soviet treaty and the respect it granted Chinese sovereignty. They initiated a series of provocations against the Soviet Union, from whom they hoped to isolate China for the benefit of their imperialist masters.

[17] Marshal Chang Hsüe-liang, the son of Chang Tso-lin, headed the Chinese administration in Man-churia after his father was assassinated by the Japanese on 4 June 1928.

[18] American monopolies gained control of the Shanghai Electric Company in 1928 and of the Shanghai Telephone Company at the end of 1929; in 1929 a group of American aircraft companies, partners in the Curtis Company, entered into a joint American-Chinese company created in China—the Chinese National Aircraft Corporation.

Following the example of Chang Tso-lin and other northern warlords, the Nanking authorities set up unacceptable conditions for the establishment of Soviet diplomatic and commercial organizations on Kuomintang territory. The Soviet consulate in Shanghai was raided in October 1927 and that in Canton in December, five staff members being killed in the latter incident. In the same month the Nanking government closed down all Soviet consulates and organizations throughout the territory which it controlled.[19]

Provocations against the C.E.R. were renewed in 1928 and intensified in the following year. The Soviet Consulate-General in Harbin was raided by the police on 27 May 1929; all visitors on the premises were arrested, and the staff of Soviet economic organizations were declared to be Comintern agents who had convened for a 'meeting of the Third International.' The money and personal belongings of the consular staff, as well as diplomatic documents were confiscated, and the consulate employees were physically assaulted.

On 10 July 1929 the Chinese authorities raided the C.E.R. and seized the telegraph line along the entire railroad, thus cutting off telegraphic communications with the U.S.S.R.; they also closed down the Soviet Trade Delegation and the branch-offices of *Gostorg* (Governmental Foreign Trade Bureau), *Tekstil'sindikat, Neftesindikat,* and *Sovtorgflot.* Lui Jun-huang, President of the C.E.R. board of directors, demanded that the C.E.R. director hand over his functions to a person designated by him, in violation of the agreements of 31 May and 20 September 1924 on the temporary administration of the C.E.R.[20] When this claim was rejected by the Soviet administration, Lui Jun-huang illegally dismissed the director, his aide and the heads of the various departments, and replaced them by his own henchmen, mostly White Russian exiles.

At the same time the reactionary Chinese government concentrated along the border strong forces, including White Russian detachments, ready to invade the Soviet Union.

Chang Kai-shek's speech of 15 July 1929 to the Central Committee of the Kuomintang on the subject of Sino-Soviet relations was the signal for renewed provocative acts against the Soviet Union. In complete defiance of the facts and against the dictates of common sense Chang Kai-shek tried to convince the Chinese people that not the imperialist powers but the Soviet Union constituted a threat to China. He crudely misrepresented the agreements on the joint Sino-Soviet administration of Russian property—the C.E.R.—and, in effect, called for its seizure.

The Nanking government disregarded Soviet proposals for an immediate con-

---

[19] On 20 December 1927 the Nanking authorities prohibited Chinese firms from contacting Soviet trade organizations in Shanghai, and all the latter's employees were ordered to quit their jobs under threat of arrest.

[20] According to article 1 of the 31 May 1924 Agreement on the temporary administration of the C.E.R. and the identical article 1, point 6, of the Mukden agreement, all issues concerning the C.E.R. were to be discussed and decided by a board of ten, and any decision required at least six votes to become effective; the president of the Board (a Chinese citizen) and his aide (a Soviet citizen) were to 'deal together with all the board's affairs and both are to sign all documents issued by the board.'

ference on all issues related to the C.E.R., an end to the arbitrary acts committed by the Chinese authorities and the release of all Soviet citizens under arrest. Nanking, obviously acting on orders from imperialist circles, not only rejected all such proposals, but, on the contrary, made moves to increase the tension along the Sino-Soviet border and to trigger off an open conflict.

The Soviet Union thus saw no point in continuing relations with the Nanking government, which neither recognized nor fulfilled the obligations it had assumed. On 17 July 1929 the Soviet government severed diplomatic relations with Nanking and took the following steps entailed by this decision:

1) the recall of all Soviet diplomatic, consular and commercial representatives from Chinese territory;

2) the recall of all Soviet representatives from the C.E.R.;

3) the interruption of all railroad connections between China and the Soviet Union;

4) the immediate expulsion of all Nanking's diplomatic and consular representatives from the Soviet Union.

The Soviet government declared at the same time that it reserved for itself all rights ensuing from the Sino-Soviet treaties of Peking (31 May 1924) and Mukden (20 September 1924).

Even this stern warning, however, did not deter the Kuomintang reactionaries. Having become a blind pawn in the game played by international imperialism, and mainly by the United States, they openly advocated violation of the 1924 Sino-Soviet treaty and constantly provoked incidents along the Soviet border. In order to mislead world opinion and justify their seizure of the C.E.R., representatives of American monopolies and the Nanking authorities endeavored to discredit the joint Sino-Soviet administration of the railroad.[21]

C.E.R. property incurred heavy losses during the Kuomintang and White Russian administration. The Soviet government was thus obliged to declare that the Nanking and Mukden governments would be considered fully responsible for all material losses and other consequences of the seizure and arbitrary management by the Chinese authorities and the White Russians.

The Soviet Union warned all foreign governments that it 'would not recognize, after the C.E.R. was seized by the Chinese authorities, any transactions concerning the railroad concluded by these authorities or their agents, or any obligation undertaken by them in the railroad's name.'[22]

Provocations by Kuomintang military detachments and White Russian forces

---

[21] When the Soviet administration assumed the joint management of the C.E.R. in 1924, it had found it in debt to the sum of 13 million rubles and technologically in an advanced state of neglect. In five years of Soviet administration, the railroad's income increased from 37 million rubles in 1924 to 65 million in 1928. The debt was then entirely paid off and the Chinese authorities received 48.5 million rubles, not including the 20 million lost by the devaluation of the Chinese dollar. The board expended in the same period more than 36 million rubles on improvements.

[22] Extract from the declaration of the deputy People's Commissar of Foreign Affairs of the U.S.S.R. on 15 August 1929 to representatives of the Soviet press (*The Sino-Soviet Conflict of* 1929, p. 39.—Litizdat NKID. 1930 [Russ.]).

along the Soviet border became systematic at the beginning of November 1929. Kuomintang troops stationed in the area of Manchouli station and along the Argun [Erhkuna Ho] river fired on Soviet border patrols and civilians. At the same time White Russian armed groups based in China increased their raids against Soviet border outposts in the Maritime Territory.

International reactionary circles tried to present as indicative of weakness and fear of taking resolute reprisal action the Soviet efforts to restore by peaceful means its legal rights issuing from mutually assumed obligations. By increasing tension along the border, the Nanking government and its imperialist protectors wanted to force the Soviet government to make concessions on the C.E.R. issue and thus abrogate the 1924 Sino-Soviet treaty. Having unsuccessfully tried all possible channels for a peaceful settlement of the dispute, the Soviet Union had no choice but to take the strongest measures against the insolent acts of international reactionary circles. On 17 November 1929 detachments of the special Soviet Far Eastern Army stationed in the Transbaikal and Maritime territories repulsed the Kuomintang forces and pursued them on Chinese territory. More than 8,000 soldiers and 300 Kuomintang officers were disarmed, and 10,000 rifles were taken, together with many field guns, large amounts of ammunition and other equipmment.

This counterattack demonstrated to the world the military power and skill of the Soviet Union. The imperialists had miscalculated when they aspired to weaken Soviet positions in the Far East with the help of Kuomintang and White Russian forces. Moreover, the imperialist camp lacked the unity required for effecting a large-scale anti-Soviet aggressive campaign. Japan, the nearest imperialist power to the Soviet Union in the Far East, looked suspiciously upon the increasing American influence in China and Manchuria; Japan did not desire an armed conflict with the Soviet Union, for this could reduce her power at a time when American influence in China was increasing. On the other hand the United States and France, who had actively instigated the Sino-Soviet conflict, did not possess sufficient military forces based in the Far East to give them superiority in an eventual conflict with the Soviet Union.

The Kuomintang reactionaries were thus compelled to cease their anti-Soviet provocations, and, under the pressure of progressive Chinese circles, to seek a peaceful solution to the conflict. The Mukden authorities took the first step: on 19 November 1929 an agent of the Soviet People's Commisariat of Foreign Affairs in Harbin was informed by the Harbin diplomatic corps of Chinese readiness to open peace talks with representatives of the Soviet government.

The Soviet Union's answer again stressed its desire to find a peaceful solution to the conflict with the condition that the *status quo ante* be restored with respect to the C.E.R., on the basis of the 1924 Peking and Mukden treaties. On 26 November 1929 Chang Hsüe-liang informed the Commissariat of Foreign Affairs that he accepted these prior conditions. A representative of the Mukden authorities arrived on 1 December 1929 in Nikolsk-Ussuriiski [later named Voroshilovsk, today Ussuriisk] for a meeting with a representative of the Soviet government, the Commissariat agent in Khabarovsk.

Negotiations were concluded by the signing of a Protocol between the Soviet and Mukden governments on 3 December 1929. It contained Chang Hsüe-liang's declaration on the agreement of the Mukden government 'to respect strictly the 1924 Mukden and Peking treaties in their entirety and in their separate clauses' and the decision to dismiss Lui Jun-huang (who had implemented the illegal decisions of the Kuomintang authorities) from the presidency of the C.E.R. Board. The Protocol also stated that the Soviet Union agreed to nominate new Soviet representatives to the posts of C.E.R. director and deputy-director after Lui Jun-huang was dismissed, and reaffirmed the Soviet Union's steadfast determination to respect the Sino-Soviet treaties.

The peaceful solution of the conflict and the restoration of the Sino-Soviet treaties did not suit United States, French and British imperialist circles. They attempted to interfere, at first through the Nanking government, and later by direct action, in order to disrupt the Sino-Soviet negotiations. The Soviet authorities rebuffed these attempts, sending the following note to the United States, Britain and France: 'The Soviet government declares that the Soviet-Manchurian conflict[23] can be solved only by direct negotiations between the Soviet Union and China on the basis of conditions already known to China and accepted by the Mukden government, and that it will permit no intervention in these negotiations or this conflict.'[24]

This firm stand and the widespread public discontent in China with the Kuomintang's unsavory policies predetermined a favorable outcome for the Sino-Soviet negotiations, which ended with the signing of the Khabarovsk Protocol on 22 December 1929, containing the following basic points:

1) the C.E.R. was to recommence operations according to the stipulations of the 1924 Sino-Soviet treaties;

2) all Soviet citizens arrested by the Chinese authorities after 1 May 1929 were to be released immediately; the Soviet government also undertook to release the Chinese nationals arrested in retaliation;

3) the Chinese authorities were to disarm the White Russian armed gangs immediately and expel their organizers and instigators from the three eastern provinces (Manchuria);

4) both parties were to reopen consulates—the Soviet Union in the three eastern provinces and the Chinese in the Soviet Far East;

5) the Soviet economic organizations operating before the conflict in the three eastern provinces and the Chinese commercial enterprises in the Soviet Union were to renew their normal activity wherever it had been interrupted by the conflict over the C.E.R.;

6) a Sino-Soviet conference was to open in Moscow on 25 January 1930 to settle all issues between the two parties.

---

[23] [Manchuria, the three eastern provinces, was in fact at that time controlled by the Nanking National Government headed by Chang Kai-shek and the Kuomintang Party, and there was not the least hint of Manchurian autonomy. The 1929 conflict was fully a 'Sino-Soviet' one.]

[24] *Foreign Policy of the U.S.S.R. in 1917-1944.* Vol. 3, pp. 404-405. Moskva. 1944 [Russ.].

The C.E.R. board met on 10 January 1930 for the first time after the settlement of the conflict and decided to apply the Khabarovsk Protocol to the operation of the C.E.R. The clauses concerning the reopening of Chinese and Soviet consulates and of commercial and administrative organizations were also implemented at the beginning of 1930.

The Chinese began to delay implementation of the other obligations undertaken in the Protocol. The Nanking and Mukden governments made no efforts to disarm the White Russian detachments and expel their organizers and instigators from Manchuria. Moreover, armed groups amply supplied with money and equipment by imperialist circles continued to be organized on Manchurian territory. The Whites flagrantly operated around the western branch of the C.E.R., attacked railroad agents and establishments and hindered its normal functioning. Finally, General Diterikhs, nominated by the Paris emigrée organization as commander of the Far Eastern detachment of the so-called Russian Military Union, arrived in Harbin.

The reactionary Kuomintang authorities did everything in their power to sabotage the coming Sino-Soviet conference. Instead of opening on 25 January 1930, as stipulated by the Khabarovsk Protocol, the Moscow conference began only on October 11; the Nanking delegates then endeavored to modify the status of the C.E.R. despite the stipulation of the Khabarovsk Protocol and of the 1924 treaty, and they refused to discuss other pending issues.

The head of the Nanking delegation, Mo Teh-hwei, refused to discuss the normalization of diplomatic and commercial relations, invoking the pretext that he had received no authority to do so, and left Moscow on 15 December 1930.

Negotiations reopened in Moscow on 4 July 1931, but the Nanking representatives continued to limit all discussions to C.E.R. issues; purchase of the railroad by China, for example, was the subject of all the discussions held between July and October 1931. In accordance with the basic principles of Soviet foreign policy, the Soviet representatives agreed to sell C.E.R. property to the Chinese government on the condition that it would be purchased with Chinese funds and that the railroad would thus really become Chinese property.

The Nanking government's reluctance to reestablish normal diplomatic relations led to the suspension of the conference in October 1931, without any results having been achieved. Nanking did not wish to modify its anti-Soviet policy and continued to obey the dictates of imperialist powers without heeding the real interests of the Chinese people.

SINO-SOVIET ECONOMIC RELATIONS DURING THE JAPANESE INVASION OF MANCHURIA

The reactionary Kuomintand ruling clique, representing the interests of the landowners and the collaborating bourgeoisie, continued its relentless suppression of the Chinese people's anti-imperialist and anti-feudal movement. This policy disrupted the Chinese economy and harmed the country's position in world affairs.

Peasants continued to be dispossessed of their land throughout the territory controlled by the Nanking government. Sample data for a number of areas show that in 1930 approximately 70 percent of peasant households were poor, possessing not more than 10 percent of the tillable land area. The volume of Chinese foreign trade was affected by the world economic depression and decreased by almost 50 percent between 1928 and 1931, i.e., from US $1,553,000,000 to US $796,600,000. Exports were hit more severely than imports (they dropped from US $703,900,000 to US $309,200,000, compared to a decrease from US $849,100,000 to US $487,400,000 for imports). This led to a further deterioration of the balance of payments and made the country increasingly dependent on imperialist banks and monopolies.

This economic collapse was accompanied by increased penetration of foreign capital into all the main branches of the Chinese economy. Foreign investments in China were estimated at US $3,242,500,000 in 1931, compared to US $1,610,300,000 in 1914, an increase of more than 100 percent.

Foreign investments centered mainly in Manchuria, where Japanese capital was predominant, and along the Yangtze Kiang, where British investments had the upper hand.[25] American investments, which up to 1928 had not constituted more than 4 to 5 percent of the foreign capital invested in China, began to increase from this year on. Americans made massive purchases of Chinese state bonds from foreign firms and infiltrated into many regions in the guise of missionary and 'philanthropic' organizations. Their influence in Manchuria also increased considerably.[26]

The conflict between imperialist powers for the domination of China flared up with renewed vigor. The rivals attempted to evict each other and use every available method to reach a single goal—the colonization of China.

The strategy of each imperialist government and the tempo of its encroachments were determined by its power and the readiness of its rivals. The United States, for example, had to take into consideration their military inferiority in the Far East, their lack of strong naval bases in China and the relatively modest role played by American capital in the Chinese economy. In view of these factors, American imperialism tried to enlist the support of any other country, while it concealed its predatory aims behind various democratic proclamations on the 'preservation of Chinese territorial integrity,' the necessity of creating a 'centralized Chinese national government,' etc., in order to curry favor with the Chinese public and thus consolidate its position. The American monopolies did not refrain from seeking the support of Japanese imperialism, even though Japan was, in the broader context of foreign policy, the United States' most important rival in the Far East.

The Japanese ruling circles were much more confident. Japan's proximity to China, her powerful naval bases and forces on her own territory, in Formosa and in

---

[25] British investments were valued at US $1,189,200,000 in 1931, or 36.7 percent of all foreign investments; Japanese investments reached US $1,136,900,000, or 35.1 percent.

[26] The American share of imports into Manchuria was 8.1 percent in 1929, i.e., approximately the same as that of all the European capitalist countries taken together (8.6 percent); this share reached 70 percent with respect to some types of industrial railroad equipment and motor vehicles.

South Manchuria, as well as her considerable investments in Manchuria and Central China[27] placed her in an advantageous position.

Considering the international situation favorable for her, in 1931 Japan decided to speed up preparations for the aggreesion against China, which had been planned long before. Japanese political circles feared that any further delay would be to the advantage of American capitalism, which was strengthening its control over the Nanking government. Japan also feared further development of the revolutionary agitation for the liberation of China, which would constitute a serious menace to colonialism.

The Japanese invasion of Manchuria was launched in the autumn of 1931. After having provoked incidents in Mukden, the Japanese began on September 18 to implement their plans for seizing Manchuria and making it into a strategic base for aggression against the rest of China and the Soviet Union. While occupying Manchuria, Japan declared that she intended to 'deliver China from the Communist threat' and 'protect the interests' not merely of Japanese but of all other foreign possessions in China. This raised hopes in American, British and French imperialist circles that the Japanese aggression would be directed against the Soviet Union and would also be a spearhead against the popular Chinese revolutionary agitation.

In delineating the official American position, President Hoover stated that had the Japanese declared openly that they could no longer observe the Washington Agreement since order was not restored in China, half the country was bolshevized and cooperating with Russia, that Japan's very existence would be endangered if, in addition to having Bolshevik Russia in the north, they would be flanked by an eventually bolshevized China, and that they therefore asked permission to restore order in China, then [stated Hoover,] the United States would not have raised any objections.[28]

On 1 March 1932 Japan proclaimed the creation of the Manchurian puppet state of Manchukuo with Pu I[29] as its provisional ruler.

The invasion of Manchuria led to widespread popular agitation in China against Japanese aggression. Detachments of volunteers against the Japanese occupation forces formed at the appeal of the Communist Party, notwithstanding decrees of the Nanking government proclaiming a policy of nonresistance to Japan. Even the Kuomintang troops were receptive to the Communist Party's appeals. In January 1932 the Nineteenth Army of the Kuomintang, morally strengthened by the rising wave of popular indignation, put up a heroic opposition to the Japanese attack on Shanghai. Progressive elements in all classes of Chinese society became gradually

---

[27] Of the US $912,800,000 which constituted total Japanese investments in China in 1930, US $550,200,000 (60.3 percent) were invested in Manchuria and US $362,600,000 (39.7 percent) in the rest of China.

[28] *Relations in the Far East in* 1870-1945, p. 414. Moskva. 1951 [Russ.].

[29] After the invasion of Manchuria the Japanese 'abducted' Pu I, last emperor of the Manchu (Ch'ing) dynasty, from Peking and brought him to Manchuria, planning to use him as a cover for setting up a 'movement for the autonomy of Manchuria.' An 'All-Manchurian Convention' was staged in Mukden on 29 February 1932, before which Pu I was brought forth as provisional ruler—regent of Manchukuo. The creation of Manchukuo was proclaimed on March 1 and Pu I elected regent on March 3.

convinced of the necessity of rallying the nation's forces in order to save China from enslavement by Japanese imperialism.

The heroic struggle of the Chinese people against the Japanese aggressors was warmly supported by Soviet public opinion. The Soviet people believed that only under the leadership of the Chinese Communist Party could the Chinese people put an end to imperialist coercion.

At the end of 1932 the Soviet government sheltered a Chinese army commanded by Su Ping-wen, which had been forced to retreat to Soviet territory in the area of Manchouli station. The Soviet Union rejected Japanese allegations that Su Ping-wen was a common criminal and, as such, liable to extradition.

The First Five-Year Plan was then nearing completion ahead of schedule. From the backward peasant country which it had been under the tsarist regime, Russia was becoming an industrial nation, capable of producing itself most of the equipment it required. The volume of industrial production in 1932 had reached 26 percent of its prewar level and 202 percent of its 1928 level. The ratio of industrial to agricultural production had changed completely. Industrial production had reached 48 percent of the total in 1927/28 and increased to 70 percent in 1932; the share of heavy industry rose in the same period from 44.5 to 53 percent. Large ferrous and nonferrous metal industries, chemical factories, power plants and aircraft industries had been created and complex machine tools and instruments were being produced locally.

At the completion of the First Five-Year Plan, the Soviet engineering industry, which constituted the core of the country's industrial development, had developed by 450 percent above the 1927/28 level and by 1,000 percent compared to prewar figures.

The completion of the First Five-Year Plan was of great importance not only to the Soviet people but also to the workers of the entire world. The successful development of socialism in the Soviet Union convinced them of the correctness of the way indicated by the Communist Parties and of the advantages of the socialist system and showed the world the immense forces which a free nation could put to use. Higher goals in the industrialization of the Soviet Union and the development of the Soviet economy were set up by the Second Five-Year Plan.

The Soviet Union's voice in international affairs became stronger as the economy developed. In 1931-1932 the Soviet Union signed nonaggression pacts with Afghanistan (24 June 1931), Finland (21 January 1932), Poland (25 July 1932) and France (29 November 1932). It actively opposed all forms of militarization; the Soviet delegation at the international conference on disarmament (11 February-23 July 1932) introduced a proposal for general and complete disarmament, and recommended that even if this proposal were to be rejected, the convening countries should at least destroy all weapons which could be used for aggression (tanks, long-range artillery, aircraft carriers, heavy bombers, warships of over 10,000 tons, etc.). The delegation warned the conference that the situation which had developed in the Far East after the Japanese invasion of Manchuria could lead to a new war.

While the Soviet Union's economy continued to develop successfully, the capitalist countries felt the effect of a prolonged economic depression. The imperialist powers, and Japan among them, had no compunctions about solving their domestic and foreign problems at the expense of the Soviet Union. The Japanese government rejected a Soviet proposal for a nonaggression pact and occupied Manchuria in violation of its obligations under the Treaty of Portsmouth.[30]

Despite the official Japanese statement that it would do nothing likely to damage Soviet interests on the C.E.R., Japanese troops crudely interfered in the dealings of the Soviet administration and disturbed normal operation of the railroad. On 7 July 1932 the Manchukuo authorities, instigated by their Japanese advisers, seized the Reloading Laoshaokow Landing[31] of the C.E.R. At the demand of Japanese representatives, the Manchukuo police tore up the tracks at Manchouli station between the C.E.R. and the Transbaikal railroad.

Without abandoning any of their aggressive anti-Soviet plans, the Japanese imperialists nevertheless had to reckon with Soviet military power, and therefore chose underdeveloped China as their main target for the time being. Having occupied North Manchuria, the Japanese militarists began to prepare their aggression against North China. The Chinese people perceived ever more clearly that their country stood in mortal danger, that Kuomintang policy only encouraged Japanese aggression, and that Japanese imperialism had decided to colonize China. The propaganda of the reactionary Chang Kai-shek clique asserting that the 'red menace' was the main danger was not accepted even by the Chinese ruling classes. The seizure of Chinese industrial and commercial enterprises, of railroads and ports (including Huludao port, then still under construction) in Manchuria, and the forcible eviction of Chinese peasants from a number of areas clearly revealed the real intentions of the Japanese imperialists.

On the other hand, Chinese ruling classes could no longer disregard the peaceful policy consistently pursued by the Soviet Union, which had led to the signing of nonaggression pacts with almost all the neighboring countries. The continuation of an openly anti-Soviet policy would have unmasked the Nanking government as a traitor to the national interests. The Nanking authorities could thus no longer defer the normalization of Sino-Soviet relations, which had already been discussed at the Moscow conference in October 1930.

Notes were exchanged on 12 December 1932 between the Soviet and Nanking governments on the reestablishment of diplomatic relations. Litvinov stated: 'The Soviet government proved its friendly attitude toward China, when it was the only state to release China from the inequitable treaties, extraterritoriality, and other rights extorted by tsarist imperialism, and agreed to transform the railroad concession obtained by the tsarist government on Chinese territory into a commercial enterprise

---

[30] According to article 3 of the Russo-Japanese peace treaty signed at Portsmouth on 5 September 1905 and validated by the Soviet-Japanese agreement of 20 January 1925, Japan had no right to station troops in Manchuria outside the Liaotung [Leased] Territory.

[31] [This landing was situated at the junction of the C.E.R. Harbin-Changchun line and the Sungari river near the Laoshaokow station (later closed down) on the south bank of the Sungari near the railroad bridge. Freight was transferred at this point from the railroad to ferries, and vice-versa.]

under joint Soviet and Chinese administration. The Soviet government was motivated by feelings of disinterested friendship when it established relations with the Chinese Republic in 1924. The same feelings, and not any passing considerations, dictate the present reestablishment of diplomatic relations.'[32]

SINO-SOVIET ECONOMIC RELATIONS BEFORE THE JAPANESE
INVASION OF CHINA PROPER

Although the Nanking government had yielded to Chinese public opinion in re-establishing diplomatic relations with the Soviet Union, it did not abandon its anti-Soviet policy and continued to prevent further development of the historical economic and political ties between the two peoples.

In the field of domestic policy, Nanking continued to combat the people's democratic movement led by the Communist Party. Between June 1932 and February 1933, 90 divisions, numbering approximately 500,000 men, were mobilized for a fourth campaign against the Chinese Workers' and Peasants' Army. In the autumn of 1933, after the failure of this venture, Chang Kai-shek mobilized one million men with the support of the United States, Britain, and other imperialist powers; these forces, staffed by German generals commanded by H. von Seeckt, attacked the 'soviet areas' of China.[33]

The campaigns against the 'soviet areas' were initiated by the Kuomintang reactionaries at a time when the Japanese militarists were invading North China. The Nanking government, rejecting the Communist Party's proposal for the unification of all the armed forces of China against the Japanese occupation troops, disgracefully capitulated to the Japanese army at Tangku and recognized the Japanese occupation of Manchuria. Subsequent negotiations with Japan led Nanking to even greater concessions: it agreed to open a railroad link between China and Manchukuo, establish commercial relations with this puppet state and prohibit all anti-Japanese agitation in China.

The treasonable policy of the Nanking government with regard to Manchuria and North China and the calculated passivity shown by the League of Nations encouraged Japanese imperialism to new ventures. A violent anti-Soviet campaign developed in Japan, advocating immediate aggression against the Soviet Union. Having enlisted the support of European and American imperialist circles, the Japanese militarists thought the time ripe for seizing the Soviet Far East and Eastern Siberia.

The Japanese militarists enacted their aggressive plans by increasing their provocative acts against the C.E.R. They seized the rolling stock and forced the administration to transport Japanese troops free of charge. On 31 May 1933 the Manchukuo

---

[32] Excerpt from an interview with Litvinov, People's Commissar of Foreign Affairs, on 12 December 1932.

[33] [These 'soviet areas' had nothing in common with the Soviet Union. The term designates areas in a number of Chinese provinces where the communists had set up 'soviets' (Suweiai in Chinese) on the Russian model. To avoid confusion this term is placed in quotation marks.]

police commanded by Sato, a Japanese official, interrupted communications between the C.E.R. and the Ussuri railroad, and thus cut off all transit operations through Vladivostok.

It was well known from official Japanese documents that Japanese diplomatic and military circles were deploying constant efforts to undermine and abrogate the 1924 Sino-Soviet treaty which defined the status of the C.E.R.

The Soviet government repeatedly protested against the outrages committed by the Japanese-Manchurian militarists against the C.E.R., and warned them that they would be held wholly responsible for any damage to the railroad. The Soviet authorities continued to respect all the clauses of the Sino-Soviet treaty and firmly opposed all attempts by the Japanese-Manchurian administration to undermine the agreement.

It became impossible, however, to maintain the normal operation of the C.E.R. while Japan was occupying Manchuria. After the interruption of the direct railroad link between Manchuria and the Soviet Union, the C.E.R. remained connected only to the Manchurian and Korean railroads, controlled by the Japanese army. The Chinese representatives on the railroad directorate and board were no longer delegated by the Chinese authorities, but were mere henchmen of the Japanese occupation officials, who endeavored to direct the operation of the railroad contrary to the interests of China and the Soviet Union.

It became increasingly difficult for the Soviet representatives in the C.E.R. administration to fulfil their obligations. In September the Japanese-Manchurian authorities again arrested several important Soviet C.E.R. officials. Their representatives in the C.E.R. administration falsified inspection sheets and leveled various accusations at the Soviet staff members; without informing the Soviet railroad administration of the content of these documents, they ordered the Manchu-Japanese[34] police to arrest the Russian officials.

It became completely evident that the Manchu-Japanese militarists were doing all in their power to increase tension in the Far East and ultimately to provoke war against the Soviet Union. This warmongering encouraged by the imperialist circles was, however, countered by the Soviet Union's consistently peaceful aims. Soviet foreign policy was not based on short-term considerations: it expressed the basic interests of the Soviet people.

In order to limit opportunities for anti-Soviet provocations, the Soviet government examined the possibility of selling the C.E.R. and officially proposed such a step to the Manchu authorities at the beginning of May 1933. Negotiations for the purchase of the C.E.R. continued for more than two years. The Manchurian authorities, backed by the Japanese militarists, not wishing for any peaceful settlement of the C.E.R. issue, strove to break off negotiations. They hoped to reach deadlock on the determination of the value of the railroad.

After repeated interruptions of negotiations and protracted delays, the Manchu authorities proposed a sum of 140 million *yen,* or approximately 70 million gold

---

[34] [*Manchu* is used here to designate the Manchukuo authorities, and has nothing to do with the *Manchu* (Ch'ing) regime before 1912.]

rubles for the C.E.R.; actual construction costs had reached 411,691,976 gold rubles, or almost 1 billion *yen*. The Soviet Union, however, was interested mainly in the political consequences of the transaction, and not in its commercial aspect. It considered it necessary to remove all cause for tension between the Soviet Union and Japan and thus delay, if only temporarily, an armed conflict in the Far East. The Soviet government therefore consented to the sale, and an agreement which stipulated the payment of 140 million *yen* to the Soviet Union (in commodity deliveries) and 30 million *yen* in compensation to the Soviet railroaders was signed on 23 March 1935.

The Soviet government considered that the Japanese invaders had, and could have, no future in China, that they would at some time be expelled, and that all difficulties between a liberated China and the Soviet Union, owing to the proximity and the historic ties between the two countries, would then be settled for the best interests and in light of the traditional friendship between the two peoples.

After the sale of the C.E.R. and the departure of Soviet commercial and industrial representations from Manchuria, the economic ties between the Soviet Union and China were broken off almost completely along the entire Soviet-Manchurian border. In order to put an end to all contacts between border populations, the Japanese military clique evicted Chinese citizens from the areas neighboring upon the Soviet frontier and set up Japanese military settlements there. The Japanese invaders of Manchuria thus temporarily succeeded in cutting off the Chinese and Soviet population from each other and in forcibly breaking off their historical ties across this important border.

Trade between the Soviet Far East and China could then continue only by sea, through Vladivostok and the eastern Chinese ports. There were, however, certain difficulties even there. Soviet commerce in Shanghai, Tientsin and other ports was interfered with in various ways by the British and the Americans, who controlled the customs and foreign trade of the Nanking government. The legal status of the Sino-Soviet trade remained indefinite. The Soviet Union could not trade with China on the same basis as it did with other countries—through the Trade Delegation, the governmental trade monopoly. The offices of *Tsentrosoyuz* and *Eksportkhleb* remaining open in East China could not replace the Trade Delegation, which had been closed down in 1927, and they carried out limited commercial operations which concerned only the small range of items in which these organizations usually dealt.

The Nanking government openly refused to restore commercial relations with the Soviet Union to their normal state and disregarded the Soviet proposal, advanced at the 1930 Manchurian conference, for the signing of a commercial treaty. Nanking's reactionary domestic and foreign policy aroused the indignation of Chinese progressive circles. The lack of normal commercial relations affected Sinkiang province most severely, since it was removed from China's industrial centers and needed foreign markets for its products.

After breaking off diplomatic relations with the Soviet Union in April 1927, the Nanking government discontinued the commercial negotiations which had opened in 1926 between representatives of Sinkiang province and the Soviet consul at Urumchi [Tihwa]. In the autumn of 1931, when the Japanese invasion of Manchuria had given new impetus to patriotic popular agitation in China, progressive circles became insistent in their demands for the reestablishment of diplomatic and commercial relations with the Soviet Union. Many firms and local public figures made proposals to Soviet representatives in Sinkiang for the reopening of commercial negotiations, in order to establish a legal basis for the Soviet-Sinkiang trade, which had reached important proportions.

Faced with this current of public opinion, the Nanking authorities were compelled to open negotiations with the Soviet government on normalization of commercial relations between the Soviet Union and Sinkiang province, although the issue of commercial relations with China as a whole was omitted. Negotiations were concluded on 1 October 1931 by an exchange of notes between the representatives of the Nanking Ministry of Foreign Affairs in Sinkiang province and the People's Commissariat of Foreign Affairs of the Soviet Union.

These notes, temporarily serving in lieu of a commercial treaty, touched upon the main issues of commercial relations between the Soviet Union and Sinkiang. The Chinese side stated: 'In view of the territorial contiguity and the historical interest in the development of economic relations between Sinkiang, a province of the Chinese Republic, and the Union of Soviet Socialist Republics, as well as of the repeated declared wishes of both our governments for the development of trade between Sinkiang and the Soviet Union, the Sinkiang Provincial Government, pending the conclusion of a commercial treaty between the Chinese Republic and the Soviet Union, undertakes the following agreement with the government of the Union of Soviet Socialist Republics:

1) freight and passenger transport between Sinkiang province and the Union of Soviet Socialist Republics will take place in accordance with the existing laws of China and the Soviet Union through the border points of Irkeshtam or Turugat Pass, Hocheng [Hoerhkwosze], Bakhty and Zimunay (May-Kopchegay).

'...3) The Sinkiang Provincial Gogernment agrees to authorize Soviet economic organizations and Soviet citizens to trade freely in the districts of Kashgar [Shufu], Ili [Kuldja], Tarbagatai [Chuguchak], Altai [Chenghwa, or Sharashume] and Urumchi [Tihwa] and to authorize them to send representatives or agents from the above districts to the towns of Yarkend [Yehcheng, or Soche], Turfan, Qara Shahr [Yenki], Hotien [Khotan] and Aqsu [Wensuh] in order to conduct commercial operations with local merchants and commercial enterprises and supervise their execution...'[35]

The note expressed the hope that the Soviet government would cooperate in the fields of agronomy and live-stock breeding, would export to Sinkiang industrial and communications equipment required for the economic development of the province, and would also authorize Sinkiang merchants to send goods in transit from East China to Sinkiang and back through Soviet territory.

The note dispatched by the representative of the Soviet People's Commissariat

---

[35] Excerpt from the note dispatched on 1 October 1931 from Urumchi by Mr. Chen, representative of the Ministry of Foreign Affairs of the Chinese Republic in Sinkiang province, to the representative of the People's Commissariat of Foreign Affairs of the Soviet Union.

of Foreign Affairs confirmed the Soviet government's agreement to the conditions set forth by the Chinese side and also stated: 'The government of the Union of Soviet Socialist Republics agrees to authorize the unlicensed and untaxed importation to the Soviet Union by Sinkiang merchants of all goods originating in Sinkiang, for their sale to Soviet governmental organizations, except for products the importation of which is forbidden by existing laws... The government of the Union of Soviet Socialist Republics, taking into account the interests of the Sinkiang economy, agrees to authorize the transit of Chinese goods from East China to Sinkiang through Soviet territory...'[36]

This agreement established a definite legal basis for the operation of Chinese and Soviet firms and organizations and favorably affected commodity circulation between the Soviet Union and Sinkiang province. In 1937 this trade constituted most of the Soviet Union's total trade with China.

SINO-SOVIET TRADE IN 1928-1936

Soviet Trade with Northeast (Manchuria) and East China. After the closing down of of the Soviet Trade Delegation and its branch in East China in 1927, Soviet organizations experienced difficulties in their commerical dealings with this area. The commercial ties established after 1924 by the Soviet organizations with Chinese firms in Shanghai, Tientsin, Hankow and Canton [Kwangchow] were interrupted. Up to 1933 all Soviet trade organizations in China proper could deal only through the Shanghai office of *Tsentrosoyuz* (All-Russian Union of Consumers' Societies), which had at first imported mainly tea and a number of other Chinese products, but had sold hardly any Soviet products. Many Soviet goods, including timber, furs, and reindeer antlers reached the Chinese market through Dalny, where there were many intermediaries, brokers and agents of various firms.

Many Chinese firms endeavored, however, to maintain direct contact with Soviet trade organizations and avoid intermediaries. Joint Sino-Soviet commercial companies could, in their opinion, be one form of such direct cooperation. In 1928 a group of Chinese firms proposed to Soviet representatives the creation of a joint Sino-Soviet company for the cale of various Soviet products in China.[37] The pro-

---

[36] Excerpt from the note dispatched on 1 October 1931 by Slavutskii, representative in Urumchi of the People's Commissariat of Foreign Affairs of the Soviet Union, to the representative in Sinkiang province of the Ministry of Foreign Affairs of the Chinese Republic.

[37] This step was advocated by the six following important Chinese merchants: 1) S.T.Wang, honorary member of the Shanghai Association for the Sale of Korean Ginseng, member of the Hong Kong Chamber of Commerce, president of the Shantung Association in Shanghai and director of the Lung Tai Co. (Hong Kong). 2) G.F.Chiang, president of the North China Association in Canton, member of the Newchwang [Yingkow] Society for the Sale of Ginseng, director of the Chiang Shun Hsi Co. in Newchwang, Shanghai and Canton. 3) S.J.Liu, member of the New China Trading Company in Weihaiwei [Weihai] and Chefoo [Yentai], director of the Yu Tai Tung Co. in Chefoo and Weihaiwei. 4) L.D.Wang, director of the Fu San Shang Co. of Chefoo, Shanghai and Antung. 5) S.H.Chih, director of the Tung Shun Co. of Chefoo. 6) S.M.Chu, member of the Tientsin Association for the Sale of Timber and Lumber.

moters planned to include products such as reindeer antlers, crabs, trepang, sea kale, ginseng, musk and humpback salmon, to a total value of 2 to 3 million rubles. Negotiations were held in the same year in Manchuria between Chinese firms and *Dal'gostorg* for the creation of a joint Sino-Soviet commercial company for the export of soybean, vegetable oil and oilcake from Manchuria.

A number of Chinese firms also opened stores specializing in Soviet products. Large stores selling Soviet fishery products, caviar, confectionery, Siberian furs, cotton and linen fabrics and yarn, etc., opened in Harbin in 1930-31.

These moves initiated by Chinese business circles for the development of economic ties between the Soviet Union and China were not supported by the Nanking government. In the central and southern regions of China, i.e., the areas in which Nanking was most influential, foreign trade was controlled mainly by American monopolies, and in Manchuria and North China it was dominated by the Japanese. The sale of any foreign product in Shanghai required the services of American firms. In 1935 *Tsentrosoyuz* was thus compelled to sell Soviet pig iron and electric motors through the American Trading Company and Soviet telephone equipment through the Chinese Electric Company, a branch of the Shanghai Telephone Company, controlled by the United States.

In Manchuria and North China, in addition to the direct administrative measures taken by the Japanese military clique for limiting the commerce of all third parties, Japanese firms resorted to extensive smuggling. The Chinese market was thus flooded with cheap Japanese goods on which no duties had been paid; consequently, other countries encountered difficulties in selling their goods. In 1934-35 products such as sugar, fabrics, artificial silk thread, paper, aspirin, sewing-machines and others sold on the Shanghai market were mainly Japanese.

The Japanese occupation of Manchuria led to the transfer of the region's foreign trade into the hands of Japanese capitalism. Importation of various foreign products (including Chinese goods) was authorized only insofar as Japanese firms could not meet the local demand or when the imported goods were required by the Japanese army. Exports were also strictly controlled. Manchurian products were first exported to Japan or to countries from which Japan purchased strategic raw materials and equipment and was obliged to repay in kind.

In 1934 the 'Manchukuo government' established a special 'Bureau of Monopolies' and passed a law which made most importation into Manchuria a government monopoly; 'governmental' organizations were also set up for 'state purchases' of agricultural produce (soybean, grain, etc.).

Soviet trade organizations found it extremely difficult to operate in Manchuria under such conditions. Purchases of soybean and oilcake by *Eksportkhleb* for importation to the Soviet Union via Vladivostok were interrupted in 1934, and the offices of this bureau were closed down in Fuchin [Fugdin] and at other points along the border, and finally in Harbin. The Soviet Trade Delegation in North Manchuria (Harbin), which directed the activity of all the Soviet economic organizations in this region, was closed in September 1935. Only one Soviet commercial representative then remained open throughout North China and Manchuria—the office of the

Trade Delegation in Dalny, itself a branch of the Soviet Trade Delegation in Japan.

These circumstances, which prevented Sino-Soviet commercial relations from remaining normal, gradually led to a reduction in the volume of trade between the Soviet Union and East and Northeast (Manchuria) China; in 1936 this volume dropped to less than one-ninth of its 1929 value (after price corrections).

SOVIET FOREIGN TRADE WITH EAST AND
NORTHEAST (MANCHURIA) CHINA IN 1929-1936
(in thousand rubles)

Year	Soviet exports	Soviet imports	Total value
1929	6,952	18,124	25,076
1930	12,493	8,432	20,925
1931	11,064	6,931	17,995
1932	8,086	5,888	13,974
1933	7,171	2,639	9,810
1934	2,055	3,440	5,495
1935	509	3,539	4,048
1936	573	12,791	13,364

The period immediately following the October Revolution had been characterized by the predominance of Soviet imports over exports in the China trade; during the First Five-Year Plan, on the contrary, Soviet exports to East and Northeast China were greater than imports from these areas. This change in the import-export ratio was due to general changes in the composition of Soviet exports during this period,

SOVIET IMPORTS FROM EAST AND NORTHEAST (MANCHURIA) CHINA[38]

Goods	1929		1932		1936	
	tons	thous. rubles	tons	thous. rubles	tons	thous. rubles
Grain	14,356	989	13,420	1,062	—	—
Flour, groats	2,338	259	17,064	1,555	—	—
Tea	18,012	14,146	5,968	2,634	4,079	3,121
Animal fats	952	473	—	—	—	—
Undressed leather	386	432	—	—	—	—
Vegetable oil	1,420	478	151	59	393	774
Nonferrous metals	—	—	—	—	2,702	4,015
Tungsten ore	—	—	—	—	1,339	3,601
Raw cotton	555	433	—	—	1	6
Wool	179	262	115	115	—	—
TOTAL	39,963	18,124	39,788	5,888	8,881	12,791

[38] From Soviet customs statistics for the corresponding period.

which marked the beginning of Soviet industrialization. Industrial equipment became the main item exported, reaching 51.2 percent of total exports in 1930 (2,374 million out of 4,637.5 million rubles) and 60.1 percent in 1932 (2,909 out of 3,083.5 million rubles); importation of foodstuffs, previously the main items imported from China, decreased at the same time.

Tea, which had constituted the main Russian import throughout the history of Russian-Chinese trade, now lost its rank to items such as tungsten ore and non-ferrous metals.

The composition of Soviet exports to East and Northeast China also underwent important changes.

Despite the continuing economic depression in the capitalist countries, Soviet exports to China in 1932 increased both in value and in volume compared to the 1929 level.

The increase of Soviet exports to China after 1929 was due mainly to products of the Soviet Far East: fish, timber and canned food; this was accompanied by a decrease of textile exports, which were produced in the central regions of the Soviet

SOVIET EXPORTS TO EAST AND NORTHEAST (MANCHURIA) CHINA[39]

Goods	1929		1932		1936	
	tons	thous. rubles	tons	thous. rubles	tons	thous. rubles
Fish	1,195	,253	12,032	1,110	—	—
Black caviar	2	12	7	34	—	—
Red caviar	15	23	36	22	—	—
Lumber	2,069	91	44,979	752	—	—
Plywood	245	42	397	31	—	—
Other lumber	22,233	517	85,308	999	3,128	58
Canned food	26	20	1,389	496	—	—
Tobacco products	39	96	181	149	—	—
Wine	47	33	9	2	—	—
Confectionery	50	69	208	45	—	—
Salt	475	35	2,492	110	—	—
Coal	102,770	968	45,948	280	400	8
Petroleum products	4,410	552	93,766	2,150	—	—
Matches and matchwood	104	33	126	24	—	—
Cement	1,744	55	—	—	—	—
Pottery, porcelain, glass	11	8	1,179	95	—	—
Cotton fabrics	1,088	2,480	470	1,155	—	—
Electrometallurgical products	215	104	17	17	59	218
Unprocessed metals	20	5	189	89	—	—
Thread	12	111	48	82	—	—
Chemical and pharmaceutical products	3	18	477	33	54	272
TOTAL	138,396	6,952	291,510	8,086	3,654	573

[39] From Soviet customs statistics for the corresponding period.

Union in 1929 constituted 35.6 percent of total Soviet exports to East and Northeast China. Soviet exports of so-called secondary items (chemical and pharmaceutical products, including those used in traditional Chinese medicine—reindeer antlers, ginseng, deer tails, trepang, mollusks, etc.—porcelain, glass, tobacco products, etc.) to China also increased during this period.

The swift development of Soviet industry made it possible to export industrial products during the First Five-Year plan to neighboring Asiatic countries, including China. *Eksportkhleb* concluded agreements in Shanghai in 1935-1936 for the sale of a sample lot of Soviet machine tools, electric motors, as well as telephone and other types of equipment.

Circumstances remained unfavorable for Soviet exports to China while Japan occupied the Northeast and part of the North, and Japanese, American and British monopolies predominated in Central China and in the south of the country. After the closing down of the Soviet organizations in Northeast China (Manchuria), Soviet trade with this area and with East China ceased almost completely. Sales through the Dalny branch of the Soviet Trade Delegation in 1936 were limited to products used in Chinese popular medicine; a certain amount of industrial equipment was sold through the Shanghai office of *Eksportkhleb*.

SOVIET FOREIGN TRADE WITH SINKIANG PROVINCE IN 1929-1936[40]
(in thousand rubles)

Year	Exports to to Sinkiang	Imports from from Sinkiang	Total volume of Soviet trade with Sinkiang
1929	16,396	16,435	32,831
1930	16,027	16,033	32,060
1931	13,954	10,212	24,166
1932	15,698	12,305	28,004
1933	10,856	18,822	29,678
1934	4,730	5,945	10,675
1935	6,049	4,550	10,599
1936	36,145	25,671	61,816

Soviet trade with Sinkiang Province in 1929-1936. While Chinese foreign trade, severely affected by the depression and the drop of market prices, decreased by approximately 50 percent from 1929 to 1935, the volume of Soviet trade remained almost constant, decreasing by less than 10 percent. Moreover, the Soviet-Sinkiang trade began to increase from 1931, after the conclusion of a temporary commercial agreement (the exchange of notes between the representative of the Chinese Ministry of Foreign Affairs and the Consul-General of the Soviet Union).

Soviet-Sinkiang trade contracted sharply in 1934 due to the beginning of hostilities in January of that year between the forces of the Sinkiang Provincial Government

---

[40] From Soviet customs statistics for the corresponding period.

and General Ma Chu-ying.[41] After the end of hostilities and the reestablishment of economic relations between the various regions of Sinkiang there was a renewed expansion of trade, particularly of Soviet exports.

The demand for Soviet products increased noticeably in 1935 with the beginning of highway construction in Sinkiang and the creation of a number of municipal services and manufacturing industries. The Sinkiang provincial administration, wishing to promote industrial development, began to encourage the creation of large companies entrusted with purchasing Soviet equipment and materials.

An agreement for bilateral commodity deliveries reaching 22 million rubles for each party was concluded in May 1935 between *Sovsin'torg,* the Soviet association for trade with Sinkiang, and the Sinkiang purchasing company Tuchankungssu.[42] *Sovsin'torg* was to supply on credit within two years equipment for macadamization, electric power stations and leather industries as well as other Soviet products, while Tuchankungssu undertook to pay off the debt in Sinkiang goods (wool, live-stock, animal casings, furs, etc.) within five years of the inauguration of the enterprises built with the Soviet equipment. Since Tuchankungssu did not possess a sufficient network in the remote areas of the province, it reserved the right to commission a number of Sinkiang firms and individual merchants to supply goods to the Soviet Union within the framework of the agreement. This agreement between *Sovsin'torg* and Tuchangkungssu favorably affected the development of commercial relations between the Soviet Union and Sinkiang and promoted the economic development of the province. It ensured the uninterrupted sale of its agricultural products at equitable prices and for a long period.

The Soviet Union completed its equipment supplies according to the terms of the agreement by the middle of 1936. In view of this fact a second agreement was concluded on 1 July 1936 between *Sovsin'torg* and Tuchankungssu for supplementary deliveries of Soviet commodoties to a value of 8,760,000 rubles at the same conditions as in the previous agreement.

Although imports of Soviet equipment, motor vehicles and industrial materials were increasing, the most important items bought from the Soviet Union, remained, as before, articles of general consumption.

The decreased value of Soviet exports to Sinkiang in 1936 compared to 1929 was caused mainly by the sharp drop of prices during the depression years. Evaluation of 1936 exports in 1929 prices shows that Soviet exports to Sinkiang increased to 96.8 million rubles in 1936 compared to 71.8 million in 1929. The items exported by the Soviet Union in 1936 covered a wider range. Cotton fabrics still remained the main

---

[41] A provincial government was set up in Sinkiang on 12 April 1933, headed by *tupan* [military Governor-General] Shen Shih-tsai. General Ma Chu-ying, who had connections with the Japanese military clique, was designated Commander of Sinkiang's eastern region (Hami [Qomul]). Ma Chu-ying soon initiated a rebellion against the Sinkiang Provincial Government; it was finally suppressed in 1934, but a few rebel detachments continued to operate in the Hami area as late as 1935.

[42] The agreement between *Sovsin'torg* and Tuchankungssu stipulated commodity deliveries valued at 5 million gold rubles by each party; at the new rate of exchange introduced in 1935, this equaled 21.9 million rubles.

item among Soviet exports, but clothing and linen, footwear, tanned leather and dyes were also shipped; exports of confectionery, chemical and pharmaceutical products, tobacco products, thread and other goods also expanded.

SOVIET EXPORTS TO SINKIANG PROVINCE[43]

Goods	1929		1932		1936	
	tons	*thous. rubles*	*tons*	*thous. rubles*	*tons*	*thous. rubles*
Cotton fabrics	2,331	9,529	2,358	11,236	3,279	14,023
Woolen fabrics	—	—	—	—	180	833
Clothing and linen	—	—	—	—	77	1,274
Thread and cotton yarn	9	69	26	197	62	452
Footwear	—	—	—	—	240	1,835
Tanned leather	—	—	—	—	164	499
Sugar	3,110	1,682	1,766	978	2,934	1,327
Tea	—	—	—	—	1,032	2,030
Confectionery	100	109	40	54	324	447
Tobacco products	98	362	319	42	285	906
Pottery, porcelain, glass	560	420	295	519	418	499
Rubber products	68	286	36	161	83	317
Dyes	—	—	—	—	44	115
Chemical and pharmaceutical products	14	20	19	17	178	242
Matches	215	119	238	96	270	246
Petroleum products	1,187	338	743	142	4,309	1,059
Cars, motorcyles, bicycles	—	—	—	—	330	659
Agricultural machinery and parts	—	—	—	—	1,058	413
Ferrous metals and metal products[44]	3,442	1,811	1,679	1,088	1,996	1,183
Equipment, apparatus, instruments	—	—	—	—	434	965
TOTAL	12,502	16,396	8,006	15,698	22,786	36,145

The hostilities which flared up from 1933 to 1936 between the Sinkiang provincial authorities and generals Ma Pu-fang and Ma Chu-ying interrupted almost completely the province's economic ties with East China, and Chinese firms began either to carry tea to Sinkiang by transit through the Soviet Union or to purchase it from the Soviet organizations. Tea became a relatively important and stable item of Soviet export to Sinkiang from 1936 on.

The appearance of new items (motor vehicles, industrial equipment, agricultural

[43] From Soviet customs statistics for the corresponding period.

[44] The item 'Ferrous metals and metal products' includes mainly pig iron in 1929 and 1932 and ironware in 1936.

machinery) among Soviet goods in 1936 and the increased quantities of petroleum products exported to Sinkiang characterized trade at this stage.

The nature of Sinkiang's exports to Soviet Russia remained much more stable. Live-stock and animal husbandry products, as well as cotton, raw silk and other agricultural goods were still the main items.

SOVIET IMPORTS FROM SINKIANG PROVINCE[45]

Goods	1929		1932		1936	
	tons	thous. rubles	tons	thous. rubles	tons	thous. rubles
Wool	6,746	8,584	4,571	4,896	4,539	5,791
Small live-stock and cattle	8,674	2,211	14,151	3,334	19,337	7,050
Fine undressed leather	1,713	2,030	1,317	1,576	2,223	2,653
Animal casings	1	4	1	3	195	3,542
Furs	24	145	24	330	231	3,174
Cotton	2,971	2,854	899	767	1,075	1,130
Raw silk	9	216	52	883	58	263
Hair	21	46	3	6	433	965
Rugs	—	—	—	—	13	108
TOTAL	20,440	16,435	21,238	12,305	28,498	25,671

As in the case of exports, the value of imports was much smaller in 1936 than in 1929 when expressed in current prices, but if this value is calculated in 1929 prices, imports are found to have reached 74 million rubles compared to 72 million in 1929. Analysis of data for the separate items fully corroborates this increase.

Animal casings became a new item in Soviet imports from Sinkiang in 1936. This valuable raw material, which remains a profitable item despite long-distance freight rates, had previously been exported almost exclusively to Europe or America through East China. When Sinkiang was cut off from East China, casings began to be exported to the Soviet Union or to Western Europe through the Soviet Union. Furs and rugs, which previously had been exported through West China (furs) or India (rugs) to Western Europe and the United States, began to follow the same route.

The predominance of Soviet exports over imports to Sinkiang in 1935-1936 is explained, as stated above, by the commodity deliveries of *Sovsin'torg* within the framework of the credit agreement with Tuchankungssu.

*   *
*

1) Sino-Soviet economic relations were to a certain extent affected by the accession to power of the Kuomintang reactionaries, led by Chang Kai-shek. The Kuomintang (Nanking) government followed an anti-Soviet foreign policy. Repeated provoca-

---

[45] From Soviet customs statistics for the corresponding period.

tions by the Kuomintang authorities against Soviet representatives in China finally led to the severance of diplomatic relations and the almost complete cessation of Soviet commercial operations in the regions of China proper controlled by the Kuomintang.

Chinese business circles unsuccessfully attempted to overcome these setbacks in the development of economic relations with the Soviet Union which had been caused by the imperialist powers and the Nanking government.

2) The Japanese invasion of Manchuria severely affected Sino-Soviet economic relations. Japanese imperialism, which had seized Manchuria with the connivance of the Nanking government, set up a colonial regime and made conditions impossible for the continuation of normal economic relations with the Soviet Union. By various provocative acts against the Soviet officials and workers of the C.E.R. and raids against the railroad, the Japanese military clique disrupted its operation; they also removed the legal Chinese representatives from the railroad administration. In order to avoid any pretext which could force the Soviet Union to war, the Soviet government decided to sell the C.E.R. to the Manchukuo administration, since the Kuomintang government had waived its sovereign rights to Manchuria. The Japanese monopolies behind the Manchu administration offered to pay approximately one-seventh of the real value for the C.E.R. For the sake of peace the Soviet government accepted this proposal.

The evacuation of Soviet C.E.R. workers and officials and the closing down of Soviet trade organizations in Manchuria led to the interruption of economic relations between the Soviet Union and Manchuria.

3) The continuation of Sino-Soviet trade through the Sinkiang border proved that this trade developed successfully wherever the pressure of imperialist circles on China slackened and wherever the imperialist powers could not set up artificial barriers between the two countries.

Soviet trade with Sinkiang province increased between 1925 and 1936 both in total value and in the range of items involved.

CHAPTER SEVEN

ECONOMIC RELATIONS BETWEEN THE SOVIET UNION AND CHINA FROM 1937 TO 1949 (FROM THE JAPANESE INVASION OF CHINA PROPER TO THE ESTABLISHMENT OF THE CHINESE PEOPLE'S REPUBLIC)

THE FAR EASTERN SITUATION ON THE EVE OF THE JAPANESE INVASION OF CHINA PROPER

TENSION in the Far East continued to mount in 1937. Encouraged by America's 'neutrality' and by the treasonable connivance of the Chang Kai-shek clique, the Japanese imperialists pushed their aggression even further and frantically prepared for a 'big war.' Having secured an alliance with Nazi Germany,[1] Japanese imperialist circles thought the time was ripe for their extensive plans to take over China.

The Japanese considered this step feasible only if they could diminish Soviet power in the Far East, deprive the Soviet Union of her Far Eastern territories, and thus cut her off from China, Korea and Southeast Asia. A preliminary attack against the Soviet Union was advocated by most Japanese army generals, and in particular by General Araki.[2]

At the end of 1936 and the beginning of 1937 Japanese provocations along the Soviet Far Eastern frontier intensified and clashes ensued between Japanese-Manchurian forces and the Soviet border guards. Japanese imperialist circles tried to justify their anti-Soviet policy with pat utterances about combating communism, desiring to protect China from the Soviet Union's influence, and so on. Japan's nefarious imperialist policy was doomed to failure.

After the successful completion of the Second Five-Year Plan (1933-1937), the Soviet Union had become an economically independent country technologically capable of meeting all its economic and defense requirements. While the volume of industrial production of the capitalist countries barely passed the 1929 level in 1937 (102.5 percent) as a consequence of the depression, Soviet industrial production in 1937 reached 372 percent of the 1929 level and 588 percent of the 1913 level.

The authority of the Soviet Union in the field of international affairs was considerably enhanced at the same time. Capitalist governments were compelled to acknowledge that the most important world issues, including the Far Eastern pro-

---

[1] An Anti-Comintern Pact was concluded between fascist Germany and Japan on 25 November 1936; each party undertook to take steps against the Comintern—the democratic movement of European and Asiatic nations.

[2] General Araki Sadao served as War Minister in 1931-1933 and Minister of Education in 1938; he led the anti-Soviet military group.

blem, could not be settled without Soviet participation. A naval agreement was signed on 17 July 1937 between Britain and the Soviet Union. Statements were exchanged on 21-28 July 1937 between President Roosevelt, in the name of the United States, and the government of the Soviet Union, expressing the common views of both parties as to the necessity of preserving peace and organizing collective security. Notes were exchanged on 4 August 1937 between the United States and Soviet governments concerning commercial relations, stipulating the mutual, unconditional and unlimited application of the most-favored-nation clause.

A different attitude toward the Soviet Union was advocated at the same time by American, British and French reactionary imperialist circles, who, in their desire to undermine the economy of the socialist state and weaken the position of their rivals, favored unleashing a war between the Soviet Union on the the one hand and Japan and Germany on the other.

The Soviet Union could not help but notice the contradictions between the public declarations of American and British politicians and the activities of the imperialist circles. On the one hand, Secretary of State Hull declared that the United States opposed the application of force by any nation to further its policies and interference in the internal affairs of other nations. He added that the United States stood for the settlement of all international issues by peaceful negotiations and agreements.[3] At the same time United States financial magnates continued to supply the Japanese army in China with strategic raw materials, and traded secret military patents; American banks, commercial monopolies and advisers of the Nanking government crudely interfered in China's internal affairs and trampled on the Chinese people's most elementary sovereign rights.

Although American, British and French ruling circles did in fact admit that Japan was not fulfilling her obligations and was violating Chinese sovereignity, this was not due to opposition to this aggression or to their support of the Chinese people's struggle for national independence. They opposed the Japanese invasion of China because it endangered their own multimillion dollar investments in China, which brought in large profits and afforded political advantages. Moreover, American, British and French ruling circles had no compunctions about utilizing Japanese militarism to preserve the semicolonial status of China, and would have applauded the aggression had it been directed openly against communism in China or against the Soviet Union.

The Soviet people and their government adopted a different attitude toward Japanese aggression. The Soviet Union had the warmest sympathy for the Chinese people's just struggle against Japanese aggression and was ready to maintain close and friendly relations with the Chinese people. It was the responsibility of the Nanking government, which followed an anti-national policy and continued to co-operate with the Japanese in the suppression of the Chinese democratic movement, that Sino-Soviet economic relations failed to develop sufficiently and remained unregulated.

---

[3] From the declaration of Secretary of State Hull to the American press on 16 July 1937.

THE JAPANESE INVASION OF CHINA PROPER AND THE DOMESTIC
SITUATION IN CHINA

The invasion of North China by Japanese troops in July 1937 modified the Chinese situation. Events proved clearly to all strata of Chinese society that Japanese imperialism was set on transforming China from a semicolony, in which the interests of a number of imperialist powers clashed, into a Japanese colony.

Mao Tse-tung declared in May 1937: 'Of all the conflicts between the imperialist powers and China, that between China and Japanese imperialism has become particularly acute. Japanese imperialism has begun to implement a policy of total enslavement of China. In view of this fact, the conflicts between certain imperialist countries and China have become less important, while those between the same countries and Japanese imperialism have come to the fore.'[4] The Chinese people's struggle against Japanese imperialism became national in scale. The demands contained in the Chinese Communist Party declaration of 1 August 1935 for an end to the civil war and the establishment of a government of national defense became vital goals in the eyes of the entire nation.

The continuing Kuomintang sabotage of the Communist Party's proposal for the creation of a united anti-Japanese national front aroused widespread indignation in all strata of Chinese society, including the Kuomintang troops themselves.

The Chinese Communist Party summoned the Chinese people to a decisive counterattack against the Japanese occupation forces. 'Peking and Tientsin stand in danger! North China stands in danger! The Chinese people stand in danger!' stated an appeal launched by the Communist Party two days after the Lugoutsao events.

At the end of August the Eighth National-Revolutionary Army, commanded by Chu Teh and Peng Teh-hwai, entered the northern part of Shansi province and near Pingsingkwan defeated a Japanese division commanded by General Itagaki. This, the first victory of Chinese troops against the Japanese invaders, had an enormous effect on the morale of the Chinese people and convinced them of the possibility that Japanese aggression could be successfully resisted.

The Communist Party's prestige grew by leaps and bounds. Although the Party set up its main military bases in the north and northeast, far from the important industrial centers and densely populated areas, its voice was heard throughout China. The Nanking government, no longer able to reject the proposal for the creation of a united anti-Japanese front, finally consented in September 1937 to cooperate with the Communist Party on the basis of the declaration made in August by the Party Central Committee.[5]

---

[4] Mao Tse-tung. *Selected Works,* Vol. 1, pp. 449-450 [Russ.].

[5] In August 1937 the Chinese Communist Party sent to the Kuomintang Central Executive Committee a proposed program for a united front on the basis of the following conditions: defeat and eviction of the Japanese interventionists from China; general mobilization of all the nation's resourses; introduction of a democratic governmental system; abolition of exacting taxes and various duties; reduction of land rents and usury; creation of a united anti-Japanese national front which would include all the parties and groups representing all strata of the population, on the basis of cooperation between the Kuomintang and the Communist Party in the war of liberation.

At the beginning of 1938 the Nanking government was partially reorganized on the program for the united front, which had been accepted by both sides; a National Political Council was set up on 1 July as a consultative body, with the participation of Communist representatives (Mao Tse-tung, Tung Pi-wu and others) and representatives of other parties and political groups.

SINO-SOVIET RELATIONS IN 1937-1941

Analyzing China's domestic and international situation after the Japanese invasion of the northern areas, Mao Tse-tung appealed in December 1935 for national unity and the immediate formation of an anti-Japanese popular front. He also said: 'We need the help of foreign nations in our anti-Japanese war, and first and foremost of the Soviet people, who will of course help us, for we have common vital interests.'[6]

Conditions for the establishment of friendly relations between the Soviet Union and China improved as the anti-Japanese national front was gradually strengthened and the Communist Party's influence increased throughout the country. A nonaggression pact, giving moral support to China—then isolated by the imperialists—was concluded between the Soviet Union and China on 21 August 1937, just after the Japanese invasion of China proper.

While the United States and Britain continued to support Japan by supplying military equipment and strategic raw materials, the Soviet Union undertook the mutual obligation 'to extend no direct or indirect aid' to any state attacking China 'throughout the entire conflict and also to refrain from conducting any activities and from concluding any treaties which could be used by the aggressor or aggressors to the detriment of the country attacked.'[7] This agreement consolidated China's international position and demonstrated to progressive circles throughout the world that the Soviet Union stood on the side of the Chinese people and considered its struggle to be just.

Soviet representatives at the Brussels Conference (3-24 November 1937), convened by the signatories to the Washington Treaty,[8] supported the Chinese proposal for economic sanctions against Japan. They stressed the increasing danger presented by aggressive states[9] and called for the cooperation of peace-loving nations against aggression. Although the Soviet and Chinese proposals were rejected by the other members of the conference, which limited itself merely to noting Japan's violation of the Nine Power Treaty and calling for the 'suspension of hostilities and the use of

---

[6] Mao Tse-tung. *op. cit.,* Vol. 1, p. 290.

[7] From article 2 of the nonaggression pact between the Union of Soviet Socialist Republics and the Chinese Republic, signed in Nanking on 21 August 1937 (*Foreign Policy of the U.S.S.R.,* Vol. 4, pp. 290-291 [Russ.]).

[8] Japan, who had been a signatory to the Washington Treaty, refused to take part in the Brussels Conference. The Soviet Union, not a signatory to the agreement, was invited to the conference in view of her interest in Far Eastern issues.

[9] A protocol by which Italy joined the Anti-Comintern Pact concluded between Germany and Japan on 25 November 1936 was signed in Rome on 6 November 1937.

peaceful methods,' the Soviet Union's firm stand and its friendly attitude toward China had a noticeable effect on world opinion.

China's economic situation deteriorated after the loss of Shanghai and Nanking. The loss of important industrial centers disorganized her foreign trade. British and American commercial and banking monopolies which controlled the economy of Central China did not leave the Japanese-occupied territory and actively traded with Japan. In 1938 the United States supplied almost half of the value of imports to the areas occupied by Japan and their share reached 53 percent in 1939.

Throughout this most difficult period in the Chinese people's struggle against the Japanese the United States and Britain remained the main suppliers of strategic raw materials and alimentary products for the occupied territores, i.e., for the Japanese army. At the same time, commercial operations between these countries and the free Chinese areas diminished.

EXPORTS OF STATEGIC RAW MATERIALS AND ALIMENTARY PRODUCTS TO THE JAPANESE-OCCUPIED AREAS IN 1939[10]

Countries	Petroleum products (in million liters)	Cotton	Wheat	Wheat flour
		(in thousand tons)		
Dutch Indies	144.4	—	—	—
United States	55.9	36.4	167.5	143.9
Japan (including Korea and the Liaotung peninsula)	34.0	0.4	—	23.5
India (including Burma)	—	148.9	—	
Australia	—	—	298.7	171.5
Brazil	—	50.6	—	—
Egypt	—	8.2	—	—

United States and British imperialist circles appeared increasingly distrustful of China as the anti-Japanese popular front was gradually strengthened and democratic agitation increased. Even after the Japanese had occupied Shanghai, an extremely important region of British and American investments, the United States and Britain did not abandon hope of reaching an agreement with Japan for the joint exploitation of China, since Japanese imperialism was relatively weak from the economic point of view. They feared the victory of the Chinese people and the consolidation of a free and democratic China.

American and British politicians saw that China could defeat Japan only if all her popular forces were united on a democratic basis. This in turn meant that after the Japanese defeat, Britain and the United States would find themselves faced with a powerful democratic China which would not tolerate imperialist domination.

---

[10] Chinese customs statistics for 1940 (*The Trade of China*, Vol. 1, part 1, pp. 77-83).

On the one hand, Britain and the United States suffered serious losses as a result of the Japanese invasion, and the trade and profits of Anglo-American companies possessing large enterprises in occupied territories decreased. On the other hand, they feared the increasing authority of the Chinese Communist Party. These circumstances explain the dual policy of American and British imperialism.

From the formation of the united anti-Japanese national front to 1940 the United States practically boycotted China and floated only one US $25 million loan to be repaid in long-term Chinese tung oil exports.

The Soviet Union maintained an entirely different attitude toward China. It not only gave its moral support, but also granted extensive material aid. The Soviet Union granted two loans of US $50 million each to China in 1938, to be paid off in five years in Chinese goods (at a yearly interest of 3 percent). According to the agreement signed on 1 March, the first loan was to be repaid, between 31 October 1938 and 31 October 1943, and the second loan, concluded on 1 July, was to be repaid between 1 July 1940 and 1 July 1945. A third agreement was also concluded for a Soviet loan of US $150 million to be paid off in Chinese commodity deliveries between 1 July 1949 and 1 July 1952 (the 3 percent interest was calculated from 1 July 1939). These loans enabled China to purchase industrial products, petroleum products, motor vehicles, aircraft and various types of armaments from the Soviet Union.

A commercial treaty[11] was signed on 16 June 1939 between China and the Soviet Union; according to the Sino-Soviet agreement of 31 May 1924, the conclusion of this treaty had been set for 1924. This was China's first equitable commercial treaty, which settled on a reciprocal basis all the commercial, maritime and legal issues between individual and juristic persons of both parties. The treaty applied the most-favored-nation clause to both contracting parties[12] as concerned export-import operations, customs and duties, the use of warehouses, the determination of methods for the checking and analysis of goods, the establishment of customs classification and the interpretation of the tariff (articles 1,2 and 4). The treaty also granted most-favored status to the ships of both parties in their ports with regard to the use of wharves and port services and the imposition of customs and other taxes.

Following established international practice as to trade with the Soviet Union, the Chinese government recognized the Soviet state monopoly of foreign trade; the commercial treaty therefore established a trade delegation attached to the Soviet Embassy in China, with branch offices in Tientsin, Shanghai, Hankow, Canton and Lanchow.

The Soviet Union granted in its turn the same status to Chinese merchants, industrialists, and individual and juristic persons residing on Soviet territory as that established by Soviet law for individual and juristic persons of any third country.

---

[11] The treaty became valid on 16 March 1940, when the ratified copies were exchanged in Chungking.

[12] Exchanged notes appended to the Commercial Treaty specified that the status of most-favored-nation granted by China to the Soviet Union designated the status granted by China to other nations after 1928, i.e., after the formal repeal of the inequitable treaties.

The Sino-Soviet commercial treaty laid solid foundations for the development of trade between the two states and consolidated China's position in its relations with other countries. Sino-Soviet trade expanded considerably during this period, in spite of unfavorable conditions resulting from the Japanese occupation of all Chinese ports and the Japanese naval blockade.

In addition to the economic assistance of the three loans, the Soviet Union's firm and consistent attitude toward Japan, which it condemned as an aggressor, was also an important factor.

While hostilities against China continued, Japanese imperialism did not abandon its plans for the occupation of the Soviet Far East, which would have made it master of East Asia. In 1938 Japan attempted to invade Soviet territory near Lake Khasan[13] and to advance toward Vladivostok. Violent fighting raged in this area for three weeks (from 29 July to 18 August) between Soviet border detachments and the invading Japanese-Manchukuo forces; the latter were finally defeated and thrown back to Manchuria.

In 1939 the Japanese imperialists were also driven back from the Halhain Gol river, on the Mongolian-Manchurian border. In an attempt to cut off the Far Eastern Territory from Siberia, Japanese troops began reconnaissance patrols on 11 May and later attempted to breach the Soviet-Mongolian defenses, having concentrated large forces supported by tanks, artillery and planes. The Japanese suffered heavy losses in the violent fighting, hundreds of their tanks and planes were destroyed, and finally, between 21 and 28 August, the entire Japanese force was surrounded and wiped out by the Soviet-Mongolian army. The four-month battle of Halhain Gol was Japan's first major military defeat. It threw confusion into the ranks of the Japanese army, which had prided itself on its invincibility, and seriously affected its morale, while it gave an inspiring example to the Chinese people.

Mao Tse-tung wrote at the end of 1939, in an analysis of the Soviet Union's role and importance for China: 'Since the beginning of hostilities against the Japanese aggressors, not one imperialist government granted us sincere assistance; the Soviet Union alone has helped us with military aircraft and material resources.'[14] 'The Soviet Union has not only signed a nonagression pact with China, but has actively begun to assist China in its struggle against the imperialist aggressors.'[15]

SINO-SOVIET TRADE IN 1937-1941

Sino-Soviet economic relations were considerably broadened by the loan agreements and the commercial treaty.

In spite of transport difficulties caused by the Japanese occupation of Canton (22 October 1938) and the transfer of the Chinese government from Wuhan to Chung-

---

[13] [In the Japanese, Chinese and some of the Western literature this is designated by the name of 'battle of Changkufeng heights,' a knoll also called Zaozernaya in Russian.]

[14] Mao Tse-tung. *op. cit.,* Vol. 3, p. 190.

[15] *Ibid.* p. 82.

king (25 October 1938), the Soviet government fulfilled its obligations for the supply of armaments and various war materials within the framework of the first loan in 1938, and for the second loan in 1938 and the first half of 1939.

Until the fall of Canton and the occupation of the southern sea coast deliveries were mostly by sea and partly by the Sinkiang-Kansu motor road passing through Northwest China. After the interruption of maritime communications with South China, all traffic had to pass through the northeast. In order to continue armament, fuel and equipment deliveries the Soviet Union assisted China in the construction of macadam roads. Soviet motor convoys began to follow the Hocheng-Lanchow 2,700 kilometer route. Soviet organizations assisted China in building gas stations, unloading installations and warehouses along the convoy route.

In Sinkiang province, far from the front lines, the Chinese government concentrated its reserves for the war against Japan. In the Sinkiang area of Tushantze, Soviet geologists discovered oil fields and set up an oil-refinery. Soviet armaments reached the most active combat area on the Chinese front, in the north, where the Eighth National Revolutionary Army stopped the Japanese advance to the northwest and firmly held its positions in Shansi.

Subsequent events showed, however, that the ruling Chang Kai-shek clique did not profit from the favorable situation which the Soviet Union had helped to create. In violation of the united front program, which had been approved by the 2nd session of the National Political Council of the Chinese Republic (November 1938), the Kuomintang government again ignited the civil war and attempted to compromise with the Japanese.

Influenced by the Munich agreement, Chang Kai-shek attempted through the mediation of Carr, the British ambassador in China, to reach an agreement with Japan for 'peace and an alliance' on the basis of a declaration by the Japanese Prime Minister, Konoe Fumimaro. Even after the failure of these negotiations owing to the strong opposition of the anti-Japanese popular front, the Chang Kai-shek clique continued its conciliatory policy, and hostilities practically ceased along the Kuomintang front in 1939. Wishing at the same time to favor the imperialist and reactionary camp, the Kuomintang government interrupted the supply of equipment to the Eighth and Fourth National Revolutionary armies[16] and attacked them at several points.

The Soviet government could not disregard these actions; it had assisted the Chinese people in their struggle against the Japanese aggressors and had helped to maintain the united anti-Japanese national front, and could not now tolerate the use of its equipment by the Chang Kai-shek clique for the suppression of the progressive forces in China. In 1940 the Soviet Union thus found itself obliged to halt the military supplies within the framework of the third loan (total deliveries for this loan reached only US $73,176,000 instead of the US $150 million originally stipulated).

---

[16] [The Eighth Army was called *Paluchun,* or Army of Eastern Direction, and the Fourth, *Hsinssuchun,* or New Fourth Army.]

Chinese commodity deliveries in payment of the loans. According to the credit agreements, the Chinese government was to repay the Soviet loans by deliveries of Chinese goods; the principal and interest on the first loan were to be repaid beginning in 1938, payment of interest for the second loan began in 1938 and the principal on 1 July 1940; as for the third loan, interest payments began in 1939 and the principal on 1 July 1942.

Commodity deliveries to the Soviet Union were entrusted by the Chinese government to governmental organizations and organizations in which the state had an important share, which had been created in 1938 and 1939 with the imposition of governmental control on most import-export items. Nonferrous and rare metals were supplied by the Commission of National Resources of the Ministry of Economic Affairs, tea was supplied by the China Tea Company, and other products (silk, tung oil, bristles, wool, undressed leather and furs) by the Fu Hwa (Rich China) and Fu Hsin (Renaissance) companies, which later merged (1942) into the Fu Hsin company.

Contracts for commodity imports to the Soviet Union in payment for the loans were handled from the Soviet side by the agency of *Eksportkhleb,* which had been transferred from Shanghai to Chungking (only a small office remained open in Shanghai), under the general direction of the Soviet trade representation which had opened after the signing of the Chungking commercial treaty in December 1939.

Chinese goods were assembled in the south at Hong Kong; Chinese organizations shipped tea to Hong Kong from the central and southern provinces on small ships and junks from the provincial ports of Kwangtung and Fukien, tin was shipped from Yunnan, antimony from Hunan, tung oil, silk and bristles from Szechwan,

EXPORTS FROM UNOCCUPIED CHINA (EXCEPT SINKIANG)
TO THE SOVIET UNION IN 1938-1941

Goods	Unit	1938	1939	1940	1941
Tungsten concentrate	million rubles	3,964	4,600	1,600	4,500
Tin	,,	1,085	1,900	1,400	3,000
Mercury	,,	—	—	50	100
Antimony	,,	4,075	—	—	—
Zinc	,,	593	—	—	—
Tung oil	,,	568	1,500	2,000	3,600
Wool	,,	—	1,700	4,600	4,200
Raw silk	,,	—	35	24	61
Bristles	,,	57	—	50	209
Tea	,,	7,993	7,800	12,700	1,300
Fine undressed leather	thousand pieces	400	33	915	784
Furs	million rubles	—	0.5	0.9	0.3
TOTAL	million rubles	39.0	63.1	76.6	86.1

tungsten from Kiangsi, Kwantung and Kwangsi, etc. Branch offices of the four Chinese companies dealing in these commodity deliveries were opened in Hong Kong. The British government authorized the establishment of the Soviet *Eksport-*

khleb organization, which received the goods and shipped them to Odessa and Vladivostok.

In addition to these deliveries by maritime routes, goods began to be dispatched in the autumn of 1938 also through Lanchow-Urumchi. This route was used at first only for wool, collected by the Chinese companies in the northwestern provinces of Kansu, Tsinghai [Koko Nor] and Ninghsia.[17] Subsequently, other Chinese products, such as tungsten, raw silk, bristles, furs and undressed leather, began to be imported to the Soviet Union through the northwest as it became difficult to keep the southern maritime routes open.

A stock center was created in Singsingsia, on the border of Kansu and Sinkiang provinces, for the reception and shipping of Chinese goods, and a wool-washing plant opened in the town of Hami [Qomul] in Sinkiang. In spite of the Japanese block-ade of the seacoast and the interruption of traffic through Burma following the Anglo-Japanese agreement of 1 July 1940, the commercial relations between unoccupied

SOVIET EXPORTS TO SINKIANG PROVINCE IN 1937-1941

Goods	1937 tons	1937 thous. rubles	1938 tons	1938 thous. rubles	1939 tons	1939 thous. rubles	1941 tons	1941 thous. rubles
Cotton fabrics	2,998	12,981	4,265	18,916	2,738	11,651	3,092	15,122
Woolen fabrics	54	421	68	607	60	609	52	555
Silks	103	876	52	452	46	448	—	—
Clothing, linen	92	1,151	75	674	49	751	143	1,859
Tanned leather	127	340	71	331	91	402	75	407
Footwear	143	841	190	1,156	156	1,118	194	1,360
Sugar	3,547	1,393	3,928	1,526	2,841	1,220	3,166	1,575
Tea	1,509	2,611	1,223	1,223	1,261	3,024	408	1,691
Confectionery	207	316	172	272	182	379	194	463
Tobacco products	249	674	239	711	355	1,050	237	1,066
Pottery, porcelain, glass	568	612	944	748	467	427	758	714
Paper	678	587	1,225	1,032	788	480	836	635
Petroleum products	5,964	1,404	8,142	2,138	11,659	3,280	12,396	4,906
Ferrous metals and products	3,112	1,945	3,665	2,018	1,778	804	2,936	1,824
Agricultural machinery	515	238	315	120	262	109	625	488
Metal-cutting lathes	20	58	25	65	2	2	22	79
Electric motors and parts	129	346	115	295	72	238	71.1	389
Motor vehicles and bicycles	603	1,284	641	1,503	303	709	355	1,014
Telegraph, telephone and radio equipment	35	171	49	216	1	6	7	71
Other machines, equipment and instruments	144	628	272	88	88	281	275	1,267
TOTAL	25,733	34,753	29,596	43,381	27,364	33,107	33,240	47,097

[17] [Today the Ningsia Hui Autonomous Region. 'Hui' or 'Hwei' is the Chinese name of the people known in Anglo-American literature as Tungans, or Dungans.]

SOVIET IMPORTS FROM SINKIANG PROVINCE IN 1937-1941

Goods	1937		1938		1939		1940		1941	
	tons	thous. rubles	tons	thous. rubles	tons	thous. rubles	tons	thous. rubles	tons	thous. rubles
Small live-stock (thousand head)	253.6	3,804	437.1	7,445	478.1	8,993	478.1	9,233	563.0	10,785
Cattle (thousand head)	20.6	—	17.8	2,250	15.7	2,153	22.3	2,042	24.3	2,528
Horses (thousand head)	3.8	—	0.04	479	4.4	—	—	—	1.2	132
Sheep's wool	3,757	4,869	5,376	7,806	3,620	6,756	4,423	9,685	4,316	10,430
Camel hair	258	654	563	1,543	437	1,341	418	1,338	399	1,294
Goat's wool	63	178	77	204	63	176	76	234	62	191
Coarse undressed leather (thousand pieces)	41.4	671	49.9	439	61	773	82	977	68	695
Fine undressed leather (thousand pieces)	1,435	3,213	1,793	3,600	1,674	3,175	1,865	3,852	1,935	4,090
Furs	—	1,495	—	1,203	—	2,009	—	2,312	—	2,116
Peltry	—	1,936	—	1,779	—	1,581	—	1,657	—	2,326
Cotton fibers	1,286	1,489	1,538	1,749	2,699	2,612	2,554	2,166	1,202	1,210
Fruit (dry)	61.2	1,393	84.4	1,532	86	1,712	97	2,173	92	1,995
Raw silk	187	225	312	289	277	208	386	274	414	248
Animals casings (thousand bundles)	1,910	—	2,116	3,515	1,791	2,870	1,791	2,459	1,580	2,361
Oilseeds	856	402	1,609	484	1,638	590	2,371	726	1,413	434
TOTAL	28,990	25,774	36,438	35,197	—	41,700	—	47,100	—	43,700

China and the Soviet Union thus expanded instead of decreasing. In 1941, the year of the German aggression against the Soviet Union, the Chinese organizations greatly increased their deliveries of important strategic materials such as tungsten concentrate, tin, mercury, and of wool, undressed leather and other goods.

Economic relations of the Soviet Union with Sinkiang Province in 1937-1941. Progressive Sinkiang organizations, such as the *League for Combating Imperialism,* did not follow the reactionary Kuomintang policy. They demanded the mobilization of the nation's forces, as had been stipulated by the program for a united anti-Japanese front, and the strengthening of friendly ties with the Soviet Union. The Sinkiang authorities strove to develop trade with the Soviet Union and achieved a relatively important degree of economic development by putting to good use the deliveries of Soviet industrial and transport equipment and of products for general consumption. With Soviet assistance three saw-mills, three electric power-plants, two telephone exchanges, one radio station in Urumchi, one flour-mill in Kuldja, one printing and lithograph plant in Urumchi, two teaching workshops, etc., were built in Sinkiang in 1937-1938.

The economic development of the province was boosted by the conveyance of armaments, fuel and other materials from the Soviet Union to China proper and the export of Chinese products to the Soviet Union. These factors led to a considerable increase of the volume of Soviet-Sinkiang trade.

Soviet exports to Sinkiang increased in 1938 because most of the commodity deliveries stipulated by the credit agreements signed on 16 May 1935 and 1 July 1936 between *Sovsin'torg* and the Sinkiang purchasing firm of Tuchankungssu took place that year. These deliveries were completed at the end of 1939, and subsequent Soviet export transactions were normal commercial operations which paid for products bought in Sinkiang.

DEVELOPMENT OF THE MAIN ITEMS OF AGRICULTURAL PRODUCTION IN SINKIANG FOR 1936-1940

Goods	Unit	1936	1939	1940
Small live-stock	thous. head	12,921	13,930	16,368
Cattle	thous. head	818	1,388	1,308
Horses	thous. head	740	772	804
Gross yield of wheat	thous. tons	—	418	446
Gross yield of rice	thous. tons	—	803	973
Gross yield of corn	thous. tons	—	254	300
Gross yield of *kaoliang* [sorghum chinense]	thous. tons	—	62	65
Gross yield of raw cotton	thous. tons	—	20	28

The value of exports to the Soviet Union remained considerably lower than that of imports at the time of the Soviet deliveries within the framework of the credit agreements. After 1939, however, when Sinkiang began to refund the debt, the value of the exports at first almost equaled and later passed that of the imports from the Soviet Union.

The increase in the exports of cattle, grain, wool, undressed leather and other agricultural produce and game was made possible by achievements in economic development. The agricultural production of Sinkiang increased considerably in all the major items in 1939-1940.

Sinkiang's policy of friendly relations with the Soviet Union advanced the economy. Sinkiang was becoming China's powerful rear area in her struggle against Japanese imperialism.

ECONOMIC RELATIONS BETWEEN THE SOVIET UNION AND CHINA
DURING THE SECOND WORLD WAR

The German attack on the Soviet Union on 22 June 1941 interrupted the Soviet Union's normal economic relations with many capitalist countries. Military requirements, as well as the temporary Nazi occupation of Belorussia, the Ukraine, Moldavia, the Baltic Region, Crimea and certain areas of the Russian Federation and of the Caucasus, transformed the Soviet economy in the eastern regions of the Soviet Union, and modified the currents of foreign trade.

The trade routes with China remained unchanged. A new route for commodity traffic through Iran and from there by sea through the Indian Ocean became particularly important during the war years.

The enterprises which had been evacuated from the western and central regions of the country to Siberia and Central Asia, as well as the new wartime industries created in these areas, enabled the Soviet Union to continue deliveries of many industrial products usually exported to China. On the other hand, the unoccupied northwest provinces of China, which possessed important reserves of raw materials (wool, leather, etc.), were also in need of the Soviet market. In spite of the difficult military situation for both countries, objective conditions existed for the continuation of commercial relations, and both parties were interested in the development of mutual trade.

The situation developed differently, however, in actuality. The ruling Chang Kai-shek clique conducted an anti-democratic and treasonable domestic policy and renewed its previous hostile attitude toward the Soviet Union.

After hostilities had broken out in the Pacific (7 December 1941), the Kuomintang government formally declared war on Germany, Italy and Japan (9 December 1941), but ruling Kuomintang circles did not hide their sympathy for Nazi Germany. Their anti-Soviet attitude found its expression in Kuomintang foreign policy. The executive *Yuan* (the supreme executive organ of the Kuomintang government), presided over by Chang Kai-shek, refused to ratify a Sino-Soviet agreement for the construction of an aircraft plant in Sinkiang. The Kuomintang interrupted almost completely all relations with the Soviet Union through Sinkiang from the end of 1942 and put an end to commodity deliveries through this route.

The Kuomintang government simultaneously intensified its attacks against the Eighth Army and the regions occupied by the New Fourth Army. American military assistance, which China began to receive after Pearl Harbor, was used by the Kuomintang to reinforce its troops blockading the regions held by the Eighth and Fourth armies.

The Kuomintang reactionaries also launched at this time a campaign against the revolutionary organizations in Sinkiang province and compelled the Sinkiang administration to sever economic relations with the Soviet Union. In 1942 General Shen Shih-tsai, virtual ruler of Sinkiang, destroyed all democratic organizations and at Chang Kai-shek's behest organized mass executions of Chinese revolutionaries. A bloody civil war began in Sinkiang; the insurgents fiercely resisted the reactionary Kuomintang forces and set up democratic districts in the areas of Kuldja, Chuguchak [Tahcheng] and Sharasume [Altai, or Chenghwa].

The operation of Soviet trade organizations and the work of Soviet experts, particularly in the Tushantze oil fields and in other industries, became impossible throughout the territory controlled by Shen Shih-tsai. Chinese organizations, firms and individual merchants maintaining relations with Soviet commercial organizations were subjected to various persecutions, and individual arrests were made.

The Chang Kai-shek clique endeavored to curry favor with Japanese imperialism and German fascism by its anti-Soviet and anti-democratic policy. It strove to prove that the Kuomintang reactionaries had common ideals with the fascists[18] and to conclude a separate peace with Japan. In these difficult times for the Soviet people, the Kuomintang reactionaries became the accomplices of Nazi Germany against the Soviet Union, completely forgetting the disinterested assistance which the Soviet Union had extended to China. By taking measures toward the severance of economic ties between Northwest China and the Soviet Union, they hoped to create additional difficulties for the Soviet people and bring about a Nazi victory.

In these circumstances the Soviet Union could neither maintain normal commercial ties with China, including the neighboring province of Sinkiang, nor disregard the hostile acts committed by the Kuomintang reactionaries against Soviet trade representatives and experts. In May 1943 the Soviet government protested strongly against the hostile activities of the Sinkiang Kuomintang authorities, closed down its trade organizations in Sinkiang and withdrew all its commercial representatives and experts from the province.

Meanwhile, events on the Soviet-German front and in China itself turned against Nazi Germany and the Chang Kai-shek clique. The defeat of the fascist hordes at Stalingrad and the subsequent 1943 Soviet summer offensive near Kursk placed Germany in a very difficult position, gave the Soviet Union the advantage, and decided the favorable outcome of the war. The Soviet Union played a major role in

---

[18] In March 1943 Chang Kai-shek published his book entitled *China's Fate,* which attempted to prove that communist and liberal ideas were unacceptable for China, and stressed the superiority of the ancient moral values of the East. This book found enthusiastic critics in Japan. Japanese imperialist circles perceived the sir ''arity of Chang Kai-shek's views to their program for the creation of a 'Greater East Asia.'

the liberation of Europe from Nazism. Its victories also had a decisive effect on the situation in the Pacific.

During the same period the Chinese democratic movement gained strength under the Communist Party's leadership. The Eighth and New Fourth armies were then the main military units fighting against Japanese imperialism. After the fall of Wuhan 64 percent of the Japanese forces stationed in China and 95 percent of the Japanese puppet troops were occupied with operations against these two armies. Even the Japanese aggressors were forced to recognize the importance of the communist-led armies. In March 1943 the Japanese weekly, *Tokyo Domei Sekai Shuho,* wrote 'In our opinion, the Chinese Communist Party is the real force which has opposed Japan from the very first. Chungking is only an apparent center of resistance to Japan; in fact, it is the Communist Party—this main force force of the anti-Japanese front —which has brought China and Japan to their present situation.'[19]

The Chinese democratic forces not only successfully opposed the Japanese aggression, but also coped with the Kuomintang reactionaries' 'third anti-communist campaign.'[20] Agitation against the bloody Kuomintang dictatorship increased throughout the country. The disintegration of the Kuomintang army, the desertion of important detachments to the enemy and the rout of Chang Kai-shek's forces from the large-scale Japanese offensive in the south of China at the beginning of 1944 placed the Kuomintang reactionaries in a difficult position.

At a session of the National Political Council in September 1944, the Communist Party, supported by other democratic groups, demanded the abolition of the one-party Kuomintang dictatorship and the creation of a democratic coalition government as the only measure capable of creating an independent, free and powerful new Chinese state. The Communist Party appeal for the establishment of a coalition government was taken up by the masses and became the central demand of all democratic groups and parties.

Soviet public opinion expressed its warmest sympathy for the Chinese democratic forces in their struggle for final victory against Japanese imperialism and the democratization of China.

In negotiations with the Chinese Communist Party, the Kuomintang refused to discuss the most important issues—the democratization of the regime—and succeeded in obtaining a reduction of the Eighth and New Fourth armies and the removal of the authorities elected by the people in the liberated areas.

The Kuomintang policies did not change in the least and became even more dependent on the American monopolies, which were granted special rights and extensive possibilities for capital investment in all branches of the economy.

---

[19] Chen Po-ta. *Chang Kai-shek, Enemy of the Chinese People.* p.163 [translated from Chin. to Russ.].
[20] The Kuomintang armies launched a campaign against the liberated areas in the summer of 1943. Their attack was unsuccessful against the increasing military power of the Eighth and the New Fourth armies and was also hampered by the development of the democratic movement and the changes of the international situation after the victories of the Soviet army.

THE YALTA CONFERENCE AND THE WAR BETWEEN THE SOVIET UNION
AND JAPAN

The Soviet Army reached the Oder in January 1945. The final defeat of Germany and the complete liberation of Europe from fascist tyranny were at hand.

Hostilities continued in the Pacific. Japanese troops still occupied Indonesia, Indochina, Malaya and China. Shigemitsu, the Japanese Minister of Foreign Affairs, assured the 85th session of the Japanese parliament in a speech in January 1945 that the war alliance with Germany and her partners was becoming even stronger, and that Japan would continue fighting to the final victory.

The Japanese militarists continued their attempts to provoke the Soviet Union to war. The 500,000-strong elite Kwantung Army[21] was stationed in Manchuria along the Soviet border and thus menaced the Soviet Union in the Far East.

The Yalta Conference took place in February 1945 with the participation of the Soviet Union, the United States and Britain. On 11 February the leaders of the three powers signed an agreement according to which the Soviet Union would open hostilities against Japan within 2 to 3 months after the capitulation of Germany, with the following conditions:

1) maintenance of the *status quo* in Outer Mongolia (the Mongolian People's Republic);

2) restoration of the Russian rights which Japan had violated by her treacherous attack in 1904, viz.:

a) restitution of the southern part of Sakhalin Island and all the neighboring islands to the Soviet Union;

b) internationalization of the port of Dairen (Dalny), with the protection of the Soviet Union's dominant interests; renewal of the lease on Port Arthur as a Soviet naval base;

c) joint operation of the Chinese Eastern Railroad and the South Manchurian Railroad with an outlet to Dairen, on the basis of a joint Sino-Soviet company which would ensure the Soviet Union's dominant interests. China was to remain at the same time fully sovereign in Manchuria;

3) transfer of the Kuril Islands to the Soviet Union.[22]

It was stipulated at Yalta that President Roosevelt should reach an agreement with the Chinese government on all the points concerning the Monogolian People's Republic, Dairen, Port Arthur, the C.E.R. and the S.M.R. The Soviet Union agreed at the same time to conclude a pact of friendship and alliance with China to assist the Chinese armed forces to liberate their land from the Japanese yoke.[23]

---

[21] [Kwantung is the name for the southern tip of the Liaotung peninsula. From 1905 to 1931 the Japanese forces were stationed only on this leased territory and were designated by the term of 'Kwantung Army.' After the total occupation of Manchuria, all the Japanese forces in this area were thus designated up to 1945. It should not be confused with Kwangtung, one of the southern Chinese provinces.]

[22] *Foreign Policy of the U.S.S.R. Collected Documents,* Vol. 5, pp. 537-538 [Russ.].

[23] *Foreign Policy of the U.S.S.R. Collected Documents,* Vol. 5, p. 554 [Russ.].

The Soviet government advised the Japanese government on 5 April 1945 that it rescinded the Japanese-Soviet nonaggression pact signed on 13 April 1941, i.e., before the German aggression against Russia and the opening of hostilities between the Japanese and Anglo-American forces.

After the defeat and capitulation of Germany, it became possible for the Soviet Union to start the necessary military preparations in the Far East to carry out the obligations undertaken by the Yalta Agreement. The Potsdam Declaration, which demanded unconditional Japanese surrender, was a last warning to Japan. On 8 August 1945 the Soviet Union sent a declaration to the Japanese government stating that 'the Soviet Union would consider herself at war with Japan' from 9 August. Soviet forces opened hostilities on that date.

Negotiations between the Soviet and Chinese governments for the conclusion of the treaties and agreements discussed at Yalta had opened on 30 June 1945 and were nearing conclusion. A Treaty of Friendship and Alliance was signed in Moscow on 14 August; the Soviet Union and China were to fight Japan together, and undertook not to open separate negotiations with Japan and not to conclude without mutual consent any armistice or peace treaty with any Japanese government which would not reject all aggressive policies. The treaty also stipulated mutual assistance if one of the contracting parties 'became involved in military activities against Japan as a result of the latter's aggression'

The following documents were also signed on the same date: an agreement re-organizing the C.E.R. as the joint property of the Soviet Union and China and the joint management of this property for 30 years on a parity basis; an agreement concerning the use of Port Arthur as a joint naval base, the defense of which was entrusted by China to the Soviet Union for a period of 30 years; an agreement concerning Dalny (Dairen) port, and a number of other documents.

The agreements and treaties concluded laid firm foundations for the development of Sino-Soviet relations. They were designed to protect both parties from Japanese aggression. The Soviet people and progressive circles in China warmly greeted the outcome of these negotations; they clearly understood that only close cooperation between the two nations could put an end to the war and establish peace in this area of the world.

SINO-SOVIET TRADE IN 1942-1945

The disloyal, anti-Soviet Kuomintang policy during the war years also affected Sino-Soviet trade. From the latter half of 1942 the Kuomintang organizations discontinued their commodity deliveries to the Soviet Union from the provinces of Kansu, Ningsia, Tsinghai [Koko Nor] and Sinkiang.

The northwest provinces of Kansu, Ningsia and Tsinghai were protected in the west by the forces of the Eigth National Revolutionary Army, and remained free from Japanese occupation. These provinces were important producers of wool, the main item supplied to the Soviet Union through Northwest China. Increasing stocks of wool and other animal husbandry products accumulated yearly in the northwest provinces, which were cut off from the industrial centers (Shanghai, Tientsin, Nanking). This reduction of sales unfavorably affected the development of animal husbandry.

The Kuomintang clique disregarded these factors and set up a military barrier in the western part of Kansu province in order to oppose the popular movement; it isolated the northwestern provinces of China proper from Sinkiang with the troops of the reactionary general, Ma Pu-fang.

Conditions were somewhat different in Southwest China, which supplied tungsten concentrate, tin, bristles, silk and a number of other products to the Soviet Union. The Commission of National Resources continued to ship considerable quantities of tungsten concentrate, tin and mercury to the Soviet Union by air to India and from there by sea to south Iran.

EXPORTS FROM UNOCCUPIED CHINA (EXCLUDING SINKIANG) TO
THE SOVIET UNION IN THE WAR YEARS

Goods	*Units*	1942	1943	1944	1945
Tungsten concentrate	thousand tons	3.0	2.9	6.7	2.2
Tin	thousand tons	0.6	3.8	0.5	0.4
Mercury	thousand tons	0.1	0.1	0.1	0.03
Tung oil	thousand tons	0.7	—	—	0.5
Wool	thousand tons	2.4	1.2	0.2	—
Raw silk	tons	15	79	56	39
Furs	million rubles	0.3	—	0.7	—
Peltry	million rubles	1.5	0.6	1.3	0.2
Fine undressed leather	thousand pieces	—	—	100	—
Bristles	tons	—	123	316	130
Tea	thousand tons	—	—	0.4	0.1
TOTAL	million rubles	51.8	104.6	143.2	62.5

As a result of the closure of the northwest route by the reactionary Kuomintang clique, the Chinese side did not fulfil its obligations in commodity deliveries to the Soviet Union during the war years. The Kuomintang government did not refund the credits granted by the Soviet Union and in 1945 it still lagged behind stipulated deliveries by US $22.5 million.

Soviet-Sinkiang trade in 1942-1945. Trade between Sinkiang Province and the Soviet Union during the Second World War falls into two periods—before and after June 1943, when the Soviet trade organizations were forced to withdraw.

Soviet commodity deliveries in the war years reached a maximum of 47.1 million rubles in 1941. Deliveries decreased to 21.9 million rubles, i.e., by almost 250 percent, in 1942, mainly as a result of the hostile attitude of the Kuomintang toward Soviet trade organizations and the persecution of Chinese firms and individual merchants who dealt with the Soviet Union.

The volume of Sinkiang exports to the Soviet Union was relatively large in 1942 (reaching 45.4 million rubles), owing to deliveries by the Sinkiang government in payment for the credit granted by *Sovsin'torg* to Tuchankungssu in 1935 and 1936.

SOVIET EXPORTS TO SINKIANG PROVINCE IN 1942-1945

Goods	Units	1942	1943	1944	1945
Cotton fabrics	thousand meters	9,811	2,661	1,840	3,933
Woolen fabrics	thousand meters	99	9	19	33
Silks	thousand meters	544	82	47	45
Clothing	thousand rubles	1,099	2,343	167	129
Sugar	tons	2,202	309	40	402
Green brick tea	tons	69	10	3	16
Cigarettes	million units	41	32	5	12
Footwear	thousand pairs	7	8	4	2.2
Benzine	tons	1,338	42	—	491
Pottery and porcelain	thousand pieces	61	—	6	32
Paper	tons	684	60	2.7	27
Tires	sets	996	16	19	229
TOTAL	thousand rubles	21,900	11,600	3,300	7,700

Soviet trade with the areas of Sinkiang controlled by the Kuomintang ceased almost entirely in the second half of 1943. Trade began to develop at the same time with individual merchants and firms in areas controlled by the anti-Kuomintang administration. These operations remained limited, however, and the total volume of trade was insignificant.

SOVIET IMPORTS FROM SINKIANG PROVINCE IN 1942-1945

Goods	Units	1942	1943	1944	1945
Wool	tons	4,864	811	157	2,089
Cattle	thousand head	18.1	0.5	18.3	41.4
Small live-stock	thousand head	4,81.0	2.5	469.4	315.5
Horses	thousand head	50.2	2.2	19.0	25.5
Coarse undressed leather	thousand pieces	49.8	0.54	1.1	5.1
Fine undressed leather	thousand pieces	1,548	12.7	7.3	118
Furs	thousand rubles	1,319	31	33	386
Peltry	thousand rubles	1,781	38.5	58.6	629
Dried fruits	tons	228	14	1.3	1.1
Raw silk	tons	82	13	—	0.2
TOTAL		56.4	3.3	23.2	22.5

The decrease of Soviet exports to Sinkiang was due mainly to the almost complete interruption of sales of industrial products and transport equipment, as well as to a decrease in the quantities supplied of Soviet petroleum products, cotton fabrics, sugar, paper and other goods. The decrease of imports from Russia affected the economy; speculation developed, and led to inflation and economic disorganization. Prices of cotton fabrics and footwear increased one hundred fold between 1944 and 1946, sugar prices thirty-five fold, etc.

The decrease of exports to the Soviet Union, particularly exports of animal husbandry products, also affected the economy unfavorably.

All exports to the Soviet Union decreased in 1944-1945, except for cattle and small live-stock supplied by the Sinkiang authorities in payment for property purchased from the Soviet trade organizations when they closed down. The interruption of wool exports (the main item exported by the province) to the Soviet Union had a particularly unfavorable effect on local agriculture and prices dropped sharply, since connections with other markets, including that of China proper, had been cut and domestic consumption remained low.

During the war years the anti-national policy of the Kuomintang clique, who had not served the real interests of the Chinese people or met the needs of the anti-Japanese struggle, thus interrupted the normal Sino-Soviet commercial relations.

SINO-SOVIET ECONOMIC RELATIONS DURING THE THIRD
REVOLUTIONARY CIVIL WAR IN CHINA (1946-1949)

During August 1945 Soviet forces defeated the elite Japanese Kwantung Army and occupied Manchuria and the northern part of Korea. The defeat of the Japanese forces in Manchuria severely affected the morale of the entire Japanese army, which could no longer put up any serious resistance in other regions of China.

The Chinese People's Revolutionary Army launched an offensive in the North and toward Nanking and Shanghai. In their swift advance, detachments of the Eighth People's Revolutionary Army liberated Kalgan [Changkiakow], Chengteh and Chihfeng [Unlan Hada][24] and other cities. Detachments also reached liberated Manchuria.

The defeat of the Japanese occupation forces in Manchuria decided the outcome of the war in the Pacific. The Japanese government was compelled to sign an act of unconditional surrender on 2 September 1945 in Tokyo.

The Chinese people enthusiastically greeted the news of the surrender as a great event for China, exhausted by her 14 years of war against the Japanese aggressors. They believed that the expulsion of the Japanese would liberate China from imperialist domination and permit them to build a new life in their homeland. The Chinese people warmly hailed the Soviet Army, whose heroic struggle had helped them to avoid complete enslavement.

Subsequent events, however, only brought new tribulations. During the war against Japan the American monopolies had obtained Chang Kai-shek's consent to an open-door policy in China. The American imperialists and the Chang Kai-shek clique were interested in maintaining the semifeudal and semicolonial status in China, and in suppressing the people's revolutionary movement which fought against

[24] [The Russian text erroneously indicates here 'Chefoo,' on the Shantung peninsula.]

this regime. The Kuomintang government became to an increasing extent an agent of American imperialism. Having obtained financial and military aid from the United States, Chang Kai-shek prepared his offensive against the liberated areas of the country.

In order to play for time and consolidate their forces, the Kuomintang reactionaries concealed their plans in the first few months after the defeat of Japan, and proclaimed their intention of making a number of concessions to the democratic organizations. Mao Tse-tung was invited to negotiate with Chang Kai-shek in Chungking at the end of August 1945. An agreement was concluded on 10 October 1945 between the Kuomintang and the Communist Party establishing 'peace and a national front.'

A communique issued after these talks stated that both parties had agreed to set up a Political Consultative Council, which was to 'put an end to the political wardship[22] and establish a constitutional form of government... reach an agreement on the future of the country, discuss a program for peace and national reconstruction, and convene a national assembly.'

The perfidy of the Kuomintang assurances became evident only a few days after the signing of the agreement. Under cover of the negotiations with the Communist Party, which continued for 43 days, the Kuomintang reactionaries mobilized an army of 800,000-1,000,000 men and launched a swift offensive.

However, China's democratic forces had also been growing. The anti-popular forces were met by the heroic People's Liberation Armies (as the Eighth and New Fourth armies were then called), supported by the laboring masses of the Chinese people. This marked the beginning of the Third Civil War, provoked by the Kuomintang reactionaries with the support of American imperialism.

The civil war flared up when Soviet and American troops were still stationed on Chinese territory, with the accord of the Chinese (Kuomintang) government, in order to complete the capitulation of all Japanese forces. The civil war and the Kuomintang government's nonrecognition of the local authorities elected in the areas where Soviet troops were stationed made it difficult for the Soviet military administration to carry out its tasks. In these circumstances, which included the participation of American troops in the civil war, the Soviet government proposed talks with the United States on the Chinese situation.

The Moscow Conference of Soviet, American and British foreign ministers in December 1945 stressed the necessity of ending the civil war in China by achieving national unity and the democratization of all governmental organs. A meeting between the Soviet Minister of Foreign Affairs and the US Secretary of State re-

---

[25] Throughout the entire period of its authority, the Kuomintang government did not convene a national assembly and ruled without a constitution. Holding the same opinion as the imperialist governments, which held that the Chinese people were unprepared for democratic self-government, the Kuomintang reactionaries proclaimed that until the convening of a national assembly China would remain in the 'wardship' of the Kuomintang, which would administer the national affairs in the country's name. Article 1 of the Kuomintang government program published in 1928 stated: 'During the period of political wardship, the national congress of the Kuomintang will rule the country and exercise governmental power in the name of the people.'

resulted in 'complete agreement as to the desirability of evacuating Soviet and American forces from China as quickly as is possible and compatible with the ful- filment of their obligations and responsibilities.'[26]

In accordance with this agreement, the Soviet government began the evacuation of its forces from Manchuria in March-April 1946, with the consent of the Chinese side. The last detachment of Soviet troops left the Pogranichnaia (Suifenho) station for the Maritime Territory on 3 May of the same year.

The American government, however, not only deferred the withdrawal of its troops from China after the conclusion of the Moscow agreement, but on the con- trary dispatched new forces and extensive military supplies to the Kuomintang armies.[27] American planes and ships transferred to South Manchuria large Kuo- mintang forces with modern equipment, which succeeded in seizing the most import- ant towns: Mukden [Shenyang], Changchun, Szepingkai [Szeping], Fushun, and others. The murderous regime which the Kuomintang instated in South Manchuria with American assistance paralyzed the economic development of the region.

In flagrant violation of the agreement concluded with the Soviet Union for the joint administration of the Chinese Changchun Railroad (C.C.R.), the Kuomintang and their American advisers seized the railroad. The C.C.R. Board in Changchun found itself in difficult straits and the Soviet members of the administration were forced to leave for home at the end of April 1946 (after the evacuation of Soviet troops from Changchun on April 14-15).

Kuomintang China became increasingly dependent upon American imperialism. On 4 November 1946 the United States signed with the Kuomintang government a 'Treaty of Friendship, Commerce and Navigation' which the Chinese people called the 'new twenty-one conditions.'[28]

A number of economic and military agreements between the Kuomintang and the United States (aviation treaty of December 1946; agreement of July 1947 concerning the administration of the Yunnan-Indochina railroad and the construction of a Szechwan-Yunnan railroad; treaty of 16 October 1947 on international customs and trade etc.), which tightened American control of the Chinese economy.

United States interference in Chinese domestic affairs and seizure of key positions in the Chinese economy aroused the indignation of the Chinese laboring masses and bourgeoisie. Many strata of Chinese society cooperated in the struggle against the Kuomintang reactionaries and the American interventionists. The ranks of the People's Liberation army swelled rapidly; the reactionary forces constantly de- creased.

The Soviet government consistently exerted pressure for the withdrawal of Ameri- can troops from China. The Soviet delegate in the United Nations Security Council, A. Gromyko, declared on September 23: 'The stationing of American troops in

---

[26] *Foreign Policy of the U.S.S.R. Collected Documents*, Vol. 6, p. 108 [Russ.].

[27] More than US $5 billion of armaments and military equipment were imported to China by the United States in 1945-1948.

[28] Alluding to the 'Twenty-one demands' raised by Japan in 1915.

China, which is unjustified in the present conditions, and their interference in China's domestic affairs have evoked a wave of protest from wide circles of Chinese society... All these voices must be heard. It is impossible to disregard them. They raise a problem which involves more than just China and the United States.'[29]

In a letter of April 1947 to the US Secretary of State, G. Marshall, the Soviet Ministry of Foreign Affairs, referring to the decisions of the December 1945 Moscow conference, pointed out that the United States had not fulfilled its obligations as to the withdrawal of American troops from China although more than one year had passed since the conference, and demanded the discussion of this issue at a joint meeting of the Soviet, American and British foreign ministers.

Meanwhile, the Kuomintang was progressively demoralized, despite the American aid. Manchuria and Inner Mongolia were liberated at the end of 1948. Fearing imminent defeat and realizing how unpopular American policies were, the Kuomintang government attempted evasive tactics in the last days of its existence and tried to enlist in in its favor the authority which the Soviet Union had gained in international affairs. On 8 January 1949 the Kuomintang Minister of Foreign Affairs requested that the Soviet Union act as mediator in peace talks between the Kuomintang government and the Chinese Communist Party. The Deputy-Minister of Foreign Affairs of the Soviet Union, A. Vyshinsky, received the Kuomintang ambassador on 17 January 1949 and handed over the Soviet answer; it stated that the Soviet Union maintained its steadfast respect of the principle of non-intervention in the domestic affairs of other states, did not find it expedient to accept the role of mediator, and considered that the restoration of national unity concerned the Chinese people alone.[30]

Reestablishment of Soviet foreign trade organizations in China and reopening of Sino-Soviet trade. Soviet foreign trade organizations renewed their activities in the large commercial and industrial centers of Central, North and Northeast China after the Japanese surrender and the liberation of these areas. Offices of the Soviet trade delegation reopened in Shanghai, Harbin and Mukden at the end of 1945. The Soviet associations *Eksportkhleb, Intourist, Dal'vneshtrans* [Far Eastern Foreign Transport Bureau], *Dal'bank* and others renewed their activity in Manchuria at the same time, and the Soviet Trade Delegation was transfered from Chungking to Nanking in June 1946.

The civil war provoked by the Chang Kai-shek clique with American assistance, however, obstructed Sino-Soviet trade. In the coastal regions of Central, South and North China held by the Kuomintang foreign trade was controlled by American monopolies, and China did not enjoy equal rights in commercial operations. Chinese commercial and industrial enterprises could not compete with the powerful American monopolies and were doomed to bankruptcy.[31]

---

[29] *Foreign Policy of the U.S.S.R. Collected Documents,* Vol. 6, p. 656 [Russ.].
[30] *Foreign Policy of the U.S.S.R. in* 1949, pp. 39-40—Moskva. 1953 [Russ.].
[31] American dumping on the Shanghai market in 1945 and 1946 resulting in the closing down the Kiao Fu match plant, the Ta Lung and Ya Chung wool industries, and ten knitted-goods factories, including the Chung Kuo, Li I, Hwa An and Fu Kang enterprises.

The throng of American advisers and instructors who controlled all the branches of the economy throughout Kuomintang territory afforded the United States an exclusive status and ensured the domination of American capital. The United States' share in Chinese foreign trade in 1946 was 57.1 percent of Chinese imports and 38.7 percent of her exports. All the main items of Chinese export were a monopoly of the Kuomintang trade bodies. These products were either exported to the United States in payment for American loans or were sold for cash, which the Kuomintang businessmen deposited in American banks.

SOVIET EXPORTS TO CENTRAL CHINA IN 1946-1949

Goods	Units	1946	1947	1948	1949
Paper	thousand rubles	13.3	9.1	14.4	10.3
Products for Tibetian medicine	thousand rubles	3,992	6,465	—	875
Sea products	thousand rubles	1,814	3,225	—	32
Window glass	thousand m²	—	—	113	—
TOTAL	thousand rubles	21,964	40,549	34,765	39,607

The Kuomintang reactionaries were hostile to trade with the Soviet Union. Continuing to control all export-import operations, they hindered Chinese firms trading with the Soviet Union. Soviet trade with the territory controlled by the Kuomintang authorities remained sporadic throughout 1945-1949 and involved only small lots of Russian goods which entered China mainly through Hong Kong.

CHINESE DELIVERIES TO THE SOVIET UNION IN PAYMENT FOR LOANS (1946-1949)

Goods	Units	1946	1947	1948	1949
Tungsten concentrate	tons	4,748	4,485	2,430	625
Tin	tons	858	719	—	81
Antimony	tons	—	1,000	200	400
Tung oil	tons	4,188	2,999	3,018	1,625
Raw silk	tons	103	59	95	56
Wool	tons	—	728	—	—
Bristles	tons	395	295	242	333
Tea	tons	—	748	2,738	793
Furs peltry	thousand rubles	—	919	—	—
TOTAL	million rubles	87.2	78.0	48	17.4

The Kuomintang government did not respect its obligations as to commodity deliveries to the Soviet Union in payment for the 1938-1939 loans. On 1 July 1946 the Chinese still owed US $19 million, and this debt continued to increase yearly, although the Kuomintang authorities disposed of important commodity resources in the postwar period.

Of China's total credit obligations to the Soviet Union—US$201,779,000 (US $173,176,000 principal and US$28,603,000 interest)—commodities valued at US $161,990,000 were delivered to the Soviet Union between 1 December 1938 and 31 October 1949.

Soviet organizations did not make any commercial purchases in 1946-1949 in the territory controlled by the Kuomintang.

Commercial operations of Soviet organizations in North Manchuria. The situation differed with respect to Soviet foreign trade with Manchuria. In spite of the Kuomintang's attempts to suppress the people's revolutionary movement with the assistance of American imperialist circles and to establish the Kuomintang dictatorship in Southeast China, North Manchuria (to the north of Changchun) and the north of the Liaotung peninsula remained firmly in the hands of the People's Liberation Army, which set up organs of a people's government. Cut off from North and Central China, the people's democratic areas of the northeast needed industrial products, petroleum products and certain types of industrial raw materials. On the other hand, North Manchuria produced soybean and other agricultural surpluses. Consequently, the Chinese commercial firm, Tungsing, and other enterprises began to establish commercial ties with Soviet foreign trade bodies at the end of 1946.

The first deal for commodity deliveries was concluded on 21 December 1946 between the foreign-trade organization, *Eksportkhleb,* and the Tungsing company. From December 1946 to October 1947 the latter delivered various alimentary products for a sum of 23.4 trillion southeast *yüans* [the southeast or Manchurian *yüan* was called *Tungpeiliutungchuan*]. In the same period *Eksportkhleb* delivered to the Tungsing company cotton fabrics, raw cotton, petroleum products, salt, coal and various industrial products for a sum of 29.1 trillion southeast *yüans.*

As the provinces of Northeast China were gradually liberated from the Kuomintang and the economy of the democratic areas was consolidated, the volume of trade of Chinese companies and firms with the Soviet foreign trade organizations increased. A trade delegation of the Manchurian people's democratic authorities visited Moscow in July 1949 and signed a one-year agreement for mutual commodity deliveries between the Soviet Union and Manchuria.[32]

Part of the grain purchased in Manchuria *kaoliang* [Sorghum chinense], soybean, *hsiaomitze* [Italian millet—*Setaria italica* supsp. *maxima*] was shipped through Vladivostok or North Korea to the Liaotung peninsula, which remained cut off from North Manchuria in 1947 and 1948.

Volume of foreign trade carried on by I.I. Tschurin & Co., Ltd. The firm of I.I. Tschurin & Co., Ltd, participated to a certain extent in the North Manchurian trade with the Soviet Union; Soviet foreign trade organizations became shareholders of the firm in November 1945.[33]

[32] *Foreign Policy of the U.S.S.R. in* 1949, p. 124. Moskva. 1953 [Russ.].
[33] After the branch of I.I. Tschurin and Co. in the Soviet Far East was closed in 1928, the owners set up the Joint Association of the Commercial Firm I.I. Tschurin & Co. in Manchuria. After the Japanese

In 1946-1947 I.I. Tschurin & Co. reopened large general stores (in Harbin, Dalny [Talien], Mukden [Shenyang], Kiamusze, Tsitsihar, Mutankiang, Hailar [Hulun], Suifenho [Pogranichnaia], at Manchouli station and at a number of other points along the border) and processing plants (one distillery, one brewery, sausage and confectionery factories, and other enterprises). However, the distance from the industrial centers of North and Central China and the closing of most Chinese enter-

VOLUME OF TRADE BETWEEN THE NORTHEAST COMPANIES (MANCHURIA, EXCLUDING THE LIAOTUNG PENINSULA) AND SOVIET FOREIGN TRADE ORGANIZATIONS IN 1947-1949

		Units	1947	1948	1949
I.	Soviet imports from the northeastern provinces	million rubles	201.7	346.5	470.7
	Soybean	thousand tons	298.2	366.2	568
	Kaoliang	thousand tons	33.5	25.9	0.6
	Hsiaomitze	thousand tons	21.7		6.1
	Corn	thousand tons	95.6	140.2	84.1
	Wheat	thousand tons	82.1	44.4	4.2
	Meat	thousand tons	7.4	3.5	3.4
	Rice	thousand tons	15.4	44.3	28.7
	Vegetable oil	thousand tons	6.3	5.3	18.5
	Bristles	tons	32	27	110
II.	Soviet exports to the northeastern provinces	million rubles	212.1	327.5	445.2
	Cars, motorcycles, bicycles	million rubles	10.4	26.3	34.5
	Industrial equipment	million rubles	1.0	15.6	24.6
	Ferrous metals	thousand tons	0.07	3.9	17.1
	Petroleum products	thousand tons	8.4	46.6	52.4
	Chemical products	million rubles	0.5	1.8	25.9
	Rubber and rubber products	million rubles	—	7.0	9.8
	Drugs and medical supplies	million rubles	1.8	3.2	5.7
	Sugar	thousand tons	1.4	3.2	5.9
	Paper	thousand tons	1.5	3.0	10.4
	Cotton	thousand tons	6.5	12.9	11.8
	Wadding	thousand tons	2.6	5.6	3.9
	Cotton fabrics	million meters	21.1	30.5	19.8
	Cotton yarn	million meters	0.6	1.9	287
III.	Total volume	million rubles	413.8	674.0	915.9

occupation of Manchuria, the association was compelled to reduce its activities and found itself in difficult financial straits. The British Hong Kong—Shanghai Bank, with Japanese cooperation, profited from this to acquire all the association's property at a very low price. In 1937 the Hong Kong—Shanghai Bank reorganized the association into a joint-stock company, I.I. Tschurin & Co. At the beginning of the war in the Pacific the Japanese seized the company and created another joint-stock company bearing the same name. After the defeat of Japanese imperialism, the Chinese government proclaimed as illegal all seizure and 'acquisition' of property by the Japanese during the war, and reinstated previous owners with their rights. In November 1945 the representative of the Hong Kong-Shanghai Bank in Harbin sold the stock of I.I. Tschurin & Co. to Soviet foreign trade organizations for 4,614,000 *yüan*. The company was reorganized in 1947, increased its stock to 220,000,900 *yüan* and offered 2,200,000 hundred-*yüan* shares. These were purchased by the following Soviet foreign trade bodies: *Dal'intorg* (Far-Eastern Foreign Trade Bureau)—1,605,000 shares, *Eksportkhleb*—540,000 shares, *Mezhkniga* (International Publishing House)—11,120 shares, and *Dal'vneshtrans*—43,880 shares.

prises during the Japanese occupation prevented I. I. Tschurin & Co. from supplying its enterprises and stores with locally produced industrial raw materials and products. In these circumstances the people's democratic administration authorized the joint-stock company to purchase industrial products from the Soviet Union, to be repaid in alimentary products (grain, meat, etc.). The firm's volume of foreign trade remained relatively low, the volume of operations with Soviet foreign trade organizations reaching 5.5 million rubles in 1947, 17.4 million in 1948 and 38.4 million in 1949.

Commercial operations between Soviet organizations and the enterprises and firms of North China and the Liaotung peninsula. The Liaotung peninsula remained cut off from North and Central China and from the liberated areas of North Manchuria up to the liberation of South Manchuria from the Kuomintang (November 1948). This region was thus compelled to import from abroad all the raw materials and equipment necessary for its industry, and alimentary and industrial products for general consumption. Commercial bonds were established in 1946 between Soviet foreign trade bodies and enterprises of the Liaotung peninsula (the *Dal'dok* plant, the industrial commercial company *Kvantunryba* [Far Eastern Fisheries], *Dal'energo* [Far Eastern Energy Works], locomotive works, etc.).

Commercial operations between Liaotung firms and industries and the Soviet foreign trade associations expanded beginning in 1947, and regular deliveries were initiated within the framework of long-term agreements. Representatives of the Soviet foreign trade body, *Dal'intorg,* and Liaotung commercial organizations concluded annual agreements for the delivery of industrial raw materials, equipment and alimentary products by the Soviet Union in exchange for local Liaotung industrial products, salt and other items. Economic conditions improved in the Liaotung peninsula as South Manchuria and North China were gradually liberated by the People's Army, and the democratic Liaotung authorities then succeeded not only in meeting local requirements by purchasing Chinese raw materials and alimentary products, but also in exporting some types of alimentary products to the Soviet Union and North Korea. Moreover, the industrial reconstruction and development of Dalny required increasing imports of industrial equipment, petroleum products, motor vehicles and other goods. In 1949 the annual volume of the foreign trade of the Liaotung peninsula with Soviet organizations reached 200 million rubles.

After the liberation of Peking in January 1949 the people's democratic authorities began to organize foreign trade in North China as well. A board for the control of foreign trade—the North China Foreign Trade Company—was created in Peking in the spring of 1949. The reestablishment of railroad connections between Peking and Mukden enabled North China to maintain commercial relations both with the northeast and with the Soviet Union. The first commercial operations between the North China Foreign Trade Company and Soviet foreign trade associations (*Dal'intorg, Eksportkhleb*) were concluded in September 1949 and involved commodity deliveries valued at 31 million rubles by each side. These deliveries were effected in the last quarter of 1949.

Volume of trade of Soviet foreign trade organizations with Sinkiang province in 1946-1949. The domestic situation in Sinkiang remained tense at the beginning of 1946. An agreement was signed on 2 January 1946 between the Kuomintang administration and the democratic authorities of the Kuldja territory which put an end to hostilities and stipulated the peaceful settlement of political and economic issues. As elsewhere, however, the Kuomintang used these negotiations to play for time and concentrate their forces against the people's democratic movement. Having agreed to the establishment of a provincial democratic government for the entire province of Sinkiang, in April 1946 the Kuomintang placed at its head the reactionary Maksud, who advocated separating Sinkiang from China and incorporating it into Pakistan. American representatives traveling to Sinkiang as journalists, consular employees, etc. (Stevenson in the middle of 1947, Page in the autumn of the same year) granted considerable assistance to the Maksud government. Shipton, the British consul, broadened the scope of his 'activities' in that period in the south of the province.

In the summer of 1947 the Kuomintang reactionaries launched a new campaign against the democratic organizations. On June 30 an armed gang destroyed an Urumchi club belonging to the Uighur educational association. In September 1947 armed groups led by large feudal landowner, ex-Governor Osman of the Sharasume [Altai, or Chenghwa] region, raided and destroyed the city of Sharasume and the surroundings regions. At the same time the central Kuomintang government dispatched new detachments to Sinkiang and began to prepare an offensive against the people's democratic forces in the province.

The representatives of the democratic regions (Kuldja, Chuguchak [Tahcheng], Sharasume) thus had no choice but to withdraw from the provincial government in August 1947 and leave Urumchi. This split also caused agitation within the Kuomintung camp. Those Kuomintang public figures who recognized the treachery of Chang Kai-shek's policies advocated the continuation of peaceful and democratic rule in Sinkiang; they clearly understood that a civil war would severely affect the province's economic situation. A progressive group in the Sinkiang administration (Chang Chih-chung, Lui Tse-chung and others) stood for the reopening of trade with the Soviet Union and the establishment of friendly relations.

Before the severance of relations with the democratic authorities Chang Chih-chung, Governor-General of Sinkiang, had sent a proposal on 4 November 1946 to the Soviet Consul General in Urumchi for the reopening of the Soviet-Sinkiang trade and the creation of joint Sino-Soviet companies on a parity basis to prospect for and extract metals and oil. This proposal came to nothing since it was opposed by the Kuomintang warlord clique which controlled the province. The Kuomintang reactionaries unleashed a defamatory press campaign against the Soviet Union in order to bring about the severance of relations and tried to convince the Sinkiang population of the necessity of turning to the United States and other imperialist powers for assistance.

Trade between the Soviet Union and the areas of Sinkiang controlled by the Kuomintang was completely interrupted. Relations between Soviet organizations and the border areas controlled by the people's democratic administration developed in an entirely different manner, and commercial firms and individual merchants continued to maintain ties with the branch offices of the Soviet foreign trade association, *Sovsin'torg*. As in previous years, Chinese merchants drove cattle to the border, shipped wool, undressed leather, furs and other goods to the border points, and concluded operations with *Sovsin'torg* for the exchange of cotton fabrics, silks, sugar, petroleum products, and other Soviet goods.

Commerce between Sinkiang merchants and *Sovsin'torg* remained exclusively a barter trade. In some cases such as the purchase of live-stock and wool, *Sovsin'torg* granted credit for one season to the Chinese merchants while the goods were being prepared.

COMMERCIAL OPERATIONS OF SOVIET FOREIGN TRADE ORGANIZATIONS
WITH SINKIANG PROVINCE IN 1946-1949

		Units	1946	1947	1948	1949
I.	Soviet imports from Sinkiang	million rubles	23.8	22.1	30.4	36.0
	Cattle	thousand head	48.2	21.3	34.7	35.2
	Small live-stock	thousand head	334.9	399.9	344.5	319.3
	Wool	tons	1,267	1,697	1,061	1,166
	Coarse undressed leather	thousand pieces	106	63	25	23
	Fine undressed leather	thousand pieces	520	495	379	412
	Animal casings	thousand bundles	516	829	642	631
	Furs and peltry	thousand rubles	1,240	2,195	1,391	1,299
	Animal fats	tons	184	159	215	291
	Vegetable oil	tons	75	7	648	413
	Wheat	thousand tons	1.7	2.4	21.1	31.4
II.	Soviet exports to Sinkiang	million rubles	23.8	22.1	30.4	36.0
	Cotton fabrics	thousand meters	6,102	7,942	10,410	12,449
	Silks	thousand meters	165	65	261	244
	Clothing	thousand rubles	358	394	348	601
	Sugar	tons	1,159	1,954	909	1,129
	Tea	tons	186	94	132	167
	Cotton yarn	thousand spools	1,266	2,003	1,672	1,761
	Matches	thousand excise crates	6.7	31.4	22.5	5.3
	Petroleum products	tons	1,599	741	600	1.46
III.	Total volume of trade	million rubles	47.6	44.2	60.8	72.0

The volume of the Sinkiang border trade remained relatively stable in 1946-1947 and was handled by a number of minor Chinese merchants residing in the Sinkiang towns close to the Soviet border. Chinese merchants from cities deep inside Sinkiang began to take part in this trade in 1948 and particularly in 1949, and the volume of trade with the Soviet Union began to increase noticeably.

*   *

*

1) Sino-Soviet economic relations changed considerably between 1937 and 1949.

The Soviet Union continued as always to regard sympathetically and to assist the Chinese people's struggle for independence, freedom and democracy.

Sino-Soviet relations improved during this period, when historical factors led to the formation of a popular anti-imperialist front in China, and Chinese foreign policy was being liberated to some extent from the control of imperialist powers and began to represent the national interests. Thus in 1937-1938 the Kuomintang and the Communist Party cooperated and set up a united popular front against Japanese imperialism, and the Chinese government sought a rapprochement with the Soviet Union; agreements for Soviet loans to China and a Sino-Soviet commercial treaty were concluded. In 1945 the Kuomintang reactionaries again were compelled to take into account the Chinese people's democratic movement, and Chinese foreign policy took a common stand with the democratic forces in the international arena; China joined the Three-Power Agreement between the Soviet Union, the United States, and Britain against Japanese imperialism.

Sino-Soviet relations deteriorated and economic ties were broken off when reactionary forces gained the ascendancy in China, the Chinese government lost contact with the democratic movement and its foreign policy served foreign interests. Thus in 1942-1943 the Kuomintang government disbanded the progressive democratic organizations of Sinkiang province and made conditions impossible for the continuation of economic ties between China and the Soviet Union through Northwest China. In 1946-1948 the Kuomintang clique unleashed a civil war in China with American support, let itself be dominated in its foreign policy by American imperialist circles and interrupted completely all commerce between the territory which it controlled and the Soviet Union.

2) Throughout the entire period of existence of the reactionary Kuomintang regime the Chinese people continued their unflagging struggle for democratic reforms and an independent foreign policy. A people's democratic administration which fulfilled the revolutionary aspirations of the Chinese people was set up under the leadership of the Communist Party on the territories liberated from the Kuomintang.

As the democratic areas consolidated and expanded, the artificial barriers set up by the Chinese reactionaries to prevent cooperation with the Soviet Union were eliminated and the traditional friendship between the two mighty neighbors was restored.

At the time of the victory of the people's democratic revolution, relatively important commercial ties had already been established between Soviet foreign trade organizations and the areas of China liberated by the People's Democratic Army which bordered on the Soviet Union; these ties laid foundations for a new period of friendly and close cooperation between the Soviet and the Chinese peoples.

CHAPTER EIGHT

ECONOMIC RELATIONS BETWEEN THE SOVIET UNION AND CHINA AFTER THE ESTABLISHMENT OF THE PEOPLE'S REPUBLIC OF CHINA

THE INTERNATIONAL AND DOMESTIC SITUATION ON THE EVE OF THE ESTABLISHMENT OF THE PEOPLE'S REPUBLIC OF CHINA

THE defeat of fascist Germany and militarist Japan undermined world imperialism and decisively influenced the development of the popular democratic movement for national liberation in the countries liberated from Hitlerism and in the colonial and semicolonial territories.

People's democratic republics, states of a new type, based on an alliance of the working classes and the peasantry under the leadership of the former and following the road of socialist development, were established and developed successfully in both the East and West. Socialism thus spread beyond the boundaries of a single country and became a worldwide system.

The Soviet people's historic victory in World War II demonstrated to the entire world the invincible vital force of the socialist system and its incomparable advantages over capitalism. After the conclusion of the war, the Soviet Union implemented through its own resources and without any foreign credits a plan for the rehabilitation and further development of its economy. Despite the destruction of highly productive areas temporarily occupied by the Nazi armies, a destruction which occasioned a 23 percent decrease in Soviet 1946 industrial production relative to the prewar (1940) level, the Soviet Union succeeded in rebuilding its industry in the first three postwar years; in 1949 the prewar production level was surpassed by 63 percent for means of production and 7 percent for consumer goods, i.e., a total increase of 41 percent. The high productivity of the socialist mode of production was clearly confirmed by the rapid growth of the gross national product.

The Soviet Union, a workers' state knowing no economic crises or upheavals, which is successfully developing its economy in the interests of the people, a fraternal union of many nations settled on territories which differ in geographic and economic conditions and a great power steadfastly pursuing a policy of peace, equality and mutual respect of the interests of large and small states, has set an inspiring example for the workers of the world.

Its first-class industry and highly skilled scientific and technical workers have enabled the Soviet Union to extend comprehensive assistance to other people's democracies and to help speed up their economic development.

The economic reconstruction and development of the Soviet Union and the people's democracies have strengthened the forces militating for peace, socialism and democracy. The influence of the Soviet Union and the people's democracies in international affairs has thus grown immeasurably.

In its struggle against internal reaction and imperialism, the Chinese people received the warmest cooperation and support of the socialist countries. In the East, North and Northwest, the territories liberated from the reactionary Kuomintang could rely on their rear, and they were guaranteed against any imperialist attack from that direction.

GROWTH OF SOVIET GROSS PRODUCT
COMPARED TO THAT OF TSARIST RUSSIA[1]
(in 1926/27 prices)

Year	Billion rubles
1913	21.0
1926	21.7
1940	128.3
1950	177.0

The imperialist forces also lost ground along the southern borders of China. A powerful movement of national liberation followed the defeat of Japanese imperialism in the neighboring countries of Southeast Asia. The peoples of Indochina, Indonesia, Burma and India rose against colonial enslavement in a struggle for freedom, independence and democracy. Imperialist powers who had previously possessed colonies in this area and militated anew for colonial supremacy could no longer use the territories as military bases nor could they compel the local populations to oppose the revolutionary movement in China.

The consolidation of the socialist countries and the growth of movements of national liberation in Southeast Asia created favorable conditions for the successful conclusion of the Chinese people's struggle.

The Chinese Communist Party, guided by the revolutionary doctrine of Marxism-Leninism as adapted to the special conditions of China, and skilfully taking advantage of the favorable international situation, led the workers' revolutionary struggle against the semifeudal and semicolonial system in China.

The Party's policy in the period of the new democratic revolution was contained in the resolutions passed by its 7th Congress, held in Yenan in April 1945. Mao Tse-tung stated in his report to the congress: 'At the present stage of China's historical development we communists are in agreement with the opinion of the great majority of the population concerning the following matters. First, the system of government in China should not be feudal, fascist, or undemocratic—not a dictator-

---

[1] Zhukovskii, Ya. *The Rise of the Material and Cultural Standard of Living in the New Five-Year Plan for 1946-1950.*—Published by the Higher Party School of the Central Committee of the All-Union Communist Party of Bolshevics. 1951 [Russ.].

ship of big landowners and the upper bourgeoisie...Second, it is impossible to establish in China—and therefore one should not try to establish—a democratic dictatorship of the old type, controlled only by the national bourgeoisie; this is so because, on the one hand, the national bourgeoisie in China is extremely weak both economically and politically, and on the other hand, there has long since emerged in China a new factor, the class-conscious Chinese proletariat, which has demonstrated its power in the political arena, is leading the broad masses of the peasantry, the urban petty bourgeoisie, the intelligentsia and other democratic elements, and is itself guided by the Chinese Communist Party.'[2]

Mao Tse-tung pointed out in the same report that the necessary socio-economic conditions for the introduction of a socialist system did not yet exist in China; the Chinese Communist Party thus set as its immediate goal the establishment of a governmental system based on a democratic alliance between the members of a united front supported by the great majority of the population under the leadership of the working class; the transition to higher stages of social development—socialism and communism—was part of the program for subsequent development. He said: 'We communists have never concealed our political aims. The program for our further struggle, our maximum program, aims at raising China to a higher stage—the stage of socialism and communism.'[3]

Subsequent events fully confirmed the correctness and vitality of the political line adopted by the 7th Congress of the Chinese Communist Party. The laboring masses of the Chinese people rallied in millions to the Communist Party and joined the struggle against the reactionary Kuomintang for the establishment of a people's democratic republic.

Chang Kai-shek's temporary military superiority at the beginning of the Third Civil War[4] could not alter the general trend of events. China's ancient reactionary system hampered economic and political development and did not accord with the interests of either the laboring classes or the national bourgeoisie. It became obvious to the majority of the Chinese people that any consolidation of the reactionary Kuomintang regime would reinforce the semicolonial and semifeudal status and would destroy the people's hopes of building an independent, democratic state.

On 10 October 1947 the Chinese National Liberation Army in an appeal to the whole nation called for the overthrow of the reactionary Kuomintang regime and the establishment of a people's democratic republic. On the same day the Chinese Communist Party published the main clauses of the land law, proclaiming the abolition of the system of feudal exploitation in agriculture and introducing an agrarian system based on the principle 'to each tiller his own field.' The implementation of the land reform in the liberated territories abolished the landowner class and consolidated the government organs of the people's democratic regime. The democratic reforms applied in these territories elicited the revolutionary enthusiasm of the

---

[2] Mao Tse-tung. *Selected Works*, Vol. 4, pp. 501-502 [Russ. ed.].
[3] Mao Tse-tung. *op.cit.*, Vol. 4, p. 507.
[4] The Third Civil War in China covers the period from 1946 to 1949.

laboring masses and swelled the ranks of class-conscious fighters in the National Liberation Army.

Despite extensive United States military assistance to the reactionary Kuomintang and the direct intervention of American troops in the Chinese civil war, even in 1948 the odds were clearly in favor of the National Liberation Army. After the successful occupation of Shenyang (Mukden) Northeast China [Manchuria] was completely cleared of Kuomintang troops by the National Liberation Army by November 1948. This was followed by the decisive Kuomintang defeat on the southern front at Soochow [Hsüchow] (7 November 1948-10 January 1949) which opened the way to Nanking. Peking, Kalgan [Changkiakow] and Tientsin were liberated between 5 December 1948 and 31 January 1949.

Military defeat led to the disintegration of the reactionary Kuomintang camp. Seeking a respite which would enable it to take advantage of recently promised American assistance,[5] the Chang Kai-shek clique attempted a 'peace maneuver.' On 1 January 1949 Chang Kai-shek offered to open peace talks with the Chinese Communist Party, continuing all the while to concentrate the remnants of his battered forces along the mighty barrier of the Yangtze Kiang.

The Central Committee of the Chinese Communist Party published on 14 January 1949 a statement which exposed the criminal maneuvers of the Chang Kai-shek clique. The Party agreed to open peace talks with the Kuomintang authorities provided they would accept eight conditions; these included the punishment of war criminals, the reorganization of all reactionary armies in conformity with democratic principles, the confiscation of bureaucratic capital [riches amassed by top government officials], the implementation of agrarian reform, the convening of a political consultative council devoid of any reactionary elements with the aim of setting up a democratic coalition government.

The conditions proposed by the Communist Party for the peaceful unification of China were supported by all the nation's progressive organizations. Fifty-five representatives of various democratic parties and Chinese political groups published a declaration which supported them in full.

The delegates sent by the Kuomintang government for the peace talks with the Communist Party (April 1949) agreed in principle to these conditions (after having requested certain mitigations concerning the war-criminals clause and nominations to top positions in the Kuomintang army and the state machinery). However, the proposals were not ratified by the Kuomintang.

Further negotiations were pointless. On 20 April 1949 Mao Tse-tung, chairman of the National Revolutionary Military Committee of China, and Chu Teh, Commander-in-Chief of the National Liberation Army, ordered a general offensive. On 21 April 1949 units of the National Liberation Army numbering approximately 300,000 men successfully crossed the Yangtze Kiang and took up positions between Wuhu and Anking [Hwaining]. Nanking, capital of the Kuomintang government,

---

[5] The United States Congress passed a law in April 1948 authorizing aid to the Kuomintang clique amounting to US $463,000,000.

was liberated on 23 April. Having passed the world's mightiest water barrier—the Yangtze Kiang—and captured the main cities of Central China—Nanking, Wuhan (May 17) and Shanghai (May 27)—the National Liberation forces launched a final offensive to the South and Southwest and destroyed the enemy's last strongholds.

The outcome of the many years of struggle had been clear from the start. Under the experienced leadership of their heroic Communist Party the Chinese people had achieved their final victory. The plans of the Chinese reactionaries and their imperialist masters for keeping China in chains had failed. The great Chinese nation, which had drawn itself up to its full stature and squared its mighty shoulders, set out confidently on the road to freedom, independence, socialism and the strengthening of fraternal bonds with all peoples of the world.

THE ESTABLISHMENT OF THE PEOPLE'S REPUBLIC OF CHINA

As the country was progressively cleared of the Kuomintang forces, preparations were being made under the leadership of the Chinese Communist Party to convene the People's Political Consultative Council.[6]

At the end of September 1949 more than 600 delegates representing all Chinese democratic parties and political groups, popular organizations, the National Liberation Army, and various regions and nationalities, as well as Chinese citizens living abroad, met in Peking for the session of the People's Political Consultative Council. The delegates represented all strata of the Chinese people and its progressive parties and organizations. Thus, the session could realize the authority of the All-Chinese Assembly of People's Representatives and carry out the functions with which it was entrusted.

From 21 September to 1 October 1949 the first session of the council adopted its Organizational Statute and General Program, passed a law on the organization of the Central People's Government of the People's Republic of China, elected the All-Chinese Committee of the People's Political Consultative Council, and the Central Governmental Council of the People's Republic of China, approved the national flag and emblem and proclaimed Peking the capital.

Mao Tse-tung, elected President of the Central Governmental Council, proclaimed on 1 October 1949 the establishment of the People's Republic of China and informed the governments of all countries that the only legal government representing the

---

[6] The form of popular representation through the Political Consultative Council was chosen because it was both popular and generally understood. A Political Consultative Council, representing various parties and political groups, had been established in December 1945 on the basis of an agreement concluded on October 10 of the same year between the Chinese Communist Party and the Kuomintang. This council was originally to have organized a democratic coalition government and implemented the resolutions of the National People's Front. Chang Kai-shek's reactionary clique used its political monopoly during the Kuomintang rule to paralyze the council's activities and prevent it from implementing its own resolutions. The new Council was set up on a different basis, that is, without the participation of the reactionary classes and their political parties. It was to represent all the progressive organizations fighting for a people's democracy and Chinese independence and was to express the will of the great majority of the Chinese people.

entire Chinese people, 'wishes to establish diplomatic relations with any foreign government respecting the principles of equality, mutual benefit and mutual respect of territorial integrity and sovereignty.' This marked the official establishment of the great People's Republic of China—a dictatorship of the people's democracy, led by the working class, based on alliance of workers and peasants and rallying all the democratic classes and all nationalities.

In accordance with the general program adopted on 29 September 1949 by the first session of the People's Political Consultative Council, all enterprises of economic importance and monopolistic branches of the national economy, such as railroads and communications, as well as large industrial enterprises and banks which had formerly been the property of bureaucratic capital, were declared the property of the entire nation, and constituted the basis of the governmental socialist sector. The people's government also ensured the coordination and regulation of other economic sectors while conferring a dominant and guiding role to the state-owned sector.

In the sphere of foreign relations, the People's Republic of China proclaimed its intention of ensuring the nation's independence, freedom, territorial integrity and sovereignty, of defending peace throughout the world, supporting peaceful cooperation between nations and leading the struggle against the imperialist policies of aggression and war. It therefore expressed its desire to align itself with all peace-loving and freedom-loving countries, and above all with the Soviet Union, the people's democracies and the oppressed nations.

The new Chinese government stated its preparedness to hold negotiations and establish diplomatic relations on the basis of equality, mutual benefit and the mutual respect of territories and sovereignty with all foreign governments which would sever their relations with the Kuomintang clique (expelled and overthrown by the Chinese people) and would adopt a sincere attitude toward the People's Republic of China.

The government also declared itself ready to reexamine the treaties and agreements concluded by the former Kuomintang government with other states and recognize, abrogate, revise or renegotiate them accordingly.

In reconstructing the national economy, which had been destroyed by the war and the Kuomintang's depredations and setting it on the path of independent development, the Chinese government established its control over foreign trade and protected the nation's industry and agriculture from the destructive effects of foreign capitalist competition.

The founding of the People's Republic of China opened a new page in the life of the Chinese people. For the first time in their long history they had assumed power, liberated themselves from the burden of the exploiting classes and imperialist forces and set out on the path of free, independent and democratic development. The Chinese people's victory dealt a serious blow to world imperialism. The imperialist powers lost their control of China's extensive material resources, and could no longer extract enormous profits from the laboring Chinese people. Finally, the defeat of the Kuomintang reactionaries and of the imperialists was by no means limited to the territory of China. The liberated Chinese people began to have a tremendous revolutionary influence on the struggle of other oppressed Asiatic nations, imbuing in them a belief in ultimate victory, and showing them the way toward liberation from colonialism.

The forces of socialism and democracy have increased beyond all measure since the establishment of the People's Republic of China. The achievements of the Chinese people constituted the greatest victory of the oppressed laboring masses since the Russian October Revolution. A powerful socialist camp, led by the Soviet Union and the People's Republic of China, was thus established over a quarter of the world's surface, with a population of more than 900 million.

The birth of a free people's democracy in China brought about radical changes in Chinese relations with the Soviet Union. The policy of equality and respect for the rights of large and small nations proclaimed by the October Revolution and constantly pursued by the Soviet Union had received the sympathy and support of the the Chinese people; after the victory of the Chinese revolution it found comprehensive application in the relations between the Soviet Union and the new Chinese government.

The establishment of the People's Republic of China destroyed the artificial barriers in the way of the development of Sino-Soviet friendship which had been set up by Chinese militarists and the Kuomintang reactionaries for the benefit of their imperialist masters.

The relations between the Soviet Union and China accorded with the basic interests of both peoples and were based on the political and economic identity of their aims.

ESTABLISHMENT OF DIPLOMATIC AND ECONOMIC RELATIONS BETWEEN THE SOVIET UNION AND THE PEOPLE'S REPUBLIC OF CHINA

The Soviet Union was the first state to establish diplomatic relations with the People's Republic of China. On 1 October 1949 the Chinese Minister of Foreign Affairs, Chou En-lai, dispatched a message to the Soviet government containing the declaration of the Central People's Government on the establishment of the People's Republic of China and its desire to establish diplomatic relations with foreign states; the Soviet government informed China on 2 October 1949 of its decision to establish diplomatic relations. The Soviet Deputy-Minister of Foreign Affairs, Gromyko, stated in this note: 'Having considered the proposal of the Central People's Government of China, the Soviet Government, motivated by its firm desire to maintain friendly relations with the Chinese people and being convinced that the Central People's Government of China expresses the will of the great majority of the Chinese people, informs you that it has decided to establish diplomatic relations between the Soviet Union and the People's Republic of China and to exchange ambassadors.'[7]

Once diplomatic relations had been established, both governments were faced

---

[7] *Establishment of the People's Republic of China. Documents and Materials*, p. 68. Moskva.—Gospolit-izdat. 1950 [Russ.].

with a number of questions arising from their policy of peace and the radical change of the Far Eastern situation; the form of their political, economic and cultural co-operation also had to be determined. It was decided to examine these problems not through the usual diplomatic channels but by personal meetings between the heads of government and other leading statesmen. Moscow was chosen for these Sino-Soviet talks. A delegation of the Chinese government headed by Mao Tse-tung, President of the Central People's Governemnt of the People's Republic of China, left Peking for Moscow at the beginning of December 1949.

The Soviet people gave a rousing and sincere welcome to the Chinese governmental delegation; it greeted the first official representatives of the victorious Chinese people as the heroic sons of revolutionary China.

The Chinese delegation arrived in Moscow on 16 December 1949. Speaking at the Moscow railroad station before the Soviet representatives meeting the delegation, Mao Tse-tung declared: 'A deep and lasting friendship exists between the great peoples of China and the Soviet Union. For almost thirty years the Soviet people and the Soviet government have repeatedly contributed to the liberation of the Chinese people. This fraternal friendship which the Soviet people and the Soviet government have manifested toward the Chinese people in days of severe trial will never be forgotten.'

Conversations held in an extremely friendly and open atmosphere were concluded on 14 February 1950 by the signing of the following documents:

1) a treaty of friendship, alliance and mutual assistance between the Soviet Union and the People's Republic of China;

2) an agreement between the Soviet Union and China concerning the Chinese Changchun Railroad, Port Arthur and Dalny;

3) an agreement between the government of the Soviet Union and the Central People's Government of the People's Republic of China concerning a loan to China;

4) an exchange of notes on the transfer to China of property acquired by Soviet economic organizations from Japanese owners in Manchuria, as well as of all the buildings of the former Russian military compound in Peking.

The treaty and agreements stressed both parties' desire to consolidate the fraternal relations between their peoples and develop them in a spirit of indestructible friendship and cooperation for the good of both countries and for the strengthening of peace and security for all nations.

The treaty of friendship, alliance and mutual assistance was designed to strengthen the friendship and cooperation between the Soviet and Chinese people in order to prevent the rebirth of Japanese imperialism and eliminate the possibility of any new aggression by Japan or any other state which might ally itself in any way with her for such a purpose. It provided that 'if one of the contracting parties were to be attacked by Japan or states allied with the latter, and were thus to find itself in a state of war, the other contracting party would immediately render military and other assistance by all the means at its disposal...' (article 1).

In addition to solving the main political issues, the treaty established a firm basis for the development of comprehensive economic and cultural cooperation resting on the principles of equality, mutual benefit, mutual respect of national sovereignty and territorial integrity and nonintervention in domestic affairs. In accordance with stipulations of the treaty and with the above principles, both governments undertook the obligation to 'develop and consolidate the economic and cultural relations between the Soviet Union and China, to extend all possible economic assistance to each other and promote the necessary economic cooperation' (article 5). The treaty was to remain valid for 30 years and could be renewed automatically for further 5-year periods unless one of the parties indicated its unwillingness one year prior to the expiration of the current term.

Taking into account the radical change of the Far Eastern situation following the defeat of Japanese imperialism, the overthrow of the reactionary Kuomintang government and the transformation of China into a people's democratic republic, the Soviet and Chinese governments decided to reconsider the problems raised by the Chinese Changchun Railroad (C.C.R.), Port Arthur and Dalny.

The existence of the People's Republic of China—a peace-loving democratic state which had established friendly relations with all freedom-loving nations and countries of the world—constituted a reliable guarantee for the preservation of peace and security in the Far East. Whereas under the reactionary Kuomintang regime the territory of Manchuria had been used by the imperialist powers as a base for aggression against China and the Soviet Union, after the victory of the people's democratic system in China Manchuria became an integral part of China and of the northeastern region, maintaining close economic ties with the Soviet Far East and Eastern Siberia.

The agreement on the C.C.R., Port Arthur and Dalny stated the Soviet Union's decision to transfer to the Chinese government without any compensation all its rights to the joint administration of the C.C.R. together with all the railroad property belonging to the Soviet Union; this was to take place after the conclusion of a peace treaty with Japan, but in any case no later than at the end of 1952. For the remaining period of joint administration of the C.C.R., both parties agreed to apply the principle of parity in the alternate nomination to executive positions on the board of directors and administration.[8]

The parties agreed that within the same period (i.e., by the end of 1952 at the latest) Soviet troops would be withdrawn from the joint naval base at Port Arthur and all the installations transferred to the Chinese government; the Soviet Union was to be compensated for all expenditure for the reconstruction and building of installations after 1945.

The Soviet and Chinese governments decided that the question of Dalny Port, which had been prolcaimed an international port by the Yalta Agreement of 11 February 1945, would be examined after the conclusion of a peace treaty with Japan. The

---

[8] Formerly executive positions on the C.C.R. had been distributed on a parity basis for the entire term of the treaty. Thus, for example, the president of the board of directors was Chinese and his deputy a Soviet citizen; the director of the railroad was a Soviet citizen and his deputy a Chinese one. By the terms of the new agreement each of the above positions would be occupied for one year by Chinese or Soviet nationals alternately.

Soviet government agreed in this context to transfer to China in 1950 all the property in Dalny either leased or temporarily used by the Soviet Union at conditions to be specified within three months after the agreement became effective.

The third document signed in Moscow played no less an important role in strengthening the friendly ties between the Soviet Union and China. This was an agreement to grant China a loan of US$300 million or 1,200 million rubles,[9] the most important loan ever granted to China by any foreign state. Soviet deliveries to China were to promote the reconstruction of the most important branches of the economy. The Soviet Union was to deliver in five years (1950-1954) equipment and materials for electric power stations, metallurgical and machine-tool plants, coal mines, railroads, motor transport and other branches of the economy, for the entire amount of the loan.

The loan was granted at particularly favorable conditions. Taking into account the tremendous damage inflicted by the prolonged military activities upon the Chinese economy, the Soviet government granted the loan at an interest rate of only one percent, conditions without precedent in the financial practice of either the Soviet Union or China. As stipulated by article 3 of the loan agreement, China was to pay off the debt in ten equal yearly installments from 31 December 1954 to 31 December 1953. Payments of interest computed from the utilization date of the corresponding part of the loan were to be at half-yearly intervals. Both the loan itself and the interest were to be repaid either in deliveries of raw materials and tea to the Soviet Union at prices established on the basis of world market rates, or in gold or US dollars.

The Soviet and Chinese people greeted with joy and deep satisfaction the signing of the treaty and agreements of 14 February 1950. They considered these documents to be an expression of genuine fraternal cooperation between the Soviet Union and of the People's Republic of China, Saifuddin Azizov, Deputy Prime -inister of the for coexistence in peace and lasting friendship.

The friendly relations between the Soviet Union and China were thus formalized by the treaty and agreements. The general principles of the coordinated policy of both parties concerning the Far East and all important international problems involving the interests of the Soviet Union and the People's Republic of China were thus succinctly and clearly formulated, and the further development of economic cooperation between the two peoples was delineated.

After the departure of Mao Tse-tung, Chou En-lai and some other members of the delegation on 17 February 1950, Li Fu-chun, Deputy Prime Minister of the Northeastern [Manchurian] government, Yeh Chi-chwang, Minister of Commerce of the People's Republic of China, Saifuddin Azizov, Deputy Prime Minister of the government of Sinkiang Province and a group of Chinese experts remained in Moscow for the continuation of negotiations with Soviet ministries and officials on concrete issues of trade and economic cooperation.

---

[9] The amount in rubles was not specified in the agreement; it was calculated after the establishment of a new rate of exchange for the ruble on 1 March 1950 (US$1 = 4 rubles).

These negotiations were concluded on 27 March 1950 by the signing of three agreements setting up Sino-Soviet joint-stock companies:[10]

1) an association for the extraction of nonferrous and rare metals in Sinkiang (its abbreviated Russian name was *Sovkitmetall* and the Chinese name *Chungsuchinshukungssu*) which would deal in the prospection, extraction and processing of nonferrous and rare metals;

2) a company for the prospection, extraction and processing of petrolium, gas and subsidiary petroleum products in Sinkiang (abbreviated Russian name *Sovkitneft* and Chinese name *Chungsuchihyukungssu*);

3) a company for the organization and operation of civil airlines (*SKOGA* in Russian and *Chungsuminhangkungssu* in Chinese) which was to set up and operate the following lines:

a) Peking - Shenyang (Mukden) -Changchun - Harbin - Tsitsihar - Hailar [Hulun] - Chita;

b) Peking - Taiyuan - Sian [Siking] - Lanchow - Suchow [Kinchuan] -Hami [Qomul] - Urumchi [Tihwa] - Kuldja - Alma - Ata;

c) Peking - Changkiakow [Kalgan] - Ulan Bator - Irkutsk.

These joint Sino-Soviet companies were to be set up on a parity basis, both sides participating equally in capital investment and administration.[11]

In addition to accomplishing the production tasks facing these companies during this initial reconstruction period of the Chinese economy, they also undertook to train qualified Chinese technical and administrative personnel. The agreements stipulated (article 17 of the agreement on *Sovkitneft* and *Sovkitmetall* and article 14 of the agreement on *SKOGA*) that the companies would either open technical schools and courses or send Chinese citizens to learn in the Soviet Union. The companies thus played the role of important educational institutions, preparing Chinese specialists not only for their own requirements but also for other Chinese organizations.

A commercial treaty was signed on 19 April 1950 as a result of negotiations between the Chinese Minister of Commerce and the Soviet Ministry of Foreign Trade; the treaty defined the general legal basis for commercial operations between the Soviet Union and the People's Republic of China. It fixed the mode of commodity deliveries (on the basis of lists of commodities fixed once a year), of price calculation (on the basis of prices on the world market), the mode of payment (through the Soviet

---

[10] A fourth agreement was signed on 28 July 1951 between the Soviet government and the Chinese Central People's Government for the creation in Dalny of a Sino-Soviet joint-stock ship-repairing and ship-building company, *Sovkitsudostroi* (*Chungsutsaochuankungssu* in Chinese). This company used as its basis the *Dal'dok* plant, reconstructed by the Soviet military administration in 1946. The plant had originally been built by Russians in 1903 at the same time as the completion of construction of the Chinese Eastern Railroad.

[11] During the initial period of the companies' activity (the first three years for the *Sovkitmetall* and *Sovkitneft* and two years for the *SKOGA*), both parties made provisions for the lack of qualified Chinese personnel; the managing directors of the companies were therefore Soviet citizens and their deputies Chinese. In the same period Chinese citizens were designated as presidents of the companies and were to control their operation in general; their deputies were Soviet citizens. For the three following years these functions were to be reversed.

State Bank and the People's Bank of China), and other related issues. An agreement was also reached concerning the transit of goods through the territory of both parties, the legal status of the Soviet Trade Delegation in China and the activity of the commercial attaché of the Chinese Embassy in the Soviet Union; mutual commodity deliveries for 1950 were also negotiated.

Two other agreements were concluded in 1950 concerning working conditions for the following Soviet specialists in China: a) instructors and advisers to Chinese organizations (agreement of 27 March 1950), and b) specialists for technical assistance in the assembly and operation of Soviet equipment (agreement of 25 October 1950).

The Sino-Soviet agreements concluded in the first year of existence of the People's Republic of China thus covered a significant number of political and economic problems and determined the concrete form and the further development of friendly relations between the Soviet Union and China.

SINO-SOVIET ECONOMIC RELATIONS DURING THE PERIOD OF
RECONSTRUCTION OF THE CHINESE ECONOMY (1950-1952)

The Japanese invasion of China and the war led by the reactionary Kuomintang clique against the Chinese people severely affected the national economy. The volume of industrial production in 1949, at the establishment of the People's Republic of China, was 50 percent below the highest level reached before the liberation; this reduction was most severe in heavy industry since most of the factories had been completely or partly destroyed. The level of industrial production in 1949 was thus 70 percent of its previous maximum level in the cotton industry, 85 percent in the match industry and 65 percent in paper production; production dropped to 17 percent of the previous maximum level for pig iron, 18 percent for rolled metal, 38 percent for petroleum and 50 percent for coal.

Agriculture was also severely affected. In 1949 the total yield of alimentary products reached 74.6 percent of the prewar value, and the cotton harvest dropped by 48 percent. The destruction and neglect of the irrigation system led to the danger of extensive flooding and droughts in all the main agricultural areas of the country, particularly the Hwang Ho and Hwai Ho river valleys.[12]

The People's Republic of China also faced problems in other branches of the national economy. The greedy Kuomintang plutocrats, who had accumulated millions in American banks, had brought the country to bankruptcy and completely disrupted monetary circulation. In May 1949 one US dollar was worth 40 million Chinese dollars *(fapi)*.

---

[12] Under the pretext of the need to stop the Japanese advance in 1938, the Chang Kai-shek government ordered its troops to destroy the southern dike of the Hwang Ho, which as a result streamed into the Hwai Ho; the joint torrent flowed into the Yangtze Kiang, flooding an enormous area of fertile land which remained under water for 9 years. In 1949 floods and drought affected approximately 120 million *mu* [a unit of area equivalent to 0.0631 hectares] with a population of approximately 40 million persons.

The economic situation changed radically after the eviction of the Kuomintang reactionaries from mainland China and the establishment of the People's Republic of China. The nationalization of industries and banks owned by Japan and bureaucratic capital, and of railroads, communications and other important economic branches enabled the Chinese government to control the main branches of the national economy; it could therefore organize the reconstruction of the economy and ensure the dominant role of the socialist sector, which constituted the mainstay of the people's democratic state.

The creation and consolidation of a state-owned socialist industry on the one hand, and the abolition of all the rights and privileges of imperialist powers and foreign subjects on the other, reflected the completion of the Chinese people's anti-imperialistic struggle and the construction of a new and independent economy. In addition to solving the issue of imperialism, the Chinese government also abolished the feudal landowning class by transforming the semifeudal agrarian regime into a system of peasant holdings, in accordance with the principle of 'the land to those who work it.'

The plenum of the Chinese Communist Party Central Committee in June 1950 fixed a period of approximately 3 years for agrarian reform and the reconstruction of the national economy. The Chinese people set to work to achieve these aims with great enthusiasm and energy, in order to proceed onward to extensive planned socialist construction. Foreign trade was also geared to this purpose. Having established control of foreign trade, the Chinese government authorized the importation mainly of products required for the reconstruction of industry, transportation, communications and other branches of the national economy which could not be produced locally. Importation of luxury items or of light industrial products competing with Chinese goods was either limited or entirely prohibited. Equipment for the reconstruction of the metallurgical, machine-tool, power and chemical industries, metals, petroleum and other vital industrial raw materials, as well as products for general consumption were the main items imported by China.

In the first year of its existence the Chinese government succeeded in considerably increasing its foreign trade. The expansion of trade with the Soviet Union and the European people's democracies was accompanied by the reopening of commercial relations with capitalist countries, which still continued to play a dominant role in Chinese foreign trade. They accounted for 74 percent of total foreign trade in 1950; at this date the southern and central provinces traded almost exclusively with capitalist countries. The restoration and expansion of foreign trade enabled the Chinese government to meet in 1950 the country's demands for such items as metals, petroleum-products, rubber, motor vehicles, etc., mainly by imports from abroad.

The further development of foreign trade encountered, however, serious setbacks. The achievements of the Chinese people in the reconstruction of their independent state provoked the ire of imperialist circles, particularly American monopolies, which hoped to restore China to its former status with the assistance of the venal Chang Kai-shek clique. The northeastern provinces were menaced by the attack on the Korean People's Democratic Republic in June 1950 and the occupation of Formosa.

On 1 February 1951 the United Nations passed an illegal resolution dictated by the United States which proclaimed the peace-loving Chinese people an 'aggressor,' and on 18 May 1951 the plenary session of the General Assembly voted for an American resolution for an embargo on all trade with the People's Republic of China.

In their policy of military and economic aggression against the People's Republic of China, the reactionary circles led by the American imperialists attempted to undermine China's new economic and political regime. They assumed that the Chinese government would be unable to obtain the necessary economic and technical assistance from the Soviet Union and other socialist countries and that trade with the socialist countries could not substitute for commercial relations with the United States, Britain and other capitalist states, which had previously been China's main importers and exporters.

Subsequent events belied these hopes. As had frequently been the case in the past, monopolistic circles did not sufficiently take into account the enormous potentialities of the powerful, free, diligent and talented Chinese people. They also underestimated the technical and scientific achievements of the Soviet people and the possibilities offered by the Soviet Union's socialist industry.

At the end of the postwar Five-Year Plan in 1950 the value of the Soviet Union's industrial production passed the 1940 level by 73 percent; the manufacture of production facilities had increased by 105 percent and that of consumer goods by 23 percent.

In 1951 the Soviet Union began to implement its Fifth Five-Year Plan of industrial development (1951-1955), which aimed at raising the volume of production by approximately 70 percent over that of 1950.[13] The construction of the biggest hydroelectric station in the world—the Kuibyshev power station producing approximately 2 million Rw, with a yearly power output of almost 10 billion kwhr—was begun in 1950, and of the Stalingrad hydroelectric plant—producing approximately 1,700,000 kw, with a yearly output of almost 10 billion kwhr—in 1951.

In 1952 the Soviet Union produced approximately 25.1 million tons of cast iron, 34.5 milli n tons of steel, 26.8 million tons of rolled metal, 300.9 million tons of coal, 47.3 million tons of petroleum and 119.1 billion kwhr of electric power.

The swift reconstruction and development of the Soviet economy and the achievements of the Chinese economy created a basis for the expansion of commercial relations. In the very first year following the conclusion of the Sino-Soviet agreements the volume of trade between the two countries reached 170 percent of its 1949 level; it increased to 236 percent in 1951 and to 282 percent in 1952.

Sino-Soviet trade constituted 23.4 percent of the Chinese total foreign trade in 1950, 38.5 percent in 1951 and 51.5 percent in 1952. The value of Sino-Soviet trade in 1952 was almost double that of China's trade with all the capitalist countries; the Soviet Union had thus become China's main partner in the field of foreign trade.

---

[13] The volume of industrial production during the 1951-1955 period increased in fact by 85 percent; the manufacture of production facilities expanded by 91 percent and that of consumer goods by 76 percent. —*Report of the Central Committee of the Communist Party of the Soviet Union to the 20th Party Congress*. Stenographic account, Vol.1, 0. 43. Moskva. 1956 [Russ.].

The Soviet Union's increasing share in Chinese foreign trade is not merely a consequence of the boycott by the United States, Britain and other dependent capitalist countries. The Soviet Union supplies China with all the necessary modern technical industrial equipment, materials, and varied commodities at mutually

VOLUME OF TRADE BETWEEN THE SOVIET UNION AND
THE PEOPLE'S REPUBLIC OF CHINA
(in million rubles)

	1950	1951	1952
Soviet exports to China	1,552.8	1,905.1	2,200.1
Soviet imports from China	765.1	1,327.7	1,655.0
Total volume of trade	2,317.9	3,232.8	3,855.1

advantageous conditions. In addition to these supplies, the Soviet Union grants fraternal technical assistance to the Chinese people for the reconstruction and expansion of its industries, transportation and other branches of the economy and for the application of the most recent scientific and technical discoveries; it also imparts the experience gained by the Soviet people who have set up a powerful socialist economy in a short period.

Sino-Soviet trade exemplifies new forms of socialist relations between states, based on friendly cooperation and the desire to help one another in economic development.

The Sino-Soviet commercial agreements and contracts provide for commodity deliveries over periods of one year or more at fixed prices calculated for each item on the basis of world market rates. The long terms of the Sino-Soviet agreements, the stable prices set for the listed items and the fixed trade conditions exclude any of the speculation common in capitalist practice and fully meet the requirements of planned economy in both the Soviet Union and China.

Clearly, since the volume of trade has increased and the list of items has expanded, the Soviet and Chinese foreign trade organizations have to supplement and modify the agreements and treaties, sign new contracts or invalidate previous ones and modify the term or the geographic distribution of commodity deliveries; such corrections remain, however, relatively minor and do not noticeably affect the constant increase of Sino-Soviet trade.

The nature of Chinese imports from the Soviet Union has been determined by the need to reconstruct the Chinese economy, satisfy the most urgent requirements of the Chinese people and create a firm basis for further economic development. Industrial equipment which increased in value from 165.3 million rubles (10.6 per cent) in 1950 to 609.4 million (27.7 percent) in 1952 thus became the most important item of Chinese imports from the Soviet Union. The supply of equipment complexes for the complete equipment of reconstructed or newly created industries in machine tools, machinery, apparatus and various mechanism has increased yearly. The proportion of equipment complexes passed from 0.2 percent of the total value of

Soviet exports to China in 1950 to 6.6 percent in 1952. The same period also saw an increase of the following Soviet exports to China: ferrous metals, which increased from 80.3 to 265.6 million rubles, petroleum and petroleum products—from 199.4 to 607.5 thousand tons, nonferrous metals—from 12.3 to 62 million rubles and ferrous alloys—from 5 to 21 million rubles.

As the Chinese economy gradually recovered the local demand for a number of products was met to an increasing extent by domestic production. This primarily applied to textile products. Thus, in 1952 China produced 4,465 million meters of cotton fabrics, i.e., 47 percent more than in the year of maximum prewar production. This enabled China to reduce considerably her imports from abroad; those from the Soviet Union decreased in 1952 to 13 million rubles (0.6 percent of total Soviet exports to China) compared to 14.9 million rubles in 1950. Although domestic paper production passed the maximum prewar level and reached 372 thousand tons, imports from the Soviet Union continued to expand, reaching 66.3 million rubles in 1952, compared to 16.2 million rubles in 1950.

SOVIET EXPORTS TO CHINA IN 1950-1952

Groups of commodities	1950		1951		1952	
	million rubles	%	million rubles	%	million rubles	%
Equipment and machinery	165.3	10.6	430.6	22.6	609.4	27.7
Equipment complexes	4	0.2	128.9	6.8	145.7	6.6
Ferrous metals	80.3	5.2	199.8	10.5	265.6	12.1
Nonferrous metals	12.3	0.8	66.3	3.5	62.4	2.7
Cable and wire	26.3	1.7	23.5	1.2	11.8	0.5
Petroleum products	44.6	2.9	155.7	8.2	129.1	5.9
Chemical products	26.5	1.8	64.1	3.4	39.7	1.8
Paper	16.2	1.0	44.5	2.3	66.3	3.0
Cotton	6.7	0.4	44.8	2.4	—	—
Cotton fabrics	14.9	0.96	59.2	3.1	13	0.6
Sugar	17.5	1.1	11.8	0.6	9.8	0.4
TOTAL	1,552.8	100	1,905.1	100	2,200.1	100

The Sino-Soviet protocols on the volume of trade in 1951 and 1952 and the protocol on Soviet commodity deliveries to China within the terms of the loan agreement of 14 February 1950 provided in addition to the commodity deliveries, for increased technical assistance to China.

The Soviet Union offered technical assistance to China in varied fields. At the request of the Chinese government, Soviet organizations dispatched specialists who were to share their experience with various Chinese industries, institutions, institutes for scientific research and higher education, assist Chinese specialists in the technical operation of industries and institutions and train Chinese technical personnel. The Soviet organizations which had undertaken to assist in the construction of Chinese industries sent specialists to China for research and planning, the assembly and operation of equipment and the teaching of technological processes. Soviet scientific, planning and industrial enterprises filled various orders and commissions of Chinese organizations in the Soviet Union (consultations, projects and drafts, laboratory tests, etc.). Chinese organizations sent Chinese citizens to study in Soviet educational institutions and gain practice in the technological processes used in Soviet industries. As the Chinese scientific and technical organizations gradually took form, the Soviet Union began to grant patents and licenses for inventions and improvements, to share its advanced scientific and technical achievements.

During the period of Chinese economic reconstruction (1950-1952), Soviet organizations assisted in the reconstruction and creation of more than 50 important industrial works, a number of which were partially or completely operating by the end of 1952. These included the Anshan metallurgical complex, the Fengman[14] hydroelectric station and the thermoelectric power stations in Penhsihu [Penki], Taiyuan, Sian, Chungking and Changchow.

The new industrial works built with Soviet assistance during the reconstruction period included the Fushin thermoelectric power station (September 1952), the Harbin linen spinning and weaving plant (October 1952) and the Urumchi motor vehicle repair plant (December 1952).

Soviet specialists also participate in the building and construction of other enterprises on the basis of Chinese projects and plans in other branches of the economy, such as transportation, agriculture, finance, scientific research. In 1950-1952 Soviet specialists took part in the elaboration of an irrigation project on the Hway Ho river, helped in the construction of a 3-kilometer bridge on the Hwang Ho, the re-reconstruction of northeastern and northern railroad lines, the creation of more than ten large state-owned animal farms, the establishment of various courses for scientific and technical personnel in industry, transport and agriculture, the organization of institutes for scientific research and in the solution of many other technical problems. The *People's China* wrote in December 1952: 'There is not a a single branch of the new democratic economy in which the rich Soviet experience has not been extensively applied.'[15]

Trade between the Soviet Union and China developed bilaterally. Except for the loan granted to the Chinese government by the agreement of 14 February 1950 for the payment of equipment and materials purchased from the Soviet Union, all other payments for Soviet commodities and technical assistance were made in commodity deliveries.

The volume of Soviet imports of Chinese goods increased by 116 percent from 1950 to 1952, from 765.1 million to 1,655 million rubles, and the number of items exported also increased considerably. In the first year following the establishment of the People's Republic of China, when many highly important export branches of the Chinese economy, such as the mining, silk growing and tea industries had only begun

---

[14] [On the Sungari River, near the town of Kirin.].
[15] *People's China*, No. 23, p. 3. 1952 [Russ.].

to recover and communications between the northern and southern areas still remained sporadic, exports to the Soviet Union were limited mainly to agricultural products from North and Northeast China: soybean accounted for 25 percent of exports, vegetable oil for 6 percent and other products of the Northeast [Manchuria], for approximately 20 percent.

SOVIET IMPORTS FROM THE PEOPLE'S REPUBLIC OF CHINA IN 1950-1952

Groups of commodities	1950		1951		1952	
	million rubles	%	million rubles	%	million rubles	%
Raw alimentary materials	268.5	35.1	345.1	26	499.3	30.2
Alimentary products	86.8	11.3	92	6.9	229	13.8
Nonferrous and alloyed metals, concentrates	81.8	10.7	183.2	13.8	292.2	17.7
Textile raw materials and semifinished products (silk, wool, jute, ramee etc.)	67.9	8.9	121	9.1	155.4	9.4
Textile products (silks and woolens, knitted wear, etc.)	—	—	14.3	1.1	59.2	3.6
Raw materials of animal husbandry (bristles, undressed leather, guts, etc.)	39.7	5.2	68.3	5.1	125.5	7.6
Chemical products	5.8	0.8	5.1	0.4	9.5	0.6
Handicraft wares	—	—	—	—	1.5	0.1
TOTAL	765.1	100	1,327.7	100	1,655.0	100

As the Chinese economy gradually recovered and the territorial unification of the country progressed, exports increased and their composition changed. Nonferrous metals and alloys (tungsten, tin, antimony), produced in South and Southwest China were the second item in importance among Chinese exports to the Soviet Union in 1952 (17.7 percent). The proportion of soybean exports dropped to 12.9 per-percent, although their value continued to increase (from 194.2 million rubles in 1950 to 213 million in 1952); peanuts, mainly produced in Shantung province, began to play an important role, reaching 8.9 percent of the total volume of Chinese exports to the Soviet Union. Exports of tea (4.6 percent), raw silk (3.1 percent), meat and meat products (3.8 percent), mainly originating in Central and South China, showed a sharp increase in 1952.

The list of Chinese exports to the Soviet Union began to include such items as citrus fruit, pineapples and bananas grown in the remote subtropical areas of South China, handicraft products of Shanghai and Canton, ramee hemp from Central China, tobacco, rosin and many other items which had not been previously exported to the Soviet Union.

In view of the constant expansion of its domestic production and the improvement of living conditions, the Soviet Union was able not only to supply China with the necessary resources for the reconstruction and development of her economy, but also to become the most important buyer of many of the commonly exported Chinese products. The hopes of British and American imperialist circles of preventing the economic reconstruction of the People's Republic of China by their embargo came to nothing. Fraternal cooperation with the Soviet Union and the other people's democracies enabled China to surmount all obstacles, not only to import all the equipment and materials she needed but also to find new markets for her exports. In the words of Chinese Minister of Foreign Trade, Yeh Chi-chwang, 'The uninterrupted expansion of our foreign trade justifies our foreign trade policy and shows the failure of the embargo imposed by American imperialism in its attempt to intimidate us. But the American imperialists have made a serious error. Their embargo has in fact enabled us to end the semicolonial dependence of China's economy and to open the way for economic independence. Anyone can see today that the embargo has not affected us in the least but has on the contrary incurred losses to those countries who followed this American policy.'[16]

The successful development of Chinese trade with the Soviet Union constituted a firms basis for the indestructible and mutually beneficial economic relations between the two countries. In contrast to the preceeding period, when, due to certain historical circumstances, Sino-Russian trade had remained mainly a local border trade, it now developed on a national scale. It became so considerable in volume and the number of items involved, that it extended to all the main branches of the economy of both countries and began to exert a decisive influence on their foreign trade as a whole.

BEGINNING OF EXTENSIVE PLANNED ECONOMIC DEVELOPMENT IN THE PEOPLE'S REPUBLIC OF CHINA

During the first three years of existence of the People's Republic of China, the Chinese people not only succeeded in entirely reconstructing the national economy but also in certain branches in surpassing the highest preliberation production level. The volume of industrial production in 1952 passed the highest pre-1949 level by the following percentages: 21.9 percent for electric power, 36.3 percent for petroleum, 46.1 percent for steel, 67 percent for rolled metal, 5.5 percent for cast iron, 154 percent for cement, 47 percent for cotton yarn, 98.3 percent for cotton fabrics, 125 percent for paper, 12 percent for cigarettes, 11 percent for matches and 6 percent for flour.

The gross volume of industrial, handicraft, agricultural and subsidiary peasant production increased in 1952 by 77 percent (in fixed prices) compared to 1949; modern industrial production increased by 178.6 percent and agricultural production (including subsidiary peasant handicrafts) by 48.5 percent.

During the reconstruction period agrarian reforms and the abolition of the feudal mode of production were effected throughout a territory with an agricultural population of more than 450 million persons, with the exception of a number of areas in-

---

[16] Yeh Chi-chwang. Collected articles *New China's Economic Achievements in Three Years* (1949-1952), p. 99. Peking. 1953 [translated from Chin. to Russ.].

habited by national minorities. The last privileges of the imperialist powers were abolished, and all enterprises previously owned by bureaucratic capital were nationalized and became governmental socialist enterprises.

In 1952 the gross product of the state-owned industrial sector, not counting the joint state and private industries and the cooperative sector, accounted for 41.5 percent of the total Chinese gross national product; the People's Government thus possessed a solid economic basis for the transition to planned economic development which ensured steady progress toward socialism.

The international position of the People's Republic of China also became stronger. The danger of war, which could have spread from Korea to China's Northeastern provinces [Manchuria], was successfully averted. The finest sons and daughters of the Chinese people took up the struggle against the aggressors. Fighting in the ranks of the People's Volunteer Corps, they defeated together with Korean People's Army the interventionists who had invaded North Korea.

The Chinese people's just fight against aggression in the northeast and the seizure of Formosa and their efforts for peace throughout the world elicited the warmest sympathy of all peace-loving nations toward China and enhanced its authority and prestige as a peace-loving and freedom-loving great power.

In 1952 the Central Committee of the Chinese Communist Party set forth the party's general line for a transitional period during which China was to become a powerful socialist state by means of gradual urban and rural socialist reorganization. After nationwide discussions, the party's general line was adopted in September 1954 by the first meeting of the first session of the All-Chinese Assembly of People's Representatives; it thus became the state program and was included in the Constitution. The introduction to this Constitution states: 'The period from the establishment of the People's Republic of China until the construction of a socialist society is a transitional period. The main goals of the state in the transitional period are the gradual achievement of the socialist industrialization and the gradual implementation of socialist reorganization in agriculture, domestic industry and in capitalist production and commerce.'

The Chinese people regarded socialist industrialization, especially the development of heavy and machine-tool industry, as a primary goal in the development of the Chinese economy. Li Fu-chun, Deputy-Chairman of the State Council and Chairman of the State Planning Committee, stated in his report on the First Five-Year Plan: 'Only by creating a powerful modern heavy industry, producing ferrous metal products, machine tools, electricity, fuel, nonferrous metal products, the most important chemical products, etc, will we be able to produce various types of modern industrial equipment and ensure the technological reconstruction of our heavy and light industries. Only then shall we be able to supply our agriculture with tractors and other modern agricultural machinery and fertilizers, ensure the technological reconstruction of our agriculture...our transport system..., and strengthen our national national defense.'[17]

---

[17] Supplement to the journal *People's China*, No. 17. 1955 [Russ.].

The First Five-Year Plan for the development of the Chinese economy covered the period from 1953 to 1957.[18] The plan essentially provides for the creation of a basis for the socialist reorganization of agriculture, domestic industry, private industry and trade.

The total sum assigned for economic and cultural development for the period of the First Five-Year Plan was fixed at 76,640 million *yüan,* or 21,875 tons of gold. Capital investments were assigned 42,740 million *yüan,* or 55.8 percent of the total, the rest was devoted to prospection, capital repairs of existing industrial and transport enterprises, training of qualified personnel and other requirements.

In the industrial field the plan concentrated all efforts on the implementation of 694 projects; 156 of these were industrial projects executed with Soviet assistance (research, planning, supply of basic technical equipment, assembly and operation of enterprises). According to the plan, the Chinese gross volume of industrial production was to increase in value by 98.3 percent between 1952 and 1957 and reach 36.0 percent of the value of total industrial and agricultural production at the latter date compared to 26.7 percent in 1952. Particular attention was given to the creation of industries in the interior areas, near the sources of raw materials. As is generally known, since Chinese industry had developed under the control of foreign capital and had been greatly influenced by the imperialist powers, most of the industries were concentrated in the coastal provinces. In 1952, at the end of the reconstruction period, industrial production in the coastal provinces accounted for more than 70 percent of the total value of industrial production. In order to correct this situation,

MAIN TYPES OF INDUSTRIAL PRODUCTION OF THE
PEOPLE'S REPUBLIC OF CHINA

Types of industrial production	*Units*	1952	1957 *(planned)*
Steel	million tons	1.35	4.12
Electric power	billion kwh	7.26	15.9
Coal	million tons	63.53	112,985
Generator equipment	thousand kw	6.7	164
Metallurgical equipment	thousand tons	—	8
Metal lathes	thousand units	14	13
Cement	million tons	2.86	6
Paper (factory produced)	thousand tons	372	665
Cotton fabrics	million pieces	111.63	163.72
Sugar (including domestic production)	thousand tons	451	1,100

[18] The project for the First Five-Year Plan of Chinese industrial development was elaborated by the Central Committee of the Chinese Communist Party, discussed in March 1955 by the All-Chinese Party Conference and then brought after a number of corrections to the State Council of the People's Republic of China. The State Council discussed and adopted the plan at its plenary session and remitted it for examination and adoption to a session of the All-Chinese Assembly of People's Representatives. The second session of this forum, held in Peking on 5-6 July 1955, heard Li Fu-chun's report on the Five-Year Plan and adopted the latter.

472 of the 694 industrial projects set up by the First Five-Year Plan were to be built in the interior regions and 222 projects on the coast.

In addition to the enlargement and reconstruction of the Anshan metallurgical complex, which forms the mainstay of the Chinese metal industry, the First Five-Year Plan provides for the construction of two new metallurgical complexes in the interior regions—in Paotow and in the Wuhan area. One automobile factory, 15 thermo-electric power stations of more than 50,000 kw each and 31 coal mining enterprises with a yearly rated capacity of more than one million tons each were to be built in 1953-1957; two heavy machinetool plants, 39 relatively large textile factories and many others were to be erected within the same period.

MAIN TYPES OF AGRICULTURAL PRODUCTION OF THE
PEOPLE'S REPUBLIC OF CHINA

Types of agricultural production	Units	1952	1957 (planned)
Grain	million tons	154.4	181.6
Soybean	million tons	9.5	11.2
Cotton	million tons	1,304	1,635
Cattle	million head	56.6	73.6
Horses	million head	6.1	8.3
Sheep and goats	million head	61.78	113.04
Pigs	million head	89.77	138.34

In the field of agriculture, the First Five-Year Plan provides for a 23.3 percent increase in value of agricultural production, including subsidiary industries. It stipulates the establishment of 91 state-owned mechanized farms and 194 tractor stations, the construction of 13 large reservoirs and earth- and stoneworks totaling 1,300 million cubic meters along various rivers. Large projects for the control and utilization of the Hwang Ho river waters have already been started.

The Five-Year Plan stipulates that by 1957 up to one third of all peasant farm-steads will be included in agricultural cooperatives. These cooperatives are to become the main source of agricultural produce and ensure the transition from small-scale production to extensive collective agricultural production.

The First Five-Year Plan set up an urgent program which would enable China's laboring masses to solve the main problems of the transitional period. The free Chinese people led by the Communist Party industriously competed to realize the impressive goals of the First Five-Year Plan.

Instead of the 694 large industrial projects stipulated by the Five-Year Plan, 455 of which were to have been entirely completed by the end of the period, the actual number of projects started has reached 800, and 500 of them will be entirely completed by the end of 1957.[19] The gross volume of industrial and agricultural produc-

---

[19] Report by Liu Shao-chi to the 8th Congress of the Chinese Communist Party. Peking.—Publications in Foreign Languages. 1956 [Russ.ed.].

tion is to increase in 1957 by more than 60 percent above its 1952 value, and the gross volume of industrial production (including domestic industries) is to account account for approximately 50 percent of the gross national product.[20]

The Chinese people's labor achievements enabled them to reach in 1956 the level of industrial production planned for 1957. Chou En-lai stated in his report to the 8th Congress of the Chinese Communist Party that the plan for industrial production would be passed by approximately 15 percent in 1957; steel production would then reach 5.5 million tons, electric power 18 billion kwhr, coal 120 million tons, metal lathes 30,000 units, etc.

The Chinese people also achieved great success in the transformation of agriculture. The completion ahead of schedule of the yearly sections of the Five-Year Plan in the field of industrialization made possible the development of cooperative agriculture, without which difficulties might have arisen in the supply of industrial raw materials and of alimentary products. The resolutions of the sixth plenum of the Central Committee of the Chinese Communist Party on 11 October 1955 stated: 'Industry is developing at a rapid pace. Facts show that if the cooperative movement in agriculture does not follow the tempo of industrialization, if the production of grain and industrial crops lags behind, our socialist industrialization will encounter increasing difficulties.'[21]

A mass movement developed in the countryside under the direction of the Communist Party for the creation of agricultural cooperatives. Of the 120 million peasant farmsteads existing in June 1956, 110 million or 91.7 percent formed agricultural cooperatives: 35 million were absorbed into lower producers' agricultural cooperatives and 72 million into higher ones.[22]

As a result of the socialist reorganization of agriculture, the Chinese gross grain yield, including soybean, reached 174.8 million tons in 1955, i.e., 20.4 million tons more than in 1952, and cotton production passed 1.5 million tons, or 214 thousand tons more than in 1952.[23]

The goals set by the First Five-Year Plan required the mobilization of the Chinese people's energy and resources and the expansion of China's foreign relations, especially those with the Soviet Union and other socialist countries. In appreciation of the assistance granted to China by the Soviet Union and the people's democracies in the period of the First Five-Year Plan, Chou En-lai, Chairman of the State Council, stated in his report to the 8th Congress of the Chinese Communist Party: 'The powerful Soviet Union and the people's democracies have given us enormous assistance in the implementing of our First Five-Year Plan. In this period the Soviet Union granted us loans at favorable conditions, assisted in the planning of 205 industrial projects and the supplying of most of the requisite equipment, sent us many excellent specialists and also gave us considerable technical aid in other fields.'

[20] Report by Chou En-lai to the 8th Congress of the Chinese Communist Party 'Proposals for a Second Five-Year Plan of Economic Development,' Peking.—Publications in Foreign Languages. 1956 [Russ. ed.].
[21] *Pravda,* 31 October 1955.   [22] Report of Liu Shao-chi to the 8th Party Congress.
[23] Report of Chou En-lai to the 8th Party Congress.

SINO-SOVIET ECONOMIC COOPERATION AFTER THE BEGINNING
OF LARGE-SCALE CHINESE ECONOMIC DEVELOPMENT

The large-scale planned economic development undertaken by the People's Republic of China created a number of new problems. At this stage in the development of the Chinese economy the main issue was no longer the reconstruction of existing enterprises for which more or less technically familiar equipment had been supplied; China now undertook to build new industries and industrial branches which required complex modern equipment and highly qualified technical personnel. In addition to continuing her imports of modern industrial equipment, China needed increasing technical and scientific assistance to master the new equipment, study new technological processes and learn the requisite methods for building large industrial plants and directing their operation.

The Chinese government decided to coordinate the Five-Year Plan with the volume and rate at which they received equipment and technical and scientific assistance from the Soviet Union and the people's democracies.

The Soviet and Chinese governments began negotiations in August 1952 concerning the expansion of economic cooperation in view of the new problems created by China's transition to large-scale economic development. A Chinese governmental delegation headed by Chairman of the State Administrative Council and Minister of Foreign Affairs, Chou En-lai, arrived in Moscow on 17 August 1952. The delegation also included Deputy-Chairman, Chen Yun, Deputy-Chairman of the Financial-Economic Committee of the State Administrative Council, Li Fu-chun, and the heads of various ministries and departments.

The Chinese governmental delegation and the accompanying officials held talks with Soviet leaders and representatives of Soviet science and industry and studied the operation of Soviet ministries, departments, economic organizations and large industrial enterprises in Moscow and other Soviet cities. The delegation visited the Lenin Volga-Don canal, toured the reconstruction project in Stalingrad and other construction projects in various areas of the country.

The conversations between the Chinese delegation and the Soviet government covered many economic issues. Before determining the scope and form of Soviet assistance within the framework of the first Chinese Five-Year Plan of economic development it was found necessary to elaborate various programs and conduct a number of preliminary studies. During its month-long visit, the delegation held general talks with the Soviet government on the further development of Sino-Soviet economic cooperation, and explained its government's requirements as to technical assistance and the volume of industrial equipment supplies which China planned to receive from the Soviet Union during the 1953-1957 period. The delegation left Moscow on 22 September 1952 after the conclusion of these talks; a group of important ministry and department officials headed by Li Fu-chun remained in Moscow in order to reach agreements on concrete issues.

A Chinese trade delegation headed by the Foreign Trade Minister, Yeh Chi-chwang, arrived in Moscow on 2 November 1952 for negotiations on the Sino-

Soviet volume of trade and Soviet supplies for 1953 within the framework of the loan. The trade delegation also negotiated an additional program of Soviet assistance and mutual commodity deliveries for 1953.

A protocol on the volume of Sino-Soviet trade for 1953 was signed in Moscow on 21 March 1953; a protocol appended to the treaty of 14 February concerning a loan and an agreement which provided for Soviet assistance in the expansion of existing electric power plants and the construction of new ones were also signed on the same day. Agreement was subsequently reached concerning all other issues related to Soviet assistance during the First Five-Year Plan. The Soviet government agreed to grant economic and technical assistance in the building and reconstruction of 91 new plants (more than 50 of which were already being built), which were to form the nucleus of the Chinese industrial program. They included large-scale metallurgical, machine-tool, power, chemical and other plants. It was also decided to develop with Soviet aid new industrial branches such as an automobile industry, an aircraft industry, turbine production, etc.

After negotiations had been concluded and the Chinese representatives had returned to Peking, the Chinese Central People's Governmental Council heard and approved at its session of 15 September 1953 a report by Li Fu-chun, member of the Chinese governmental delegation, concerning the negotiations.

The enormous achievements of the Chinese people, their inexhaustible energy, willpower and efforts for socialist development ensured not only the implementation of the Five-Year Plan but its fulfillment ahead of schedule.

An assessment of Chinese economic development in 1953 showed that the gross volume of industrial and agricultural production had increased by 14.4 percent compared to 1952 instead of the 8.7 percent set by the Five-Year Plan.

The international situation in the Far East improved in the middle of 1954 after the Geneva Conference. Thanks to the efforts of peace-loving nations, the consistently peaceful policy of the Soviet Union and the People's Republic of China and the spirit of conciliation shown at that time by the British and French representatives, the Geneva Conference between the Soviet Union, the People's Republic of China, Britain, France and other interested countries decided on 21 July 1954, in spite of American opposition, to put an end to hostilities in Indochina and reach a peaceful settlement of political issues in Vietnam, Laos and Cambodia.

Talks held by the Chinese Premier, Chou En-lai, with Nehru and Ho Chi Mink in the course of his visit to India, Burma and the Vietnamese Democratic Republic constituted an important contribution to peace throughout the world, and particularly in Asia. They stressed the common goals of these countries in their policy of peace based on five principles (mutual respect of territorial integrity and sovereignty, nonaggression, noninterference in domestic affairs, equality, and mutual benefit in peaceful coexistence) and strengthened the common front of peace-loving Asiatic countries.

The implementation of the initial Five-Year Plan ahead of schedule enabled the planning organizations to provide for additional construction of industrial plants for the coming five years; China consequently required additional industrial equipment and trained technicians. On the other hand enterprises which had begun to operate accumulated experience and swiftly formed technical and administrative staffs in productive branches which had traditionally existed in China, who could thus assist in the development of such industries in other friendly countries.

New possibilities appeared for the expansion of Sino-Soviet cooperation. The visit of an official Soviet delegation to China in September-October 1954 constituted an important step in the development of Sino-Soviet economic relations. The delegation included the First Secretary of the Central Committee of the Communist Party of the Soviet Union and member of the Presidium of the Supreme Soviet, N. S. Khrushchev (who headed the delegation), the First Deputy-Chairman of the Council of Ministers, N. A. Bulganin, the Deputy-Chairman of the Council of Ministers, A. I. Mikoyan, and a number of other personages; it arrived in Peking on 29 September 1954 for the celebration of the fifth anniversary of the People's Republic of China.

The cordial reception given to the Soviet delegation by the leaders of the Chinese Communist Party, the Chinese government and the numerous representatives of the workers of the Chinese capital expressed the sincere fraternal feelings of the entire Chinese people toward the nations of the Soviet Union.

In his speech at the ceremonial session held in Hwaijentang Hall, N. S. Khrushchev, head of the delegation, stated: 'We Soviet people consider it our fraternal duty to assist our friend and brother, the Chinese people, to consolidate their people's democratic state and build socialism. This is why each of your achievements in the construction of a new China greatly gladdens the Soviet people. The Chinese people may be confident that the Soviet people will also remain their reliable and trustworthy friend in the future, and will extend comprehensive assistance and support in the effort for the further consolidation and development of the People's Republic of China.

'Common goals in the struggle for socialism and communism, common goals in the struggle for peace between nations, the free and independent development of all nations, an ideology of friendship between nations—all greatly promote the strengthening of ties between countries, cement the unity of free nations. The role played by the fraternal friendship of the peoples of the Soviet Union and the People's Republic of China is an extremely important one.'[24]

The Soviet delegation immediately opened talks with Chairman of the State Council and Minister of Foreign Affairs, Chou En-lai, Deputy-Chairmen Chen Yun, Peng Teh-hwai, Teng Tze-hwei, Teng Hsiao-ping and Li Fu-chun on the subject of Sino-Soviet relations and the international situation. President Mao Tse-tung, Vice-President Chu Teh and the Secretary of the Central Committee of the Chinese Communist Party and Chairman of the Permanent Committee of the All-Chinese Assembly, Liu Shao-chi, also participated in the talks.

Negotiations were concluded on 12 October 1954 by the signing of a number of documents which expressed the common views of both governments on international

---

[24] *Pravda*, 1 October 1954.

problems and defined the further development of fraternal cooperation between the two peoples:

1) 'the joint declaration of the Soviet and Chinese governments on Sino-Soviet relations and the international situation;'

2) 'the joint declaration of the Soviet Union and Chinese governments on relations with Japan;'

3) 'the Sino-Soviet communiqué on the withdrawal of Soviet military forces from the joint naval base of Port Arthur and the transfer of this base to the People's Republic of China;'

4) 'the Sino-Soviet communiqué on the transfer to the People's Republic of China of the Soviet share in the joint companies;'

5) 'the Sino-Soviet communiqué on the signing of an agreement for scientific and technical cooperation;'

6) 'the Sino-Soviet communiqué on the construction of the Lanchow-Urumchi-Alma-Ata railroad and the organization of direct connections;'

7) 'the joint communiqué of the Soviet government, the People's Republic of China and the Mongolian People's Republic on the construction of a railroad from Tsining to Ulan-Bator and the organization of direct communications;'

8) the agreement on the grant of a long-term loan to the Chinese government by the Soviet government;

9) the protocol on the organization of Soviet assistance to China for the construction of 15 additional industrial plants and the increase of equipment supplies for 141 plants;

10) an exchange of letters concerning the gift of technical equipment to the Chinese people for the organization of large-scale grain farming.

1) In the common declaration on Sino-Soviet relations and the international situation both governments stated that the cooperation between the Soviet Union and the People's Republic of China promotes the economic and cultural development of both countries, the further consolidation and expansion of their mutual friendship and therefore strenthens peace and security in the Far East and throughout the world.

Both governments declared themselves united in their desire to continue their participation in all international forums promoting the cause of peace and to act in a concerted manner in all issues concerning the interests of both parties.

Both governments noted the importance of the Geneva Agreement which settled the Indochina issue and appraised the aggressive policy of the United States against China, Korea and other Asiatic and Pacific nations; the declaration stated in this context that both governments 'find it necessary to declare that the Soviet Union and the People's Republic of China base and will continue to base their relations with Asiatic and Pacific countries as well as with other states on the strict observance of the mutual respect of sovereignty and territorial integrity, mutual nonaggression, mutual nonintervention in domestic affairs, equality, mutual benefit and peaceful co-existence; this opens extensive possibilities for the development of beneficial international cooperation.'

2) The common declaration concerning relations with Japan stated that the United

States was openly violating the Potsdam agreement in compelling Japan to sign the San Fransisco 'peace treaty' and other illegal agreements; the Soviet and Chinese governments expressed in the name of their peoples their deepest sympathy toward Japan and their confidence that the Japanese people would find enough strength to free themselves from foreign dependence, bring about the rebirth of their homeland and strive to normalize economic relations and cultural ties with other countries, mainly with their neighbors. 'The governments of the Soviet Union and of the People's Republic of China,' stated the declaration, 'base their policy toward Japan on the principle of peaceful coexistence between states whatever their social structure, being convinced that such a step accords with the vital interests of all nations. They stand for the development of extensive commercial relations with Japan at mutually benefical conditions and the establishment of close cultural ties with that country.'

3) In view of the new international situation in the Far East after the end of hostilities in Korea and Indochina, as well as the increasing defensive potential of the People's Republic of China, the declaration concerning the Port Arthur naval base stated: 'The governments of the Soviet Union and China, in accordance with the present developing relations of friendship and cooperation between the two states, have agreed to the withdrawal of Soviet military forces from the joint naval base of Port Arthur, and all installations in this area are transferred without compensation to the government of the People's Republic of China.' It was agreed that the withdrawal of Soviet troops and the transfer of installations be completed by 31 May 1955.

4) The Soviet and Chinese governments concluded that in view of China's economic development and the increasing number of trained Chinese technical personnel, certain forms of Soviet assistance had no further utility. Four joint Sino-Soviet companies had been created in 1950-1951, when the newly established People's Republic of China was faced with the necessity of reconstructing its economy: a company for the extraction of nonferrous and rare metals in Sinkiang, a company for the extraction and processing of petroleum in Sinkiang, a company for the construction and repair of ships in Dalny and a company for the organization and operation of civil airlines.

The Sino-Soviet companies, which had made use of modern Soviet economic experience, rapidly succeeded in organizing their branches of activity, considerably increasing production and raising their general technical level; they thus contributed to the reconstruction and development of the Chinese economy. The communiqué concerning the transfer to China of the Soviet Union's share in these joint companies stated: 'Today, when China has reconstructed its economy and is successfully implementing the First Five-Year Plan, the Chinese economic organizations have accumulated the necessary experience and may independently direct the enterprises of the joint companies; the governments of the Soviet Union and the People's Republic of China have reached an agreement according to which the Soviet share in the joint Sino-Soviet companies will be transferred in full to the People's Republic of China on 1 January 1955. Payments for this share will be made over several years in deliveries to the Soviet Union of goods usually exported from China.'

5) Both governments acknowledged that it had become possible to expand econ-

omic cooperation. Negotiations which opened in Moscow and were concluded in Peking led to the signing of an agreement for scientific and technical cooperation between the two countries.

According to this agreement, both governments were to profit from their experience in all economic branches and were mutually to exchange all technical documents without any compensation (the only payment stipulated was to cover the cost of the copies), exchange technical information and specialists for technical assistance and thus learn of each other's scientific and technical achievements.

The implementation of this agreement was to be ensured by a Sino-Soviet commission of seven representatives for each party, which was to elaborate measures for scientific and technical cooperation and present recommendations to both governments. The commission was to meet not less than twice a year, alternately in Moscow and Peking.

The agreement was concluded for five years and could be extended for a further five-year period in accordance with the desires of both parties.

6) The Soviet and Chinese governments, endeavoring to strengthen further economic and cultural ties, agreed to build in the near future a railroad from Lanchow to Alma-Ata through Urumchi. The section running through Chinese territory, from Lanchow to the border, was to be built by the Chinese government, and that running from Alma-Ata to the border by the Soviet government. The Soviet side agreed to grant comprehensive technical assistance to China for the construction of the section passing through Chinese territory.

7) The joint communiqué of the Soviet government, the People's Republic of China and the Mongolian People's Republic stated that the three governments had agreed to finish the construction of a railroad from Ulan Bator to Tsining which would be carried out, as stipulated by the agreement of 15 September 1952 between the three governments, by the Soviet Union and the Mongolian People's Republic for the section on the latter's territory and by the Chinese government for the section on Chinese territory; it was also agreed to open direct communications along this railroad in 1955.

8) During the visit of the Soviet governmental delegation to China an agreement was signed for the grant of a long-term loan to China which was to be used for the payment of the increasing Chinese purchases of Soviet industrial equipment and other commodities. This new loan involved a sum of 520 million rubles.

9) A protocol was also signed for Soviet assistance to China in the construction of 15 additional industrial plants and the increase of equipment deliveries for 141 plants built with Soviet assistance within the framework of previous agreements. These additional deliveries of equipment were to reach more than 400 million rubles.

10) In the name of the Soviet Union the Soviet governmental delegation expressed the desire to impart the experience gained by the Soviet people in the development of virgin and unused lands by sovkhozes; as a sign of the fraternal friendship between the Soviet and Chinese people and in order to mark the fifth anniversary of the People's Republic of China, the delegation offered in the name of the Soviet people the necessary equipment for setting up a grain sovkhoz with a sowing area of 20,000

hectares. The letter on this subject stated the Soviet government's agreement to the dispatch of Soviet specialists to China who were to help in the organization of grain farming and production during the first year of this project.

The Soviet governmental delegation visited various areas in the north, northeast, east and south of China.[25]

The new Sino-Soviet agreements signed on 12 October 1954 were of great importance for the further development of economic and cultural relations between the two countries. They established a program for the radical improvement of transport facilities between the two neighboring states, laid the basis for a comprehensive exchange of scientific and technical experience and delineated the future expansion of Sino-Soviet trade.

Implementation of these agreements was begun at the exact dates set. The protocols concerning volume of trade in 1955 (signed on 11 February 1955) and 1956 (concluded on 27 December 1955) provided for a considerable increase of commodity deliveries; these included Soviet deliveries of equipment complexes by the terms of the loan agreement of 12 October 1954 and increasing imports of Chinese products to the Soviet Union. The protocol on the volume of trade for 1956 provided, in addition to an increase of mutual deliveries, for freight transport along a new route—by transit through the Mongolian People's Republic along the Ulan Bator—Tsining railroad. The Sino-Soviet commission for scientific and technical cooperation began its sessions in December 1954; the number of mutual visits of scientific delegations and individual scientists and specialists increased considerably as a result of its activity.

The visit of a Soviet governmental delegation to China headed by the First Deputy-Chairman of the Council of Ministers, A. I. Mikoyan, on 6-7 April 1956 constituted a further step in the development of Sino-Soviet economic cooperation.[26] During its stay in Peking the Soviet delegation continued the negotiations initiated with the

---

[25] The delegation left Peking by rail for the south on 6 October through Nanking and Shanghai and from there to Hangchow. In Nanking it visited the mausoleum of Sun Yat-sen and the common graves of the revolutionaries killed during the anti-popular Chang Kai-shek regime. In Shanghai the delegation visited the harbor and the No. 1 state-owned cotton mill. It then left for Hangchow, a health center for Chinese workers. From there it flew to Canton, where it visited the surrounding state-farms for the cultivation of rubber trees, bananas and pineapples. On the way back to Peking by air the delegates stopped at Hangkow, visited the city and toured the earthworks thrown up by the population to prevent flooding. The delegation reached Peking in the evening of 10 October.

On 13 October N. S. Khrushchev, N. A. Bulganin and A. I. Mikoyan flew from Peking to Northeast China [Manchuria], while the other members of the delegation left by air for Moscow on 13-14 October. Khrushchev, Bulganin and Mikoyan visited Port Arthur and Dalny, where they received reports from the military command and gave their views concerning the withdrawal of Soviet units from Port Arthur. They visited Soviet warships and historical battle sites. On their way to the Soviet Union through the Northeastern Chinese provinces the three members of the delegation toured the Anshan metallurgical complex and industries in Mukden, Changchun and Harbin; their visits included tours of the Changchun automobile plant, constructed with Soviet assistance, the flax mill and the tool factory. The delegation left Harbin for Vladivostok by air on 17 October.

[26] The Soviet governmental delegation reached Peking on 6 April 1956 from Hanoi and left Peking by air on 7 April 1956.

Chinese government in Moscow concerning further economic cooperation between the two countries. These talks were concluded by the signing of two agreements.[27]

The first agreement provided for Soviet assistance in the construction of 55 industrial plants in addition to the 156 already under construction by the terms of previous agreements. These new projects included metallurgical, machine-tool and chemical industries, plants producing artificial fibers and plastic, eletrotechnical and radio technical plants, plants for the production of synthetic liquid fuel, electric power stations and institutes working for the aircraft industry. The Soviet Union was to supply equipment, projects and other technical assistance for these 55 enterprises amounting to approximately 2.5 billion rubles. The agreement stipulated that this sum would be paid by the Chinese government in commodities delivered in the corresponding years: it also provided for an increase of Soviet assistance for Chinese geological surveys.

The second agreement concerned the construction of a railroad from Lanchow to the Aktogai station of the Turkestan-Siberian railroad, which was to cross the Sino-Soviet border at the Dzungarian Gates (Alashan pass) and the organization of direct communications along this line in 1960. This agreement followed up talks conducted by the Soviet governmental delegation in October 1954.

According to these agreements, the Soviet Union was to help in accelarating the projects by assisting China in the construction of the railroad through Chinese territory from Urumchi to the Dzungarian Gates; this assistance would take the form of deliveries of equipment and materials and participation of Soviet specialists in construction. China was to pay for this assistance by deliveries of Chinese commoditits at the same conditions as those stipulated by the existing commercial treaty between the two countries.

These and the previous economic agreements laid a firm basis for the development of economic relations between the Soviet Union and the People's Republic of China. They demonstrated that with the gradual economic development of both countries the economic cooperation between the Soviet and Chinese people was assuming increasing importance and was extending to the most varied branches of science and production.

TRADE AND SCIENTIFIC AND TECHNICAL COOPERATION BETWEEN
THE SOVIET UNION AND THE PEOPLE'S REPUBLIC OF CHINA
IN 1953-1955

Sino-Soviet Trade. The volume and composition of Sino-Soviet trade in 1953-1955 differed considerably as compared with the preeceding three-year period. These changes reflected the economic development of both countries and were due to the foreign trade goals which both attempted to reach at this stage of their development.

---

[27] The agreements were signed by A. I. Mikoyan for the Soviet side and Deputy-Chairman of the Chinese State Council, Li Fu-chun, for the Chinese side.

The total value of Sino-Soviet trade rose from 3,885 million rubles in 1952 to 5,544 million in 1955, an increase of 43.8 percent; Soviet exports to China increased 35 percent and Chinese exports to Russia by 55.5 percent. Chinese exports showed a greater increase because China paid in commodity deliveries not only for Soviet imports but also for technical assistance (research, planning, assembly of equipment, etc.), which increased greatly after 1954.

EVOLUTION OF THE SINO-SOVIET VOLUME OF TRADE IN 1953-1955
(1952 = 100%)

	1953		1954		1955	
	million rubles	%	*million rubles*	%	*million rubles*	%
Soviet exports to China	2,822	128.3	3,037.2	138.0	2,969.5	135.0
Soviet imports from China	1,898.9	114.7	2,313.4	140.0	2,574	155.5
Total volume of trade	4,720.9	122.5	5,350.6	138.8	5,543.5	143.8

Soviet exports to the People's Republic of China. The composition of Soviet exports to China changed considerably in 1953, that is, after the end of the period of reconstruction. By the end of 1955, 271 industrial enterprises were put into operation in China. The gross value of industrial production increased from 82,718 million *yüan* in 1952 to 110,415 million in 1955; the production of modern machinery rose in the same period from 22,049 million to 37,082 million *yüan*. China succeeded in meeting its most pressing requirements for many types of textile and alimentary products by domestic production; it thus reduced or discontinued its imports from other

SOVIET EXPORTS TO THE PEOPLE'S REPUBLIC OF CHINA IN 1953-1955

Groups of commodities	1953		1954		1955	
	million rubles	%	*million rubles*	%	*million rubles*	%
Equipment and machinery	650.2	23	795.5	26.2	894.4	30.1
Equipment complexes	180.3	6.4	372.3	12.3	542.2	18.3
Ferrous metals	290.3	10.3	351.6	11.6	327.1	11
Nonferrous metals	53.8	1.9	88.5	2.9	51.0	1.7
Wire cable	16.5	0.6	13.0	0.5	4.7	0.2
Petroleum products	178.5	6.3	180.1	5.9	316.1	10.6
Chemicals (products fertilizers, etc.)	26.7	0.9	33.3	1.1	24.8	0.8
Paper	35.7	1.3	25.0	0.8	28.8	1.0
Cotton	—	—	49.5	1.6	38.7	1.3
Cotton fabrics	1.7	0.1	6.5	0.2	—	—
TOTAL	2,822	100	3,037.2	100	2,969.5	100

countries, including the Soviet Union. This applied to cotton fabrics, the production of which rose from 89,273 to 122,331 pieces between 1952 and 1955, cotton yarn, which increased from 3,618 to 4,598 thousand bales, machine-produced paper, which passed from 372 to 556 thousand tons, tires, from 417 to 701 thousand units, sugar, from 249 to 347 thousand tons (including local domestic production) and cigarettes, from 2,630 to 3,728 thousand crates.

Total exports of Soviet rolled ferrous metals to China increased from 321 thousand tons in 1952 to 432 thousand tons in 1955; on the other hand, Soviet exports of rails, girders, small-caliber tubing and sleepers contracted noticeably after the inauguration of the rail and girder plant of Anshan and of other plants which supplied most of the domestic requirements. Soviet exports to China of thick and thin sheet steel, oil pipes and high-grade steel increased at the same time.

The structure of Soviet exports of metal lathes also changed. The total volume of these Soviet deliveries to China dropped from 1,615 units in 1952 to 684 units in 1955. The export of simple models ceased almost entirely during the same period, since China met her requirements almost entirely by domestic production, but Soviet exports of automatic and various special lathes increased yearly.[28]

Imports of Soviet mining equipment also decreased. In 1955 China began to produce various types of mining machinery including steam shovels for coal extraction from open beds, mining combines of the Soviet 'Donbass' type, mechanical loaders and drills. China not only ceased to import textile equipment but became itself an exporter to Southeast Asia and Egypt. From 1951 the Chinese textile engineering industry put out spinning mills producing one million spindles a year and 31.5 million automatic looms. At the end of 1955 electric machinery for color prints, complexes producing fabric for tires and other modern textile machinery were being produced in China.

Despite the decrease in Soviet exports of some types of industrial products, resulting from the successful Chinese production of these items, the number of different Soviet items exported to China increased as a whole and reached approximately 17 thousand at the beginning of 1956. An important part of Soviet exports in 1955 consisted of modern apparatus, high-precision products, laboratory equipment, various large-size tubing, equipment for petroleum and general prospection, high-power electromotors, X-ray equipment for medical and industrial use and many other commodities.

Petroleum and petroleum products still constitute an important part of Soviet exports to China. Despite the increase of domestic petroleum production from 436 thousand tons in 1952 to almost one million tons in 1955, imports of petroleum and

---

[28] China also made important achievements toward the end of 1955 in the production of automatic machine tools. According to the correspondent of the *New China Agency*, one of the Nanking state-owned machine tool plants produced on 20 October 1955 the first automatic lathe processing 30 units per minute. According to a report published by the *Jenminjipao* Agency on 5 November 1955, the Shanghai state-owned machine-tool plant mastered the production of special polishing machines of SK 371 type. The First Five-Year Plan for economic development provided for more than 1,500 new types of industrial products, which included more than 100 types of machine tools.

petroleum products from the Soviet Union increased in the same period from 607.5 thousand to 1,589.2 thousand tons. The most important change in Soviet exports to China, which reflected both the new stage of Chinese economic development and the expansion of Soviet technical assistance, was an increase of Soviet deliveries of equipment complexes to China.

Equipment complexes, for the complete equipment of reconstructed or new enterprises, became the most important item exported to China during the years of the planned economic development. An intrinsic part of such deliveries is the increase in comprehensive technical assistance for the construction of the enterprises destined to receive the equipment.

Deliveries of equipment complexes entail the participation of Soviet commercial, scientific and production organizations which impart their experience in the corresponding field of production and construction. Before beginning deliveries of equipment complexes the Soviet organizations must participate in the research work (determine the site of the enterprise from the rational and economical point of view study the supply of raw materials, etc) and draw up the required plans; only then, when construction is about to begin, can the equipment deliveries be effected.

These deliveries and technical assistance by the Soviet Union and other socialist countries increase China's domestic production and economic independence and reduce her reliance on imports. Deliveries of these complexes are the most characteristic expression of entirely new socialist relations in the field of foreign trade, based on mutual fraternal assistance and the granting of aid by one country at a higher level of scientific and technical development to another less developed country. The Soviet deliveries do not usually include auxiliary equipment if the latter can be produced in China. On the other hand, they are sometimes accompanied by spare parts, sets of instruments and in some cases industrial materials, particularly if a new industry is to be set up and samples must be produced.

Soviet equipment complexes accounted at first for 80 percent of the total value of equipment required by China for the construction of new enterprises; only 20 percent of the necessary equipment was produced locally. However, as Chinese production gradually expanded, the proportion of Chinese equipment for the enterprises under construction also began to grow. The proportion of Soviet equipment correspondingly dropped to 70 percent by the end of 1956 and even reached only only 50-60 percent for certain enterprises.

Despite this decrease in the proportion of Soviet equipment complexes used in Chinese enterprises under construction, the value of such exports to China increased yearly owing to the increasing volume of construction in China.

The total value of Soviet exports to China increased by 35 percent from 1952 to 1955; deliveries of equipment complexes increased during this period by 270 percent and became the most important item of Soviet export to China.

In 1953-1956 the Soviet Union delivered to China equipment complexes for 156 industrial projects and 21 production departments created with Soviet assistance. These include the main projects of the First Five-Year Plan:

In the ferrous metal industry: the reconstructed Anshan metal works, Penhsihu [Penki] works and the new metal industries in Wuhan and Paotow;

In the nonferrous metal industry: the reconstructed Anyuan tungsten works, the Kokiu tin works, the Fushun aluminium works and the Harbin rolled aluminium works;

In the engineering industry: the Changchun automobile plant, the Mukden machine-tool plants, the Tsitsihar heavy machine-tool works, the Harbin plant for electro-technical equipment, the Mukden drill works, the Harbin turbine works;

In the electrotechnical industry: the reconstructed Fengman hydroelectric station, the thermoelectric stations in Fushun, Taiyuan, Sian, Loyang, Kirin, Chengtu, Kiamusze, Kokiu, Changchun, Penhsihu [Penki], Fusin, Dalny (Talien), Paotow, Lanchow, Wuhan;

In the coal industry: coal mines in Kiamusze, Fusin, Fengfeng, Pehpiao, Sian, Tunghwa, Kisi and the coal concentrating plants in Fushun, Kiamusze, Fedgfend, Kisi;

In the chemical industry: the chemical plants of Kirin, Taiyuan and Lanchow;

In the paper industry: the cellulose paper plant of Kiamusze;

In the petroleum industry: the Lanchow refinery.

SOVIET EXPORTS OF EQUIPMENT COMPLEXES TO THE
PEOPLE'S REPUBLIC OF CHINA IN 1952-1955

	1952	1953	1954	1955
Value of equipment complexes (million rubles)	145.7	180.3	372.3	542.1
Share of these exports in total Soviet exports to China (percent)	6.6	6.4	12.3	18.3
Increase of exports of equipment complexes (percent)	100	123.7	255.5	372.1

Long-term agreements between Soviet and Chinese organizations constitute the characteristic modality of the deliveries of equipment complexes, since the preliminary projects and the construction of large industrial plants usually take several years.

Extensive deliveries of equipment complexes are therefore possible only within the framework of planned governmental construction, when the establishment of any particular enterprise is not determined by temporary considerations but is provided for by a single long-range plan of economic development on a national scale. Deliveries of equipment complexes within the framework of long-term agreements promote, in turn, state planning, and introduce an element of stability in the relations between the Soviet Union and the People's Republic of China.

Soviet imports from the People's Republic of China. The resources of the Chinese economy increased considerably in the first three years of planned economic development. Production of basic industrial items expanded from 1952 to the end of 1955 as follows: coal production from 63.5 to 93.6 million tons, cast iron from 1,900 to 3,630 thousand tons, steel from 1,350 to 2,853 thousand tons, and the gross volume of industrial production increased by approximately 100 percent. The yield of industrial crops reached approximately 184 million tons in 1955, compared to 163.9 million in 1952.

These economic achievements enabled the Chinese government to expand foreign trade and exports; Chinese exports to the Soviet Union expanded, from 1,655 million rubles in 1952 to 2,574 million in 1955, an increase of 55.5 percent.

The growth of Soviet imports from China also reflected the changes occurring at this time in the Soviet economy. The material and cultural level of the Soviet people improved considerably in the period of the Fifth Five-Year Plan. In these years Soviet national income increased by 68 percent, the real wages of Soviet workers and employees rose by 39 percent and the income of kolkhoz workers by 50 percent. Thus, despite the considerable increase in the sale of basic alimentary and industrial products to the Soviet population through the state-owned and cooperative network from 1950 to 1955 (of 220 percent for meat, 158 percent for animal fats, 222 percent for vegetable fats, 198 percent for clothing and linen and 168 percent for footwear) the demand for consumer goods could not be entirely met. In addition to increasing its domestic production, the Soviet Union was thus interested in importing many alimentary products and industrial raw materials from China.

China was also interested, in the initial period of large-scale economic construction, in increasing its exports as much as possible in order to pay for its constantly expanding industrial imports. In view of the American embargo the Chinese government had to find new stable markets for many items which had been exported in the past to Western Europe and the United States. At the same time owing to the increased domestic demand for alimentary products and raw materials the Chinese government had to reduce or completely discontinue exports of several products, including oilseeds, *hsiaomitze* [Italian millet] and *kaoliang* [Sorghum chinense].

An increase of exports, which was absolutely necessary for ensuring payment of industrial imports, could thus be achieved only by finding new export products which had either not been previously exported at all or had been so merely in small amounts, and by ensuring a stable market for these items. The Soviet Union and the other socialist countries offered China ample possibilities for developing her exports.

Certain difficulties that arose in the sale of some Chinese products on the Soviet market neccessitated some corrective measures. For example, the Soviet Union had previously imported from China only fresh eggs, while such egg products as *melange* had been exported by China to Britain and other Western countries. As China was finding increasing difficulties in marketing this commodity, Soviet organizations adapted their industry to utilize it and began to purchase it from China in large quantities. Chinese organizations also had to adapt themselves to the Soviet demand. Soviet organizations were interested in purchasing cork, for example, which had not been previously exported by China. The Chinese foreign trade organizations succeeded in organizing the collection and exporting of cork within a short time. Soviet and Chinese organizations concluded long-term agreements for certain commodities requiring special measures or large capital investments either for their export from China or their utilization in Russia; such agreements justified the sums and efforts expended. These factors led to an expansion and modification of Chinese exports to the Soviet Union.

Alimentary raw materials constituted the main item of Chinese export to the Soviet Union in 1952, reaching 449 million rubles or 30.2 percent. The value of these items decreased during the two following years, and although it expanded again in 1955 and reached 475 million rubles, their relative increase was much smaller than that of other export items and they constituted at this date only 18.5 percent of the total value of exports to the Soviet Union.

Chinese exports of alimentary products to the Soviet Union increased at the same time from 229 to 652 million rubles and their share in total Chinese exports to the Soviet Union grew from 13.8 to 25.3 percent. The increase was greatest in exports of products such as rice, meat, fresh and canned fruit, egg products, fats, etc.

Nonferrous metals and alloys remained one of the main Chinese export items throughout the entire period (17.7-18.4 percent) and the value of these exports rose from 292 to 474 million rubles. Exports of tungsten, molybdenum and mercury increased considerably.

SOVIET IMPORTS FROM THE PEOPLE'S REPUBLIC OF CHINA IN 1953-1955

Groups of commodities	1953		1954		1955	
	million rubles	%	*million rubles*	%	*million rubles*	%
Raw materials for alimentary products	489	25.7	463	20	475	18.5
Alimentary products	355	18.7	594	25.7	652	25.3
Nonferrous and alloyed metals, concentrates	403	21.3	427	18.5	474	18.4
Textile raw materials	232	12.2	222	9.5	238	9.2
Textile products	69	3.6	149	6.4	234	9.1
Animal husbandry raw materials (bristles, un-dressed leather, casings, etc.)	70	3.7	99	4.3	107	4.3
Chemical products	15	0.8	14	0.6	26	1.0
TOTAL	1,898.9	100	2,313.4	100	2,574.0	100

Textile raw materials (raw silk, lamb's wool, ramee, jute, etc.) as well as textile products (silks and woolens, table cloths, linen and other commodities) are an important group among China's exports to the Soviet Union. Exports of textile products also increased very rapidly from 69 to 234 million rubles), while exports of textile raw material exports decreased slightly (from 12.2 to 9.2 percent).

Together with the increase of all main items of Chinese export in 1953-1955, exports to the Soviet Union of new Chinese products also increased noticeably; this was the case for handicraft wares, haberdashery, rugs, essential oils, etc.

The Chinese Industrial and Agricultural Exhibition, held in Moscow from 11 July to 5 August 1953, played an important role in the expansion of Chinese exports to the Soviet Union. All branches of the Chinese economy were represented at the exhibition, which demonstrated the important economic changes which had occurred in China in the four years since the establishment of the People's Republic of China. The products of skilled Chinese artisans, agricultural produce from the subtropical areas, rare minerals from Tien Shan, Kunlun and the Himalayas, and many original modern industrial products presented at the exhibition interested Soviet commercial and industrial organizations; many of these items were subsequently included into Chinese exports to the Soviet Union.

Experience has shown that Sino-Soviet trade was mutually beneficial. The conditions (exchange of goods at the Sino-Soviet border at average world market prices fixed for extended periods) are advantageous to both parties. Long-term purchase and sale agreements involving large lots of commodities make it possible for each side to carry out continuous shipments, avoid stocking in railroad or port warehouses, and thus reduce stocking costs and transport losses.

Sino-Soviet trade has demonstrated its vitality and refuted the expectations of the American monopolist circles, who endeavored to undermine the economy of the socialist countries by their embargo. This policy has only promoted the search for new export items and the creation of new industries in the scoialist countries for the mutual supply of products previously imported from the United States and Britain. It has speeded up the development and consolidation of the foreign trade between socialist countries, including Sino-Soviet trade. The experience accumulated in trade under embargo conditions has demonstrated that the Soviet Union and the People's Republic of China are capable of meeting their requirements in the main industrial products and raw materials without any interruption and in sufficient amounts.

Sino-Soviet scientific and technical cooperation. Scientific and technical cooperation, the mutual exchange of experience in the fields of science and production, constituted one of the most recent forms of friendship between the Soviet Union and the People's Republic of China.

An agreement on scientific and technical cooperation was concluded on 12 October 1954 between the Soviet and Chinese governments. Special departments were set up in the foreign trade ministries of both parties to implement this cooperation. The earlier agreements providing for Soviet technical assistance to China in her industrial development, the dispatch of Soviet specialists and the training of Chinese citizens in the Soviet Union continued to be valid, but were now enlarged and supplemented in accordance with the specific program of Soviet participation in the new Chinese industrial development.

The agreement on scientific and technical cooperation provided for the mutual exchange of experience and information either unknown to one of the parties or not yet applied in production. The exchange of scientific and technical experience is achieved by the gratuitous transfer of patents and various types of documents (payments included only expenses for duplication of the documents) and the mutual exchange of information concerning the scientifiic and technical achievements of both parties. Each session of the Sino-Soviet commission for scientific and technical cooperation prepares a memorandum which lists the subjects on which information is to be exchanged and determines the measures for implementing this exchange. The commission for scientific and technical cooperation held three sessions between December 1954 and December 1955, the first and third in Moscow and the second in in Peking[29]

The Soviet Union transmitted to China scientific and technical documents concerning all branches of industry, transport and other economic activities. China in turn offered Russia documents and descriptions concerning some light industries, in particular the production of raw silk, the raising of subtropical crops, vegetables and some grain crops as well as other fields in which the talented Chinese people had gained a centuries-long experience. The delegates of both parties had the additional

---

[29] a) The first session was held in Moscow in December 1954. It established the following list of subjects for the exchange of scientific and technical information:

The Soviet Union was to transmit to China: designs for industrial buildings (metal works, engineering works, electric stations, etc.), working drafts for the production of machinery and equipment and technological documents for many types of industrial production, scientific and technical literature, standards and handbooks reflecting the accumulated experience of the Soviet Union in the field of socialist construction.

The People's Republic of China was to transmit to the Soviet Union: descriptions of the technological process and samples of wares produced by light industries, pharmaceutical industries and local industries; samples of agricultural produce, including subtropical plants, citrus fruits, vegetables, grain crops and other plants. China also offered Soviet specialists the possibility of becoming acquainted with the achievements and operation of certain branches of the Chinese economy.

The Chinese specialists who visited Moscow in order to take part in the first session for scientific and technical cooperation toured industrial enterprises and scientific institutions in Moscow, Leningrad and the Urals.

b) The second session met in Peking in July 1955 and provided for the following exchange of information:

The Soviet Union was to supply technical documents for the construction of mines, concentrating plants, electric stations, locomotive works, wagon factories, oil-refining and glass works, locomotive and wagon roundhouses and other installations, working drafts for the production of rolling-mills, pumps and other machinery, as well as technical documents concerning the production of high-grade steel and rolled metal, varnish, paints, enamel, etc.

The People's Republic of China was to supply technical documentation concerning the production of silk, cellulose, paper, concrete tubing, drying oil from tung oil, a number of alimentary and chemical products, plants for oil and essential oil crops and seeds of trees and shrubs.

c) The third session, held in Moscow in December 1955, provided for the exchange of the following information:

The Soviet Union was to submit projects for the construction of nonferrous metal plants, coal-mining industries and railroad installations; working drafts for the production of domestic, concentrating, pumping, compressing, transport, and polishing equipment and various types of agricultural machinery, equipment for the chemical industry, etc.

The People's Republic of China was to furnish technical documents concerning a number of chemical processes, working drafts for some types of textile and tobacco equipment, seed samples and a number of drug samples.

opportunity of becoming acquainted with scientific organizations and industrial enterprises.

In addition to the exchange of information provided for by the three sessions of the Sino-Soviet commission, the Soviet Union invited a Chinese delegation in March-April 1955 to Moscow, together with delegations from Poland, Czechoslovakia, Romania and the German Democratic Republic; these delegations of physicists and engineers studied Soviet scientific achievements in the field of nuclear physics and the peaceful uses of atomic energy. The Soviet government declared itself ready to extend scientifiic, technical and engineering assistance to these countries in setting up their own scientific experimental installations for the advancement of nuclear physics and the peaceful uses of atomic energy.

After the delegations had examined Soviet scientific achievements in nuclear physics, negotiations were concluded by the signing of an agreement on 27 April 1955 between the Soviet Union and the People's Republic of China[30] which provided, in addition to the experimental atomic reactor and particle accelerators which were to be delivered to China in 1955-1956, for the gift of scientific and technical documents concerning the reactor and accelerators and the granting of Soviet assistance in the assembly and operation of the nuclear reactor and its supply in fissionable and other materials.

In order to inform the Chinese population of Soviet achievements in the peaceful utilization of atomic energy the Soviet Academy of Sciences organized an exhibition on this subject in Peking from 15 June to 15 August 1956. This exhibition constituted a kind of public laboratory open to Chinese scientists, specialists and the general public.

The principle of reciprocity applied in the Sino-Soviet Scientific and technical cooperation as in Soviet cooperation with other socialist countries, does not in the least imply that the extent of the exchange is limited or that each side must offer scientific and technical information of equal value with that received. This principle implies that each side informs its partners of all its accumulated experience, all its achievements, that the most advanced partner shares its experience with the others and assists them to advance more rapidly along the road of socialist development, in order to further general progress and reinforce the socialist camp.

MAIN FACTORS DETERMINING THE SUCCESSFUL DEVELOPMENT OF
SINO-SOVIET ECONOMIC COOPERATION

The Soviet Union and the People's Republic of China are fraternal socialist countries. They are united by common goals, inspired by the same ideals of building communism. The friendship between the Soviet and Chinese people, like that between all the nations of the socialist camp, is based on a complete equality of rights and the mutual respect of national interests. By helping one another they endeavor to rein-

---

[30] Similar agreements were concluded in April 1955 by the Soviet government with the governments of Romania, Poland, Czechoslovakia and the German Democratic Republic.

force each socialist country and the socialist camp as a whole. Such relations are the embodiment of proletarian internationalism.

By the beginning of 1956 the workers of the socialist countries had considerably furthered the economic progress of their countries and were successfully developing their fraternal ties.

In 1955 Soviet foreign trade with the people's democracies reached a volume of 19.5 billion rubles, compared to 10.6 billion in 1950, Sino-Soviet trade accounting for more than 20 percent of this. At the beginning of 1956, Soviet long-term loans to the people's democracies totaled 21 billion rubles.

The successful development of Sino-Soviet economic cooperation can be attributed to common factors in the social evolution of all countries and to a number of specific geographical and economic characteristics of both countries.

1) *The common goal of the Soviet Union and the People's Republic of China—building socialism and communism.*

The most decisive factor which determines the successful development of economic relations between the Soviet Union and China is their common goals and interest in the building of socialism and communism. The Soviet Union and the People's Republic of China, striving for the maximum satisfaction of their populations' increasing demands by the continuous expansion and technical improvement of socialist production, are comprehensively increasing their foreign trade and other types of economic cooperation. The socialist planned economy of both countries takes into account the projected scope of economic cooperation and thus ensures the long-term development of economic ties. The Soviet and Chinese peoples consider economic cooperation between their countries to be a highly important factor of their social development.

One of the main goals of Soviet foreign policy defined by the 20th Congress of the Communist Party of the Soviet Union is the 'comprehensive consolidation of fraternal relations with the People's Republic of China and all the people's democracies, inasmuch as the cause of peace will be strengthened in direct proportion to the reinforcement and unification of the socialist states.'[31]

Friendship and cooperation with the Soviet Union and the people's democracies are also basic principles of Chinese foreign policy. The 8th Congress of the Chinese Communist Party, which defined policy in international affairs, found it a necessary preliminary condition to 'continue to strengthen and consolidate the eternal and fraternal friendship with the Soviet Union and all the people's democracies.'[32]

The fraternal friendship between the Soviet Union and China creates favorable conditions for the rational utilization of both countries' resources.

---

[31] From the resolutions of the 20th Party Congress on the report of the Central Committee (Stenographic report, Vol. 2, p. 416) [Russ.].

[32] . Resolution of the 8th All-Chinese Congress of the Chinese Communist Party on the political report. Peking.—Foreign Languages Editions. 1956 [Russ. ed.].

2) *Differences in economic development and geographical conditions between the Soviet Union and the People's Republic of China.*

The Soviet Union and China are the two leading socialist countries, in territory, population and resources. They are the main force which ensures the power and influence of the socialist system on the international scene.

The two countries are by no means on the same level of economic development. While the Soviet Union is a developed industrial country, China continues to remain predominantly agricultural despite the fact that its industrial output reached more than twice its maximum prewar level in 1955.

VOLUME OF BASIC TYPES OF INDUSTRIAL AND AGRICULTURAL PRODUCTION OF THE PEOPLE'S REPUBLIC OF CHINA[33]

Types of production	*Units*	*Soviet Union*		*China*	
		1955	1960 (plan)	1955	1962 (plan)
Steel	million tons	45.3	68.3	2.85	10.5-12
Petroleum	million tons	70.8	135	0.966	5-6
Coal	million tons	391	593	93.6	190-210
Electric power	billion kwh	170.1	320	12.3	40-43
Metal-cutting lathes	thousand units	117.8	200	13.7	60-65
Cotton fabrics	million meters	5,904	7,270	4,120[34]	9,400-10,400[34]
Grain[35]	million tons	—	180	183.9	262.5
Cattle	million head	67.1	—	65.95	approx. 90
Sheep and goats	million head	142.6	—	84.2	approx. 170
Pigs	million head	52.2	—	87.9	approx. 250

To socialist states, a difference in the level of economic development is not an obstacle to the development of economic relations. In the capitalist world, economically advanced countries invade the markets of less developed ones, undermine their economic development and prevent their industrialization; in the socialist world relations between economically advanced and economically backward countries are based on equality and mutual benefit. The advanced industrial socialist nations do not seek profit but endeavor to promote general progress and establish peace and fraternal friendship between nations on this basis; they therefore deem it their

[33] Data for the volume of industrial and agricultural production are taken from the statistical survey of the Central Statistical Bureau of the Soviet of Ministers of the Soviet Union 'Narodnoe khozyaistvo SSSR' (Economy of the U.S.S.R.), Moscow, 1956; data for Chinese production in 1955 are taken from the report of the State Statistical Department of the People's Republic of China, Peking, 1956 (Chin.) and those for 1962 from the proposals of the 7th All-Chinese Party Congress for the Second Five-Year Plan of economic development, Peking.—Publications in Foreign Languages, 1956 [Russ. ed.].

[34] Converted from pieces to meters (1 piece = 40 meters).

[35] Chinese data include pulses and sweet potatoes.

obligation to grant assistance to the less developed socialist countries in the creation of their industry. This principle is applied in Soviet relations with China. The Soviet Union is helping China to reach that stage of industrial development at which Chinese industry will play the main role in national production. N. S. Khrushchev stressed in his report to the 20th Party Congress: 'The Soviet Union... is taking all the necessary steps to assist the fraternal Chinese people in creating their own powerful industry.'[36]

In spite of rapid industrial development, including machine-tool production, for a number of years China will still be unable to ensure the necessary supply of equipment for the industrial plants under construction. According to Liu Shao-shi's report to the 8th Congress of the Chinese Communist Party, China will be able to meet in 1962 approximately 70 percent of its requirements in machinery and equipment. Consequently, 30 percent of the necessary equipment will still have to be imported from abroad by the end of the Second Five-Year Plan.

It is clear that importation of Soviet equipment to China will continue to increase in the future, mainly of heavy and high-precision equipment and machinery, which will still be produced in insufficient amounts by China.

The implementation of the Sixth Five-Year Plan of Soviet economic development (1956-1960) will play an important role in the further cooperation and strengthening of Sino-Soviet economic ties; the plan provides for the large-scale industrial development of Western and Eastern Siberia and of the Soviet Far East, areas which border directly on China. Within the next 10 years Siberia is to become the most important Soviet area for the production of coal and electric power, an important area for the production of aluminum, magnesium and titanium and various metallurgical, petrochemical and electrochemical industries.

The Sixth Five-Year Plan provides for the construction of the first stage of the largest hydroelectric station in the world, at Bratsk (on the Angara river), producing 3,200 million kw, the beginning of the construction of the Krasnoyarsk hydroelectric station (on the Yenisei river) of approximately the same power, as well as of three aluminum plants and two oil refineries (Omsk and Irkutsk). Five new machine-tool plants, six plants for forging and pressing equipment, four specialized foundries, two instrument plants, three plants producing abrasives, eight plants for building and highway mechanized equipment, instrument factories, one plant producing electric locomotives, and one plant producing electrical equipment for locomotives, power transformers, and high-voltage apparatus are among those plants producing machinery which will be built during the same period in Siberia and the Urals region.

Within the next two or three five-year plans Siberia will become the third metallurgical area of the Soviet Union and produce 15-20 million tons of cast iron a year; large engineering works cabable of producing all types of machinery, equipment and instruments are to be set up within the next 10 years. The creation of a powerful industrial area in the Soviet East will enable the Soviet Union to meet the increasing Chinese requirements for equipment; equipment deliveries from this area are three

---

[36]   From the stenographic report of the 20th Party Congress, Vol. 1, p. 13.

to four times swifter than from the central Russian areas and the cost of railroad freight will not be greater than shipment costs from European and American ports.

The creation of a large-scale oil-refining industry in Siberia will be of particular importance for Sino-Soviet trade. Main pipelines are to be laid from the oil-producing areas of Tuimazy and Ufa to Irkutsk during the Sixth Five-Year Plan.

Agriculture will also continue to develop in the Eastern areas of the Soviet Union. These border areas—the Far Eastern Territory, Siberia and the republics of Soviet Central Asia—possess extensive tracts of virgin land on which large-scale grain farming and animal husbandry can develop.

The proposals of the 8th Congress of the Chinese Communist Party also provide for considerable industrial development of the North, Northeast and Northwest, the areas lying closest to the Soviet border. New metallurgical complexes are to be built near the Sanmenhsia gorge and in Kansu and Tsinghai [Koko Nor] provinces. Other branches of the economy which are to be considerably developed in these areas include a petroleum industry, nonferrous metallurgy, and hydroelectric power production. Animal husbandry, particularly the raising of cattle and small livestock, is also to expand in this region.

In some cases the absolute value of Chinese production will surpass those of the Soviet Union and the people's democracies; in other cases China will have developed export items and will become an important exporter of them to the capitalist market. This will be so mainly for nonferrous and alloyed metals and for a number of agricultural products.

The enormous reserves of tungsten, tin, molybdenum, mercury, lead and other nonferrous, rare metals and alloys and increased extraction and production will

PRODUCTION OF CERTAIN ALIMENTARY GOODS IN
CAPITALIST COUNTRIES AND IN THE
PEOPLE'S REPUBLIC OF CHINA[37]
(average yearly production in 1952-1954, in thousand tons)

	Rice	Ground-nuts	Soy-bean	Tea
I. Capitalist countries	113,000	8,300	9,600	598
India	37,748	3,480	—	290
Japan	11,364	—	442	60
Indonesia	9,352	366	330	40
Burma	5,753	176	—	—
United States of America	2,412	601	8,270	—
Ceylon	533	—	—	155
II. People's Republic of China	70,183	2,400	9,500	86

[37] Data for production in the capitalist countries are taken from the handbook put out by the Scientific Institute for Statistical Research of the Soviet Foreign Trade Ministry, *Proizvodstvo vazhneishikh tovarov v kapitalisticheskikh stranakh za 1937, 1940 i 1950-1954* (Production of Main Items by the Capitalist Countries in 1937, 1940 and 1950-1954).

Data on Chinese production are taken from a report of the Governmental Department of Statistics of the People's Republic of China, Peking, 1956.

enable China to become and long remain the main supplier of these metals to all the socialist countries, including the Soviet Union.

China is today by far the leading socialist country in the production of agricultural commodities such as rice, groundnuts, soybean and tea and one of the main world producers of these items.

Soil and climatic conditions enable China to raise citrus fruit, bananas and pine-apples in large amounts; rubber trees, black pepper, cork trees and many other tropical and subtropical crops may also be grown. Such conditions are either non-existent in the Soviet Union and the European people's democracies or the growing of these crops is economically inexpedient.

Natural resources will undoubtedly be comprehensively developed by the planned socialist economy, and China will be able to produce many new products adapted to her climatic and soil conditions in amounts sufficient to meet the domestic demand and that of the other socialist countries. Consequently, the differences in geographical conditions, like the different levels of economic development of the socialist countries, constitue an additional stimulus for the mutual exchange of products which is con-stantly expanding as these countries gradually become richer.

3) *Geographic proximity of the Soviet Union and the People's Republic of China.*
The common Sino-Soviet border has been an important factor in the consolidation and successful development of economic ties between the two countries throughout the history of more than 300 years of their relations.

Past events have shown the invaluable importance of this common border, particu-larly when American imperialist circles and their satellites enforced an embargo against the People's Republic of China after the agression in Korea and the seizure of Formosa. The Soviet Union and China then carried on 95-98 percent of their total volume of trade across their common border.

The contiguity of the land borders not only permits uninterrupted commercial relations but also the passage of goods in trasit to and from third countries. The Soviet Union thus transfers freight to and from Korea along the railroads of North-east China [Manchuria], and ships goods to and from the Vietnamese Democratic Republic over the same route. China in turn may effect commercial operations through Soviet territory with all European states and with countries of the Middle and Near East.

The common border between the Soviet Union and China makes possible the joint utilization of the natural resources of the border area for the benefit of both countries. Cooperation of this type has already been initiated on the Amur river; an agreement was concluded between the two governments on 18 August 1956 for joint research projects in ore prospection, the establishment of development projects for the Amur river basin and a joint research project for the development of an economic complex on the Argun river and the upper course of the Amur.

The contiguity of borders and the rich resources of the border areas along this common frontier thus promote the stability of Sino-Soviet economic ties and create favorable conditions for their further development.

4) *Communications between the Soviet Union and the People's Republic of China.* In addition to promoting the development of friendly relations between the Soviet Union and China, the contiguity of their borders also favors convenient communications between the two countries.

Throughout the entire history of Sino-Soviet relations, communications passed mainly over the land border. Maritime routes were and today still are of importance only for economic relations between Chinese ports and the Soviet Far East and serve only slightly in China's trade with other Soviet areas. This is due to two basic factors:

Firstly, the areas along the Chinese and Soviet land frontier account for an important proportion of the Sino-Soviet trade. This was particularly the case before the foundation of the People's Republic of China, when the relatively small total volume of Soviet exports to China was supplied by the Soviet areas close to the border, and the commodities imported from China also found a market in these areas. This will probably continue to be the case in view of the large-scale Soviet industrialization in Siberia and the Soviet Far East and the considerable expansion of industrial and agricultural production in Northeast and Northwest China.

Secondly, whatever the state of the maritime routes, it remains economically inexpedient to ship Chinese commodities to the Soviet Union's European ports. This particularly applies to some types of alimentary raw materials and manufactured finished and half-finished articles of which the areas of Russia-in-Europe lying near the Black Sea and Baltic ports produce surpluses. It is also inefficient to import from China overseas to the European ports of the Soviet Union many industrial raw materials such as nonferrous metals and alloys, which may be processed in Siberia, in the Urals region or in the Soviet republics of Central Asia.

Many important Soviet export items to China and particularly equipment, are more conveniently received by China not through the ports, where no important industrial construction is as yet under way, but through the Sino-Soviet land frontier, since it is simpler to transport the Soviet products from there to the areas of large-scale industrial development in the Northeast, Northwest and North of China.

At the end of 1955 the Sino-Soviet freight turnover followed two rail routes, through the border stations Grodekovo-Suifenho [Pogranichnaya] and Otpor [Zabaikalsk]-Manchouli, two road routes along the Sary-Ozek—Urumchi and Trugart-Kashgar highways and the river routes of the Sungari, Amur, Ili and Kara Irtish.

The main freight route followed by Sino-Soviet trade is the railroad running from Harbin through the Otpor-Manchouli border stations to a connection on the main Siberian line at Ksenevskaya station. This route carries approximately 65 percent of the total freight turnover, including the Soviet commodities exported to China (except for Sinkiang province) from the European part of the Soviet Union, the Soviet republics of Central Asia (along the Turkestan-Siberia railroad, Western and Eastern Siberia, as well as Chinese freight (except for that originating in Sinkiang) imported to these areas.

The second railroad, which connects Northeast China [Manchuria] to the Khabarovsk and Vladivostok areas through Grodekovo and Suifenho, plays an important role for the Soviet Far East and the central and southern areas of Northeast China, although it carries only a relatively small amount of freight (between China and the Soviet Far East).

In addition to the Grodekovo-Suifenho railroad,[38] freight is shipped between China and the Soviet Far Eastern Territory along the Sungari and Amur rivers during the period of navigation. This waterway is particularly convenient for the shipment of high-grade coal from the Kiamusze area to Khabarovsk and Komsomolsk-on-Amur and the importation of Sakhalin petroleum and petroleum products to Northeast China.

A new railroad from Ulan Bator to Tsining (China), connecting the main Siberian line to the railroads of North China, was inaugurated on 1 January 1956.[39] This is the shortest route from Siberia to Central China. The distance from Ulan Ude (the connection between the Siberian railroad with the Ulan Ude-Ulan Bator-Tsining line) to Peking is thus 1,025 km shorter than that over the previously existing line through Harbin.

Freight shipments over the new road leading from the provinces of Kansu, Shensi, Hopeh, Honan and Szechwan are particularly expedient; the distance from these provinces to the Sino-Soviet border is thus reduced by 1,500-2,000 kilometers and the freight shipment time is 10 to 15 days shorter than over the northeastern railroad route. The Ulan Bator-Tsining railroad offers favorable possibilities for the further expansion of Sino-Soviet trade, since it now carries up to 50 percent of the freight turnover previously carried by the Harbin-Otpor [Zabaikalsk] railroad. In addition to speeding up and facilitating freight transports, the Ulan Bator-Tsining line will have a considerable influence on the economic development of the nearby areas of North China and the Mongolian People's Republic.

The 3,000 kilometer railroad line which is now under construction, passing from Lanchow to Aktogai through Urumchi and across the Sino-Soviet border, will be of great importance for the expansion of Sino-Soviet trade. The section passing through Chinese territory, from Lanchow to Urumchi (Sinkiang province), was begun in 1952; according to the Sino-Soviet agreement of 7 April 1955 the construction work was to be completed both on Chinese and Soviet territory by 1960 and a direct connection opened by that date.

This new line will pass through the areas of Northwest China. Products such as wool and undressed leather will then be shipped from the provinces of Tsinghai [Koko Nor], Kansu, Ningsia[40] and Szechwan to processing areas in the Soviet Union by the shortest route passing through Szechwan province instead of through

---

[38] [It seems an exaggeration to speak of a 'railroad' in this instance. Grodekovo is merely the last station on Soviet territory and Suifenho the first on Chinese territory; the distance between them is about 6 to 8 kilometers.]

[39] The total length of the line from Ulan Ude to Tsining is 1,702 kilometers, of which 255 kilometers pass through Soviet territory (Ulan Ude-Naushki), 1,116 kilometers through the territory of the Mongolian People's Republic (Naushki-Ulan Bator-Erhlien [Erhlien-Hoto]) and 331 kilometers through that of China (Elhlien-Tsining).

[40] [Today the Ningsia Hui Autonomous Region.]

Siberia. It will also be expedient to ship to the Soviet Union over this route commodities such as nonferrous and rare metals, raw silk, tung oil, bristles.

With the inauguration of the Ulan Bator-Tsining railroad, the turnover of freight is fully provided for at present by the existing communications between the Soviet Union and China. When the construction of the railroad passing through Sinkiang province will be completed, conditions for Sino-Soviet trade will improve considerably and four railroad routes will then ensure deliveries which are expected to be $1\frac{1}{2}$ to 2 times greater than the present freight turnover.

Since the main Soviet and Chinese industrial centers are situated near the Sino-Soviet border, reliable and convenient communications by rail will be capable of carrying the Sino-Soviet freight turnover in full, without it being necessary to develop maritime transport to any considerable extent; the Soviet Far East is an exception, for maritime routes will continue to play an important role, as in the past, to the extent that conditions in the Pacific will remain normal.

*   *

*

The economic relations between the Russian and Chinese peoples have a history of more than 300 years. Both countries have maintained friendly relations throughout this entire period; the development of foreign trade and other economic ties corresponded to the interests of both sides and rested on a firm economic basis.

The October Revolution in Russia was a historic landmark in the relations between the Soviet and Chinese peoples. It proclaimed for the first time in the history of mankind the freedom and equality of large and small nations and mobilized the resources of the Soviet Union for the implementation of these principles in its relations with other countries.

The Soviet Union was the first state to conclude (in 1924) a fair and equitable treaty with China and to show the Chinese people the road to freedom and independence. Ever since October 1917 the Soviet Union has endeavored to consolidate and expand its economic relations with China and remove all the obstacles placed in the way of Sino-Russian relations by the tsarist government.

The October Revolution had an enormous influence on China. The revolutionary movement which developed in that country led to the establishment of a revolutionary government in the South at the beginning of the 1920's led by the progressive wing of the Kuomintang inspired by Sun Yat-sen; this was followed by the establishment of democratic authorities in the areas liberated from the Kuomintang reactionaries under the leadership of the Chinese Communist Party, the heroic vanguard of the Chinese proletariat. The southern government headed by Sun Yat-sen, and later the democratic authorities of the liberated areas expressed the will of the people in implementing a policy of friendship with the Soviet Union, which led to an expansion of economic ties.

However, only after the victory of the people's democratic revolution and the establishment of the People's Republic of China did the Chinese people succeed in applying on a national scale the foreign policy which accorded with its basic interests.

From that time on, Sino-Soviet economic relations have expanded to an unprecedented extent. The volume of Sino-Soviet trade increased in six years from 2,317.9 million rubles in 1950 to 5,543.5 million in 1955, passing the level of China's maximum total foreign trade (including Manchuria) in the prewar period (1930-1937) as well as that of Soviet foreign trade with any other country.

The economic cooperation between the Soviet Union and the People's Republic of China has demonstrated its stability and vitality. It constitutes an example of socialist relations, based on the principles of proletarian internationalism and fraternal solidarity and serves the interests of peace and friendship between nations for the benefit of the progressive forces of mankind.

APPENDICES

FOREIGN TRADE OF THE SOVIET UNION WITH CHINA

(in thousand rubles)

Year	Soviet exports		Soviet imports		Volume of Sino-Soviet trade	
	In current prices	In 1950 rubles[6]	In current prices	In 1950 rubles[6]	In current prices	In 1950 rubles[6]
1697[1]	26	424	26	424	52	848
1729[1]	100	666	100	666	200	1,332
1761[2]	391	2,320	620	3,679	1,011	5,999
1800[2]	4,191	19,538	4,191	19,538	8,382	39,076
1850[3]	7,127	33,226	7,446	34,713	14,573	67,939
1893[4]	4,087	14,244	33,292	116,026	37,379	130,270
1895	5,047	17,589	41,567	144,865	46,614	162,454
1896	5,501	19,172	41,457	144,482	46,958	163,654
1897	6,430	22,409	39,274	136,874	45,704	159,283
1898	6,256	21,803	40,293	140,425	46,549	162,228
1899	7,525	26,225	43,515	151,654	51,040	177,879
1900	6,702	23,357	45,945	160,123	52,647	183,480
1901	9,711	33,844	46,903	163,462	56,614	197,306
1902	9,315	32,464	52,177	181,842	61,492	214,306
1903	22,441	78,209	56,498	196,901	78,939	275,110
1904	22,972	80,060	52,455	182,811	75,427	262,871
1905	31,588	110,087	60,549	211,019	92,137	321,106
1906	57,530	200,492	97,427	339,543	154,957	540,035
1907	26,440	92,146	89,742	312,760	116,182	404,906
1908	23,285	81,151	93,344	325,313	116,629	406,464
1909	21,782	75,912	74,607	260,013	96,389	335,925
1910	20,158	70,253	78,813	274,671	98,971	344,924
1911	25,598	89,212	82,311	286,862	107,909	376,074
1912	30,688	106,951	76,254	265,753	106,942	372,704
1913[5]	28,801	100,375	75,650	263,651	104,451	364,026
1923/24	4,668	16,268	11,149	38,855	15,817	55,123
1924/25	9,109	31,744	16,866	58,780	25,975	90,524
1925/26	17,230	60,047	31,004	108,052	48,234	168,099
1926/27	18,744	65,325	29,984	104,497	48,728	169,822
1927/28	24,481	85,319	45,265	157,753	69,746	243,072
1928 October-December	8,038	28,013	7,221	25,166	15,259	53,179
1929	23,348	81,371	34,559	120,442	57,907	201,813
1930	28,520	99,395	24,465	85,263	52,985	184,658
1931	25,018	87,190	17,143	59,745	42,161	146,935
1932	23,784	82,890	18,193	63,404	41,977	146,294
1933	18,027	62,826	21,461	74,794	39,488	137,620
1934	6,785	23,647	9,385	32,708	16,170	56,355
1935	6,558	22,855	8,089	28,191	14,647	51,046
1936	36,718	29,217	38,462	30,604	75,180	59,821
1937[7]	35,376	26,699	40,732	30,741	76,108	57,440
1938[7]	43,402	32,762	84,200	63,552	127,602	96,314
1939[7]	34,013	25,071	104,296	78,714	138,309	104,385
1940[7]	51,906	39,175	102,376	77,265	154,282	116,440
1941[7]	41,097	35,545	130,510	98,499	177,607	134,044

Year	Soviet exports		Soviet imports		Volume of Sino-Soviet trade	
	In current prices	In 1950 rubles[6]	In current prices	In 1950 rubles[6]	In current prices	In 1950 rubles[6]
1942	19,088	14,406	97,200	73,359	116,288	87,765
1943	9,207	6,949	107,900	81,434	117,107	88,383
1944	3,006	2,269	166,400	125,585	169,406	127,854
1945	7,820	5,902	84,500	63,774	92,320	69,676
1946[8]	67,309	50,800	328,068	247,600	395,377	298,400
1947[9]	405,845	306,300	424,925	320,700	830,770	627,000
1948[9]	660,377	498,400	478,588	361,200	1,138,965	859,600
1949[9]	1,054,175	795,607	759,089	572,900	1,813,264	1,368,507
1950	1,552,800	1,552,800	765,100	765,100	2,317,900	2,317,900
1951	1,905,100	1,905,000	1,327,700	1,327,700	3,232,800	3,232,800
1952	2,200,100	2,200,100	1,655,000	1,655,000	3,855,100	3,855,100
1953	2,822,000	2,822,000	1,898,960	1,898,960	4,720,900	4,720,960
1954	3,037,200	3,037,200	2,313,400	2,313,400	5,350,600	5,350,600
1955	2,969,500	2,969,500	2,574,000	2,574,000	5,543,500	5,543,500

[1] Data for caravan trade, which do not include the then negligible border trade. The value of Russia's imports has been computed on the basis of export data (imports are taken as equal to exports), since there are no independent data for the value of imports from China during this period.

[2] Trade at Kyakhta. There was practically no trade whatever at other border points and no trading caravans were sent to Peking in these years.

[3] Trade at Kyakhta and along the Sinkiang border.

[4] Data for 1893-1913 include trade between Russia and Outer Mongolia, since the latter was then part of China.

[5] Beginning in 1913, Russian trade with Outer Mongolia is not included in the data concerning Sino-Russian trade.

[6] The value of trade in 1697-1850 has been calculated in 1950 rubles by comparing the value of gold in the corresponding years to its value in 1950, namely:

Year	Price of 1 gold zolotnik	Coefficient for converting rubles of the corresponding year to 1950 rubles
1697	1 ruble	16.320
1729	2 rubles 45 kopecks	6.661
1761	2 rubles 75 kopecks	5.934
1800	3 rubles 50 kopecks	4.662
1850	3 rubles 50 kopecks	4.662
1950	16 rubles 32 kopecks	—

The value of the goods traded in 1893-1955 has been calculated in 1950 rubles on the basis of the following proportions:
a) for 1913-1935, one ruble at the 1950 exchange rate equals 3.4851 rubles.
b) for 1936, one ruble at the 1950 exchange rate equals 0.7957 rubles.
c) for 1937-1955, one ruble of the corresponding year equals 0.75472 rubles at the 1950 exchange rate. The exchange rate of the ruble remained stable after 1950.

Data on the value of gold in 1697, 1729 and 1761 are taken from Trusevich (*op.cit.*, p. 203), in 1800 from the imperial decree to the Senate dated 15 March 1800 and in 1850 from the imperial decree dated 1 March 1850 concerning the St Petersburg mint.

[7] Not including Soviet commodity deliveries within the framework of loans.

[8] Data include the commercial operations of Soviet organizations with Sinkiang and the unliberated areas of Kuomintang China.

[9] Data include the commercial operations of Soviet organizations with Sinkiang, the liberated areas of Northeast China [Manchuria] (including the Liaotung peninsula) and the unliberated areas of Kuomintang China.

CHRONOLOGY OF MAIN EVENTS IN THE HISTORY OF ECONOMIC RELATIONS BETWEEN RUSSIA AND CHINA

1618—Peking visited by the first Russian envoys of the Tomsk voivode, the Cossacks Ivan Petlin and Petr Kozylov, who received letters from the Chinese Emperor to the Russian Tsar.

1644-1646—Russian expedition to the Amur, led by Vasilii Poyarkov, traveled from Yakutsk to the Lena and Aldan rivers, through the Stanovoi range to the Zeya river and from there along the Amur to the Sea of Okhotsk.

1649-1651—Russian expedition to the Amur, led by Erofey Pavlovich Khabarov; Russian settlements founded on the Amur river (Albazin [Yaksa], Aigun).

1656-1658—Dispatch of first Russian mission to China headed by Fedor Baikov (bearing letters from the Russian Tsar to the Chinese Emperor) for establishment of diplomatic and commercial relations with China.

1658—Second Russian mission to China (headed by Perfil'ev), empowered to settle all border incidents and establish diplomatic and commercial relations with China.

1670—Arrival of the first Russian governmental trading caravan (headed by Krasikov) in Peking.

1675-1677—Dispatch of a Russian embassy to China, headed by Nikolai Spafarii, with instructions to invite the Chinese to send an ambassador to Russia and to negotiate for the opening of free trade.

1689, 24 August—Conclusion of the Nerchinsk Treaty (the first treaty between Russia and China) by Ambassador Golovin.

1693—A Russian embassy to China, headed by Izbrand Ides, received authorization from the Chinese Emperor for Russian trading caravans to visit Peking.

1719-1720—Russian embassy to China, headed by Ambassador Extraordinary Lev Izmailov.

1727, 21 August—Signing of the Sino-Russian treaty of Kyakhta.

1728—Construction of Russian trading settlement began at Kyakhta.

1730-1731—First Chinese embassy to Russia, headed by Tulishen, visited Moscow (14 January-8 March 1731).

1731-1732—Second Chinese embassy to Russia consisting of two ambassadors, Deysin and Bayantay (visited St Petersburg in April 1732).

1762, 31 July—Publication of a Russian manifesto terminating the dispatch of governmental trading caravans to Peking and authorizing private trade in furs and other commodities along the Chinese border.

1768, 18 October—Signing of the 'Supplementary Article to the Kyakhta Treaty,' abolishing customs at Kyakhta.

1792, 8 February—Signing of the 'International Protocol' which confirmed the validity of the Sino-Russian treaty of Kyakhta.

1805, December—Arrival in Canton of the first Russian ships, the *Nadezhda* and the *Neva*, commanded by the famous navigators Kruzenshtern and Lisyanskii.

1848, September—Arrival in Shanghai of the Russian vessel *Knyaz' Men'shikov*, which had sailed from the Russian port of New Archangel [Sitka] in Alaska.

1849—Expedition of the Russian navigator Nevel'skii to Sakhalin Island and the mouth of the Amur river (this expedition demonstrated the possibility of navigating the Amur and founded the outpost of Nikolaevskii, today the port of Nikolaevsk-on-Amur).[1]

1851, 25 July—Conclusion of the Sino-Russian treaty of Kuldja, which specified conditions for trade along the Sinkiang border.

1858, 16 May—Conclusion of the Sino-Russian treaty of Aigun specifying conditions for Sino-Russian border trade and regulations for navigation along the Amur, Sungari and Ussuri rivers.

1858, 1 June—Conclusion of the Sino-Russian treaty of Tientsin, which granted Russia the right to conduct maritime trade on the same footing as other Western countries.

1860, 2 November—Conclusion of the Supplementary (Peking) Sino-Russian Treaty, which established duty-free trade along the Amur, the Ussuri and thence to the Tumen Kiang river and also authorized Russian merchants to visit Peking.

1881, 12 February—Conclusion of the Sino-Russian treaty of St Petersburg by which the free trade area was extended to the province of Sinkiang, preferential duties were stipulated for exports of China tea to Russia, etc.

1895, 24 June—Publication in St Petersburg of the official Sino-Russian declaration on the grant of a loan to China by Russian and foreign banks guaranteed by the Russian government.

1896, 22 May—Conclusion of a Sino-Russian defensive alliance which provided, in addition to military and political clauses, for the construction of a railroad in Manchuria by the Russo-Chinese Bank.

1896, 27 August—Signing in St Petersburg by the Chinese ambassador and the Russo-Chinese Bank (representing Russia) of a contract for the construction and operation of the Chinese Eastern Railroad (C.E.R.).

1897, 16 August—Beginning of construction of the C.E.R.

1898, 15 March—Signing of a Sino-Russian convention on a 25-year lease to Russia of Port Arthur [Lüshunkow] and Dalny [Talien] and an extension of the concession previously granted to the Russo-Chinese Bank for the construction of a railroad to Dalny and Yingkow [Newchwang].

1901, 25 August (7 September)—Eight imperialist powers, including tsarist Russia, force China to sign the Final (Boxer) Protocol which imposed a 450-million *tael* indemnity on China.

1903, 1 (14) July—Completion of construction of the C.E.R. and beginning of operation.

1905, 23 August (5 September)—Signing of a Russo-Japanese treaty by which tsarist Russia leased Port Arthur, Dalny and their surrounding areas and territorial waters to Japan (the lease included public property and installations, such as the southern line of the C.E.R. up to the Kwanchengtze [Changchun] station).

1907, 31 July (13 February)—Signing of the Russo-Japanese General Political Convention which provided (in its secret clauses) for the delimitation of tsarist Russia's and Japan's 'interests' in Manchuria.

1910, 21 June (4 July)—Signing of the Russo-Japanese agreement on the joint preservation of the *status quo* in Manchuria.

1912—Tsarist banks joined the International Banking Consortium created by British, American, French and German banks (the U.S. banks left the consortium after Russia and Japan joined).

1912, 11 (24) August—The government of tsarist Russia informed the Chinese Ministry of Foreign Affairs of Russia's unilateral decision to extend the validity of the 1881 treaty of

---

[1] Former Chinese name—Miaoerhcheng.

St Petersburg (which had expired after 10 years) for another 10 years, i.e., to 20 August 1921.

1917-1918, December-March—Negotiations between the Soviet government and the Chinese embassy in Moscow—Petrograd on the basis of a Soviet proposal to abrogate all inequitable treaties concluded by tsarist Russia with China.

1917, 24 December—The Peking government published a decree prohibiting the exportation of Chinese commodities to Soviet Russia.

1918, 16 May—The Peking government headed by Tuan Chi-jui signed a military convention with Japan for the participation of Chinese troops under Japanese command in an intervention against Soviet Russia in the Far East.

1919, 25 July—Soviet appeal to China for the establishment of official relations, the abrogation of tsarist Russia's inequitable treaties, and the conclusion of new treaties on the basis of complete equality.

1920, 27 May—The Soviet administration in Central Asia and the Chinese administration of the Kuldja territory signed the Ili Protocol fixing conditions for border trade between the Kuldja territory and the neighboring Soviet areas.

1920, October—The government of the Russian Soviet Federative Socialist Republic again proposed to abrogate the treaties concluded by tsarist Russia and to establish official relations.

1921, June—Exchange of notes between the Soviet People's Commissariat of Foreign Affairs and the head of the South China government, Dr. Sun Yat-sen.

1922—Opening of *Sibdal'vneshtorg* (Siberian Far Eastern Trade Bureau) office in Harbin.

1923, June—Formation of the Soviet joint stock company, *Dal'bank* (Far Eastern Bank), in Harbin.

1924, 31 May—Signing in Peking of the Agreement on General Principles for Settling Issues between the Soviet Union and the Chinese Republic.

1924, 20 September—The Soviet Union signed in Mukden a supplementary agreement on the C.E.R. with the administration of the Three Eastern Autonomous Provinces (Manchuria).

1926, 21 January—Chinese authorities in Manchuria arrested the Soviet director of the C.E.R. and other railroad officials.

1926, September—Chinese authorities in Manchuria seized river boats belonging to the C.E.R. on the Sungari river.

1927, 6 April—The Peking police raided the Soviet embassy.

1927, December—The Nanking government closed all Soviet consulates and institutions on the territory which it controlled.

1929, July-December—Conflict over the C.E.R. provoked by the reactionary Kuomintang clique and foreign imperialists, leading to the severance of diplomatic relations between the Soviet Union and China.

1929, 22 December—Signing of the Sino-Soviet Khabazovsk Protocol on the restoration of the *status quo* on the C.E.R.

1930, 9 October-October 1931—Sino-Soviet conference in Moscow, as stipulated by the Khabarovsk Protocol, for settling controversial issues in the relations between the two countries.

1931, 1 October—Exchange of notes between the Soviet People's Commissariat of Foreign Affairs and the representative of the Nanking government in Sinkiang province fixing conditions for commercial relations between the province and the Soviet Union pending the conclusion of a commercial treaty.

1932, 12 December—Resumption of diplomatic relations between the Soviet Union and China.

1935, May—Signing of an agreement on the extension of credit amounting to 21.9 million rubles by the Soviet association for trade with Sinkiang—*Sovsin'torg*—to the Chinese firm of Tuchankungssu.

1936, July—Signing of a second agreement on the extension of additional credit by *Sovsin'torg* to Tuchankungssu of an amount of 8,760,000 rubles.

1937, 21 August—Signing of a Sino-Soviet nonaggression pact.

1938, 1 March—Signing of an agreement whereby the Soviet Union extended US$50 million credit to China.

1938, 1 July—Signing of a second agreement whereby the Soviet Union granted an additional US$50 million credit to China.

1939, 16 June—Conclusion of a commercial treaty between the Soviet Union and China.

1939, 16 June—Signing of a third agreement whereby the Soviet Union granted US $150 million credit to China.

1945, 11 February—The leaders of the three great powers (the Soviet Union, the United States and Britain) signed the Yalta Agreement defining the conditions for the Soviet Union's participation in the war against Japan.

1945, 9 August—The Soviet Union opened hostilities against Japan.

1945, 14 August—Signing of the Sino-Soviet Treaty of Friendship and Alliance providing for a joint effort against Japan, of an agreement on the joint ownership of the C.E.R. by the Soviet Union and China, an agreement on the use of Port Arthur as a joint naval base, an agreement on Dalny and other documents.

1945, October-December—Reopening of the Soviet trade delegation in Shanghai, Harbin and Mukden [Shenyang].

1946, May-June—Transfer of the Soviet trade delegation from Chungking to Nanking.

1946, 21 December—Signing in Voroshilovsk-Ussuriiskii [now Ussuriisk] of a commercial agreement between the Soviet *Eksportkhleb* and *Tungsing*—the commercial organization of the people's-democratic regions of Northeast China—for reciprocal commodity deliveries in 1947.

1949, July—Arrival in Moscow of a trade delegation of the people's democratic authorities of Manchuria and signing of an agreement with Soviet commercial organizations for reciprocal commodity deliveries in 1949.

1949, 1 October—Declaration of the Central People's Government of China on the establishment of the People's Republic of China.

1949, 2 October—The government of the Soviet Union informed the Central People's Government of China of its decision to establish diplomatic relations with the People's Republic of China.

1949, December—Transfer of the Soviet trade delegation in the People's Republic of China from Nanking to Peking.

1949, 16 December—Arrival in Moscow of Mao Tse-tung, president of the Central People's Government of China, with an accompanying delegation.

1950, 20 January—Arrival in Moscow of Chou En-lai, chairman of the State Administrative Council of the People's Republic of China.

1950, 14 February—Signing in Moscow of a treaty of friendship, alliance and mutual assistance between the Soviet Union and China for a period of 30 years, an agreement concerning the Chinese Changchun Railroad, Port Arthur and Dalny, and an agreement by which the Soviet government granted a long-term loan to the Chinese government.

1950, 17 February—Departure from Moscow of Mao Tse-tung, president of the Central People's Government of the People's Republic of China, Chou En-lai, chairman of the State

Administrative Council and Minister of Foreign Affairs, and the accompanying delegation.

1950, 27 March—Signing in Moscow of Sino-Soviet agreements on the creation of the Sino-Soviet joint-stock companies *Sovkitneft* [Sino-Soviet Petroleum Co.] *Sovkitmetall* [Sino-Soviet Metal Co.] and the Sino-Soviet Air Transport Company, as well as of an agreement which defined working conditions for Soviet specialists sent to China at the request of the Chinese government to work on industrial plants, institutions and organizations.

1950, 19 April—Signing in Moscow of a commercial treaty, of a protocol dealing with the volume of Sino-Soviet trade in 1950, and a protocol on Soviet commodity deliveries in 1950 within the framework of the loan granted by the Soviet Union by the agreement of 14 February 1950.

1950, 25 October—Signing in Peking of an agreement on the conditions of payment for the Soviet specialists sent to China for technical assistance.

1951, 15 June—Signing in Moscow of a protocol on the volume of Sino-Soviet trade in 1951 and of a protocol on Soviet commodity deliveries in 1951 within the framework of the loan granted by the Soviet Union by the agreement of 14 February 1950.

1952, 12 April—Signing in Moscow of a protocol on the volume of Sino-Soviet trade in 1952 and of a protocol on Soviet commodity deliveries within the framework of the loan granted by the Soviet Union by the agreement of 14 February 1950.

1952, 17 August—Arrival in Moscow of a Chinese governmental delegation which included Chou En-lai, chairman of the State Administrative Council (head of the delegation), Chen Yun, deputy chairman of the State Administrative Council and Li Fu-chun, deputy chairman of the State Planning Committee.

1952, 15 September—Signing in Moscow of an agreement between the governments of the Soviet Union, the Mongolian People's Republic and the People's Republic of China on the organization of direct railroad connections between the three countries.

1953, 21 March—Signing in Moscow of a protocol on the volume of Sino-Soviet trade in 1953, of a protocol on Soviet commodity deliveries in 1953 within the framework of the loan granted by the Soviet Union by the agreement of 14 February 1950, and of an agreement whereby the Soviet Union extended assistance to China for the expansion of existing electric power plants and the construction of new plants.

1953, 11 July-5 August—Moscow exhibition of Chinese industrial and agricultural achievements.

1953, 15 September—The Central People's Governmental Council of the People's Republic of China heard and approved a report by Li Fu-chun, a member of the governmental delegation which visited Moscow from August 1952 to May 1953, concerning the talks held with the Soviet government on the subject of assistance to Chinese economic development.

1954, 23 January—Signing in Moscow of a protocol on the volume of Sino-Soviet trade in 1954 and of a protocol on Soviet commodity deliveries for 1954.

1954, 29 September—Arrival in Peking of a Soviet governmental delegation led by Khrushchev, and including Bulganin and Mikoyan, for the ceremonies celebrating the fifth anniversary of the People's Republic of China.

1954, 2 October—Opening in Peking of an exhibition of Soviet economic and cultural achievements.

1954, 12 October—Signing in Peking of the following official documents: an agreement whereby the Soviet government granted a long-term 520-million ruble loan to China; a protocol by which the Soviet government undertook to assist China in the construction of 15 industrial plants and which raised the volume of equipment deliveries previously stipulated for

141 other plants; an agreement on scientific and technical cooperation and several declarations, communiqués and other documents.

1955, 11 February—Signing in Moscow of a protocol on the volume of trade between the Soviet Union and the People's Republic of China in 1955

1955, 27 April—Signing in Moscow of an agreement by which the Soviet Union undertook the planning and construction of an experimental nuclear reactor and particle accelerators in China, and supplied free of charge all the necessary technical documents relating to the nuclear reactor, the accelerators, etc.

1955, 27 December—Signing in Moscow of a protocol on the volume of Sino-Soviet trade in 1956.

1956, 1 January—The railroad between Ulan Bator and Tsining put into operation and direct freight services established from the Soviet Union to China through the Mongolian People's Republic.

1956, 6-7 April—Arrival in Peking of a governmental delegation from the Soviet Union, headed by A. I. Mikoyan.

1956, 7 April—Signature in Peking of an agreement whereby the Soviet Union undertook to assist China in the construction of 55 industrial plants and of an agreement for the construction of a railroad from Lanchow to Aktogai and the organization of a direct connection along this line by 1960.

BIBLIOGRAPHY

MARX, K. and ENGELS, F. *Mezhdunarodnye obzory* (...Kitai) (International Surveys (...China)). *Sochineniya* (Works). Vol. 3.

MARX, K. *Anglo-kitaiskii konflikt* (The Anglo-Chinese Conflict). *Ibid.*, Vol. 11. part 1.

MARX, K. *Angliiskie zhestokosti v Kitaie* (British Brutality in China). *Ibid.*, Vol. 11. part 1.

MARX K. *Torgovlya opiumom* (The Opium Trade). *Ibid.*, Vol. 11. part 1.

MARX, K. *Novaya kitaiskaya voina* (The New China War). *Ibid.*, Vol. 11. part 2.

MARX, K. *Torgovlya s Kitaem* (Trade with China). *Ibid.*, Vol. 11. part 2.

MARX, K. *Kitaiskie delu* (Chinese Affairs). *Ibid.*, Vol. 12. part 2.

ENGELS, F. *Uspekhi Rossii na Dal'nem Vostoke* (Russia's Successes in the Far East). *Ibid.*, Vol. 11. part 1.

LENIN, V. I. *Kitaiskaya voina* (The China War). *Sochineniya* (Works). 4th edition. Vol. 4.

LENIN, V. I. *Uroki krizisa* (Lessons of the Crisis). *Ibid.*, Vol. 5.

LENIN, V. I. *Padenie Port-Artura* (The Fall of Port Arthur). *Ibid.*, Vol. 8.

LENIN, V. I. *Goryuchii material v mirovoi politike* (Inflammable Material in World Politics). *Ibid.*, Vol. 15.

LENIN, V. I. *O kitaiskoi revolyutsii* (VI ('Prazhskaya') Vserossiiskaya konferentsiya RSDRP) (On the Chinese Revolution (Sixth ('Prague') All-Russian Conference of the Russian Social Democratic Workers' Party)). *Ibid.*, Vol. 17.

LENIN, V. I. *Demokratiya i narodnichestvo v Kitae* (Democracy and Narodism in China). *Ibid.*, Vol. 18.

LENIN, V. I. *Obnovlennyi Kitai* (Regenerated China). *Ibid.*, Vol. 18.

LENIN, V. I. *Krupnyi uspekh kitaiskoi respukliki* (A Great Success for the Chinese Republic). *Ibid.*, Vol. 19.

LENIN, V. I. *Probuzhdenie Azii* (Asia's Awakening). *Ibid.*, Vol. 19.

LENIN, V. I. *Otstalaya Evropa i peredovaya Aziya* (Backward Europe and Advanced Asia). *Ibid.*, Vol. 19.

LENIN, V. I. *Imperializm, kak vysshaya stadiya kapitalizma* (Imperialism: the Highest Stage of Capitalism). *Ibid.*, Vol. 22.

LENIN, V. I. *O broshyure Yuniusa* (Concerning the Brochure by Junius). *Ibid.*, Vol. 22.

LENIN, V. I. *Imperializm i raskol sotsializma* (Imperialism and the Split in Socialism). *Ibid.*, Vol. 23.

*   *

*

BULGANIN, N. A. Doklad o Direktivakh XX s"ezda KPSS po shestomy pyatiletnemu planu razvitiya narodnogo khozyaistva SSSR na 1956-1960 gody (Report on the Directives of the XXth Congress of the CPSU Concerning the Sixth Five-Year Plan for the Development of the Soviet Economy in 1956-1960). Moskva, Gospolitizdat. 1956.

KHRUSHCHEV, N. S. Rech' na torzhestvennom zasedanii v Pekine, posvyashchennom pyatoi godovshchine so dnya obrazovaniya Kitaiskoi Narodnoi Respubliki, 30 sentyabrya 1954 g.

(Speech at the Ceremonial Session in Peking Dedicated to the Fifth Anniversary of the Founding of the People's Republic of China, September 30, 1954). *Pravda,* October 1, 1954.

KHRUSHCHEV, N. S. Otchetnyi doklad Tsentral'nogo Komiteta Kommunisticheskoi partii Sovetskogo Soyuza XX s"ezdu partii (Report of the Cedtral Committee of the Communist Party of the Soviet Union to the XXth Party Congress). Moskva, Gospolitizdat. 1956.

MIKOYAN, A. I. Rech' na XX s"ezde KPSS (Speech at the XXth Congress of the CPSU). Moskva, Gospolitizdat. 1956.

MIKOYAN, A. I. Rech' na VIII Vsekitaiskom s"ezde KPK (Speech at the VIIIth All-Chinese Congress of the Chinese Communist Party). *Pravda,* September 18, 1956.

STALIN, I. V. *Voprosy kitaiskoi revolyutsii. Tezisy dlya propagandistov, odobrennye Tsk VKP (b)* (Problems of the Chinese Revolution. Theses for Propagandists, Approved by the Central Committee of the All-Union Communist Party (bolsheviks). *Sochineniya* (Works). Vol. 9.

*   *
*

MAO TSE-TUNG. *Bol'she zaboty o zhizni naroda, bol'she vnimaniya metodam raboty* (Greater Solicitude for the Life of the People, Greater Attention to Methods of Work). *Izbrannye proizvedeniya* (Selected Works), Vol. 1. Moskva Izdatel'stvo inostrannoi literatury. 1952.

MAO TSE-TUNG. *O taktike bor'by protiv yaponskogo imperializma* (On the Tactics of Fighting Japanese Imperialism). *Ibid.,* Vol. 1.

MAO TSE-TUNG. *Strategicheskie voprosy revolyutsionnoi voiny v Kitae* (Strategic Problems of the Revolutionary War in China). *Ibid.,* Vol. 1.

MAO TSE-TUNG. *Zadachi kommunisticheskoi partii Kitaya v period antiyaponskoi voiny* (The Tasks of the Chinese Communist Party during the War Against Japan). *Ibid.,* Vol. 1.

MAO TSE-TUNG. *Bor'ba za vovlechenie mnogomillionnykh mass v edinyi antiyaponskii natsional'nyi front* (The Struggle to Recruit Millions for the United Anti-Japanese National Front). *Ibid.,* Vol. 1.

MAO TSE-TUNG. *Politicheskaya liniya, prakticheskie meropriyatiya i perspektivy bor'by protiv nastupleniya Yaponii* (The Political Line, the Practical Measures and the Prospects against Japanese Aggression). *Ibid.,* Vol. 2.

MAO TSE-TUNG. *Nasushchnye zadachi, vstavshie posle ustanovleniya sotrudnichestva mezhdu gomindanom i Kommunisticheskoi partiei* (The Urgent Problems which Developed after the Establishment of Cooperation between the Kuomintang and the Communist Party). *Ibid.,* Vol. 2.

MAO TSE-TUNG. *Obstanovka, slozhivshayasya v voine protiv yaponskikh zakhvatchikov posle padeniya Shankhaya i Taiyuana, i vytekayushchie iz nee zadachi* (The Developing Situation in the War Against the Japanese Aggressors after the Fall of Shanghai and Taiyuan and the Resulting Problems). *Ibid.,* Vol. 2.

MAO TSE-TUNG. *O zatyazhnoi voine* (Concerning Prolonged Warfare). *Ibid.,* Vol. 2.

MAO TSE-TUNG. *Beseda s korrespondentom 'Sin'khuazhibao' o sovremennoi mezhdunarodnoi obstanovke* (Interview with a Correspondent of the 'Sinhwa Jipao' on the Present International Situation). *Ibid.,* Vol. 3.

MAO TSE-TUNG. *Edinstvo interesov Sovetskogo Soyuza i vsego chelovechestva* (Identity of the Soviet Union's Interests with Those of All Mankind). *Ibid.,* Vol. 3.

MAO TSE-TUNG. *Kitaiskaya revolyutsiya i Kommunisticheskaya partiya Kitaya* (The Chinese Revolution and the Chinese Communist Party). *Ibid.,* Vol. 3.

MAO TSE-TUNG. *O novoi demokratii* (The New Democracy). *Ibid.,* Vol. 3.

MAO TSE-TUNG. *Nyneshnyaya taktika partii v edinom antiyaponskom fronte* (The Present Tactics of the Party in the United Anti-Japanese Front). *Ibid.*, Vol. 3.

MAO TSE-TUNG. *O nashei politike* (Our Policy). *Ibid.*, Vol. 3.

MAO TSE-TUNG. *O mezhdunarodnom edinom fronte bor'by protiv fashizma* (The International United Front Against Fascism). *Ibid.*, Vol, 4.

MAO TSE-TUNG. *Perelomnyi moment v khode vtoroi mirovoi voiny* (The Turning Point in World War II). *Ibid.*, Vol. 4.

MAO TSE-TUNG. *O koalitsionnom pravitel'stve* (Concerning a Coalition Government). *Ibid.*, Vol. 4.

MAO TSE-TUNG. *O diktature narodnoi demokratii* (The Dictatorship of the People's Democracy). Moskva Gospolitizdat. 1949.

MAO TSE-TUNG. Rech' pri otkrytii I sessii Narodnogo politicheskogo konsul'tativnogo soveta Kitaya (proiznesena 21 sentyabrya 1949 g.v Pekine) (Speech at the opening of the First Session of the People's Political Consultative Council of China, made in Peking on September 21, 1949). In: *Obrazovanie KNR. Dokumenty i materialy* (The Establishment of the People's Republic of China. Documents and Materials). Moskva, Gospolitizdat. 1950.

MAO TSE-TUNG. Bor'ba za korennoe uluchshenie finansovogo i ekonomicheskogo polozheniya strany (Doklad na III plenume TsK KPK iyunya 6, 1950 g.) (The Effort for the Radical Improvement of the Country's Financial and Economic Situation—Report to the IIIrd Plenum of the CCP [Chinese Communist Party] Central Committee on June 6, 1950). In: *Sbornik statei 'Ekonomicheskie uspekhi Novogo Kitaya za tri goda (1949-1952 gg.)'*) (Collected Articles 'Economic Achievements of New China in Three Years (1949-1952)'). Peking, Foreign Languages Editions [in Russian]. 1953.

MAO TSE-TUNG. Rech' pri otkrytii VIII Vsekitaiskogo s''ezda KPK (Pekin, 15 sentyabrya 1956 g.) (Opening Speech of the VIIIth All-Chinese Congress of the CCP. Peking, September 15, 1956)). *Pravda*, September 16, 1956.

CHEN YUN. Nekotorye voprosy sotsialisticheskogo preobrazovaniya chastnoi promyshlennosti i torgovli v Kitae (rech' na tret'ei sessii Vsekitaiskogo sobraniya narodnykh predstavitelei (Some Problems of the Socialist Transformation of Private Industry and Trade in China—Speech at the Third Session of the All-Chinese Assembly of People's Representatives). *Jenminjipao*.

CHEN YUN. Rech' na VIII Vsekitaiskom s''ezde KPK (Speech to the VIIIth All-Chinese Congress of the CCP). *Pravda*, September 22, 1956.

CHOU EN-LAI. Doklad ob osnovnykh chertakh Obshchei programmy Narodnogo politicheskogo konsul'tativnogo soveta Kitaya (Report on the Basic Features of the General Program of the People's Political Consultative Council of China). In: *Obrazovanie KNR. Dokumenty i materialy*. Moskva, Gospolitizdat. 1950.

CHOU EN-LAI. Doklad na tret'ei sessii Vsekitaiskogo Komiteta Narodnogo politicheskogo konsul'tativnogo soveta (Report to the Third Session of the All-Chinese Committee of the People's Political Consultative Council). *Pravda*, November 4, 1951.

CHOU EN-LAI. Politicheskii doklad na chetvertoi sessii Natsional'nogo Komiteta Narodnogo politicheskogo konsul'tativnogo soveta Kitaya 4 fevralya 1953 g. (Political Report to the Fourth Session of the National Committee of the People's Political Consultative Council of China on February 4, 1953). Supplement to the journal *People's China*, No. 4. 1953.

CHOU EN-LAI. Doklad na pervoi sessii Vsekitaiskogo sobraniya narodnykh predstavitelei o rabote pravitel'stva KNR (Report to the First Session of the All-Chinese Assembly of People's Representatives Concerning the Work of the Government of the People's Republic of China). *People's China*, No. 20. 1954.

CHOU EN-LAI. Doklad na VIII Vsekitaiskom s"ezde KPK o predlozheniyakh po vtoromu pyatiletnemu planu razvitiya narodnogo khozyaistva (Report to the VIIIth All-Chinese Congress of the CCP on the Proposals for the Second Five-Year Plan of Economic Development).*Pravda,* September 19, 1956.

CHU TEH. Rech' na XX s"ezde KPSS (Speech at the XXth Congress of the CPSU). Stenograficheskii otchet (Stenogram), Vol. 1, pp. 226-231. Moskva. 1956.

CHU TEH. Rech' na VIII Vsekitaiskom s"ezde KPK (Speech at the VIIIth All-Chinese Congress of the CCP). *Pravda,* September 20, 1956.

LI FU-CHUN *Vosstanovlenie i razvitie promyshlennosti* (Industrial Reconstruction and Development). In: *Sbornik statei 'Ekonomicheskie uspekhi Novogo Kitaya za tri goda (1949-1952 gg.).'* Peking, Foreign Languages Editions (in Russian). 1953.

LI FU-CHUN. Doklad na vtoroi sessii Vsekitaiskogo sobraniya narodnykh predstavitelei pervogo sozyva o pervom pyatiletnem plane razvitiya narodnogo khozyaistva KNR (Report to the Second Session of the First Congress of the All-Chinese Assembly of People's Representatives on the First Five-Year Plan of Economic Development of the People's Republic of China. Supplement to the journal *People's China,* No. 17. 1955.

LI FU-CHUN. Rech' na VIII Vsekitaiskom s"ezde KPK (Speech at the VIIIth All-Chinese Congress of the CCP). *Pravda,* September 28, 1956.

LIU SHAO-CHI Rech' na torzhestvennom zasedanii pekinskogo aktiva, posvyashchennom prazdniku trudyashchikhsya 1 Maya (Speech at the Ceremonial Session of the Peking Party Propagandists, Dedicated to May Day, Workers' Day). Peking, Foreign Languages Editions (in Russian). 1950.

LIU SHAO-CHI. Doklad na VIII Vsekitaiskom s"ezde KPK (politicheskii otchet TsK KPK) (Report to the VIIIth All-Chinese Congress of the CCP—Political Report of the CCP Central Committee). *Pravda,* September 17, 1956.

YEH CHI-CHWANG. *Vneshnyaya torgovlya Kitaya za tri goda* (China's Foreign Trade for Three Years). In: *Sbornik statei 'Ekonomicheskie uspekhi Novogo Kitaya za tri goda (1949-1952 gg.).'* Peking, Foreign Languages Editions (in Russian). 1953.

YEH CHI-CHWANG *Vneshnyaya torgovlya Kitaya* (China's Foreign Trade) *Vneshnyaya Torgovlya,* No. 6. 1955.

*   *

*

ANDREEV, M. *Iz istorii snoshenii Rossii s Kitaem (XVII-XX vv.)* (History of Relations between Russia and China in the 17th-20th Centuries). In: *Severnaya Aziya* (Northern Asia), Bk. 5-6. 1925.

ANDRIEVICH, V. K. *Istoricheskii ocherk Sibiri* (Historical Essay on Siberia). Tomsk. 1887.

ARISTOV, N. *Promyshlennost' drevnei Rusi* (The Industry of Ancient Rus). Sankt Peterburg. 1886.

AVARIN, V. *Bor'ba za Tikhii okean. Yapono-amerikanskie protivorechiya* (The Struggle for the Pacific. Japanese-American Conflicts). Moskva, Gospolitizdat. 1947.

BAKULIN, S. N. and MISHUSTIN, D. D. Vneshnyaya torgovlya SSR za 20 let-1918-1937. *Statisticheskii spravochnik* (Soviet Foreign Trade for 20 years—1918-1937. Statistical handbook). Moskva. 1939.

BANTYSH-KAMENSKII, N. *Diplomaticheskoe sobranie del mezhdu Rossiiskim i Kitaiskim gosudarstavami s 1619 po 1792 god* (Collected Diplomatic Papers on the Relations between the Russian and Chinese Governments from 1619 to 1792). Kazan'. 1882.

BARTOL'D, V. *Istoriya izucheniya Vostoka v Evrope i Rossii* (A History of Asian Studies in Europe and Russia). 2nd edition. Leningrad. 1925.

(BICHURIN) IAKINF. *Kitai v grazhdanskom i nravstvennom sostoyanii* (China's Civil and Moral Condition). 4 parts. Sankt Peterburg. 1848.

BOLDYREV, V. G. *Finansy Kitaiskoi Narodnoi Respubliki* (The Finances of the People's Republic of China). Moskva. 1953.

EFIMOV, G. *Ocherki po novoi i noveishei istorii Kitaya* (Essays on Modern and Contemporary Chinese History). Moskva, Gospolitizdat. 1951.

GRIMM, E. D. *Sbornik dogovorov i drugikh dokumentov po istorii mezhdunarodnykh otnoshenii na Dal'nem Vostoke (1870-1945)* (Collected Treaties and Other Documents on the History of International Relations in the Far East—1870-1945). Moskva, izdanie Instituta vostokovedeniya. 1927.

IVIN, A. Sovremennyi Kitai (Contemporary China). *Novyi Vostok,* No. 5. 1924.

KARA-MURZA, G. S. *Ocherki po novoi istorii Kitaya* (Essays on Modern Chinese History). Moskva, steklograficheskoe izdanie Instituta vostokovedeniya. 1941.

KLYUCHNIKOV, SABANIN. *Mezhdunarodnaya politika noveishego vremeni v dogovorakh, notakh i deklaratsiyakh* (Contemporary International Politics as shown through Treaties, Notes and Declarations). Moskva. 1928.

KORSAK, A. *Istoriko-statisticheskoe obozrenie torgovykh snoshenii Rossii s Kitaem* (Historico-Statistical Review of Sino-Russian Relations). Kazan'. 1857.

KYUNER, N. Y. *Noveishaya istoriya stran Dal'nego Vostoka. Snosheniya s Rossiei* (Contemporary History of the Far East. Relations with Russia). Lithographed edition, Vol. 2, book 3. Vladivostok. 1910

KYUNER, N. V. *Snosheniya Rossii s Dal'nim Vostokom na protyazhenii tsarstvovaniya doma Romanovykh* (Russia's Relations with the Far East during the Reign of the Romanovs). Vladivostok. 1913.

MASLENNIKOV, V. A. *Kitai. Politiko-ekonomicheskii ocherk* (China, A Political and Economic Essay). OGIZ. 1946.

MILLERO, O. *O pervykh rossiiskikh puteshestviyakh i posol'stvakh v Kitai* (First Russian Travelers and Embassies to China). Russian translation. 1755.

PARKER, E. *China* (translated from English). Moskva. 1902.

PAVLOVICH, M. Yaponskii imperializm na Dal'nem Vostoke (Japanese Imperialism in the Far East). *Novyi Vostok,* No. 1 & 2. 1922.

POKROVSKII, F. I. Puteshestvie v Mongoliyu i Kitai Sibirskogo kazaka Ivana Petlina v 1618 godu (mnimoe puteshestvie atamanov Ivana Petrova i Burnasha Yalycheva v 1567 g.) (Voyage of the Siberian Cossack Ivan Petlin to Mongolia and China in 1618 (alleged voyage of the hetmans Ivan Petrov and Burnash Yalychev in 1567)). *Izvestiya otdeleniya russkogo yazyka i slovesnosti imperatorskoi Akademii nauk.* Sankt Peterburg. 1914.

POKROVSKII, S. A. *Vneshnyaya torgovlya i vneshnyaya torgovaya politika Rossii* (Russia's Foreign Trade and Foreign Trade Policy). Moskva. 1947.

RADISHCHEV, A. N. *O torgovle s Kitaem* (Concerning Trade with China). In: *Polnoe sobranie sochinenii* (Complete Collected Works), Vol. 2. Moskva. 1907.

RADISHCHEV, A. N. *Pis'mo o kitaiskom torge* (Letter on the Chinese Market). In: *Polnoe sobranie sochinenii* (Complete Collected Works). Vol. 2. Moskva-Leningrad. 1941.

REIKHBERG, G. *Razgrom yaponskoi interventsii na Dal'nem Vostoke (1918-1922 gg.)* (The Defeat of the Japanese Intervention in the Far East (1918-1922)). Moskva. 1940.

ROMANOV, B. A. *Ocherki diplomaticheskoi istorii russko-yaponskoi voiny* 1895-1907 gg. (Essays on the Diplomatic History of the Russo-Japanese War (1895-1907)). Moskva-Leningrad. 1947.

RUDAKOV, A. *Obshchestvo I-khe-tuan' i ego znachenie v poslednikh sobytiyakh na Dal'nem*

Vostoke (The *Ihotuan* [Boxer] Society and Its Importance in the Recent Far Eastern Events). Vladivostok. 1901.

SAMOILOV, L. M. Istoricheskie i statisticheskie issledovaniya o Kyakhtinskoi torgovle (Historical and Statistical Studies of the Kyakhta Trade). In: *Sbornik statisticheskikh svedenii o Rossii* (Collected Statistical Data on Russia). Sankt Peterburg. 1854.

SAVIN, V. P. *Vzaimootnosheniya tsarskoi Rossii i SSSR s Kitaem* (Relations of Tsarist Russia and the USSR with China). Moskva. 1930.

SEMENOV. *Izuchenie istoricheskikh svedenii o rossiiskoi vneshnei torgovle i promyshlennosti s poloviny XVII stoletiya po 1858 god* (Study of Historical Data on Russia's Foreign Trade and Industry from the Second Half of the 17th Century to 1858). Sankt Peterburg. 1859.

SEREDONIN, S. M. Istoricheskii ocherk zavoevaniya Aziatskoi Rossii (Historical Essay on the Conquest of Asiatic Russia). In: *Sbornik statei 'Aziatskaya Rossiya'* (Collected articles 'Asiatic Russia'). Sankt Peterburg. 1914.

SEVOST'YANOV G. N. *Aktivnaya rol' SShA v obrazovanii ochaga voiny na Dal'nem Vostoke (1931-1933 gg.)* (The Active Role Played by the U.S.A. in the Creation of a Hotbed of War in the Far East (1931-1933)). Moskva. 1953.

SILIN, E. P. *Kyakhta v XVIII veke* (Kyakhta in the 18th Century). Irkutskoe oblastnoe izdatel'stvo. 1947

SKAL'KOVSKII, K. *Russkaya torgovlya v Tikhom Okeane* (Russian Trade in the Pacific). Sankt Peterburg. 1882.

SLADKOVSKII, M. I. *Ocherki razvitiya vneshneekonomicheskikh otnoshenii Kitaya* (Essays on the Development of China's Economic Relations with Other Countries). Moskva, Vneshtorgizdat. 1953.

SLOVTSOV. *Istoricheskoe obozrenie Sibiri* (Historical Essay on Siberia). Sankt Peterburg. 1886.

SMIRNOV, A. M. and LYUBIMOV, N. N., editors. *Vneshnyaya torgovlya SSSR* (Foreign Trade of the USSR). Moskva, Vneshtorgizdat. 1954.

SYCHEVSKII. *Istoricheskaya zapiska o kitaiskoi granitse* (A Historical Note Concerning the Chinese Border). Moskva. 1875.

TRUSEVICH, KH. *Posol'skie i torgovye snosheniya Rossii s Kitaem do XIX veka* (Russian Diplomatic and Commercial Relations with China before the 19th Century). Moskva. 1882.

VASIL'EV, V. P. Otkrytie Kitaya (The Discovery of China). In: *Sbornik statei 'Vestnik vsemirnoi istorii'* (Collected Articles 'Herald of World History'). Sankt Peterburg. 1900.

VOITINSKII, G. N. *Kitai i pervaya mirovaya imperialisticheskaya voina* (China and the First Imperialist World War). Trudy Moskovskogo Instituta vostokovedeniya (Works of the Moscow Oriental Institute). Moskva. 1940.

VOITINSKII, G. N. *Lektsii po noveishei istorii Kitaya (1924-1948 gg)* (Lectures on Contemporary Chinese History (1924-1928)). Moskva, izdanie Instituta vostokovedeniya. 1947.

VOITINSKII, G. N., GAL'PERIN, A. L., GUBER, A. A., DUBINSKII, A. I., ZHUKOV, E. M., ZUBOK, L. I. and NAROCHINSKII, A. L. *Mezhdunarodnye otnosheniya na Dal'nem Vostoke (1870-1945 gg.)* (International Relations in the Far East (1870-1945)). Moskva, Gospolitizdat. 1951.

*   *

*

Istoricheskii obzor KVZhD (Historical Essay on the Chinese Eastern Railway). Harbin, Izdatel'stvo KVZhD. 1923.

KPSS v rezolyutsiyakh i resheniyakh s''ezdov, konferentsii i plenumov TsK (The CPSU through the Resolutions of its Congresses, Conferences and Central Committee Plenums). Parts 1 and 2, seventh edition. Gospolitizdat. 1953.

Kratkii ocherk vozniknoveniya, razvitiya i tepereshnego sostoyaniya nashikh torgovykh s Kitaem snoshenii cherez Kyakhtu (Short Essay on the Beginning, Development and Present State of Our Commercial Relations with China through Kyakhta). Moskva, izdanie kyakhtinskogo kupechestva. 1896.

Obzory vneshnei torgovli Rossii po evropeiskoi i aziatskoi granitsam za 1895, 1904, i 1914 (Review of Russia's Foreign Trade through Her European and Asiatic Borders for 1895, 1904 and 1914). Sankt Peterburg, izdanie Departamenta tamozhennykh sborov. 1897, 1906 i 1915.

Priamur'e. Fakty, tsifry, nablyudeniya. Sobrany na Dal'nem Vostoke sortudnikami obshche-zemskoi organizatsii (The Amur Territory. Facts, Data, Observations. Collected in the Far East by the Members of the General Zemstvo Organization). Moskva. 1909.

Sbornik dogovorov i diplomaticheskikh dokumentov po delam Dal'nyago Vostoka 1895-1905 *gg.* (Collected Treaties and Diplomatic Documents Concerning Far Eastern Affairs in 1895-1905). Sankt Peterburg, izdanie ministerstva inostrannykh del. 1906.

Sbornik dogovorov Rossii s Kitaem 1689-1881 *gg.* (Collected Sino-Russian Treaties 1689-1881). Sankt Peterburg, izdanie ministerstva inostrannykh del. 1889.

Sbornik dokumentov po mezhunarodnoi politike i mezhdunarodnomu pravu (Collected Documents on International Policy and International Law). Book 4. Izdatel'stvo NKID. 1933.

Sovetsko-kitaiskii konflikt 1929 goda (The Soviet-Chinese Conflict of 1929). Litizdat NKID. 1930.

Statisticheskii ezhegodnik KVZhD (Statistical Yearbook of the Chinese Eastern Railway). Harbin. 1923.

Vneshnyaya politika SSSR 1917-1944 *gg.* (Soviet Foreign Policy, 1917-1944), collected documents. 3 Vol. Moskva. 1944.

Vneshnyaya politika Sovetskogo Soyuza v period Otechestvennoi voiny (Soviet Foreign Policy during World War II). Moskva. 1946-1947.

Vneshnyaya politika Sovetskogo Soyuza, 1946 *g.* (Soviet Foreign Policy in 1946). Moskva. 1952.

Vneshnyaya politika Sovetskogo Soyuza, 1949 *g.* (Soviet Foreign Policy in 1949). Moskva. 1953.

Vneshnyaya torgovlya SSSR za period 1918-1927/28 *gg., statisticheskii obzor* (Foreign Trade of the USSR in 1918-1927/28, a Statistical Survey). Leningrad-Moskva. 1931.

Yubileinyi sbornik Kharbinskogo birzhevogo komiteta 1907-1932 *gg.* (Jubilee Collection of the Harbin Stock-Exchange Committee 1907-1932). Harbin. 1934.

*   *
*

CHEN PO-TA. *Chetyre semeistva Kitaya* (Four Chinese Families). Translated from Chinese. Moskva, Izdatel'stvo inostrannoi literatury. 1948.

CHEN PO-TA. *Chan Kai-shi—vrag kitaiskogo naroda* (Chang Kai-shek, Enemy of the Chinese People). Translated from Chinese. Moskva, Izdatel'stvo inostrannoi literatury. 1950.

CHIN PEN-LI. *Istoriya ekonomicheskoi agressii amerikanskogo imperializma v Kitae* (History of American Imperialist Economic Aggression in China). Translated from Chinese. Moskva, Izdatel'stvo inostrannoi literatury. 1951.

China Year-Book for 1921/1922 (in English). Tientsinpress. 1922.

China Year-Book (in English). Shanghai. 1926.

China Year-Book for 1928 (in English). Tientsin. 1928.

China Year-Book (in English). Shanghai. 1929.

China Year-Book (in English). Shanghai. 1938.

China Year-Book (in English). Shanghai. 1939.

FAN WEN-LAN. *Novaya istoriya Kitaya* (Modern Chinese History). Vol. 7 (1840-1901). Translated from Chinese. Moskva, Izdatel'stvo inostrannoi literatury. 1955.

Gruppa prepodavatelei Voenno-Politicheskoi Akademii Severo-Vostochnogo Kitaya. *Novaya i noveishaya istoriya Kitaya* (Modern and Contemporary Chinese History, by a group of lecturers of the Military-Political Academy of Northeast China). Translated from Chinese Moskva, Izdatel'stvo inostrannoi literatury. 1950.

HO CHING-YING. *China's Foreign Trade* (in English). Shanghai. 1935.

HU CHIAO-MU. *Tridtsat' let Kommunisticheskoi partii Kitaya* (Thirty Years of Activity of the Chinese Communist Party). Translated from Chinese. Moskva, Izdatel'stvo inostrannoi literatury. 1952.

HU SHENG. *Agressiya imperialisticheskikh derzhav v Kitae* (The Aggression of Imperialist Powers Against China). Translated from Chinese. Moskva. 1952.

HWA KANG. *Istoriya revolyutsionnoi voiny Taipinskogo gosudarstva* (History of the Revolutionary War of the Taiping State). Translated from Chinese. Moskva. 1952.

China Year-Book, 1944-1945 (in English). Shanghai. Chungking editions.

LI CHE-JEN. *Pervyi pyatiletnii plan i vneshnyaya torgovlya Kitaiskoi Narodnoi Respubliki* (The First Five-Year Plan and the Foreign Trade of the People's Republic of China), (in Russian). *Sovetskoe vostokovedenie*, No. 6. 1955.

LI CHING-YUN. Vneshnyaya torgovlya Novogo Kitaya (New China's Foreign Trade). *Narodnyi Kitai* (People's China), No. 7-8. 1951.

LIN HAI-YUNG. Sino-Soviet Trade Has Expanded Considerably during the Last Year (in Chinese). *Jenminjipao*, February 25, 1951.

LIU TA-NIAN. *Istoriya amerikanskoi agressii v Kitae* (History of American Aggression in China). Translated from Chinese. Moskva, Izdatel'stvo inostrannoi literatury. 1951.

Popular Handbook for 1952 (in Chinese). Shanghai, *Takungpao* editions. 1952.

PENG MING. *A Short History of the Friendship Between the Soviet and Chinese People* (in Chinese). Peking. 1955.

SUN HUI-CHANG. *The Plans of American Aggression in Northeast China* [Manchuria] *after the Russo-Japanese War*. Collected Historical Material on the American Aggression *Against China* (in Chinese). Peking. 1951.

WEI TZE-CHU. *British Enterprises and Their Profits* (in Chinese). Peking. 1951.

*　　*

*

CAHEN, GASTON. *Some Early Russo-Chinese Relations* (translated into English from the French). Shanghai. 1914.

DULLES, FOSTER RHEA. *Behind the Open Door*. Boston-New York. 1944.

MACNAIR, H. F. *Modern Chinese History*. Selected Readings. Shanghai. 1923.

MORSE, H. B. *The International Relations of the Chinese Empire*. 3 Vol. London. 1910 (vol. 1.), 1918 (vol. 2), 1918 (vol. 3).

MORSE, H. B. *The Trade and Administration of China*. London, New York, Bombay and Calcutta. 1920.

REMER, C. F. *The Foreign Trade of China*. Shanghai. 1926.

REMER, C. F. *Foreign Investments in China*. New York. 1933.

For Product Safety Concerns and Information please contact our EU
representative GPSR@taylorandfrancis.com Taylor & Francis Verlag GmbH,
Kaufingerstraße 24, 80331 München, Germany

Printed and bound by CPI Group (UK) Ltd, Croydon, CR0 4YY
08/05/2025
01864362-0012